Marie Robinson Wright

Picturesque Mexico

Marie Robinson Wright

Picturesque Mexico

ISBN/EAN: 9783337119904

Printed in Europe, USA, Canada, Australia, Japan

Cover: Foto ©ninafisch / pixelio.de

More available books at **www.hansebooks.com**

Señor General Don Porfirio Diaz, President of Mexico.

MEXICO

BY

MARIE ROBINSON WRIGHT

PHILADELPHIA
J. B. LIPPINCOTT COMPANY

TO

SEÑOR GENERAL DON PORFIRIO DIAZ,

THE ILLUSTRIOUS PRESIDENT OF MEXICO,

WHOSE INTREPID MORAL CHARACTER, DISTINGUISHED STATESMANSHIP, AND DEVOTED PATRIOTISM

MAKE HIM THE PRIDE AND GLORY OF HIS COUNTRY,

Is Dedicated

THIS VOLUME, DESCRIBING A BEAUTIFUL AND PROSPEROUS LAND,

WHOSE FREE FLAG NEVER WAVED OVER A SLAVE,

AND WHOSE IMPORTANCE AS A NATION

IS DUE TO THE PATRIOT

UNDER

WHOSE ADMINISTRATION MEXICO NOW FLOURISHES AND HOLDS ITS PROUD POSITION

AMONG THE REPUBLICS OF THE WORLD.

CONTENTS

CHAPTER I	PAGE
Ancient History of Mexico	17
CHAPTER II	
The Aztec Civilization	32
CHAPTER III	
Mexico in General	40
CHAPTER IV	
Customs and Characteristics	45
CHAPTER V	
In Mexico City	59
CHAPTER VI	
Churches and Shrines	67
CHAPTER VII	
Sight-Seeing in Mexico City	74
CHAPTER VIII	
The Markets and Chapultepec	81
CHAPTER IX	
The Mexican Independence Day	87
CHAPTER X	
General Porfirio Diaz	92
CHAPTER XI	
The Ministers of the Cabinet	104
CHAPTER XII	
The Ladies of the Cabinet	118
CHAPTER XIII	
The Jockey Club	122
CHAPTER XIV	PAGE
La Viga and the Suburbs	125
CHAPTER XV	
The State of Mexico	129
CHAPTER XVI	
Hidalgo	140
CHAPTER XVII	
Tlaxcala	149
CHAPTER XVIII	
Puebla	157
CHAPTER XIX	
Oaxaca	173
CHAPTER XX	
Vera Cruz	186
CHAPTER XXI	
Tamaulipas	199
CHAPTER XXII	
Nuevo León	205
CHAPTER XXIII	
Coahuila	212
CHAPTER XXIV	
Chihuahua	220
CHAPTER XXV	
Durango	231
CHAPTER XXVI	
San Luis Potosí	236

CONTENTS

	PAGE
CHAPTER XXVII — ZACATECAS	245
CHAPTER XXVIII — AGUAS CALIENTES	251
CHAPTER XXIX — QUERÉTARO	254
CHAPTER XXX — GUANAJUATO	260
CHAPTER XXXI — JALISCO	271
CHAPTER XXXII — COLIMA	284
CHAPTER XXXIII — TEPIC	289
CHAPTER XXXIV — SINALOA	297
CHAPTER XXXV — SONORA	302
CHAPTER XXXVI — BAJA CALIFORNIA	309
CHAPTER XXXVII — MICHOACÁN	315
CHAPTER XXXVIII — GUERRERO	330
CHAPTER XXXIX — MORELOS	336
CHAPTER XL — CHIAPAS	345
CHAPTER XLI — CAMPECHE	352
CHAPTER XLII — TABASCO	358
CHAPTER XLIII — YUCATÁN	363
CHAPTER XLIV — CITIES AND INHABITANTS; PECULIARITIES OF THE INDIANS; SOME NOBLE FAMILIES; LITERATURE OF MEXICO; FOLK-LORE	380
CHAPTER XLV — NATURAL ADVANTAGES	395
CHAPTER XLVI — MINERAL RESOURCES	412
CHAPTER XLVI — RAILROADS AND TELEGRAPHS	419
CHAPTER XLVIII — FINANCIAL AND BUSINESS OUTLOOK	430
CHAPTER XLIX — MEXICO AS A WHOLE	437
CHAPTER L — GENERAL SUGGESTIONS	441

LIST OF ILLUSTRATIONS

	PAGE
Señor General Don Porfirio Diaz, President of Mexico . . . . *Frontispiece*	
Hidalgo	18
Benito Juarez	21
Señor General Don Mariano Escobedo	22
Señor General Don Ramón Corona	25
Tomb of Juarez	28
The National Palace	30
The Cathedral	33
Sacrificial Stone	35
Calendar Stone	37
Correctional School, City of Mexico	40
Fountain in the Alameda, City of Mexico	41
Entrance to the Paseo de la Reforma	41
In Riding Costume—Charo Suits	42
Entrance to the Alameda, City of Mexico	42
Hall of Ambassadors, in the National Palace . . .	43
Statue of Columbus, on the Paseo	44
Patio of the National School	45
Patio of the National Preparatory School	46
A Bull-Fight	47
Fountain of the Salto de Agua	49
Commercial School	50
Patio of a School	51
Juarez Avenue	53
An Indian Girl	54
Plaza de Santo Domingo	55
Seller of Petates	56
Seller of Fowls	56
Indian from the Mountains	57
Señor Don Rafael Rebolla, Governor of the Federal District	59
Aqueduct of Belem	61
Carriage-Road to the Castle of Chapultepec . . .	62
Patio of a Private Residence in the City of Mexico	63
A Stairway in the Municipal Palace	64
Street Scene, Cinco de Mayo, showing the National Theatre in the Distance	65
The Crown of the Virgin of Guadalupe	67
The Holy Well at Guadalupe	69
The Shrine of Guadalupe	70

	PAGE
La Santísima Church	72
The National Museum	75
El Monte de Piedad	76
Statue of Cuautlmoc, on the Paseo	78
The Noche Triste Tree	79
The Arcades	81
The Gateway to Chapultepec	82
The Castle of Chapultepec	83
One of the Large Cypress-Trees in the Grove of Chapultepec	84
Sala in the Palace of Chapultepec	85
Independence Day, 16th of September	88
The Liberty Bell.—1810	89
Rurales on the 16th of September	90
National Library	95
The Palace of Mines	100
Lic. Don Ignacio Mariscal, Secretary of Foreign Affairs	104
Salon of the Secretary of Foreign Affairs	105
General Don Manuel Gonzalez Cosio, Secretary of the Interior	106
Señor Don José Ives Limantour, Secretary of the Treasury	107
General Don Francisco Z. Mena, Secretary of Communications and Public Works	108
General Don Felipe Berriozabal, Secretary of War and the Navy	109
Lieutenant-Colonel Don Manuel Mondragon, Inventor of the Famous Gun, which he presented to the Mexican Government	110
Lic. Don Joaquin Baranda, Secretary of Public Instruction	111
National Preparatory School	112
Academy of San Carlos	112
Patio of the Conservatory of Music	113
Don Iñigo Manuel Fernandez Leal, Secretary of Encouragement	114
General Pedro Hinojosa, President of Military Court	115
Señor Don Manuel Romero Rubio	116
Señora Doña Carmen Romero Rubio de Diaz, the Wife of the President of Mexico	118

9

LIST OF ILLUSTRATIONS

	PAGE
Señora Ignacio de la Torre, Daughter of the President	119
Señorita Luz Diaz, Daughter of the President	119
Captain Porfirio Diaz	120
Señora Mariscal	120
Señora Limantour	121
Señora Cosio	121
General Pedro Rincon Gallardo, President of the Jockey Club	122
Patio of the Jockey Club	123
Corridor of the Jockey Club	123
Sala in the Jockey Club	124
The Viga Canal	126
Indian Way of Carrying Children	127
Señor Gobernador-General José Vicente Villada	129
Village of Tlapacoyo	131
Garden and Palace in Toluca	134
Cumbre de las Cruces, the Place where a Great Battle was Fought	137
Señor Gobernador-General Rafael Cravioto	140
Hacienda de la Purísima, in Pachuca	141
Hacienda of San Buenaventura	142
Statue of Hidalgo	143
Mine of Real del Monte	144
The Governor's Palace	145
Zócalo in Real del Monte	147
Omitlan	148
Señor Gobernador Coronel Prospero Cohorantzi	149
Governor's Palace in Tlaxcala	150
La Parroquia	151
An Archway in Tlaxcala	152
Sacred Well of Ocotlan	153
The First Pulpit in Mexico	155
Principal Street, Tlaxcala	156
Señor General Don Mucio P. Martinez, Governor of Puebla	157
Señor Licenciado Don Agustin Fernandez, Secretary of State, Puebla	158
Interior of Cathedral in Puebla	159
Cathedral of Puebla	160
Panorama of Puebla	161
A Country Road in Puebla, showing Popocatepetl	162
Penitentiary of Puebla	162
Cholula Pyramid	163
La Maternidad, in Puebla	164
Zócalo of Puebla	165
Scene in Puebla	166
Street in Puebla	168
Intaccihuatl	169
Scene near Puebla, State of Puebla	170
Portal de Flores, Puebla	171
Señor General Don Martin Gonzalez, Governor of Oaxaca	173

	PAGE
A Beauty of Tehuantepec	174
The Big Tree at Tula	175
The Cathedral of Oaxaca	177
Ruins of the Temple of Mitla	178
Palace of the Governor	179
The Great Cotton-Mills of Oaxaca	180
Ancient Pillars at Mitla	181
Temple of La Soledad	182
Stone Carving at Mitla	184
The Juarez Garden	185
Señor Gobernador Don Teodoro Dehesa	187
The Port of Vera Cruz	188
Waterfall, Barrio Nuevo	189
Governor's Palace at Jalapa	190
Cascade of Rincon Grande	191
Hacienda of San Antonio, in Vera Cruz	192
Park and Theatre in Orizaba	193
Municipal Palace at Cordoba	194
Drying Coffee	195
Coffee Ranch in Vera Cruz	196
Alameda in Vera Cruz	197
Señor Lic. Guadalupe Mainero, Governor of Tamaulipas	199
Market at Tampico	201
Landing at Tampico	202
The Liberty Square, Tampico	203
Plaza, Tampico	204
Señor General Bernardo Reyes, Governor of Nuevo León	205
Saddle Mountain	206
San Pedro Mines, Diente Cañon, near Monterey	206
Statue of Hidalgo	207
Swan-Pond in the Alameda Porfirio Diaz, Monterey	208
Street Scene in Monterey	209
Alameda, Monterey	209
Topo Chico Hot Springs, Monterey	210
Canal in Monterey	211
Señor Lic. Miguel Cardenas, Governor of Coahuila	213
City of Saltillo	214
Plaza de San Francisco, Saltillo	215
Portales, Saltillo	216
Penitentiary, Saltillo	217
Park Zaragoza, Saltillo	218
Señor Coronel Don Miguel Ahumada, Governor of Chihuahua	220
The Arch of the Alameda, Chihuahua	221
The Palace, Chihuahua	222
The Cathedral, Chihuahua	223
Interior of the Palace, Chihuahua	224
The Bridge of San Francisco, Chihuahua	225
Part of the Archway of an Old Aqueduct, Chihuahua	226
Hidalgo's Prison, Chihuahua	227

LIST OF ILLUSTRATIONS

	PAGE
Monte de Piedad, Chihuahua	229
Señor General Don Juan M. Flores, Governor of Durango	231
Tunal, the Great Cotton-Mills of Durango, Durango	232
Public Washing-Place for the Indian Women, State of Durango	232
A Mountain of Solid Iron, Durango	233
Casa de Maximilian Damm, Durango	234
The Principal Street, Durango	235
Señor General Don Carlos Diez Gutiérrez, Governor of San Luis Potosí	237
Palace of the Governor, San Luis Potosí	238
Church and Fountain at Guadalupe	240
Cascade del Salto, San Luis Potosí	241
The Grand Theatre "La Paz," San Luis Potosí	243
Señor General Jesús Arechiga, Governor of Zacatecas	245
The Cathedral, Zacatecas	246
A General View of Zacatecas	247
The Theatre Calderon, Zacatecas	248
The Little Plaza of Villareal, Zacatecas	249
The Church of Guadalupe, Zacatecas	250
Señor Don Rafael Arellano, Governor of Aguas Calientes	251
Street Scene in Aguas Calientes	252
Kiosk in the Park of San Marcos, Aguas Calientes	252
Temple of San Marcos, Aguas Calientes	253
Church of the Ascension, Aguas Calientes	253
Señor Coronel Don Francisco Cosío, Governor of Querétaro	254
Façade of the Ruins of San Augustin, Querétaro	255
Monument to Doña Josefa Ortiz de Dominguez, Querétaro	255
Court-Yard of the Federal Palace, Querétaro	256
Aqueduct at Querétaro	257
General View of the Hercules Factory, Querétaro	258
Water-Carriers at the Public Fountain, Querétaro	259
Señor Joaquin Obregon Gonzalez, Governor of Guanajuato	260
Theatre Juarez, Guanajuato	261
A Pretty Little Home on the Road to the Presa de la Olla	262
Mummies at the Pantheon, Guanajuato	263
The Castle of Granditas, Guanajuato	264
Dam Manuel Gonzalez, Guanajuato	265
Silver-Mine of San Navier	266
The Presa, Guanajuato	267
Triumphal Arch in the Paseo at León	269
Señor General Don Luis C. Curiel, Governor of Jalisco	271
A Street in Guadalajara	272
The Palace	273
Santuario Zapopan, Jalisco	274
A Monument to Pius IX., Jalisco	275

	PAGE
The Cathedral, Guadalajara	276
Avenue leading to the Hospicio, Guadalajara	277
School of Jurisprudence, Guadalajara	279
Falls of Juanacatlan	280
Theatre Degollado, Guadalajara	282
Señor Coronel Don Francisco Santacruz, Governor of Colima	284
Hacienda of San Antonio, near the City of Colima	285
Lake Jabali, Hacienda of San Antonio	285
Indians from the Village of Suchillan, in Working Clothes	286
Indian Women from the Pueblas near Colima	286
The Governor's House in Colima	287
Street Scene, Colima	287
Plaza de la Libertad, in front of the Governor's Palace in Colima	288
General Leopoldo Romano, Governor of Tepic	289
Cathedral, Tepic	290
Cascade which forms the Tepic River, Tepic	291
Plaza at Tepic	292
Cotton-Factory "Jauja," Tepic	293
La Escondida Sugar-Factory, Tepic	294
The Village of Puga, Tepic	294
Cascade of El Ingenio, Tepic	295
Puga Dwelling, View from Factory	296
General Francisco Cañeda, Governor of Sinaloa	297
City of Mazatlan	298
Mazatlan, showing the Harbor	298
Theatre in Culiacan	299
Calle de Rosales, Culiacan	299
Plaza, Mazatlan	300
Bay of Guaymas	303
Principal Street in the City of Guaymas	304
Government Palace, Hermosillo	305
View of the City and Bay of Guaymas	306
View of the City of Guaymas	307
Coronel Rafael Garcia Martinez, Jefe Político, La Paz	309
Port of La Paz, showing the Great Pearl-Fisheries of Baja California	310
Government House, La Paz	311
Coronel Agustin Sanginés, Jefe Político, Ensenada	312
The Bay at Ensenada	313
Pier at Ensenada	313
City of Ensenada	314
Señor Aristeo Mercado, Governor of Michoacán	315
Governor's Palace, Morelia	316
Monument to Ocampo, Morelia	317
Lake Patzcuaro, Michoacán	319
Portal de Matamoros, Morelia	320
Paseo de San Pedro, Morelia	322
College of Santa Maria de Guadalupe, Morelia	323
Cathedral, Morelia	325

LIST OF ILLUSTRATIONS

	PAGE
An Entrance to the Paseo, Morelia	327
La Fzaraxacua, Uruapan	328
Señor Coronel Antonio Mercenario, Governor of Guerrero	330
In Tixtla, Guerrero	331
Chilpancingo, the Capital of Guerrero	332
Palace, Chilpancingo	333
Temple at Quechomictlipan, Omitlan	334
Girls' College, Chilpancingo	335
Señor Coronel Manuel Alarcon, Governor of the State of Morelos	336
A View of Cuernavaca	337
Aztec Monolith, Cuernavaca	338
A Bridge built by Cortez in Morelos	338
Palace of Cortez, Cuernavaca	339
Cascade of San Antonio	340
Field of Rice in Morelos	341
Borda Garden, Cuernavaca	342
Plaza, Cuernavaca	343
Field of Sugar-Cane in Morelos	344
Señor Coronel Francisco Leon, Governor of Chiapas	345
Palace, Chiapas	346
Between Ortega and La Puerta	347
Types of Indian Women in Chiapas	349
On the Road to Bonito	350
Palace of Justice, Campeche	352
Calle de Zaragoza, showing the Wall which surrounds the City	353
Plaza de la Independencia, Campeche	354
Ruins of Hoch-ob, Campeche	355
Palacio Central, Ruins of Hoch-ob, Campeche	356
General Abraham Bandala, Governor of Tabasco	358
Farm-House, Tabasco	359
Port of San Juan Bautista	359
Street in San Juan Bautista	360
San Juan Bautista	361
Government Palace, San Juan Bautista	362
Lic. Cárlos Peón, Governor of Yucatán	363
Governor's Palace, Mérida	364
Type of Yucatacos	366
Tekax	368
Mérida, Yucatán	369
Section of the Nunnery, Chichen-Tija	371
Castle, Chichen-Tija	372
Las Monjas, Uxmal	374
Mount Sebatsche	375
Façade of Las Monjas, Uxmal	376
Municipal Palace, Mérida	377
Juarez Penitentiary, Mérida	378
The Main Canal at Tlahualilo, Durango	381
Hacienda of Zaragoza, Tlahualilo, Durango	383
Ravine of Infiernillo, Interoceanic Railroad	386
Cotton-Growing at Tlahualilo, Durango	389
Picturesque Scene on the Mexican Central near Tampico	391
Interoceanic Railroad Leaving the City of Mexico	393
La Señosa Bridge, Interoceanic Railroad	398
Ravine of Metlac, Mexican Railroad	402
A Scene along the Tehuantepec Railroad	407
Coffee Plantation on the Interoceanic Railroad	410
Tunnel, Interoceanic Railroad	413
The Bend, on the Cuernavaca and Pacific Railroad	416
Major Robert B. Gorsuch	419
Across the Isthmus of Tehuantepec	421
Colonel Joe H. Hamison	422
Two Tunnels on the Interoceanic Railroad	423
Hon. Thomas Braniff	424
Along the Cuernavaca and Pacific Railroad	426
Buena Vista Station, Mexican Railroad	427
Barranca near Tres Marias, on the Cuernavaca and Pacific Railroad	428
Telegraph Office in the Federal District	429
Organos, the Large Cactus Plant, Oaxaca	431
Husking Coffee	433
Group of Tehuantepequeñas	434
Carrying Pulque	438
A Field of Maguey Plants	439
Drawing Pulque, in Tlachiquero	440

PREFATORY NOTE

WHEN, in 1892, I first visited Mexico for the *New York World*, to collect the material for their great special illustrated edition of Mexico,—the most notable feature of modern journalism,—I realized how meagre is the knowledge of the general public outside of Mexico of the beauties and resources of that fair republic, and comprehended for the first time that books on Mexico have invariably covered either limited areas of country or circumscribed periods. I determined to visit once more that garden spot of the western world, and issue the following book. For this purpose I took as my sole companion and interpreter my daughter, Miss Ida Dent Wright, and together we made a complete tour of the republic by rail- and water-ways and on horseback, travelling more than a thousand miles in the unfrequented parts of Mexico, and gathering valuable data and novel experiences at every turn.

To President Diaz and the members of his cabinet I am deeply indebted for distinguished courtesies.

To Major Robert B. Gorsuch, who has been my faithful adviser and kind friend in all matters of importance in connection with this great undertaking, I owe many thanks.

I am also indebted to Valleto & Cia, Mr. N. Winther, and Schlattman Hermanos, who have furnished me many beautiful photographs.

For valuable editorial assistance I am indebted to Miss Helen M. Winslow, and to the *World* for permission to use some of my data published August 2, 1892. I am also indebted to Mr. E. C. Butler, of the *Mexican Herald*, to Mr. E. H. Thompson, of Yucatan, to Señor Coronel Don Ramón Corona, and to many citizens of Mexico, for their unfailing and daily kindnesses.

M. R. W.

INTRODUCTORY

MEXICO, land of mystery and romance; land of mingled tradition and history; land of vast forests and fruitful valleys; of snow-capped mountains and inexhaustible mines; land of sapphire skies and unrivalled climate; land of tropic luxuriance and noble patriotic hearts; of thee would I sing; thy praises would I carry to the farthest end of the broad green earth. All countries have their virtues and their beauties; all lands have their prophets and their poets; but none more worthy are than this magic and marvellous region where nature's affluence bears perennial witness to her storied treasures, her mineral resources, her unequalled scenery, her splendid fabric of a national and imperishable importance among the free and noble countries of the world.

Although sacked by ruthless hands for centuries, Mexico is still the typical embodiment of loveliness and truth; a country of ancient and beautiful architecture, a region of Alpine snows and tropic sun, a nation of incalculable wealth and of strong and noble men; none other has a more tragic or famous past; none a more glorious and affluent future. Through all her old traditions and achievements, and against all she has suffered from oppression and grinding tyranny in the past, the illuminating light of progress is throwing the strong radiance of advancement across mountain and valley, lighting up her wonderful resources, and showing a glimpse here and there of still more wonderful possibilities in the future.

This land, thanks to the unconquerable spirit and freedom-loving temper of Mexico, to-day stands waiting for science and commerce to walk in, hand in hand, and possess it; to develop its present resources into the glorified future of which already its republican government has laid the foundations.

Mexico, fair Mexico; quaintest and most delightful spot in the whole world. A stranger within thy gates, I know thy hospitality, thy generous, whole-souled kindness, thy inestimable character, and the true manly and womanly hearts with whom thy destiny rests. Again and again have I said *adios* to thy sapphire skies and snow-crowned hills, only to be drawn back by an irresistible impulse,—an impulse of love and admiration. And by this impulse am I impelled to tell the world through these pages something of thy unrivalled charm, as a lover sings of the charms of her who has captivated his heart.

Many people have gone a little distance into Mexico and written books about it. They give us glimpses of some small portion of the Mexican country along the beaten tracks, and already mapped out by many a guide-book. This is, perhaps, one reason why no complete book on Mexico exists to-day. With all modesty, I think I may claim, after travelling through the wilds of Mexico more than a thousand miles away from the railroads, across mountains and among the native races, with no company but my daughter and the official escort kindly provided me by the Mexican governors, that in offering this book I am giving the public not only the most complete book ever written about this wonderful country, but also ample evidence that two American ladies may travel anywhere and everywhere in Mexico sure of meeting with nothing but courtesy, respect, and the kindest attention.

PICTURESQUE MEXICO

CHAPTER I

ANCIENT HISTORY OF MEXICO

FEW people outside the fair republic of Mexico know anything of its wonderful resources; its beautiful atmosphere of romance; its remarkable development; its charming, progressive men and women; its lovely natural beauties; and, least of all, of the spirit of modern enterprise that has entered in and taken possession of the land. In considering the development of this wonderful country, with a civilization in some respects older than that of the United States, the object is to present a true picture of Mexico to-day; to look into the reasons why the spirit of progress and advancement was not brought into play earlier in its history; to give some account of the wonderful and rapid development of the past few years; and to convey to the civilized world an adequate idea of the possibilities of immediate and profitable extension of existing industries, and of the introduction of new ones; for Mexico—beautiful, historic, splendid Mexico—has undreamed-of possibilities in a commercial sense, and is becoming one of the leading republics of the earth, a nation celebrated in industrial enterprise as well as artistic and natural beauty.

Why, then, with all her advantages, has not this fair land made greater progress since her settlement three hundred years ago? Why has not this country of such beauty and such resources, of wealth incalculable and noble patriotic people, developed sooner and taken her place as the literary, commercial, and educational centre of the western hemisphere, just as she is the geographical centre?

Let us look at the history of other nations for a moment. All records of the past show that different nations and races have led in civilization, in commerce, and in war at various periods in the world's great story. Egypt and Phœnicia, Assyria and Babylon, succeeded each other as masters and leaders of the known world, but the dynasty of each gave way in due course of events. Greece took her place as the ruling nation, only to be followed by Rome. Then the fall of the Western Empire, in 476, ensued; while the accession of Hildebrand, in 1073, made another turning point in history, followed by a troublous, changing, historic, kaleidoscopic picture, in which Europe and even a part of Asia were colors in the great prism of the world. Venice became mistress of the seas, and sent her ships to whiten the seas of both hemispheres. Her wealth increased, and with it her power; her traders enriched themselves from the Orient, and for a time she, too, reigned supreme. Then the fall of Constantinople closed the East to the nations of Western Europe, and her navigators had to seek new pathways to wealth, new worlds to conquer, and, most important of all, as they thought, new roadsteads to Oriental marts. Four great nations—Spain, Portugal, France, and Great Britain—each sought for this pathway. Their most experienced navigators were called into requisition, and each sought studiously for a new gate-way to the treasure-gardens of the East. Their ships sailed in every direction; their keels ploughed the seas far and near; their faith was great, and their persistence was greater; they sought with an unparalleled zeal to find out another way to the old market, or a new one to conquest and increase of trade.

Christopher Columbus was but one of the many who crossed and recrossed each other in pursuit of the same quest. Their petty quarrels and the greater ones of their sovereigns concerning the New India and its lands and inhabitants are records of history. Our own hemisphere was visited by all grades of explorers, from the religious one in the name of the Cross, to the pitiless trader who boasted the power of his king to help him,—his only condition being that he pay into the royal treasury a goodly percentage of the fruits of his expedition, gathered at the points of gleaming swords.

HIDALGO.

When these ravagers reached Mexico they met a sturdy resistance; but at last, under the colors of Spain, the great peninsula washed by two mighty oceans and its aborigines were subdued, and the contents of the strong coffers of the Montezumas went to fill the rapidly diminishing Castilian treasury. The native speech, religion, and independence were sacrificed to Rome and Spain; for against the Church and the Spanish army, hand in hand, what could the subjects of Montezuma do? The ravages of war kept up for years. Attacks external and civil on the Spanish treasury were supported or materially aided by taxes extorted from Mexico and her sister colonies of the West Indies; and while armies of men poured from Spain into Mexico, floods of silver poured from the land of the Montezumas into old Castile.

The crown of Spain had discovered here a fairy godmother. The king had only to wish, and wealth poured into the royal coffers without stint or measure.

Three centuries of Spanish rule ensued,—centuries of watchful jealousy lest other hands should profane the beauties or sack the treasures of Mexico. It is estimated that the treasures mounted to the almost incredible sum of nearly three billion five hundred millions of dollars. No wonder Spain was a careful mother to her adopted daughter. And this does not include the astonishing amounts carried off by all sorts of explorers for their own enrichment, nor the millions extorted by the Church of Rome as her tithes from the New World.

During these centuries the gold and silver seemed without limit. The East, with relentless avarice, grasped the silver; the West, with never-satisfied appetite, ate up the gold. Like the beggar of the streets, their cry was "give" more and ever more. The ability of the plunderers to extort by any means both from ancient treasuries and newly opened mines was the only limit to this ceaseless flow.

It was a wicked waste, for only the richer veins and ores were manipulated; the remainder were left for future generations, should there ever be need for more laborious process amid such bounteous profusion of wealth.

And so the glittering harvest was reaped during succeeding years, which multiplied into centuries. It was a harvest which needed not to wait for seed-time. It was always ready. Every ship was laden with it; every man who touched it became rich. And yet, to-day, lying in the depths of the mountains, flashing in the streams, or glinting in the light of open day, it is there,—every kind of precious stone and precious metal,—far exceeding in amount and value those that have ever enriched England or Asia, and are scattered in such abundance over whole districts of the United States of North America.

But, in view of these three centuries of ravage and pillage, is it any wonder that Mexico did not develop into an independent country? Yielding up her vast treasures to enrich the crowns of her oppressors, how could she gain independence or develop even the consciousness of her own strength and power?

And yet, in all the days since the Spanish conquest, agriculture, where it has been in any degree advisable to till the fields, has not been neglected. In many places it has only been necessary to touch the earth with a spade for it to respond with abundant harvests. The wants of the natives were simple, and nature ever generous. The happy inhabitants, therefore, had not found it necessary to cultivate arable lands, or to try to wrest from a rugged soil a scanty living.

Where costly jewels were the possession of the humblest, and a friendly climate not only makes slight the demand for food but produces it in the greatest profusion, agriculture would, naturally, not acquire great value; and in those years the principal ambition was for gold.

It was not until the various colonies to the north of them had achieved their independence, and had come to be known as a new nation, the United States of America, that the Mexicans began to indulge the spirit of patriotism and the desire for independence which are implanted by nature in every human breast. Other patriots had succeeded in establishing their rights to freedom and its privileges, why not they?

As the years went on, this restless desire for liberty grew among the patriots of Mexico. The fruits, the wealth, the prodigal bounty of the country were theirs, they felt, by inheritance; why should they go to enrich the coffers of a foreign country while they were kept here in poverty and oppression? In 1798 the Spanish viceroy began to discover signs of the uprising that broke out with such force a few years later, under the noble Hidalgo. Even then the Mexicans had decided in their secret hearts that Mexico should no longer be New Spain either in name or in fact. She should be free. She should govern her own country and worship in her own church. She should come into her own Kingdom of Liberty.

It was a bloody struggle, however, and one that was several times repeated ere the victory was gained and Mexico became firmly established as one of the republics of the world.

Hidalgo and his patriots made a noble fight, but internal dissensions and foreign invasions followed; the valuable mines, sacked for centuries by other rulers, had to be abandoned, and the tillable lands were left untouched. The patriots were fighting in the cause of honor and trying to wrest the crown of liberty from their oppressors, while starvation stared them in the face. It is always so in a desperate revolution. Liberty is to be won only by the sacrifice of many human lives.

And so the older patriots fought, bled, and died for their country, while their places were taken by younger men who continued the battle for progress and freedom, and only the Indians of the mountain fastnesses were left free from care or ambitions.

Mexico's history has been singularly cursed by the greed of gold and lust of power on the part of foreign potentates. Her inexhaustible treasures have, in past ages, been to her, in a sense, a curse rather than a blessing; since it was only the greed of gold which brought the cruel, grinding oppressor, who for centuries kept her under the iron heel of the conquerors. While Mexico waited, many a less favored settlement rose to the distinction of a nation, and smaller colonies rose to proud prominence.

But Mexico was oppressed and despoiled in vain. Slowly, perhaps, her courage rose to the point of resistance, but when the day of struggle came her spirit was indomitable. Beaten repeatedly, thrust down from temporary acquisitions more than once, she knew not the meaning of the word defeat. Again and again she rose fresh from discouragement; and with a persistence that was almost divine, and a courage that comes only from the God of Liberty, cried, undismayed, "Mexico shall be free! Mexico shall take her place among the independent nations of the earth!"

And so the young republic to-day stands strong and free, with the crown of liberty on her brow and the unconquerable hope of ages on her face; with eager gaze on the goal far in the distant future, with ambition in her young breast, with the lethargy of centuries thrown from her like a discarded garment, and with inspiration drawn with every breath from the spirit of modern progress, Mexico will soon rank with the mightiest nations of earth.

As relics of past ages are noble buildings and public works which put to blush any in her neighboring countries; as accomplishments of the present are her railroads, her telegraph system, her business enterprise developing with every morn; as auguries of the future are the many wise projects for developing the vast resources of the land, together with the same proud, indomitable spirit that brought her out from the land of bondage and made her a "home of the free and a land of the brave."

This is the Mexico that Hidalgo, Morelos, Juarez, Lerdo, and Ocampo died for. It is to these men that Mexico owes so much of past, present, and future achievement. Modest, brave, and unselfish, they have fought better than they knew; and to-day they are themselves the pedestal on which their goddess stands on high, seen and admired by every nation in the world.

No country can succeed without good and brave men, whose patriotism is far above any greed of gain or desire for pelf. It is such men that make the Mexico of to-day.

The history of Mexico may be divided into ancient and modern, and the latter subdivided into two periods, the colonial and that of independence. Notwithstanding the numerous theories advanced concerning the primitive inhabitants of the country, all is still wrapped in profound obscurity. Tradition and the existing remnants of ancient structures point to a more remote and perhaps a higher civilization than that which filled the early Spanish conquerors with admiration; but neither can assist in determining the name or the origin of the first immigrants. Historic ground in Mexico is not reached until the end of the sixth century; all beyond belongs to the domain of mythology. The Toltecs came to the valley of Mexico, and

ANCIENT HISTORY OF MEXICO

there built their capital, Tollan, toward the beginning of the seventh century. According to one theory they came from Guatemala; another theory represents them as crossing from Asia to America, by a chain of islands which, in remote ages, stretched at the north from the shores of the Eastern to those of the Western continent. They are described as an agricultural people, clothed in long tunics, sandals, and straw hats; not very warlike, but humane and civilized, and proficient in the highest mechanical arts; erecting gigantic edifices; having a worship not sanguinary; and inventing the system of astronomy afterward adopted by the Tezcucans and Mexicans.

The first Toltec dynasty is said to have been founded early in the eighth century by Icoatzin. After a lapse of about five hundred years, the kingdom of Tollan, reduced by civil strifes, pestilence, and famine, was divided, and many of the surviving inhabitants migrated southward. The Toltecs were the first tribe to leave a written account of their nationality and polity; they are regarded in Mexican history as the primitive nation of the country, and their epoch is taken as the starting-point of a fixed chronology of the native annals. With the downfall of their monarchy terminated the civilization of the north.

Not long afterward, the Chichimecs, described as a fierce northern tribe, living by the chase, dwelling in caverns or straw huts, monogamous, and worshipping the sun as their father and the earth as their mother, came to the Toltec country, which they did not conquer, as they met with no resistance, but merely occupied peacefully, settling in the same towns

BENITO JUAREZ.

with the Toltecs who remained from the general emigration. The descendants of these Toltecs became once more numerous and prosperous, and, taking the name of Colhuis or Culhuas, founded Colhuacan, on the margin of the lake. Between the arrival of the Chichimecs and the end of the twelfth century, tradition mentions the influx of a multitude of other northern tribes, chief among whom were the Tepanecs, who, with Atzcapozalco as their capital, established an independent state, and became gradually so powerful that in later times two of their kings usurped the throne of Tezcuco. Another of these tribes were the Techichimecs, the founders of the Tlaxcalan republic, and all of them spoke the Nahoa or Nahuatl tongue. After these came the Acolhuis, likewise of Nahoa origin, and consequently kindred to the Toltecs, and especially distinguished among all the immigrants by the Chichimecs as being the most refined. From them the latter readily learned agriculture, the mechanic arts, and town life, and the two races became so completely intermingled as at last to be confounded in one great nation in the kingdom of Tezcuco or Acolhuacan, a name indicating that not only the customs and culture of the Acolhuis prevailed, but also their language, which was incomparably more perfect than the Chichimecan.

The most important of all the tribes, the Mexicans or Aztecs, although the last to choose a permanent resting-place, had been as long in the valley as any of the sister nations. They proceeded from Aztlan, an unknown region of the north, and reached Anahuac about 1195, having made three stations, at which the ruins of *casas grandes* are still to be seen. Their first halting-place was on the shores of the lake of Teguyo or Teguayo, probably identical with the lake of Timpanogos, or Great Salt Lake, in Utah; the second was on the river Gila; and the third not far from Presidio de los Llanos. After reaching the plain of the lakes, the Mexicans led a nomadic existence for one hundred and thirty years. After a series of unsuccessful encounters, in which their numbers were greatly diminished, they laid, on the islands of the lake, the foundations of their city of Tenochtitlan, in 1325. Reduced to extreme poverty and hated by surrounding nations, they resolutely strove against ill fortune until they became numerous and powerful enough to take the offensive. They then spread desolation and slavery through many of the tribes who, in former days, had shown them little mercy. Their capital was extended and beautified to an extraordinary degree; they soon became the equals of the Tezcucans in the cultivation of the arts and sciences; their institutions, customs, religion, and even their language, were propagated wherever their power reached. The adjacent territories were invaded and occupied by Aztec garrisons. The Tezcucans were perhaps more advanced in knowledge and refinement than the Mexicans, but the latter were certainly far more powerful, and they gave their name to the whole country and to the civilization of their day.

SEÑOR GENERAL DON MARIANO ESCOBEDO.

The boundaries of the Aztec realm have never been precisely defined, but they extended northward to the country of the Huastecas, whom the Mexicans never subdued; to the northwest the empire did not reach beyond the province of Tulba, the vast tract of land beyond which was occupied by the Otomies and some Chichimec tribes; to the west it terminated at the frontier of Michoacan; on the southwest it was in general limited only by the Pacific; and the greatest length on that coast was from Soconusco to Coliman. On the Atlantic side the Mexicans possessed all that lay west of the Coatzacoalcos. The Acolhuan dominions did not form one-eighth of the Aztec kingdom. It should be observed that Ahuizotl, whose reign immediately preceded the Spanish conquest, carried his arms successfully into Guatemala, subduing that country and a portion of Nicaragua. The Tepanees, in 141 seized the Acolhuan capital, assassinated the king, and placed their own prince, Tegozomoc, upon the throne, which was transmitted to his son, Moxtla. But Nezahualcoyotl, the rightful heir, succeeded, with the aid of the Mexicans, not only in driving out the Tepanees, but in conquering their country, which they gave to their allies, the Mexicans. A league of mutual support and defence was then entered into by the princes of Mexico, Tezcuco, and Tlacopan, the conquered countries to be divided between the confederates, and the largest share to be awarded to Mexico. During a century of constant warfare this compact was adhered to with strictest fidelity. The Mexican monarch had the predominance in matters of war; the authority of the three was equal in all other concerns, and no one ever meddled with the government of the others. Toward the middle of the fifteenth century, when the Acolhuan power began to decline, the Mexican king plundered a portion of his neighbor's territory, and arrogated to himself the title of emperor, though the Tezcucan sovereigns continued to reign until the time of the conquest. These last had the prerogative of crowning those of Mexico. For the first twenty-seven years after the foundation of Tenochtitlan, the government was in the hands of a body of twenty nobles; but in 1352 it was transformed into an elective monarchy, Acamapitzin or Acamapichtle being the first king. In the beginning the power of the sovereigns was limited, and their prerogatives were very moderate; but with territorial extension and increased wealth came the introduction of court pomp and pageantry, and such despotism as characterized the reign of Montezuma I.

After the election of a king, four princes or lords were chosen from among his nearest of kin, whose voice was indispensable in all state affairs. They acted as senators, were presidents of the royal council, and one of their number was in due time elected successor to the crown, with sole reference to fitness for the office. In later times it was customary to appoint the four candidates to the government of minor states; the one elected must have been general in the army, and not under thirty years of age. When the successor was under age, the government, during his minority, was committed to the senior of the royal family most fitted for the charge, whose election was confirmed by the kings of Tezcuco and Tlacopan. Three councils or cabinets assisted the king in the administration: one for the revenue, another for war, and a third for the government of the provinces. The councillors or ministers, though necessarily of the nobility, owed their eligibility to long military service and a profound knowledge of state matters. The nobles and priests were the main supporters of the national interests; but the influence of the latter in public affairs was more limited than in some of the earlier monarchies. They had no seat in the privy council, and their functions were chiefly restricted to superstitious exercises and foretelling the issue of campaigns. But they were intrusted with the education of children, were consulted on all grave family concerns, and their social influence was almost unbounded. Profound respect for the main principles of morality was evinced by the ancient Mexicans, with whom the security rather of person than of property was largely provided for. In the uninhabited districts public inns were placed at intervals for the gratuitous accommodation of wayfarers, and boats or bridges for their convenience in crossing rivers; and when the roads were damaged by floods, they were repaired at the public expense. A complete system of supreme and subordinate tribunals existed in all the towns, and a still more perfect judicial organization in the neighboring kingdom of Acolhuacan, where a council of all the judges throughout the realm was held once in eighty days at the capital, the monarch in person presiding, for the adjudication of causes left undetermined by the lower courts.

The Aztecs were as remarkable for the moderation of their civil as for the severity of their penal code; but their laws seem to have been administered less impartially than in Tezcuco, and to have been somewhat flexible for the nobles and priests. Creditors could imprison their debtors, and had a claim upon their inheritance, but could not enslave the widows or orphans; and slaves about to be sold might free themselves by taking refuge in the royal palace. Adultery was punished with death, however noble the offender might be. For treason or any crime against the person of the monarch, embezzlement of the taxes, etc., the offender was put to death with all his kindred to the fourth degree. Murder of even a slave was always a capital crime. Drunkenness in youth was a capital offence; in persons of maturer years, though not capital, it was punished with severity; but men of seventy years, and all persons on festive occasions, were permitted the use of wine. He who lied to the prejudice of another had a portion of his lips cut off, and sometimes his ears. Finally, he who robbed in the market, altered the lawful measures, or removed the legal boundaries in the fields, was immediately put to death; and conspirators against the prince, and those who committed adultery with the prince's wife, were torn to pieces, limb from limb. The murder of a merchant or an ambassador, or any injury or insult to the latter, was sufficient cause of war. During a series of very cruel wars all prisoners were devoured or enslaved. At one time the laws were so few that the people knew them all by heart. They were represented by paintings; and the judges were attended by clever clerks, or painters, who by means of figures described the suits and the parties concerned therein.

The Mexicans had two kinds of prisons,—one for debtors and persons not guilty of capital crimes, the other a species of cage in which were confined condemned criminals and prisoners taken in war, both of whom were closely guarded; those doomed to capital punishment being sparingly fed, and the others abundantly nourished, that they might be in good flesh when led to sacrifice. For the same reason the Mexicans in battle preferred to capture their enemies alive. Polygamy was permitted, but seldom practised save by the princes and nobles.

Marriage generally required the consent of the parents of both parties, and there was a special court for divorces, in which a wife might sue. Filial affection was a characteristic virtue of the Aztecs. Except in the royal family, sons succeeded to all the rights of their fathers; if these died without male issue, their rights reverted to their brothers, and in the absence of the latter, to their nephews. Daughters could not inherit.

The government revenues were derived from crown lands set apart in the various provinces, from a tax on the agricultural products, and chiefly from a tribute consisting of provisions and manufactured articles; besides which a contribution was received from the merchants and craftsmen every twenty or eighty days. The profession of arms was one of the most esteemed, and those who died in defence of their country were regarded as the happiest.

There were four distinct grades of generals, and next below them were captains. The main bodies or regiments consisted of eight thousand men, and seem to have been divided into battalions of four hundred men each, and these into squads of twenty. They marched in admirable order; the priests were always in front, and the signal for combat was given by kindling a fire and sounding a trumpet. Their tactics were unfavorable to hostilities by night; but "force and stratagem, courage and deceit," says Prescott, "were equally admissible in war."

The first European to visit the shores of Mexico was Francisco Fernandez de Cordova, in 1517; but he discovered only the coast of Yucatan. The discovery was continued in the following year by Juan de Grijalva, in command of a squadron sent from Cuba by Velasquez, who sailed round the north coast as far as the mouth of the river Panuco, and landed on the islet on which now stands the castle of San Juan de Ulua. After his return, his brilliant account of his discovery excited the desire of conquest.

On Good Friday, April 22, 1519, Hernan Cortez landed at that part of the coast where Vera Cruz was afterward built, and founded a town to which he gave the name of Villarica de

Vera Cruz. On the very day of his landing occurred the first of a series of battles, which terminated only with the taking of the city of Tenochtitlan, August 13, 1521, and the capture of the young and valorous Guatemozin, the last of the Aztec monarchs. The other smaller states were subdued after a short resistance.

A military government was immediately established, Cortez taking the supreme command; but *ayuntamientos* (municipalities) had already been formed, the first at Villarica, and these continued independently of the new military power. Many of the laws emanating from the *ayuntamientos* still exist in full force in the Mexican republic. By a decree of Charles the Fifth, Cortez was constituted governor of the new territory, which had been named New Spain, October 15, 1522. The Indians, though converted, were distributed among the *conquistadores* and other Spanish officials and immigrants, and compelled as slaves to till the ground and labor in the mines. This system of *repartimientos*, or distributions, had already been applied and found fatal to the aboriginal inhabitants of the island of Hayti, but the Mexicans, a hardier people, did not so readily succumb.

In 1528 was inaugurated the first *audiencia*, with Nuño de Guzman as president, and four auditors. The arbitrary and oppressive measures of this body caused considerable discontent in the colony, which, coming to the ears of the emperor, led to the suppression of the *audiencias*, and the establishment of a vice-regal government in New Spain. The first viceroy, Don Antonio de Mendoza, ruled the country from 1535 to 1550.

During his administration discoveries were actively prosecuted in the north; the first money was coined in Mexico; the printing-press, the first in the New World, was introduced; the University of Mexico and several colleges were founded, and numerous important reforms were effected. Of the sixty-four viceroys who successively governed the country till 1821, only one was of American birth, Don Juan de Acuña, a native of Lima (1722-34), and the most celebrated after Mendoza was Don Juan Vicente Guemes Pacheco, the second count of Revillagigedo (1789-94). In his time were accomplished many important improvements: the streets of the principal cities were drained, paved, and lighted, and provided with a tolerably efficient police; persons of known probity were placed in the public offices; and municipal revenues were introduced.

SEÑOR GENERAL DON RAMÓN CORONA.

At the beginning of the present century, society in New Spain consisted of four classes of opposite tendencies and interests,—the pure-blooded Indians, the creoles, or pure-blooded descendants of the early Spanish settlers, the *mestizos*, or half-breeds, from the union of whites and Indians, and the Spaniards of European birth. The condition of the Indians had but little changed under the viceroys. They were compelled to pay tribute, and were held in a sort of tutelage, which ended only in the tomb. The Indian nobles, or *caciques*, were exempted from the degrading restrictions which weighed upon the others. As for the creoles, whose numbers were continually increasing, a policy due to ignorance of their real position in the community excluded them from all places of trust in the government, and even from the higher grades in the regular army. Upon such as had amassed great wealth titles of nobility were conferred, while conciliatory crosses were distributed to those of smaller fortunes; but the home government considered it imprudent to allow them to take part in the public administration, and placed it exclusively in the hands of the Spaniards.

This, with other grievances, caused profound discontent among the creoles, who would probably have resented it by open rebellion, had they not been restrained by the apprehension that the Indians, aided by the mestizos, might avail themselves of that event for the destruction of all the whites. An ineradicable antipathy had already sprung up between the creoles and the Spaniards, whom they distinguished by the sobriquet of Gachupines; yet probably no outbreak would have immediately ensued but for the events of 1818 in the peninsula. The usurpation of Ferdinand's throne by a Bonaparte was unanimously protested against by both Spaniards and creoles in Mexico; but the public mind was agitated by intemperate discussions concerning the provisional government, which the state of things made it necessary to organize; and the excitement was not a little enhanced by the imprisonment of the viceroy, Don José de Iturrigaray, suspected of a design to seize the crown of Mexico, on September 16, 1808.

After his arrest, the prestige of Spanish authority sensibly declined among the Mexicans, who began to long for independence. A conspiracy was formed, and on September 15, 1810, a revolt broke out in the province of Guanajuato, headed by a priest, Don Miguel Hidalgo, a man of great talent and considerable influence among the Indians, and a man who thus became "the Father of his Country."

The insurrection soon assumed formidable proportions, Hidalgo having at one time one hundred thousand men under arms. He finally suffered several defeats, was betrayed to his enemies (March 21, 1811), and four months later was shot in company with his companions in arms, Allende, Aldama, and Jimenez. The contest was continued by Morelos, also a priest, who called a national congress, which met at Chilpanzingo in September, 1813, and in November declared Mexico independent. On October 22, 1814, it promulgated at Apatzingan the first Mexican constitution, which is known by the name of that place.

After several defeats, Morelos was captured, carried to the city of Mexico, and executed as a rebel, December 22, 1815. For several years the contest waged among the patriots, of whom the principal chiefs were Victoria, Guerrero, Bravo, Rayon, and Teran. These were gradually driven from the field and were killed, imprisoned, or obliged to hide in the mountains, so that long before 1820 the authority of Spain appeared to be fully re-established in Mexico.

But in the course of that year the news of the revolution in Spain, and of the proclamation of the constitution which Ferdinand VII. had been compelled to adopt, renewed the agitation among the Mexicans in favor of a liberal government.

Don Agustin Iturbide, a native Mexican and a colonel in the Mexican army, who during the recent civil war had distinguished himself on the royalist side, now threw off his allegiance and began the second revolution by proclaiming Mexico independent, February 24, 1821. The revolt of Iturbide was eminently successful. In the course of a few months the whole country recognized his authority except the capital, and by a treaty signed at Cordova, August 24, 1821, with the viceroy, Don Juan O'Donoju, he obtained possession of Mexico on September 27, and instituted a regency, of which he was the head, and O'Donoju one of the members.

Eight months later, with the support of the army and the mob of the city of Mexico, Iturbide was proclaimed emperor on the night of May 19, 1822, under the title of Agustin I. His reign was short. On December 2, Santa Anna, seconded by Bravo, Guerrero, and other chiefs, proclaimed the republic of Vera Cruz; and Iturbide abdicated on March 19, 1823, rather than see the country again plunged into civil war.

The congress which had been dissolved by Iturbide, but reconvoked by him shortly before his abdication, appointed a new governor, called *poder ejecutivo* (executive power), composed of Generals Bravo, Victoria, Negrete, and Guerrero. Iturbide was condemned to exile, and embarked at Vera Cruz for London in May of the same year, just twelve months after his exaltation to the throne.

On October 4, 1824, the congress promulgated a constitution closely resembling that of the United States, by virtue of which Mexico was formed into a republic with nineteen states and five territories. General Don Felix Fernando Victoria, better known as Guadalupe Victoria, one of the most intrepid heroes of the war of independence, was the first president, and General Bravo the first vice-president. Iturbide, who had the temerity to venture back to Mexico in this year, was arrested and shot at Padilla on July 19. In 1828 the candidates for the presidency were Generals Gomez Pedraza and Guerrero; on the election of the former the opposite party took up arms, and a bloody contest ensued, which terminated in the downfall of Pedraza's government and his flight from the country, January 4, 1829. Guerrero assumed the executive functions on April 1.

The year 1829 witnessed the recognition of the Mexican republic by the United States, and an attempt made by Spain to regain possession of her lost colony. In July, Brigadier-General Barradas, with four thousand Spanish troops, disembarked at Cabo Rojo, near Tampico, but he was compelled to capitulate on September 11, his troops being disarmed and sent to Havana.

The vice-president, General Anastasio Bustamente, who was commanding a reserve corps at Jalapa for the purpose of repelling the invaders, pronounced against Guerrero, and, having succeeded in deposing him, was himself elected president in his stead, January 11, 1830. Revolutionary disturbances continued till February 14, 1831, when Guerrero, one of the principal leaders, was treacherously delivered up to his enemies and executed. His name is perpetuated in that of one of the present states of the republic.

Bustamente was succeeded by Pedraza, who in turn was deposed by Santa Anna, the latter entering office on April 1, 1833, little more than three months after the inauguration of Pedraza. Bustamente was compelled to go into exile, and with him several other personages of political notoriety.

Congress now passed laws suppressing the convents and abolishing the compulsory payment of tithes. It also proposed to appropriate the property of the church to the payment of the national debt, but this measure led to insurrections and to further complications, which ended in 1835 in the abrogation of the constitution of 1824 and the conversion of the confederation of states into a consolidated republic, of which Santa Anna was nominally constitutional president, and practically dictator.

This revolution was acquiesced in by all parts of the country except Texas, where several thousand American colonists had settled. The refusal of the Texans to submit to the centralized government, which they pronounced a usurpation, induced Santa Anna to march against them in the beginning of 1836, with an army which was defeated and annihilated at San Jacinto, April 21, the Mexican president himself being taken prisoner.

In the previous month a convention of delegates assembled at the town of Washington had declared Texas an independent republic.

The captivity of Santa Anna threw Mexico again into confusion. Bustamente, who had returned from exile, became president April 19, 1837; but in the latter part of his term the power was virtually in the hands of Santa Anna, who, after a visit to President Jackson, at Washington, had been sent back to Mexico in a United States ship of war, in 1837. He held

TOMB OF JUAREZ.

office as revolutionary provisional president from March to July, 1839, when Nicolas Bravo became president for a week.

A long period of confusion followed, during which the constitution was suspended, and the government became a dictatorship, at the head of which was alternately Santa Anna, Bravo, and Canalizo (the last two as substitutes during the frequent absences of the first), from October 10, 1841, to June 4, 1844. Constitutional government was resumed in 1844, with Santa Anna as president, under another constitution promulgated June 12, 1843. He was deposed and banished by a revolution, and was succeeded, September 20, 1844, by Canalizo, who was deposed by a revolution in December. His successor, Herrera, was also driven from office by a revolution, December 30, 1845. Herrera was succeeded by General Paredes.

During his administration war opened with the United States, in consequence of the annexation of Texas to the American Union. In May, 1846, General Taylor crossed the Rio Grande, and after a series of engagements in which the American arms were uniformly successful, Santa Anna, who had returned from exile, regained the presidency, and, taking personal command of the army, was completely overthrown. By the treaty of Guadalupe-Hidalgo, signed in February, 1848, the war was ended, and California and New Mexico were ceded to the United States on the payment therefor of the sum of fifteen million dollars.

Santa Anna again left the country, but after the new administration of Herrera and that of Arista he was recalled in 1853, and was for the fifth time elevated to the presidency, though for a short season only, for, having attempted to secure the office for life, with the right to appoint at his death his own successor, he was deposed in August, 1855, by a revolution under Alvarez, governor of Guerrero, who was at once appointed to take his place. The latter resigned in favor of Comonfort in December of the same year, and a series of revolutions ensued, chiefly instigated by the church party, whom the president made his implacable enemies by a law recommended by him and adopted in June, 1856, for the sale of the church lands and the freedom of religious belief.

In March, 1857, a new and very democratic constitution was promulgated by congress, and Comonfort was constrained to accept it, but, owing to strenuous opposition from the church party, it did not come into operation till May. Meantime the repudiation of an acknowledged debt to Spain seemed likely to involve the republic in a war with that power. The president sought in vain for aid from the United States, and conspiracies multiplied on every side. Comonfort, although confirmed in the presidency under the new constitution in September, announced in December a change of government and of constitution; and in January, 1858, he was superseded by Zuloaga, who for a while had been his supporter, and was forced to take refuge in the United States.

Zuloaga was immediately opposed by Benito Juarez, who, as chief justice of the Supreme Court, was, by the provisions of the constitution, the president's lawful successor. Juarez was defeated, but he went to Vera Cruz and there established himself as the constitutional president.

Zuloaga was constrained to abdicate in favor of Miguel Miramon, his own general-in-chief, January 1, 1859. Miramon, a successful soldier rather than a good statesman, relied solely upon the fortune of arms for the subjection of Vera Cruz. Leaving Zuloaga as provisional president, he set forth upon a series of campaigns, which terminated in that of Calpulalpam, and the triumphal entry of Juarez into the capital on January 11, 1861. Much of Juarez's success was due to the recognition of him as the head of the government by the United States. While still at Vera Cruz he began the series of reforms which rendered his administration so popular on the one hand, but, on the other, paved the way for foreign invasion. Among them stand most prominent the making marriage a civil contract, the abolition of perpetual monastic vows and of ecclesiastical tribunals, the suppression of monasteries, and the appropriation of church property to the service of the state, the total value of which was estimated at rather more than three hundred million dollars, or nearly one-half the value of all the landed property in the country. These measures were soon followed by the complete separation of church and state.

A favorable opportunity soon offered. Spain, France, and England urged claims for the reparation of injuries and losses alleged to have been sustained by their subjects resident in Mexico; and, no satisfaction having been obtained from Juarez, he was informed that a joint expedition from the three powers would be sent to demand it: a measure agreed upon by the convention of London, October 31, 1861. In December, Vera Cruz was occupied by Spanish troops from Cuba, commanded by General Prim, and in January, 1862, by French and British forces.

But it was soon discovered that the English and Spanish claims could be settled by negotiation; it was agreed that a portion of the custom receipts should be appropriated to their liquidation, and in May the forces of both these powers were withdrawn from the country. The French army remained in the republic, thereby tacitly avowing their intention to overthrow the existing form of government in Mexico. This determination appears to have been solely prompted by Almonte and other agents of the church party sent to Europe for that purpose, and it was readily concurred in by Napoleon III. The French refused to treat with Juarez, and war was declared on April 16, 1862. Almonte, appointed president by the Vera Cruz authorities, who had revolted against Juarez (June 3), was deposed, and his government dissolved on October 2, by a decree of General Forey, the French commander. Hostilities began with an attack on Puebla by the French, who were then defeated, but who, after a number of subsequent engagements of varying success, occupied Mexico City on June 10, 1863. Juarez and his ministry having removed to San Luis Potosi. A regency was formed on the 24th; on July 8 an assembly of notables was convened, with power to decide upon the form of the future

THE NATIONAL PALACE.

government of Mexico; and on the 10th it resolved, by two hundred and fifty votes against twenty, upon an hereditary monarchical government under a Roman Catholic emperor. The crown was accepted by the Archduke Maximilian of Austria, with the title of Maximilian I., Emperor of Mexico. He arrived at the capital on June 12, 1864. The republican president, continually pursued by the imperialists, arrived by successive retreats at El Paso in September, 1865, and remained there until the commencement of the following year. On March 25, 1866, the Juarez troops captured Chihuahua, and that victory was followed by a number of others.

The 1st of November, 1866, General Diaz entered his natal city, to be crowned with laurels as her liberator. On April 2, he won in Puebla another most glorious victory, which made the walls of the empire totter, as this was one of the invader's strongholds.

After repeated remonstrances from the United States government, the French troops under Bazaine were withdrawn from Mexico early in 1867, the last detachment embarking at Vera Cruz on March 16. Maximilian, now left to his own resources, deemed it expedient to leave the capital and proceed northward. Toward the end of February he set out at the head of five thousand men and reached Querétaro, which was at once besieged by General Ramón Corona and General Mariano Escobedo, with an army of twenty thousand Juarists; Mexico, Puebla, and Vera Cruz being simultaneously invested by other divisions of the republican forces.

The ill-fated emperor was captured (May 15), tried by court-martial, condemned, and shot, with his two generals, Miramon and Mejia, on June 19, 1867.

Juarez re-entered the capital on July 16, and was re-elected president in the following October. During his flight before the imperial forces in the north his term of office had expired; but he issued a wise decree prolonging his exercise of the presidential functions until it should become possible to summon the representatives for a new election.

The work of reconstruction was interrupted for a short time by an attempt on the part of Santa Anna to occupy some of the gulf ports and promote a conspiracy against Juarez, who had rejected his offer to assist him in driving out the invaders. Santa Anna was captured at Sisal on July 12, 1867, tried at the castle of San Juan de Ulua, and condemned to banishment for eight years.

The years 1868 and 1869 were marked by insurrections, pronunciamientos, and revolutions, the most formidable of which was the pronunciamiento of Angel Santa Anna, who was taken after four months of depredations and bloodshed, and shot in company with his followers. President Juarez was again elected in 1871, the opposing candidates having been General Porfirio Diaz and Don Sebastian Lerdo de Tejada. He was the first president of Mexico who held power during his full term of office.

President Juarez died July 18, 1872, and was succeeded by Lerdo de Tejada, who was overthrown by another revolution in 1876.

General Porfirio Diaz, who had ably served his country all through her latter days of stress and trial, was then placed in the chief executive office in May, 1877. At the regular election of 1880, General Manuel Gonzalez was chosen to fill the position of president, and General Diaz gave way to him on December 1. General Gonzalez served out his full term of four years, and was then succeeded by General Diaz, who was elected by popular acclamation to the highest post of honor in the gift of Mexico. Ever since that time, December, 1884, President Diaz has served his country nobly and faithfully in that position, being now in his fifth term,—a record unmatched by any patriot in any country in the world.

CHAPTER II

THE AZTEC CIVILIZATION

WE often hear it said—and spoken as an argument against the beauty and romance of the Western Hemisphere—that America is a land without traditions, without poetry, and without castles. Ignorance is the only excuse for those who utter this heresy; for in Mexico are ancient ruins of buildings that were hoary with age when the famous castles of the Rhine and the comparatively young strongholds of England were in process of erection. Away back in the middle ages, whence we imagine the romance of Europe to have emanated, there was a civilization in Mexico that was even then historic. It is an ignorance, perhaps, that may be pardoned, since even our wisest archæologists and deepest scientific students of modern times cannot yet determine the age or origin of the most ancient of these landmarks.

No more interesting people for the modern student ever existed than the Aztecs, who seem to have been the equal in intelligence and advancement of any tribe in the world at that time. The Aztecs were most sincere in the practice of their religious rites. They believed in a supreme creator, invisible yet omnipresent, but requiring numerous assistants to perform his will, each of whom presided over some special natural phenomenon or phase of human existence. They had thirteen principal and several hundred inferior deities. The dread Huitzilopochtli, the war god of the Aztecs, was the patron divinity of the race, and myriads of human victims were sacrificed to him yearly in countless pyramidal temples throughout the realm. Quetzalcoatl, a more beneficent deity, was described by the natives as a tall white man, with a large forehead and flowing beard, who taught his favored people the art of government and the various arts of peace, especially those of the husbandman and silversmith, forbade bloody sacrifices and permitted only those of bread, roses, and perfumes, and warned against robbery and all violence. This god of the air, as he was named, having incurred the displeasure of one of the other chief deities, was compelled to leave the country; but on quitting the shores of the gulf he promised to return, and the Mexicans always looked forward to the auspicious day.

After his departure from the capital he tarried at Cholula, where a magnificent temple was dedicated to him, the ruins of which are among the most curious remains of Mexican antiquities. All these divinities were represented by images of clay, wood, stone, or precious metals and gems, but of most fantastic forms, coarse and hideous; and of the minor gods of every degree hosts of images were to be found in the dwellings of both great and small. The Mexicans, with all the other polished natives of Anahuac, regarded the souls of both man and brutes as immortal. The number of priests corresponded with the number of gods and temples; ancient historians affirm that five thousand were attached to the great temple of the capital, on the site of which now stands the cathedral. There were several different orders among the priests, the

The Cathedral.

chief of all being the two high priests, whose dignity was conferred by election. The high priests anointed the king, and were the oracles consulted by him on all important state concerns.

The sacerdotal hierarchies of the several gods were quite separate, and had each a gradation of their own. The temples (teocallis) were of two kinds,—low and circular, and high and pyramidal,—on the tops of which the sacrifices took place. Torquemada estimates that there were upward of forty thousand throughout the empire, and other historians estimate their number much higher. There were hundreds in each principal city, besides the great temple with several smaller ones within its precincts. In each outlying quarter of the city were other small courts with as many as six temples, and there were temples on the mountains and at intervals along the high-roads. They were solid pyramidal masses of earth cased with brick or stone, many of them more than one hundred feet square, and of a still greater height. The ascent was by flights of steps on the outside, and on the broad, flat summits were sanctuaries containing the images of the deities and altars on which fires were continually burning. Human sacrifices, which they made on the most trivial occasions, formed the chief religious ceremony of the Mexicans and the most important duty of the priesthood.

In later days the repetition of these sacrifices became mournfully frequent; some Franciscan monks computed that about twenty-five hundred persons were annually slaughtered on the altars of Tenochtitlan and some of the adjacent towns; and "days had been observed," writes Herrera, "on which above twenty thousand had thus perished, reckoning all the sacrifices in several parts." Within the temples were schools, colleges, and apartments for the priests. A few of the priestesses took vows of perpetual celibacy. Some of the priests were permitted to marry; those of whom chastity was required were punished with death for the slightest deviation from it. When a child of two years was dedicated to Quetzalcoatl, a priest with a knife made a slight cut on its breast, to confirm the dedication. Piercing the lips and nose for the insertion of various ornaments, and plucking the hairs of the nascent beard, were common practices among the Mexicans.

For purposes of record and communication they had a species of picture-writing bearing some relation to the Egyptian hieroglyphics. They had five books written in this way: the first treating of the seasons and years; the second, of the days and festivals throughout the year; the third, of dreams, omens, and other superstitious observances; the fourth, of baptism and the names of children (for they celebrated a baptismal ceremony much like the Christian rite, in which the infant's lips and breasts were sprinkled with water); and the fifth, of the ceremonies and prognostications used at marriages. Historical knowledge was preserved by tradition aided by picture-writings; and there were, besides the multitude of regular chronicles, certain men who kept important events, genealogies, etc., in their memory, and recited them when called upon. Translations of elaborate prose productions seem to show that eloquence and rhetorical effect were aimed at by Aztec scholars; but no original compositions have been preserved. Songs perpetuating their traditions, recited at the great festivals, formed one of the foremost branches of temple education.

Their musical instruments included various kinds of trumpets, whistles of bone and clay, horns of large sea-shells, bamboo flutes, many varieties of drums, and a few stringed instruments. Theatrical performances were given on open terraces in the market-places, the stage being covered with branches of trees; masks were indispensable, and the performances were inseparably connected with the religion. The plays were partly pantomimic and partly recitative. The art of prestidigitation was highly developed. Farces and masquerades were frequently given at the temples by the merchants, disguised as frogs, beetles, birds, butterflies, etc., the entertainment ending with dancing.

The Mexicans had a simple system of arithmetical notation, in which the first twenty numbers were expressed by a corresponding number of dots. The number twenty was expressed by a flag, and larger sums were reckoned by twenties, and expressed by repeating the number of flags. The square of twenty, four hundred, was denoted by a plume; and eight thousand, the cube of twenty, by a purse or sack. The year was divided into eighteen months of twenty days each, and both months and days were expressed by peculiar hieroglyphics. Five complementary days were added to make up the three hundred and sixty-five; and for the fraction over of nearly six hours, required to make the full year, they added thirteen days at the end of every fifty-two years, or cycle, which they called xiuhmolpilli, "the tying up of years." A month was divided into four weeks of five days each. The epoch from which the Mexicans computed their chronology corresponded with the year 1091 of the Christian era. They had no astronomical instruments except the dial, but their skill in the science of

SACRIFICIAL STONE.

astronomy is shown by their knowledge of the true length of the year, of the cause of eclipses, of the periods of the solstices and equinoxes, and of the transit of the sun across the zenith of Mexico. Most of their astronomical knowledge was derived from the Toltecs. The physicians were skilful; they had knowledge of several thousand plants and of hundreds of species of birds, quadrupeds, fishes, insects, reptiles, and minerals; but they mystified their cures with superstitious ceremonies. The Spanish conquerors attest the dexterity and success of the native surgeons in dressing wounds and in bloodletting.

The merchants and military officers had a fair notion of geography; maps and charts of certain regions, of rivers, and of the whole coast, were accurately drawn or painted on cloth. Agriculture was in tolerable advancement, the want of ploughs, oxen, and other animals being supplied by simple instruments and assiduous labor. Irrigation by means of canals was very efficient. Of the various Mexican implements, almost the only ones described are an axe of copper or bronze, with just the amount of tin alloy to give it the greatest hardness attainable, and knives and swords, razors, and arrow- and spear-heads of itztli, or obsidian. They were extremely skilful in the cultivation of gardens, in which they planted fruit-trees, medicinal plants, and flowers with much taste. Among their chief productions were maize, cotton, cacao, the maguey or aloe, chile, etc. The maguey alone furnished the poor with almost all the necessaries of life: paper, thread, needles, cloth, shoes, stockings, and cordage from the leaves, the thickest part of these with the trunk furnishing besides a substantial dish, and pulque and mezcatl from the fermented juice. From the juice of the maize-stalk they prepared sugar; from the cacao they made chocolate (Aztec, chocolatl), which they formed into tablets. In mining and metallurgy they were very expert. They exercised the arts of casting, engraving, chasing, and carving in metal with great skill; and in looms of simple construction they made manta (cotton cloth) and other tissues, some of which were of exquisite fineness, interwoven with rabbit-hair and feathers, their only substitutes for silk and wool, and painted or dyed in most gorgeous colors. With the feathers of birds tastefully disposed on fine cotton webs they made garments of the utmost magnificence. Buying and selling, there being no shops, were carried on in public squares or market-places. Earthenware of every description, and suited for every domestic use, was one of the chief Mexican industries; and many of the articles were painted in showy colors and designs. No beasts of burden were used, all carrying being done either by water, chiefly on the lakes, where a marvellous number of vessels were employed, or on men's backs. The maritime commerce was probably very trifling. For the rapid transmission of news towers were erected at intervals of six miles along the high-roads, where couriers were always in waiting for despatches, which were transferred from hand to hand at each stage. Despatches were thus carried three hundred miles in a day. The different trades were commonly grouped into a species of guild. The women shared equally with the men as well in social festivities as in labor. The Mexicans were simple in dress, but given to an inordinate display of ornaments. The people were courteous and polished, and strict observers of the proprieties of life.

The ancient temple of the Aztecs in the city of Mexico occupied the site of the present cathedral. It was a pyramidal edifice, constructed by Ahuitzotli, accounts of which appear in all histories of the Spanish invasion. It occupied, with all its different edifices and sanctuaries, not only the ground the cathedral now stands on, but a part of the plaza and streets adjoining. We are told that within its enclosure were five hundred dwellings; that its hall was built of stone and lime, and ornamented with stone serpents. We hear of its four great gates, fronting the four cardinal points; of its stone-paved court, great stone stairs, and sanctuaries dedicated to the gods of war; of the square destined for religious dances, and the colleges for the priests and seminaries for the priestesses; of the horrible temple, whose door was an enormous serpent's mouth; of the temple of mirrors, and that of shells; of the house set apart for the emperor's prayers; of the consecrated fountains, the birds kept for sacrifice, the gardens for the holy flowers, and of the terrible towers composed of the skulls of the victims,—strange mixture of the beautiful and the horrible. We are told that five thousand priests chanted night and day in the great temple to the honor and in the service of the monstrous idols, who were anointed thrice a day with the most precious perfumes, and that of these priests the most austere were clothed in black, their long hair dyed with ink, and their bodies anointed with the ashes of burnt scorpions and spiders; their chiefs were the sons of kings.

It is remarkable, by the way, that their god of war, Mejitli, was said to have been born of a woman—a Holy Virgin—who was in the service of the temple, and that when the priests, having knowledge of her disgrace, would have stoned her, a voice was heard, saying, "Fear not, mother, for I shall save thy honor and my glory;" upon which the god was born, with a shield in his left hand and an arrow in his right, a plume of green feathers on his head, his face painted blue, and his left leg adorned with feathers. Thus was his gigantic statue represented.

There were gods of the water, of the earth, of night, fire, hell; goddesses of flowers and of corn. There were oblations offered of bread and flowers and jewels, but we are assured that from twenty to fifty thousand human victims were sacrificed annually in Mexico alone. That these accounts are exaggerated, even though a bishop is among the narrators, we can scarcely doubt; but if the tenth part be the truth, let the memory of Cortez be sacred, who, with the Cross, stopped the shedding of innocent blood, founded the cathedral on the ruins of the temple, which had so often resounded with human groans, and, in the place of these blood-smeared idols, enshrined the mild form of the Virgin.

It was encompassed by a stone wall about eight feet high, ornamented on the outer side by figures of serpents in basso-rilievo, and pierced on the four sides by gate-ways opening on the four principal streets. Over each gate was an arsenal, and barracks near the temple were garrisoned by ten thousand soldiers. The temple itself was a solid, pyramidal structure of

CALENDAR STONE.

earth and pebbles, coated externally with hewn stones. It was square, its sides facing the cardinal points, and was divided into five stories, each of which receded, so as to be smaller than that below it. The ascent was by a flight of one hundred and fourteen steps on the outside, so contrived that to reach the top it was necessary to pass four times round the whole edifice; and the base of the temple is supposed to have been three hundred feet square. The summit was a large area, paved with broad, flat stones. On it were two towers or sanctuaries, and before each was an altar, on which a fire was kept continually burning. The top of this remarkable structure commanded a superb view of the city, lake, valley, and surrounding mountains.

Inside the museum, to-day, one may see the old Aztec calendar, a round stone covered with hieroglyphics, undecipherable to us, but full of meaning to countless thousands ages ago. It is a mass of porphyritic stone of ten feet diameter and circular shape. In the centre is a human head with the tongue hanging out, cut in relief. Around this head are five circles of hieroglyphic figures, intended for the computation of the different divisions of time in the calendar of the ancient Mexicans. The civil year was divided into eighteen months of twenty days each. The five intercalary days were added to the last month, and the fractions of hours were computed at the end of a cycle of fifty-two years. Thirteen years constituted a tlalpilli; four of these a cycle of fifty-two years, which were represented by bundles of reeds bound together with a string; two of these cycles of fifty-two years constituted another division of a hundred and four years, which was called an old age,—I do not remember the Mexican term. I copy the following extract of a very interesting letter upon the subject from the Abbé Hervas to Clavigero:

"The Mexican year began on the 26th of February, a day celebrated in the era of Nabonassar, which was fixed by the Egyptians, seven hundred and forty-seven years before the Christian era, for the beginning of their month Toth, corresponding with the meridian of the same day. If these priests fixed upon this day as an epoch because it was celebrated in Egypt, we have here the Mexican calendar corresponding greatly with the Egyptian.

"On the 26th of February of the above-mentioned year, according to the meridian of Alexandria, which was built three centuries after, the year properly began. The year and century have from time immemorial been regarded by the Mexicans with a degree of intelligence which does not at all correspond with their arts and sciences. In them they were certainly very inferior to the Greeks and Romans, but the discernment which appears in their calendar equals them to the most enlightened nations. Hence we may imagine that this calendar has not been the discovery of the Mexicans, but that they have received it from some more enlightened people, and as the last are not to be found in America, we must seek for them elsewhere, in Asia or in Egypt. This circumstance is confirmed by your affirmation that the Mexicans had their calendar from the Toltecas (originating from Asia), whose year, according to Boturini, was exactly adjusted by the course of the sun more than a hundred years before the Christian era, and also from observing that other nations, namely, the Chiapanese, made use of the same calendar with the Mexicans, without any difference but that of their symbols."

In the museum, also, is their "Stone of Sacrifice," with a hollow in the middle where the victim was laid, while six priests, dressed in red, with green plumes on their heads, held him down and the chief priest cut him open, took out his heart, and offered it as a sacrifice to the idol of the Aztecs. Thank Heaven! Mexico of to-day has outgrown such practices.

When the flag of the republic was unfurled in 1821, the symbol upon it was that of the old native race,—the eagle and the cactus, the emblems of the Aztecs. They were a people without means of intercommunication, of different languages, in whom was mingled the poetry of paganism with the common principles of Christianity. Their intellectual classes were selfish and inert, their subdued classes indifferent; their wants were simple and easily supplied, and therefore there was no incentive to manufactures, commerce, or education; they knew little of arms and possessed none. All this made up a reason why these people did not sooner seize their chances for building up a representative government on the ruins of hereditary despotism.

Clinging yet with the Indian pertinacity to ancient customs in dress, in traditions, and in manners, many of the common people seem to a stranger as far removed from the progress of events to-day as the fossil remains of a past age. They apply themselves to any work which interests them, but as soon as that is over they relapse again into indifference. Good or bad, the gentle, trusting, superstitious, easily yielding nature of their ancestors is repeated and continued in the descendants. Ages of misrule and oppression did not break their sweet kindliness of soul nor dull the instinctive courtesy of loyal elevation natural to the Aztec citizen.

Patriotic they are, too. In spite of their seeming indifference, a strong vein of national spirit runs through the people. Hidalgo, Morelos, Guerrero, Juarez, Diaz, are to them living embodiments of vital truths, brave lights of patriotism that no reign of terror can obliterate. They have kept alive the spirit of liberty. The eagerness with which, in the plazas of many towns, are pointed out monuments, "Chihuahua á Hidalgo" and "Tacubaya á sus Mártiros," proves all this.

There is everything to hope for a country whose people have this principle so strongly intrenched. Once let them be aroused to a proper understanding of their own importance, and the threads of their advance will be quickly woven into the strong fabric of progress.

CHAPTER III

MEXICO IN GENERAL

MEXICO, the fairy-land of tropical flowers and majestic, snow-capped mountains, opens to the view of the tourist, who has hitherto followed the beaten paths of travel, a mine of unexpected delight in its natural wealth of scenery, historic associations, marked race characteristics, and evidences of steady advancement in the van of progress. A wonderful country it is indeed, where Nature has been so lavish that she causes to grow upon its surface a vegetation so varied that it includes almost every plant of tropical lands, together with the sturdy firs of the farthest north. Some strange magic seems to hold one within its gates. Perhaps it is the dreamy poetic strain of old Spain whose traditions still tinge the country with the romance of the Cid, Manrique's lays, and the last sigh of the Moor. Echoes of the Alhambra still linger in the graceful Moorish arches of the public buildings, while the gardens of King Boabdil live again in the beautiful Alamedas with their stately trees, luxuriant vegetation, gorgeous flowers, graceful monuments, elaborate fountains, and cool shady walks.

In every city of any size is always the Alameda for the people; that of the city of Mexico being especially artistic in arrangement and the profusion and beauty of its flowers. Side by side with the pushing needs of modern civilization and progress are to be seen evidences of the artist's instinct, which finds expression in beautiful forms of architecture, instead of the solid but unsightly blocks of stone which so disfigure our large American cities.

Wonderful has been the progress of Mexico in these last fifteen years; but it has not been the rapid mushroom growth of mere sordid money-getting, which leaves no time for beautifying the cities or ministering to the artistic sense of the people. While railroads,

CORRECTIONAL SCHOOL, CITY OF MEXICO.

FOUNTAIN IN THE ALAMEDA, CITY OF MEXICO.

canals, and telegraph routes have been built, the beauty of public buildings, churches, monuments, and great public squares is not forgotten.

In its museums are stored the antiquities of the Aztecs; in its libraries are the songs and annals of its old Spanish writers; in its statues are reproduced the features and forms of its heroes. With so much "local color," variety, and picturesqueness, it is strange that this rich mine has not been more worked by the novelist, poet, and dramatist of America. Our artists journey to Spain, Algiers, and Egypt, when they might find quite as rich material at their very doors in this wonderful land of picturesque types, tropical vegetation, and splendid atmospheric effects.

True, French fashions have come among the upper classes and almost crowded out the graceful Castilian dress; still, the *mantilla* and high comb are seen to-day at high mass; the ranchero, or planter, is gorgeous in his short jacket elaborately embroidered, his slashed trousers ornamented with gold and silver lace and buttons, his wide-rimmed and sumptuously adorned hat, and his shining spurs.

The black-eyed señorita, with a rose in her hair, still peeps coquettishly from her latticed window or balcony at the cloaked gallant who twangs his lute and casts languishing glances toward his inamorata, not being permitted in any other way to voice his passion.

There are still in the moonlit nights the tinkle of guitars, the sinuous fandango, and the gypsy dance; and, above all, the towering peaks of mighty mountains, the glow of volcanic fires, and the sunsets of a tropical land.

Every one who goes to Mexico has in his note-book something like this: "Don't forget to see a bull-fight." Under the humane rule of President Diaz this brutal and revolting amusement is passing into disrepute; but still it exists, and is largely attended.

Pedro Romero, in the eighteenth century, established rules and regula-

ENTRANCE TO THE PASEO DE LA REFORMA.

tions which are still followed in conducting a bull-fight. The company is made up of the principal espada, or swordsman, four mounted picadors, four banderilleros, who manipulate the sharp, barbed goads, and two capeadors, who distract the poor beasts by waving and fluttering their cloaks. The gorgeous trappings of these men make a brilliant spectacle as they ride into the ring. The foreign visitor generally shudders and says, "How horrible!" but ends by going to see the fight and staying it out. "It is one of the institutions of the country," he says, "and one must see everything."

Among the higher classes social life in the republic is most charming. While there is considerable of ceremony and conventionality, there is also much of refinement, culture, unfailing courtesy, and delicate gallantry. The scholar, the artist, and the *littérateur* may all find congenial society. Hospitality is as generous as it is proverbial. One has only to be properly introduced to be the recipient of lavish attentions. Often gifts of flowers, birds, curios, and even valuable relics are offered with princely generosity.

In Riding Costume—Charo Suits.

The women who adorn the upper circles of society are justly noted for their personal beauty, their virtues, and their accomplishments, while their charm of manner seems a part of the poetry of this romantic land of song and story.

There is a good system of public schools and academies for higher education, and many benevolent institutions, all of which receive the earnest and substantial support of the government.

Railway and diligence lines have eliminated distances and made travelling comparatively easy, and now there is no interesting portion of Mexico that is inaccessible to the tourist.

Of the great natural resources of this country in its mines, fruits, woods, stone and marble quarries, and products of the soil, there is so much to say that further mention of these must be left to succeeding chapters.

Entrance to the Alameda, City of Mexico.

"Mexico has a world-wide reputation for its mineral wealth," says one writer. "It has given Spain untold millions, and made it one of the richest nations of the world. It has made individual millionaires in great number. It has produced since 1821 one hundred thousand tons of silver and five hundred tons of gold, of the value of four billion three hundred and twenty million dollars. When discovered by the Spanish it promised them great mineral wealth, and has kept that promise."

Mexico has all the climates of the earth, from the frozen regions of the pole, in her snow-clad mountains, to the equatorial heat of her *tierras calientes*.

What stirs the traveller to his depths when for the first time he looks down upon Mexico from afar? Beauteous she is, bathed in light, set in her lakes like some jewel in burnished

HALL OF AMBASSADORS, IN THE NATIONAL PALACE.

silver. But it is not alone nor chiefly her beauty that draws him to her, that fills him with irresistible emotion; it is that he knows himself to be looking upon another "Thebes of the hundred gates," upon a theatre of mighty events which succeed one another down the long vista of the centuries till they are lost in the mists of antiquity; it is that gazing up at Popocatepetl, where he rears his snow-crowned head like some grim despot, he realizes what bloody dramas, what idyls of love and happiness, have been played and sung at his feet in times when the pyramids of Gizeh were not so much as dreamed of. Not in sumptuous buildings, not in the beauties lavishly scattered by the hand of Nature, does that attraction consist which certain cities and places have for us; it is a something which lies deeper below the surface, a mysterious essence which makes attractive their very ugliness and defects.

Its antiquity and its variety together make Mexico endlessly interesting. The archæologist and the ethnologist both find here an inexhaustible field for their inquiring spirits. And what diversity in the views it offers, from the interminable table-land of Anahuac to the luxuriant forests of Yucatan and the picturesque ranges of Lower California! What variety! And all enriched and ennobled by the historic reminiscences evoked at every step by those mute witnesses of a civilized past which lie everywhere.

Science, commerce, and the arts draw many visitors to Mexico, but for the artistic or poetic visitor she holds treasures far exceeding those material and inexhaustible ones which in all times have roused the cupidity of the entire world. Here some little town, the time-blackened walls of its ancient church showing through the surrounding trees, melancholy, dreaming over the

STATUE OF COLUMBUS, ON THE PASEO.

past; there some castle, proud, poised upon its rock like an eagle, half hidden in century-old cypresses, whose boughs, hung with paxtle, sigh sadly to the breeze; there, again, some fortress rising from coral beds, within whose walls more tears have been shed than there are waves in the salt sea around it. Buried cities one finds, the green corn waving above them; pyramids of time-worn stone; broken columns; baths where kings have sported, carved in the solid rock; grim idols, half hidden in the prickly pears, and whose weight is calculated by tons. Gloomy temples are there like those of India and Egypt, palaces of an architecture monstrous and superb as that of Assyria, hidden in savage and virgin forests whose ever-renewed youth mocks at cities and civilization as Eternity mocks at Time.

CHAPTER IV

CUSTOMS AND CHARACTERISTICS

MEXICO was christened by the conquerors "New Spain," and to this day it has many Spanish characteristics. The city of Mexico is nearly as large as Madrid or Barcelona, and far surpasses both in novelty and interest. Outside of its wonderful picture-gallery, the finest in the world, Madrid is only an imitation Paris, while Barcelona is a bright, attractive modern business city. Mexico is all these, and, in addition, interests with Oriental scenes and suggestions. It has many of the sight-seeing attractions of Madrid, Barcelona, and gay Seville, with touches of scenes from the streets of Cairo. Guadalajara and Puebla are nearer the size of Seville, and each has manifold attractions. Guanajuato is the Mexican reminder of Toledo and Granada, perched on the rocky hill-sides, terraced, quaint, and picturesque. You hear the same language spoken as in Spain; in both countries you pay separately for each act at a theatrical performance; men smoke constantly and everywhere, as, in fact, some of the women do; while in no other country except old Spain is the bull-fight so popular an institution.

And, after all, bull-fighting seems more or less appropriate to the peculiar civilization of Mexico. The picturesque setting that is given there calls up vaguely the bouts in the amphitheatre in the days of Roman glory, and the more modern jousts and tournaments of our Anglo-Saxon forefathers.

The best place chosen in Mexico City for the contest is in Tacubaya. The amphitheatre is enclosed by a wall of adobe.

PATIO OF THE NATIONAL SCHOOL.

The sunny side of the enclosure is furnished with rows of wooden benches, but the shady side is provided with boxes for the accommodation of the grandees of the city and of distinguished visitors. The audiences are composed of all classes of society,—from the proud swell, with his four-in-hand, to the barefoot, dark-eyed, patient-faced Castilian lad. About one-fifth of the gathering is composed of women. In the boxes are beauties with olive skin and peach's bloom, their large, dark eyes lighting up with enthusiasm at exciting turns in the sport. Bands of music play lively airs, and great drums are pounded to keep the spectators satisfied during the preparations for the fray. Presently a herald, stationed in the governor's box, sounds a call, whereupon the pit opens and a troop of matadors appears. Each one wears a plumed hat, a scarlet sash, an appropriate jacket and breeches of black velvet trimmed with gold lace. A poniard hangs from his belt, a scarlet cloak upon his arm, and a pike-staff in his hand. Altogether the matador is an extremely picturesque-looking fellow, and his figure is usually lithe and dashing. Behind the matadors comes a troop of horsemen, mounted on handsome beasts decked out with the gayest trappings. Following comes a team of mules dragging a whiffletree and a long rope. This takes some of the romance and beauty out of the *ensemble*, for these mules are to drag the dead away from the field. The cavalcade stops before the governor's box and salutes his excellency, who makes a brief speech, commending their appearance and wishing them good luck. The matadors then go to a rack in front of the governor's box, upon which hang several rows of darts gaudy with colored paper rosettes and fringes. Upon this rack they hang their plumed hats, and then pause to give the spectators an opportunity to admire their attractive persons. The horsemen ride out, followed by the mules, and the beginning of the sport is close at hand. Again the pit opens, and the horsemen re-enter. A door is opened in the pit, and a bull emerges into the ring. As he lunges in one direction, two or three matadors flap their scarlet cloaks in his face; when he turns from them and bounds in another direction, he runs into the cloaks of the other matadors. In a little while his temper becomes aroused, and he runs madly across the ring and tries to clear the wall; but this, of course, he cannot do. If he will not attack his tormentors one of the horsemen rides up to him and strikes him in the face with his spear. The poor animal, maddened with pain, rushes at the blindfold horse, which he raises upon his horns and flings to the ground. The horseman knows what is coming, and dismounts just before the critical moment. After one horse is disposed of, others are brought out. When the bull grows exhausted, the matadors re-enter and tease him with their scarlet cloaks and the points of their lances. Should the bull suddenly turn, his tormentor, putting the point of his lance in the ground, vaults by its aid over the lowered horns and retreats behind some planks. The next part of the programme is to throw ornamented darts into the bull's side. The brute runs hither and thither. Soon, whoever has charge of the entertainment sounds a call, which is the death-signal. The chief matador steps forward with a red blanket and a sword, and, approaching the bull, flaps the blanket in his eyes. The bull lunges toward him, but with great precision and

PATIO OF THE NATIONAL PREPARATORY SCHOOL.

dexterity the matador jumps aside, and with one swift thrust puts his weapon into the bull's heart. The animal staggers and falls to the ground, and the matador pierces his brain with a poniard. The mules appear and are hitched to the dead beast; the band strikes up; the matadors bow to the aristocratic boxes, and clowns disport themselves in the ring till another bull is brought forth. The horses are nearly always killed, the bulls are always dispatched; but the riders and matadors seldom receive any injuries.

The Christmas customs of Mexico are uncommonly pretty and touching. The Christmas-tree is not a native institution, though it gives indications of becoming naturalized. In its stead Mexican children have what they call a pinata, which affords them just as much fun. The pinata is a large earthenware jar, which is covered with colored tissue-paper, often in such manner as

A BULL-FIGHT.

to represent a ship, a balloon, a grotesque human figure, or other object. This jar is filled with all sorts of dainties dear to children,—oranges, raisins, candy, peanuts, etc.,—and is hung up in the corridor or court-yard of the house. Each of the children and grown-up people is blind-folded in turn, and, after being turned around once or twice, has a stick placed in his or her hand and is invited to break the pinata. The other guests have to be on their guard, for the wielder of the stick is generally, after being turned round, quite out of his bearings, and often brings down his stick within an inch of the head of one of the party. He is allowed three trials, and if he is not successful the handkerchief is removed and another takes his turn. At length a crash is heard,—some one has made a true hit,—the pinata is broken and the good things fall in a shower to the ground, and a general scramble ensues among the young ones to obtain possession of as large a share as possible.

The posadas are a characteristically Mexican celebration. They commemorate the journey of Mary and Joseph from Nazareth to Bethlehem. This journey, performed by Mary mounted on an ass, which Joseph guided, is supposed to have occupied nine days. Each evening they naturally approached some dwelling to beg a night's shelter. It is this nightly episode that is commemorated in Mexican houses by the posadas, or the begging of the posada (*pedir posada*), meaning shelter, lodging, or entertainment. It is customary for a number of Mexican families to club together to celebrate the nine nights. At the appointed hour the guests assemble at one house. Each guest is provided with a taper. All the servants are invited to take part in what is regarded as a religious ceremony, for Catholicism in Mexico is a democratic and levelling element. There are no fashionable and expensive pews in Mexican churches, and one often sees the ragged beggar kneeling side by side with the inheritress of a hundred Castilian titles. A procession is formed, at the head of which are carried figures of Mary riding an ass and Joseph leading it. Overhead hovers an angel guiding the pilgrims on their way. The dresses of the holy couple are of gay-colored satin. St. Joseph is usually represented with a pilgrim's staff and gourd. The procession marches several times round the corridors of the house, intoning the Litany of Loretto, a series of poetical invocations in honor of the Virgin. When the litany is finished, two or three of the party enter the house, which, according to Mexican custom, opens on the corridor. They close the door on the rest of the party, at the head of which are the Virgin and Joseph. A dialogue in chanted verse then ensues,—this being the nightly request of the pilgrims for shelter from the cold and dangers of the road. The party outside speak in the name of Joseph and beg admittance for his wife and himself. Those within at first deny the favor, but at last relent, touched by the innocence and distress of the pilgrims. The versicles are simply sung to a tune of immemorial antiquity in Mexico. When the doors are thrown open the pilgrims are placed on an improvised altar decked with quantities of lighted tapers, shiny tinsel, and toys of small intrinsic value. All the party kneel, and prayers are recited. After that a tray is passed round containing small jars filled with candy. Each guest is invited to take one, and with this compliment the ceremony, properly speaking, ends. In the patriarchal days of the viceroys the posada was a strictly religious custom, and in a few old-fashioned families it is so still. But in most Mexican houses the posadas are only a pretext now for having a good time. The religious exercises are observed in the quickest and most perfunctory manner, and a dance and general romp follow, kept up until the early hours of the morning. The ninth night of the posadas—that is, Christmas Eve—is celebrated on the most extensive and luxurious scale of all, and generally the wealthiest of all the families that have clubbed together gives the entertainment. In memory of the night when the Saviour was born, the figure of an infant is carried in procession, and is placed in a manger between the ox and the ass in a prettily adorned cave, which is intended to represent the stable where Mary and Joseph took refuge when they found that there was no room for them in the inns.

November marks in Mexico the setting in of winter fashions. For years it has been the custom to partition off a portion of the Zócalo or the Alameda as a promenade for the rich and well-to-do. One year the whole Zócalo was enclosed and decorated with flags, mirrors, Spanish moss, and potted plants, and at night was lit with many-colored electric lights. On certain nights of the week this enclosure was frequented by all the *beau monde* of Mexico, who formed an elegantly attired throng.

The feast day celebrated by the Catholic Church on November 1 is called All Saints', and ranks as one of the most solemn of the year. It was instituted at an early period in the history of the Church as a means of doing honor to the many saints to whom it was impossible to assign a separate feast. The feast which follows on November 2 is popularly known as All Souls', and is the day for the commemoration of the faithful departed. On this day masses are said and special prayers offered by Catholics for the release of souls from purgatory. The priests wear black vestments, and in some of the churches a huge catafalque is erected in the centre of the nave.

The origin of the feast of All Souls dates back to the year 827 A.D., when Amalario, the deacon of Metz, published the office for the dead; but it was not until 998 A.D. that St. Odillon, abbot of Cluny, instituted in his churches this feast in commemoration of the faithful deceased. This feast soon prevailed in the Catholic Church. It took a rather wider range in France in the eighteenth century, when the laborers began to dedicate gratuitous work, for the benefit of the poor of All Souls' day, and offered to the Church wheat, which, according to the Pauline designation, is the symbol of resurrection.

The idea of these November feasts is not original with Mexico; it has found root in nearly every religion.

The feasts of All Saints and All Souls, although not celebrated with the *éclat* of former years, are still very interesting in certain portions of the republic, especially along the gulf coast. There the Indians are in the habit of placing upon the graves dulces, or sweetmeats, prepared with *chilacayote* and *calabazas*. The Indians place these dulces with large jars of water upon the tombs of their deceased relatives and friends during the afternoon of November 1, so that the dead—that night at least—can have something to eat and drink. This latter arrangement is similar to some of the customs of Germany and Central Europe.

FOUNTAIN OF THE SALTO DE AGUA.

"Responsos" are not given everywhere in the churches, as in Mexico City, and recited over a skull. Out in the country district they are given in the cemeteries by some priest. Armed with a bough of aromatic hyssop and his well-thumbed breviary and his ready rosary, the priest visits the tombs, sprinkles upon them some holy water, and recites a Latin prayer or two. Receiving his "medio," he is jostled on to the next grave.

The "ofrenda," or offering, is, singular to say, of Aztec origin. The Aztecs were in the habit of cremating their dead; and they kept the ashes in an urn with fragments of precious metals, emeralds, etc., also putting in food and catlis, together with bows and arrows and a quantity of a great golden-hearted flower called the *zempoalzoichitl*, which can be found growing in Mexico profusely at this day. This flower is used to decorate the sepulchres in company with white roses, the ruby "*flor de noche buena*," the haughty hortenses and velvety forget-me-nots, as well as violets, geraniums, and marguerites. In the country districts the ofrenda is much more elaborate than in the city. The women make handkerchiefs and napkins curiously embroidered, also wax figures more or less hideous, and offer these with trays of sweetmeats on the graves. Candles are also used by thousands in the little *panteóns* or cemeteries of the country. Among the simple folk in these Indian villages the local poets write up more or less readable "poetry," which is also included in the offering to the dead. In some isolated portions of Mexico this custom prevails to such an extent that the children beg money from their parents to buy fruit for that purpose, or else, they say, the departed will come on Halloween and pull their little feet. It is impossible to give an idea of all the curious customs and incidents that prevail in the rural districts of Mexico with respect to the observance of these holidays. Halloween in Mexico does not partake of the mischievous and jocose character of the day in the United States and England.

Among the characteristic sights of these days peculiar to Mexico are the strange toys sold on the streets and in stalls. They consist of skull and cross-bones of sugar adorned with gold leaf, lath coffins surrounded with priests and acolytes and containing a skeleton, miniature catafalques, altars, etc. Many of the coffins are so arranged that by pulling a string the lid opens and the dead man sits up. No Mexican child is content without one of these toys. The mozos and domestic servants also look at this time for their festival, to which they give the name of *calavera* (skull). It is a carnival of death; a mingling of levity with sadness.

COMMERCIAL SCHOOL.

It is the custom to visit on All Souls' day the graves of departed relatives and friends, to place wreaths and candles round about, and to offer prayers. Any one of Mexico's cemeteries offers an interesting scene on that day. The French cemetery, where many of Mexico's wealthiest families have their vaults, is one mass of beautiful wreaths. The grave of Minister Romero Rubio, who was recently interred there, is hardly visible beneath the load of floral offerings. The tomb of Juarez, in the San Fernando cemetery, receives many mementos from admirers of the great Liberal statesman. The cemetery of Tepeyac, near Guadalupe, where lie the remains of Santa Anna and members of many of Mexico's first families, is visited by a throng of devout mourners, bearing costly wreaths. The abundance of trees which darkens the English cemetery even at mid-day makes it eminently harmonious with the tendency to sober meditation. This cemetery contains the tombs of the first Englishmen, almost the first foreigners, that ever came to this country, away back in the twenties. The American cemetery is near the English. There is a monument to the American soldiers who perished in the valley of Mexico in 1847. This receives its floral offerings on Decoration Day. But if the tourist or resident wishes to see a characteristically Mexican celebration of All Souls', he should go to the great Dolores cemetery. Except on very few tombs, he will find no French creations in the way of wreaths, but abundance of coarse yellow flowers. In some parts of the country it is the custom of the common people to place meat and drink near the grave on the eve of All Saints'. But this is obviously a pagan survival, which the clergy have endeavored to uproot.

All good Americans are interested in the American cemetery in Mexico. Out beyond the southwestern limits of the city, on the boundary line formed by what is known as the Calzada de la Verónica, is this little patch of ground which possesses such peculiar interest for Americans, and especially for those who reside in Mexico. Though on Mexican soil, it is American in the fullest sense of the word, for the full and perfect title therein is vested in the United States, and its management and control are in the hands of the War Department at Washington. Mexico is the only country on earth where the United States possesses a title to land for such purposes, and exercises authority over foreign soil. It was in 1873 that the cemetery was subjected to the rules and regulations affecting United States national cemeteries. It was established in 1851, under an act of Congress approved September 28, 1850.

The seven hundred and fifty soldiers who were killed by the enginery of war on the plains of Mexico are buried together in a single grave. In memory of these, a simple granite shaft about six feet high has been raised. It stands on a square pedestal made of dark granite. On one side is the inscription,—

PATIO OF A SCHOOL.

TO THE MEMORY
OF THE
AMERICAN SOLDIERS
WHO PERISHED IN THIS VALLEY IN 1847,
WHOSE BONES,
COLLECTED BY THEIR COUNTRY'S ORDER,
ARE HERE BURIED.

On the other side is a marble tablet inserted in the granite, on which is written without comment,—

CONTRERAS
CHURUBUSCO
MOLINO DEL REY
CHAPULTEPEC
MEXICO.

In addition to these seven hundred and fifty soldiers, five hundred and seventy-five have been buried in the cemetery whose names are all recorded, though, owing to the absence of monuments, the exact location of each body cannot be given.

To obtain the right to bury there it is necessary to secure a permit from the United States consul-general, the permit being a voucher for the citizenship of the deceased. In addition to this, another permit has to be obtained from the civil authorities, which is a mere formality, as Americans, living or dead, have always received magnanimous treatment and the kindest consideration from district authorities as well as from those of the general government. No graves are sold, and the selection of the last resting place lies with the superintendent. No charge is made and no expense incurred. The United States government pays the employees and superintendent out of the annual appropriation, and the friends of the deceased are at liberty to express affection by the adornment of the graves with monuments and flowers.

The funeral customs of Mexico are a source of constant interest to strangers in that land, as the burial of the dead is a ceremony of great display. The poor rent handsome coffins, which they have not the means to buy, and transfer the body from its temporary casket to a cheap box before it is laid in the grave. Invitations are issued by messenger, and advertisements of funerals are published in the newspapers or posted at the street corners, like those of a bull-fight or a play. Announcements in faultless Spanish are sent to friends in big black-bordered envelopes, and are usually decorated with a picture of a tomb.

There is a very pretty custom in Mexico by which all people who call upon a mourning family must dress in deep black. You are ushered through the darkened rooms into the presence of the bereaved lady, and find her charmingly and tenderly cordial and friendly. This is but one of the many pleasant ways the Mexicans have of paying honor to the memory of their beloved dead.

During the month of November, in every village of Spain and her former colonies, the traditional legend of Don Juan Tenorio, dramatized by Don José Zorrilla, is put on the stage. The sentimentality of this piece seems to have an irresistible fascination for Spanish taste. It is impossible to understand the Spanish character without having read or heard of this extraordinary play. It has been said that every youth of Spanish descent would be a Don Juan, and every Spanish maiden a Doña Ines. It is sincerely to be hoped that this is not true, for the exploits of Juan in a more prosaic age and country would inevitably have qualified him for the gallows. The drama of Don Juan is now, however, a little off color, and is not attended by the *beau monde*. Indeed, it is pronounced by the best people of Mexico somewhat vulgar. But in the days of Maximilian things were otherwise; the emperor was a great admirer of the drama, and at his invitation the author Zorrilla once came to Mexico to superintend some private productions of Don Juan at the castle of Chapultepec. Maximilian never tired of hearing this fantastic drama.

Its author, Don José Zorrilla, was a really distinguished Spanish poet, and it is not to be supposed that he himself sincerely approved the false glitter and the absurd and vulgar bombast which are the chief ingredients of Don Juan. But, as Johnson said of Dryden, he probably knew it was bad enough to please, his aim being merely to satisfy the public.

Don Juan Tenorio is the history of a lifetime. The play opens in a low Seville dive, where Don Juan Tenorio and Don Luis Mejia exchange wagers on their pre-eminence in crime, a wager which Don Juan wins, for he proves that he has killed thirty-two men and won seventy-two pretty women, while Don Luis lags behind with only twenty-three men killed and fifty-six conquests. Don Juan then makes another bet, stranger still, and this time the life of one or the other is the stake,—viz., that he will rob Don Luis of his lady-love, Doña Ana del Pantoja; and he succeeds.

Don Juan was in love with Doña Ines Ulloa, daughter of the comendador de Calatrava, Don Gonzalo de Ulloa, who had agreed to give him her hand, but in disguise he had been present at the orgy in the dive and heard the recital of Juan's villanies, so he resolved to shut up his daughter forever in the cloister where she had been educated. Don Juan scales the walls of the convent and carries off the lady. He afterward kills in a duel the old comendador, as well as his rival, Don Luis Mejia, and Doña Ines dies of grief.

In the second part of the drama Don Juan visits the graveyard where all his victims are buried. He is at first inclined to be a little overawed by his surroundings, but afterward he breaks into defiant blasphemies, and invites the dead comendador to sup at his table. To his amazement, the marble figure surmounting the monument accepts the invitation, and the revelry of that night is interrupted first by a strange knocking, and then by the entry into the supper-room of the murdered man's ghost. And how does Don Juan end? Not on the gallows, as might have been hoped, but in a duel with Captain Centellas, and his soul, when claimed by his satanic majesty as his due, is rescued by the spirit of Doña Ines, with a calcium ballet in Paradise performed by nymphs of a very material and earthly order.

No doubt "Don Juan" is a correct portraiture of the age and country in which the scene is laid. The time is 1545.

Even to this day the Indians observe a fiesta on the 21st of August in memory of the tortures to which Cuautemoc and his cousin Tlacopan, Prince of Texcoco, were subjected by Cortez,

JUAREZ AVENUE.

who endeavored to force from Cuautemoc the secret of the hidden treasure. The monument dedicated to Cuautemoc on the Paseo has a relief representing Cuautemoc and Tlacopan standing upon stone slabs, with their feet hanging over flames of fire. Around the tortured warriors are clustered the Spaniards, anxiously awaiting the secret which Cuautemoc never disclosed. "Do not be weary," he said to his tormentors; "he who has resisted famine, death, and the wrath of the gods is not capable of humiliating himself now like a weak woman; the treasury of the kings of Mexico I submerged in the lake four days before the siege of the city, and you will never find it."

One of the Easter customs is the hanging in effigy of Judas Iscariot, which is done everywhere in the country, from the plazas of the large cities down to the smallest hamlet. The Catholic citizens attire themselves in deep mourning throughout all of Holy Week, and on Saturday these grotesque figures of him who betrayed his Lord are brought out everywhere and hung. After this they are burned with all the contempt due to the betrayer of his Master.

A peculiar custom of the country is the "Bando." From time immemorial it has been the fashion in Mexico to proclaim publicly any changes in the government; this was the custom long before the day of newspapers, and is still followed, on instructions from the war department. This is done in Mexico City, soon after the election of the President, in the following order. A division is organized consisting of two brigades, one of infantry and one of cavalry, accompanied by a light Maxim battery. The chief of staff is attended by an adjutant with two captains and three subalterns. The infantry brigade is commanded by its general, accompanied by two captains and two subalterns. The cavalry brigade is led by its general, a major, two captains, and two subalterns; and a platoon of mounted gendarmes accompanies both generals. The "Bando" is inaugurated at nine in the morning. The aldermen and city notary accompany the military parade in carriages, affixing the proclamation at certain street corners, and otherwise making known the result of the presidential election to the inhabitants of the city, with proper formalities and the pomp and circumstance of military parade. This is a curious and highly interesting custom.

Mexican women of the better class are noted for their beauty; and everywhere the young girls are exquisitely pretty. The slender oval of the face, the rich olive of the cheek, the long, sweeping, dark lashes over superb eyes, glowing at once with passion and tenderness, the low forehead with its rippling mass of dusky hair, the slender neck, the lithe form, the springing step, and the dainty foot make them like a poet's dream of darkly brilliant loveliness, and not to be measured by any other type in the world.

AN INDIAN GIRL.

Among the upper classes of Mexico will be found as high a degree of social and intellectual refinement as exists in Paris; as quick a reception and as cordial a knowledge of the arts and literature as people of the busy cities of the United States have acquired. Their wealth is lavishly displayed; their taste is exercised to a degree equal to that of any other people in the world; and the interior of many of their dwellings furnishes a glimpse of happiness and cultured elegance that, with their less active temperament, they enjoy more than do their northern neighbors. Yet these people, who receive the latest Paris fashions and literature by every steamer, still cling to some ancient customs. Social law restricts intercourse between the sexes, as in the Latin nations of Europe, and Pedro makes love to Mercedes through his father and hers; and a parent chooses his son-in-law as he selects his business partners or the directors in a bank. The people are noted for their good manners, their politeness, and their courtesy to strangers. They make excellent hosts, and they throw their houses open to their guests with the most hearty generosity. Few even of the poorest but have a very respectable whiteness in their shirts and drawers, and the towels and napkins which they use abundantly about their baskets of cakes and dulces are snowy as laundry work can make them. They are, besides, beautifully embroidered with the exquisite fine drawn-work for which the women of Mexico are celebrated. It is astonishing what beauty and value are often added to coarse and common material in this way. The bodices and short-sleeved chemises of the young girls, and even the woollen petticoats of the Indians, are almost invariably ornamented, either in colors or in white. The ease and accuracy with which intricate designs are conceived or followed from some minute strips of patterns are astonishing. The field laborers are usually dressed in white cotton, fashioned into short trousers and sleeveless shirts. The women are covered to the eyes in the long blue scarf or rebozo, which is part of the national costume. Half-naked children, with dark skins and glorious eyes, play about grated door-yards which open into small patios or court-yards beyond, bright sometimes with shrubs and flowers. The men, with wide-rimmed sombreros and gay serapes, keep a grave, dark-eyed imperturbability; or a mounted caballero rides on his small but fiery horse as if the two were but a single creature full of superb motion. The man wears a broad sombrero brilliant with silver braid, and his short, loose velvet jacket is bright with rows of silver buttons, as are also the wide velvet trousers which lose themselves in stirrups of fringed silver.

The very poor live within four walls of dried mud, on a floor of the same material. Anywhere upon this a fire of mesquite fagots may be kindled to cook the tortilla, which forms almost the sole food of a large class. A few crockery utensils for cooking and eating, a handbrush for sweeping, some water-jars and baskets, perhaps a bundle of maguey fibres for a bed, and the furniture is complete. The serape is a cloak by day and covering by night. But, best of all, here live patience, kindliness, and content, three graces hard to account for with such meagre plenishing.

And such are some of the aspects of life in Mexico. Wander forth in the morning almost any day in the year and you will find the blue sky a free expanse above, with the foliage lazily

PLAZA DE SANTO DOMINGO.

swaying against it; birds—yellow, or black with orange and crimson spots—singing or chattering in wild freedom. There is a glimpse of water, into which the sun drops beams through the foliage. Plants and trees of all sorts break the scene into fascinating patterns. Flowers in bloom beautify and scent the dream.

Or it is evening, and electric lights cast a half shadow silent as a tomb; the trees and flowers and birds sleep,—a mysterious quiet and suggestion of luxuriant foliage that appeals to one in a certain mood; but all is gay about. Then the old moon swings up from behind the ragged wall, between the heavy arches of trees, and the scene that you thought perfect is enhanced. The moon grows bigger and the scene lighter, and this, you remember, is but one day in beautiful Mexico.

Everywhere the people are cheerful and simple in their ways of living. They all attend church, and are devotional in habit. Doubtless more prayers are said in Mexico in a single day than in all of the United States together; and yet some people in the latter country want to send missionaries to Mexico!

In several different places, including Guanajuato, Mexico has a display of comparatively modern mummies and catacombs. The practice prevails, as in some European cities, of renting tomb space for the use of a corpse. In Mexico, if at the expiration of the original term there is no renewal of the lease, the corpse is dumped into an extensive underground chamber. If in the dry air the evicted mummifies, he stands against the wall; if he tumbles to pieces, his bones join the vast miscellaneous heap. The Guanajuato catacomb is ghastly enough to satisfy the most exacting connoisseur of the gruesome and blood-thirsty. In some of the mummies which have recently been examined jade teeth have been found, which is thought to be a proof that the Aztec princes used to be supplied by their dentists with handsome jade teeth, whenever their own pearly ones failed, just as the dentist of to-day supplies my lady with an ivory crown-tooth in place of her natural one.

The Mexican beggars are not to be compared in deformity with those of Constantinople, or in persistency with those of Killarney, but they maintain a fair European average in both respects, and cause the American visitor who has been abroad to remember them in Mexico. Cortez, distinguishing Cholula from other Aztec cities, said he saw there "multitudes of beggars such as are to be found in the enlightened capitals of Europe." Since the conquest, all the other Mexican cities seem to have attained Cholula's distinction, and now proudly display these evidences of European enlightenment.

SELLER OF PETATES.

SELLER OF FOWLS.

Then there are street scenes of a strange and foreign aspect to the American, such as black street-car hearses and street-car funeral hacks. There are also curious street signs, rude but vigorous and highly colored pictures depicting scenes suggestive of the business conducted within, and in appropriate names in staring letters as trade-marks, so to speak, of the different stores. Imagine, for instance, "The Last Days of Pompeii" as a business sign, or "The Sacred Heart of Jesus," which is the name of a score of establishments, ranging from a saloon to a flour-mill; and what do you think of these as names of streets?—"Crown of Thorns Street," "Fifth of May Street," "Holy Ghost Street," "Blood of Christ Street," "Body of Christ Street,"

"Mother of Sorrows Street," "Street of the Sacred Heart," "The Heart of Jesus Street," "Street of the Love of God," "Jesus Street," "John the Baptist Street."

Other governments might well take pattern from the Mexican parliament. No other government in the world has one like it in point of courtesy and dignity. The Mexican legislature holds its sessions in the evenings. The seats of the members are arranged in semicircular rows, and the presiding officer and officials of the house sit upon a large dais, or platform. At each side of the platform is a sort of pulpit, from which very formal addresses are delivered; but unpretentious discussions taking a conversational and unimpassioned form are conducted on the floor of the chamber. The orchestra and the galleries are divided into boxes, which are reserved for spectators; but it is only a rare occasion that brings outsiders to listen to the deliberations of their rulers. There is much etiquette in the parliament: members appear in evening dress; there is no confusion: there is seldom any rude or improper language like that which so often disgraces other deliberative assemblies. Speakers are courteous, even-tempered, and apparently conscious of the dignity of their position. More than three-fourths of the assemblage are white, and the Aztec blood is hardly traceable in the remainder. As a rule, men of character, means, and social position seek legislative honors, and hence it is a strong point with them to be careful about their honor. Extreme dignity and decorum mark the proceedings, which are always short and practical. The legislature meets twice in each year, in the spring and in the fall. The House of Representatives has one member for every forty thousand inhabitants, and the Senate has one senator for each state in the republic.

Perhaps nowhere else in the world is graceful horsemanship so common as in Mexico. The Mexican of adventure first thinks of a dashing horse, with showy saddle, gay saddlecloth, and gleaming bridle and bridoon, bits, and rings. Then this high-spirited horse with his flashiest accoutrements is not complete without a rider "to match." The Mexican accordingly arrays himself in a bright sash, a flowing cloak like that of a mediæval cavalier, and a broad-brimmed sombrero. As he dashes along the streets of Mexican cities he suggests the gaudiest kind of butterfly, and he is often found beyond the city on the plains. In the United States territory he is the envy of the cowboy, and receives the sincerest form of flattery,—namely, imitation. It is not unusual to find an ordinary American citizen, after three months' absence on the plains, so completely metamorphosed as to be hardly distinguishable from a Mexican.

INDIAN FROM THE MOUNTAINS.

A word should be spoken of the patient little burro, too, the most sedate and serious object one meets in Mexico. He is everywhere to be found. On his stout little back is loaded freight of all kinds; and he often carries packs much heavier than himself. One driver can manage twenty of these plodding fellows, so gentle and patient and trustworthy are they. And yet they never ask anything in return.

In all the Mexican towns of any size there is a Plaza de Armas, or Central Plaza, in which the band plays nearly every evening, and whither every one goes. On one side of this plaza is invariably the cathedral; on two of the other sides, if the town is a state capital, the governor's palace and the palace of the state legislature and the supreme court; and on the fourth side, large stores or handsome private residences. According to the custom of the country there, "an endless chain" of girls, in groups of two, three, or four, promenade in one direction, with a similar chain of young men going in the opposite direction, while the older people sit on the benches and seats. Thus every girl can be seen in succession by every young man in the other chain; and both parties make good use of their eyes. Where any mutual liking is evinced, or any encouragement shown, the girl's home is ascertained, and then the smitten youth takes to "playing bear," as it is called. That is, he promenades at certain hours back and forth beneath the narrow balcony on which, in this delightful climate, the inamorata sits in front of her apartment. He casts from time to time amorous glances, for he is not allowed to call at the house. If he receives encouragement, or thinks he does, he contrives in some way to transmit a letter. The first letter is never noticed. The second letter is answered by the same underground route, and either terminates or encourages his suit. If the girl's father approves, the youthful parties are then permitted to meet in the presence of some discreet elderly person until the preliminaries have been settled and the engagement announced. The marriage is not valid in law unless celebrated before the civil authorities, and as the women usually insist on being married by a priest, the hymeneal knot is thus usually twice tied in Mexico, as in France.

In Guadalajara there is a double walk-way around the plaza. By tacit consent, on the outer one of these the young men and maidens of the lower classes, the wearers of the serapes and rebozos, promenade, with their endless chains going in opposite directions, while at the same time, on the inner walk, separated from the outer one by a row of seats, the young people of the upper classes do the same in their American or French costumes. In some other cities this matter is tacitly arranged by one class promenading around one plaza and the other class around another; and in still other towns by one class promenading on certain nights and the other on certain other nights.

In Mexico there is a marked absence of those race distinctions which exist in the United States and many parts of the Old World. There are social inequalities, and sharply marked, but the social distinctions arise not from caste, but from those causes which create social distinctions in any country where the people are of the same race, as in France or England. Juarez, the greatest man Mexico has produced, was a full-blooded Indian; Diaz, the present able president, is part Indian, while many of the most distinguished men have been of pure Spanish descent.

CHAPTER V

IN MEXICO CITY

"SEE Naples and die," the Italians used to say of their famous and lovely city. "See Mexico and live" is the motto of young Mexico.

Other cities are, like Jerusalem of old, "beautiful for situation;" others have magnificent buildings, wide streets, and natural beauties. But when the traveller first looks on Mexico, as he approaches from afar, he experiences a new stir of the imagination, a new strain at the heart-strings. For are not here some of the relics of the oldest civilization of this continent? Not only does he feel a mysterious quality of attraction for her beauty, bathed as she is in tender clinging lights, and set like a jewel in burnished silver lakes and emerald hills, but he recalls with a thrill of eager emotion that here was the first theatre of mighty contest between Europe and a coming civilization,—a contest that was but the forerunner of final American independence.

Popocatepetl itself seems to glint down through a vista of centuries and wear a cap made up of the mists of antiquity. The mighty king of volcanoes has known such bloody scenes, such despotic wars, such idyls of love and passion, such dreams of happiness and depths of woe, that even the grim snow-crowned monarch suggests poetry, romance, and a thousand tender reminiscences.

Throughout the country one experiences the same feeling before many a time-honored city or fortress, and gazes at relics innumerable. Here it is a village, old and peaceful before Cortez's time, or an ancient church where members of his army may have worshipped. There it is the ruin of some old Aztec temple or a relic of the Toltecs. Everywhere little towns gleam through embowering

SEÑOR DON RAFAEL REBOLLA,
GOVERNOR OF THE FEDERAL DISTRICT.

foliage, ancient cypresses wave their moss-hung branches in the breeze, buried cities lie calmly under growing cornfields, broken columns point upward through the cacti, grim idols grin in unexpected places, and beauteous fields of living green alternate with virgin forests of mahogany or costly dye-woods.

Everywhere the air is poetic and dreamy with age, and the traveller is in an enchanted land of balmy air and soft Italian skies.

It has been said that nowhere in the world can a more splendid scene be presented than the first view of Mexico, the new city of the ancient Montezumas. Against a magnificent sky that defies all attempts of the painter's art are outlined minarets and domes and spires. Belfries and towers mark the numerous churches and gorgeous palaces; and the brightly painted houses, the gleaming lake in the background, and the snow-crowned mountains beyond, all go to make up a picture never to be forgotten,—a fit approach to this magnificent and stately capital.

Neither does it disappoint the traveller, as do so many cities with a fine view from afar. Oriental in effect as it certainly is, it does not dwindle, like too many cities of the East, into a vulgar, squalid town as one approaches. Switzerland furnishes no more beautiful mountains or lakes than those which surround this city; England and France show no more beautiful villages. And yet it is like neither Paris nor London. Mexico is distinctive and individual.

It is a Western city of Eastern sumptuousness in architecture. The wide, handsome streets are clean, and wholesome as well; electric lights and street-cars are seen in every part of the town; hundreds of magnificent churches testify alike to the wealth and the morality of the people; and the magnitude and beauty of the public buildings tell of a modern enterprise and ambition that place the city on a level with the foremost capitals in America.

It appears from history that the Aztecs discovered this fair valley about the twelfth century, having come down from the north.

Fair indeed was the new country; and here they chose to settle, some establishing homes on the lake-shore and others pushing on to the mountains. Anahuac they named the whole region; but it was by no means vacant and awaiting their arrival. Other tribes had settled there long before, and these resented the appearance of the upstart Aztecs. They hovered about, however, loath to leave so lovely a spot, until, according to tradition, they saw a superb eagle, with outstretched wings, mounted on a nopal which clung to a crevice in a rock. In his beak he held a viper, which he was rapidly devouring. This sign was taken by them as a token from their gods that they should found a city. Probably there were more or less internal disruptions, but at last, in 1325, they established their city, calling it Tenochtitlan, in honor of their high priest.

"Mexico," to which the name of the city was afterward changed by the Aztecs, came from Mexitli, the god of war. These men always honored the nopal, and soon after claiming the city raised a temple near it, afterward the Teocalli, which greatly astonished the Spaniards. Cortez spoke of the city as being of the size of Cordova or Seville. At least, it had a population of three hundred thousand when the Spaniards discovered it. There was a magnificent imperial palace, with twenty gates, walls of porphyry, fountains, and baths. Its sculptured roofs were of pine and cedar; and gold, silver, and precious stones were used in its furnishings. There were also a high-priest's palace (the temple of Texzatlipoca) and several other important and handsome public or semi-public edifices. There was an aqueduct from Chapultepec, and another from Churubusco, supplying drinking-water to the city.

But all this magnificence was razed to the ground as soon as the Spaniards had subjugated

AQUEDUCT OF BYLKH.

Montezuma and his people. Even after the siege the destruction was continued. Cortez divided the land among the invaders, and, after having chosen certain places for churches, ordered the erection of a cathedral upon the very ruins of the grand Teocalli or Aztec temple. With the aid of his multitudinous Indian allies, whose hatred of the Aztecs led them to work with zeal, seven-eighths of the city had been levelled to the ground in a few weeks, and when he determined to rebuild the city, he soon had four hundred thousand Indians at work.

This first cathedral, threatened as it was by repeated attacks, served the Spanish worshippers until 1626, when the newer and grander sanctuary was sufficiently safe for a transfer of the holy sacraments. When this was done with all due pomp and ceremony, the temporary cathedral was destroyed, leaving only the stone outlines of the Teocalli.

CARRIAGE-ROAD TO THE CASTLE OF CHAPULTEPEC.

In the National Museum are two of these blocks which served as pedestals or columns of the old Aztec temple. One is curiously inlaid with feathers, the other is sculptured with snakes.

The city of Mexico is said to be the finest built city on the American continent. In some respects it certainly is so. In the principal streets the houses are all constructed according to the strictest architectural rules. The foundations of the city were laid and the first buildings were erected by Cortez, who did everything well which he attempted,—from building a house or writing a couplet to conquering an empire. Many of the finest buildings in Mexico are still owned by his descendants. The public square is said to be unsurpassed by any in the world; it contains some twelve or fifteen acres paved with stone. The cathedral covers one entire side, the palace another; the western side is occupied by a row of very high and substantial houses, the second stories of which project into the street the width of the pavement; the lower stories are occupied by the principal retail merchants of the city. Most of these houses were built by Cortez, who, with his characteristic sagacity and an avarice which equally characterized him in the latter part of his life, selected the best portion of the city for himself.

The President's Palace, formerly the palace of the viceroys, is an immense building three stories high, about five hundred feet in length, and three hundred and fifty feet wide; it stands on the site of the palace of Montezuma. Only a very small part of this palace is appropriated to the president; all the public offices are here, including those of the heads of the different departments, ministers of war, foreign relations, finance and justice, the public treasury, etc.

But the cathedral, which occupies the site of the great idol temple of Montezuma, offers a striking contrast. It is five hundred feet long by four hundred and twenty feet wide. It would be superfluous to add another to the many descriptions of this famous building which have already been published. Like all the other churches in Mexico, it is built in the Gothic style. The walls, several feet in thickness, are made of unhewn stone and lime. Upon entering it, one is apt to recall the wild fictions of the Arabian Nights: it seems as if the wealth of empires was collected there.

The cathedral of the city of Mexico may be compared in size with the vast cathedral of Seville, and that of Puebla, in beauty of interior, with the best of Spain. The only church in the world that, beyond question, exceeds in size the Mexican cathedral is St. Peter's at Rome. The Seville cathedral is three hundred and ninety-eight feet by two hundred and ninety-one feet, and the nave is one hundred and forty-three feet high. Baedeker gives the Mexican cathedral's dimensions as four hundred and twenty-five feet by two hundred feet;

PATIO OF A PRIVATE RESIDENCE IN THE CITY OF MEXICO.

height, one hundred and eighty-five feet; towers, two hundred and eighteen feet high. The Mexican cathedral is, therefore, higher and longer than that of Seville, but not so wide. The Seville structure occupies a larger area; but a part of that vast building has fallen in, and is in the hands of workmen, who may be engaged upon it for centuries. According to Baedeker's figures, the Mexican cathedral ranks in the class of Seville and Milan, surpassed only by St. Peter's, and surpassing not only all other Spanish cathedrals, but every other in the world, including St. Paul's, London, St. Sophia, Constantinople, and the cathedral of Cologne. The city of Mexico has over sixty churches, and Puebla, the sacred city, with not over a hundred thousand population, has as many. Not only are these structures notable for their number, but many are impressive in size, architecture, and adornment. They were founded in a cathedral-building age, and constructed according to the plans of Spanish architects, at a time when Mexico was pouring countless millions into the coffers of Spain, and when there was no lack of money for the most extravagant projects.

When Church property was nationalized by Juarez, and monasteries and nunneries were suppressed, it was found that three-fourths of the wealth of the republic had gone into the hands of the Church. The moneys, and to some extent the rich adornment, of the churches were affected by Juarez's reform; but still these structures are, as in Spain, the country of wonderful cathedrals, the sights most proudly pointed out to the tourist. There are churches in the most inaccessible spots, on the summits of pyramids, the vast artificial mounds which formed the favorite foundation of temples of Aztec sun-worshippers; and thus the church edifices are numerous beyond conception, though many have long ago been disused or fallen into ruin.

But to return to the city of Mexico. The modern cathedral belongs to the Doric order. The architecture is severe and grandiose. The interior is composed of five naves, which gradually increase from the central to the lateral ones, which are occupied by fourteen chapels. The high arches are supported on fluted columns, the middle one being decorated with a capital of the greatest beauty, on which the visitor can admire paintings in distemper by the celebrated Jineo representing the Assumption of the Virgin in different groups, composed of the patriarchs and the most celebrated women of sacred history. The tabernacle is a modern work, far from being in harmony with the severe style of the older edifice. The principal façade of the cathedral—that toward the south—has three portals, which are composed of two orders of architecture, the first Doric and the second Ionic, ornamented with statues, bas-reliefs, pilasters, and capitals in white marble. The towers, which are over two hundred feet in height, are also composed of two architectural orders, the first Doric and the second Ionic, and are crowned with bell-like structures. The cornices of the towers in the different parts of the edifice support beautiful balustrades, with pilasters surmounted by magnificent urns and handsome statues. The statues on the towers represent the doctors of the Church, and those of the centre portal, where the clock is, the theological virtues.

A STAIRWAY IN THE MUNICIPAL PALACE.

The plan of the cathedral is a Latin cross, five hundred feet long and nearly two hundred feet high. It was estimated by a Spanish historian that over sixty thousand men had perished in human sacrifices upon its site. The building alone cost two million dollars, and the decorations far more. When these massive foundation-stones were laid, Queen Elizabeth was monarch of

England; Philip II. reigned over Spain, Charles IX. in France; Cervantes was writing "Don Quixote;" Titian and Paul Veronese were painting their masterpieces; the Turks were overrunning the plains of Hungary with the intention of wiping Christendom out of existence; Poland was a mighty empire, extending from the Baltic to the Black Sea; Sir Francis Drake was just beginning his career as a navigator, and Sir Philip Sydney was writing "Arcadia"; the first pipeful of tobacco had not been smoked in Europe; there were no telescopes; Shakespeare and Spenser, Beaumont and Fletcher, Ben Jonson and Bacon, were in their prime, and Russia was a savage and insignificant power.

As you walk through the building, on either side there are different apartments filled from floor to ceiling with paintings, statues, vases, huge candlesticks, waiters, and a host of

STREET SCENE, CINCO DE MAYO, SHOWING THE NATIONAL THEATRE IN THE DISTANCE.

other articles made of gold or silver. This, too, is only the every-day display of articles of least value; the more costly are stored away in chests and closets. What must it be when all these are brought out, with the immense quantity of precious stones which the church is known to possess? And this is only one of the churches of the city of Mexico, where there are between sixty and eighty others, some of them possessing little less wealth than the cathedral. It should also be remembered that all the large cities, such as Puebla, Guadalajara, Guanajuato, Zacatecas, Durango, San Luis Potosi, all have a proportionate number of equally gorgeous establishments.

But the immense wealth which is thus collected in the churches is not by any means all, or even the larger portion, of the wealth of the Mexican Church and clergy. They own very many of the finest houses in Mexico and other cities (the rents of which must be enormous), besides valuable real estates all over the republic. Almost every person leaves a bequest in his will for masses for his soul, which constitute an encumbrance upon the estate, and thus nearly all the estates of the small proprietors are mortgaged to the Church. The property held by the Church in mortmain is estimated at fifty millions.

The streets in Mexico are exceedingly wide,—much more so than is necessary, considering that they are not obstructed, as is the case in many cities, by drays and wagons.

The sidewalks are uncommonly narrow. The streets are all paved with round stones, the sidewalks with very rough flat ones. The houses on the principal streets are all two or three stories high. The elevation of the rooms from the floor to the ceiling—eighteen to twenty feet—gives to a house of two stories a greater height than we are accustomed to see in houses of three. The roofs are all terraced, and have parapet walls three or four feet high. The walls are built of rough stones of all shapes and sizes, and large quantities of lime mortar. They are very thick,—in ordinary buildings from two to three feet, and in the larger edifices of much greater massiveness. The foundations of most of the largest buildings are made with piles. Even these foundations are very insecure; and it is surprising that they are not more so, with such an immense weight of stone upon such an unsteady foundation. The streets cross one another at right angles, dividing the whole city into squares. Each of these squares is called a street, and has a separate name. In most of these streets there is a church, which gives name to the street in which it stands. In many instances these churches and convents (that of San Augustin, for example) cover the whole square,—not with separate buildings, but one single edifice, with the usual patio or court, an open space in the centre. There is not, I believe, a house in the city without this court, of greater or less dimensions, in proportion to the size of the building. There is only one door on the lower floor, and none on the outside of the upper story. The door is very strongly built, and high enough for a coach to pass through. It opens into the patio, through which you pass to the steps leading to the upper stories, where almost everybody lives, except the lowest classes.

At the period of the conquest the water of the lakes flowed through all the streets of the city, which were crossed in canoes or on bridges. Inundations of the city to the height of several feet were of frequent occurrence. These inundations were caused by the overflowing of the lakes San Cristobal and Zumpango, and the rush of their waters into the bed of the lake of Tezcuco, on an island in which the city of Mexico was, and near the border of which it is now situated. The city has been drained, and there is no longer the disadvantage of overflow.

Since the establishment of Mexican independence the city has been the scene of several revolutions and insurrections, and a number of important battles have been fought in the vicinity, the most noted being those of Contreras and Churubusco, August 20, 1847, and of Chapultepec, September 13, fought between the American army under General Scott and the Mexican army under General Santa Anna. After this battle the Americans occupied the city and held it until the ratification of the treaty of Guadalupe Hidalgo, in May, 1848.

CHAPTER VI

CHURCHES AND SHRINES

MOST of the churches in Mexico are beautiful pieces of architecture. Although they often mingle the Italian, Moorish, and Gothic schools, they yet preserve a delightful harmony of design and do much toward accentuating the picturesque beauty of the country. The façades are exquisitely finished in fine carving cut by loving hands into the delicate soft stone. The domes are either brilliant or soft with burnished tiles, and the light and graceful towers and belfries against the sapphire Mexican sky, make up a picture never to be forgotten by the artistic soul.

Inside there is often to be seen some fine hand-carving; silver railings and candelabra, rare old Spanish paintings, rich tapestries, and dainty ornamentations give a matchless *tout ensemble*. The high altar always rises under the great cathedral dome; the choir-room is in the nave, handsomely wrought in carved woods and furnished with wrought-metal screens. From high up on the wall the dim light filters down through small windows, while the slow monotone of a Gregorian chant floats from dawn till dark among the arches of the great building. And all the time reverent and loving worshippers glide in for a moment's prayer in the solemn hush, or glide out again to the world outside with souls refreshed and strengthened; for over all is a mystical, religious atmosphere so natural to the place that many a weary soul gladly welcomes a sanctuary here, and in the solemnity and hush girds on its armor anew.

"Our Lady of Guadalupe" is one of the most beautiful buildings in the world. Of course it is not so large or imposing as the cathedral, but it is artistically perfect. Instead of the balustrade of gold it has one of pure silver, and of the same size as that in the cathedral. Most of the vases, waiters, candlesticks, and other service are of silver also. The legend of the Virgin of Guadalupe runs thus:

THE CROWN OF THE VIRGIN OF GUADALUPE.

In the year 1531 an Indian, Juan Diego (John James), was going to Mexico early in the morning, and as he was passing over the mountains three miles from the city he saw a female descending from the clouds. He was terribly frightened, of course, but the figure, which turned out to be the Virgin Mother, told him not to be alarmed, that she was the Virgin Mary; that she had determined to become the patron saint of the Mexican Indians, and to take them under her special protection; and that he must go to the city and tell the bishop that she wished to have a church built at the foot of the mountain and dedicated to her as the patroness of the Mexicans. The poor Indian flew to the city, and when admitted into the presence of the bishop delivered the message. The bishop was incredulous and drove him off. The next day he met the Virgin at the same place, and told her that the bishop would not believe him. "Very well," said she; "do you meet me here to-morrow at the same hour, and I will give you a proof which the bishop will not doubt."

Punctual to his appointment, Juan Diego went the next day and had another interview with the Virgin. She told him to go up to the top of the mountain, and he would find the ground covered with roses, with which he should fill his apron and carry them to the bishop. The Indian found the roses, and, as none had ever grown there, they were, of course, placed there by a miracle; he filled his apron and went again to the bishop, confident in the miraculous evidence of the truth of his statements which he carried with him. When he opened his apron of coarse maguey cloth to exhibit the roses he found that there had been painted upon it, by another miracle, a portrait of the Virgin, dressed, not like the poor carpenter's wife, but in a gorgeous cloak of blue velvet with stars of gold all over it. The bishop could hold out no longer. The church was ordered to be built. The Indians all contributed whatever they had, and came into the fold by thousands. The patron saints of the Mexicans were not mere common mortals; the Mother of God herself was theirs. The original miraculous portrait in a rich frame of gold inlaid with diamonds and pearls is still to be seen in the church which was built, and every Mexican has one of more or less value in his house, and of every variety, from the cheap engraving to the most costly painting; below the picture are these characteristic Latin words: "*Non fecit taliter omni nationi.*"

The material on which the image is formed is a coarse product of the maguey plant, such as is still used by the Indians for their wraps and for other domestic purposes. The image is painted on this rough canvas, without any sizing or preparation. In fact, the canvas is transparent, the same image showing on both sides. At various times the picture has been examined by a committee of experts, composed of distinguished artists and scientific men, and they have deposed under oath that they could not account either for its production or for its preservation. The image exhibits peculiar characteristics of painting in oil, in water-color, in distemper, and in relief. In fact, these four dissimilar kinds of painting are discernible in different portions of the same canvas; and, in addition to this, the gilding which appears in the stars embroidered on the garment and in the texture of the robe itself, as well as in the rays of light which issue from the figure, is not applied according to any known process, and seems rather to have been woven into the fibre than painted on it. Besides the curious commingling of dissimilar kinds of painting on the same canvas, there is another peculiarity about the picture: for years it was exposed, without any covering, not only to the smoke of censers and innumerable candles, but to the damp air, charged with saltpetre, which continually arises from the neighboring lakes and marshes, and which affects and corrodes the hardest substances; and yet, after a period of more than three hundred and sixty years, this product of the maguey plant, which ought to have perished long ago, is still in a state of perfect preservation.

At this day you can hardly enter a shop in the city of Mexico without finding a lamp burning before a picture of Our Lady of Guadalupe. You can hardly enter a church without seeing an altar erected in her honor. Indeed, the Provincial Council of Antequera or Oaxaca specially ordains that no church shall be built in the entire province without its special altar in honor of Our Lady of Guadalupe.

Every diocese in Mexico dedicates the 12th of every month to Our Lady of Guadalupe, and every year sends thousands of devout pilgrims to her shrine. When the patriot priest Hidalgo, who is called the Washington of Mexico, began the fight for independence in 1810, his standard and his battle-cry were "Our Lady of Guadalupe." The revolution itself, although it despoiled every other church in Mexico, has ever respected this shrine of Our Lady. In one word, the Virgin of Guadalupe has taken such hold on the Mexican people that to attempt to dislodge her from their affections would be to tear out their hearts by the roots.

The church has now become the Lourdes of Mexico. From the time of the opening of the little chapel which first housed the painting it has been a favorite object of pilgrimage to the Mexicans, and many are the miracles of healing through the intercession of Our Lady of Guadalupe. The Holy See, however, was slow in giving official recognition of the miraculous nature of the picture. It was not until the year 1663, one hundred and thirty years after the apparition, that Pope Alexander V. granted the petition of the Mexican bishops that the 12th of December should be set apart forever as the feast of the Madonna of Guadalupe in Mexico. But the final triumph of Our Lady of Guadalupe came when the sovereign pontiff Leo XIII. granted the petition of the Mexican bishops for the public coronation of the miraculous picture. This was the event which brought together thirty-eight archbishops and bishops, of whom seventeen

THE HOLY WELL AT GUADALUPE.

were from the United States, hundreds of priests, and fifty thousand of the laity from all parts of Mexico, as well as from the States, on the morning of October 12, 1895.

It was, indeed, a remarkable occasion. The archbishops and bishops, arrayed in cope and mitre and bearing their crosiers, took their seats in the chancel of the church. At the appointed hour the rich crown prepared for the occasion was borne from the sacristy into the church and sanctuary by twelve of the first ladies of Mexico, and formally presented to the canons of the basilica. The crown was formed of gold and gems contributed by the Mexican ladies of wealth, who for this purpose parted with jewels which were not only of high intrinsic value, but were prized on account of having been long in their families.

The crown is what is termed an "imperial diadem," and stands two and a half feet high and measures four feet in circumference. The rim at the base consists of twenty-two enamelled shields, representing the twenty-two dioceses of Mexico. Above this is a circle of angels issuing from roses of massive gold. Between the angels and supported by them are six enamelled shields, on which are emblazoned the arms of the six archbishops of Mexico. Behind the angels, and extending to the apex of the crown, forming the imperial diadem, are alternate festoons of gold roses and diamond stars. These cluster at the top under an enamelled geographical globe, on which Mexico and the Gulf are represented. Above comes a Mexican eagle grasping the globe with one talon, while with the other it holds aloft a diamond cross. At the top of the cross is a ring by which the crown is held by a cherub over the painting. The shields are surrounded with diamonds, and between the shields are rows of sapphires and emeralds. In the breast of each angel flames a ruby. This crown is said to be the finest piece of work of its kind in religious art in existence. The maker has offered eighty thousand francs to any one who will discover two roses or leaves alike in the whole work.

The abbot and canon of the basilica, on receiving the crown, bound themselves and their successors by oath to preserve it for the purpose for which it was given. The papal brief authorizing the coronation was then read, and the crown was blessed by the Archbishop of

THE SHRINE OF GUADALUPE.

Mexico, vested in full pontificals. A solemn pontifical mass by the same illustrious prelate was then celebrated. After the mass a procession was formed of all the clergy and their assistants, the archbishops and bishops, and celebrants of the mass. The crown, borne aloft by the canons, was accompanied by the entire procession through the crowded basilica and outside the church, making a circuit of the building, and returning to the sanctuary. Then the two archbishops who were deputed by the Holy See to put the crown in place ascended a platform some thirty feet above the pavement, and the glorious diadem was suspended over the miraculous picture of Our Lady of Guadalupe. At the moment of the coronation the enthusiasm of the congregation and all present could not be restrained. The whole assemblage shouted together, "Viva Dios!" "Viva Madre di Dios!" "Viva México!" and the entire congregation burst into tears and sobs for joy that the long-looked-for and long-prayed-for honor had at last been done to their beloved Madonna of Guadalupe. At this point all the bishops ascended the altar steps one by one and laid down their crosiers and mitres as an act of homage to the Mother of God; and at the same hour all the bells of Catholic Mexico—from the Rio Grande to the Gulf, from the Atlantic to the Pacific—rang out the glad tidings that the Madonna of Guadalupe was crowned.

The interior of the church of Guadalupe is of the Doric order, and has three aisles, divided by eight pillars. There are eighteen arches, the centre one forming the dome of the edifice. The church runs from north to south, and has three great gates, one fronting Mexico and two others at the sides. Its length is, perhaps, two hundred and fifty feet, and its width about one hundred and thirty. In the four external angles of the church are four lofty towers, from the midst of which rises the dome. Three altars were at first erected, and in the middle one, destined for the image, was a sumptuous tabernacle of silver gilt, in which were more than three thousand two hundred marks of silver, and which cost nearly eighty thousand dollars. In the centre of this was a piece of gold weighing four thousand and fifty castellanos (an old Spanish coin, the fiftieth part of a mark of gold), and here the image was placed, the linen on which it is painted guarded by a silver plate of great value. The rest of the temple has riches corresponding.

It appears that the present sacristy of the parochial church dates back to 1575, and was then a small chapel, where the miraculous image was kept, and where it remained until the beginning of the next century, when a new church was built, to which the image was solemnly transported. Even when enclosed in the first small sanctuary its fame must have been great, for, by orders of the archbishop, six dowries of three hundred dollars each, to be given to six orphans on their marriage, were annually drawn from the alms offered at her shrine. But in 1629 Mexico suffered the terrible inundation which destroyed so large a part of the city, and the excellent archbishop, D. Francisco Manzo, while devoting his time and fortune to assist the sufferers, also gave orders that the Virgin of Guadalupe should be brought into Mexico and placed in the cathedral there, then of very different dimensions from the present noble building, occupying, it is said, the space which is now covered by the principal sacristy. When the waters retired and the Virgin was restored to her own sanctuary, her fame increased to a prodigious extent. Copies of the divine image were so multiplied that there is probably not an Indian hut throughout the whole country where one does not exist. Oblations and alms increased a thousandfold; a silver throne, weighing upward of three hundred and fifty marks, and beautifully wrought, chiefly at the expense of the viceroy, Count of Salvatierra, was presented to her sanctuary, together with a glass case (for the image), considered at that time a wonder of art. At the end of the century a new temple, the present sanctuary, was begun. The second church was thrown down, but not until a provisional building (the actual parish church) was erected to receive the image. The new temple was concluded in 1709, and is said to have cost from six to eight hundred thousand dollars, collected from alms alone, which were solicited in person by the viceregal archbishop, D. Juan de Ortega y Montanez. Two private individuals in Mexico gave, the one thirty, the other fifty, thousand dollars toward its erection.

In 1802, some part of the walls and arches began to give way, and it was necessary to repair them. But first, under the direction of the celebrated sculptor Tolsa, a new altar was erected for the image. His first care was to collect the most beautiful marbles of the country for this purpose. The black he brought from Puebla, and the white, gray, and rose-colored from the quarries of San José Vizarron. He also began to work at the bronze ornaments, but because of the immense sums of money necessary to its execution the work was delayed for nearly twenty years. But, in 1826, it was recommenced with fresh vigor. The image was removed, meanwhile, to the neighboring convent of the Capuchins, and the same year the altar was concluded, and the Virgin brought back in solemn procession in the midst of an innumerable multitude. This great altar, which cost from three to four hundred thousand dollars, is a concave hexagonal, in the midst of which rise two white marble pillars, and on each side two columns of rose-colored marble of the composite order, which support the arch. Between these are two pedestals, on which are the images of San Joaquin and Santa Anna, and two niches containing San José and San Juan Bantista. Above the cornices are three other pedestals, supporting the three archangels, Michael, Gabriel, and Raphael; and above St. Michael, in the midst of cherubim and seraphim, is a representation of the Eternal Father. The space between the upper part of the altar and the roof is covered with a painted crimson curtain held by saints and angels. The tabernacle in the centre of the altar is of rose-colored marble, in which the image is deposited, and all the ornaments of the altar are of gilt, bronze, and silver.

There are at Guadalupe the church of the Capuchin Nuns, and the churches of the Hill and of the Well, all in such close conjunction that the whole village, or city, as it calls itself, combine to make one religious establishment or confraternity, belonging to these temples and churches, united in the worship of the Virgin, and commemorating the "miraculous apparition" manifested to the chosen Indian, Juan Diego.

LA SANTÍSIMA CHURCH.

The shrine of the Virgin of Guadalupe is the most precious and sacred in all the republic: embodying this most beautiful and significant of legends as it does, pilgrims flock to it in a never-ceasing stream.

A rival shrine, in popular interest at least, is that of the celebrated Virgin de los Remedios. It is on a mountain a few miles out of Mexico. The view from it is superb, commanding the whole plain. The church is old and very picturesque as it stands in gray, solitary state in the midst of a quiet expanse.

This Virgin was brought over by Cortez, and when he displaced the Indian idols in the great temple of Mexico and caused them to be broken in pieces and the sanctuary to be purified, he solemnly placed there a crucifix and this image of the Virgin; then, kneeling before it, he gave solemn thanks to heaven, which had permitted him thus to adore the Most High in a place so long profaned by the most cruel idolatries.

It is said that this image was brought to Mexico by a soldier of Cortez's army called Villafuerte, and that the day after the terrible Noche Triste it was concealed by him in the place where it was subsequently found. At all events, the image disappeared, and nothing further was known of it until, on the top of a barren and treeless mountain, in the heart of a large maguey, it was found by a fortunate Indian. Its restoration was joyfully hailed by the Spaniards. A church was erected on the spot. A priest was appointed to take charge of the miraculous image. Her fame spread abroad. Gifts of immense value were brought to her shrine. A treasurer was appointed to take care of her jewels, and a camarista to superintend her rich wardrobe. No rich dowager could die in peace until she had bequeathed to Our Lady of Los Remedios her largest diamond or her richest pearl. In seasons of drought she is brought in from her dwelling in the mountain and carried in procession through the streets.

Wax candles are always burning before her shrine, and maids of honor are in attendance. Her whole wardrobe and jewels are worth more than a million of dollars, among them being different petticoats of diamonds, pearls, and emeralds.

CHAPTER VII

SIGHT-SEEING IN MEXICO CITY

THERE is so much to see in Mexico City that it is impossible to describe everything or to say definitely which point of view is most interesting. After the cathedral, however, the stranger usually seeks out the National Museum, where may be seen the sacrificial stone, which has already been referred to in these pages.

Indeed, some writers have said that of the sights in the city of Mexico the Museum may be considered the first and most important. To an antiquary it presents many curious things. It contains many Indian antiquities,—the instruments of war used by the Mexicans at the period of the conquest, bows and arrows, lances, swords, cotton armor, and their wooden drums, the sound of which is described by Bernal Diaz as "like a sound from hell."

The most curious of these is the sword described by Bernal Diaz as "*espada como navajas*," a sword like razors. It was a wooden staff, four or five feet long, with four blades, about ten inches in length and shaped like a razor, inserted on each side at right angles with the staff. These blades are made of obsidian volcanic glass, in which the country abounds, and which is not distinguishable from the glass of a black bottle, and is quite as brittle. Yet Bernal Diaz says that he has seen a horse's head cut entirely off with one of these swords. There is also in the Museum a mask made of this very fragile material and having the polish of the finest glass.

There are some curious specimens of the paper used by the ancient Mexicans, made of one of a species of the cactus (of which there are in Mexico nearly two hundred varieties). with their still more curious hieroglyphic writing upon it. It is much to be regretted that no Rosetta stone has yet been discovered which furnishes a clue to Mexican hieroglyphics. If this is ever done, most important information may be obtained not only as to Mexican history, but also as to the creation and the history of the human race.

Not only the discoverers of Mexico, but those also of every other country on this continent, found the natives familiar with all the leading events in the history of man up to the Deluge. Everything afterward was a perfect blank. With some of them the story of Adam and Eve in the garden was almost identical with the scriptural account. There is in the Museum of Mexico an ancient Mexican painting of the Deluge, the conception of which is very striking. Among other things we see the bird with a branch in its claw. A miniature copy of it may be seen in the Spanish edition of the Abbé Clavigero's history of Mexico.

The armor of Cortez is there also. This was the armor in which he had fought all the bloody battles in that most romantic achievement of all history,—the conquest of Mexico. In reading the history of the conquest of Mexico by Bernal Diaz,—the most enchanting book in any language. combining the beauties of Ossian and Froissart,—one seems to know personally many of the old Spanish heroes.

Bernal Diaz was one of the officers of Cortez, and kept a regular journal, which he afterward wrote out more fully. He came from the province of Old Castile, where every one spoke and wrote with great purity; and his history is the most reliable authority upon the conquest of Mexico. The letters of Cortez are the reports of the commander of an army, and therefore, in some degree, wanting in details. Gomara obtained his facts from conversations with Cortez and others of the conquerors, and the book of Solis is more a romance than a history. But Bernal Diaz describes what he saw personally,—scenes in all of which he was an actor,—and in the simple style of an old soldier recounting his battles by the fireside, with occasionally passages of great beauty and eloquence.

The armor of Pedro Alvarado, the greatest of Cortez's captains, is also in the Museum. In looking at one of these coats of mail the incredulity with which one reads the accounts of the battles of the conquest, when a hundred Spaniards resisted such swarms of Mexicans, is very much diminished. The armor formed a perfect covering of polished steel for the whole body, leaving the wearer vulnerable only at the joints; and with such arms as the Mexicans used it must have been an accident, and a very rare one, that it was penetrated. The horse was almost as effectually protected. Besides the covering of other parts, all his body from the saddle back was protected with an anquera, which was made of the thickest bull's hide, and which was attached to the saddle, and covered all the rump of the horse down to his hocks.

THE NATIONAL MUSEUM.

The lower part of this anquera had small pieces of iron attached to it like fringe, which jingled like bells. This last was an invention of Cortez's to strike his Indian enemies with terror.

Nothing better illustrates the tenacity with which the Spaniards adhere to all their old customs and habits, which has made them so striking an exception to the advancement observed in every other country in this age of progress, than the fact that these anqueras are still in general use in Mexico. No horse is fully caparisoned without one. And this is by no means confined to the military, for private gentlemen also use them,—many of them costing a sum which would seem incredible,—bedizened with a profusion of silver and sometimes of gold.

It was Alvarado whose extraordinary personal beauty led the Aztecs to give him the name of Tonatiuh (the sun). He survived the completion of the conquest, and became Adelantado of Guatemala. He had projected a large expedition of discovery in the Pacific Ocean, on which the ships were all ready to sail, when he went to suppress an insurrection among some of the Indian tribes. As he was ascending a mountain, on the sides of which the Spaniards and Indians were engaged in battle, one of the horses was wounded, and, tumbling down the mountain, fell upon and crushed Alvarado. Nothing could be more touching than the account by Bernal Diaz of his death and the grief of his wife. There is a street in Mexico which still bears his name, and commemorates the extraordinary leap which he made across one of the canals from which the bridge had been removed on the Noche Triste. It is called "El salto de Alvarado" (Alvarado's leap). Bernal Diaz says, however, that Alvarado never made the leap, active as he was. Whether he made the leap or not, he was a glorious hero, such as the world has not often seen since the discovery of gunpowder, which has had pretty much the same effect upon individual heroism as the discovery of the art of printing has had on eloquence.

The story of "Alvarado's leap" is as follows. On that "sad night" (July 1, 1520), the rain falling in torrents, the moon and stars refusing their light, the sky covered with thick clouds, Cortez commanded the silent march of his troops. Sandoval, the unconquerable captain, led his vanguard, and the stern hero, Pedro de Alvarado, brought up the rear. A bridge of wood was carried by forty soldiers, to enable the troops to pass the ditches or canals, which must otherwise have impeded their retreat. It is said that in choosing the night for this march Cortez was guided by the counsels of an astrologer. Be that as it may, the first canal was happily passed by means of the portable bridge. The sentinels who guarded that point were overcome; but the noise of the struggle attracted the attention of the vigilant priests, who in the silence of the night were keeping watch in the temple. They blew the holy trumpets, which called to arms and awakened the startled inhabitants from their slumbers. In a moment the Spaniards were surrounded by water and by land. At the second canal, which they had already reached, the combat was terrible. All was confusion, wounds, groans, and death, and the canal became so choked with dead bodies that the rear-guard passed over them as over a bridge. We are told that Cortez himself swam more than once over the canal, regardless of danger, cheering on his men, giving out his orders, every blow aimed in the direction of his voice, yet cool and intrepid as ever in the midst of all the clamor and confusion and darkness. But, arrived at the third canal, Alvarado, finding himself alone and surrounded by furious enemies, against whom it was in vain for his single arm to contend, fixed his lance in the bottom of the canal, and, leaning against it, gave one spring to the opposite shore.

EL MONTE DE PIEDAD.

An Aztec author and contemporary of Cortez says that when the Indians beheld this marvellous leap and saw that their enemy was safe, they bit the dust, "*comieron tierra;*" and that the children of Alvarado, who was ever after known as "Alvarado of the leap," proved in the course of a lawsuit before the judges of Tezcuco by competent witnesses the truth of this prowess of their father. In an annual called the "Mosaico Mexicano" there are some curious particulars concerning the "Noche Triste." It is said that the alarm was given by an old woman who kept a stall, and mention is made of the extraordinary valor of a lady called Maria de Estrada, who performed marvellous deeds with her sword, and who was afterward married to Don Pedro Sanchez Farfan. It is also said that when the Indians beheld the leap they called out, "Truly this man is the offspring of the sun;" and that this manner of tearing up the ground and eating earth by handfuls was a common Indian mode of expressing admiration.

I have already mentioned the great sacrificial stone upon which human victims were offered to the Aztec gods. It is some four feet high and eight feet in diameter, of circular form, with figures in relief elaborately cut on the top and sides. It is the best specimen of sculpture among the antiquities of Mexico. It is a curious question how the Aztecs were able to cut stone without other instruments than those made of copper, jade, and obsidian.

Custom demanded that the captive or other victim to be sacrificed should fight seven of their best gladiators. If he was victorious his life was spared, but if vanquished he was placed on this stone and his heart taken out, and whilst yet palpitating it was offered to their god. That this was really the sacrificial stone there can be no doubt, as the Spaniards were themselves made to witness the sacrifice at one time of sixty-two of their companions who fell into the hands of the Mexicans at the battle of the "Narrow Causeway" in Mexico, where Cortez was in such imminent peril. Bernal Diaz thus describes the scene:

"And again the great drum of Huichilobos (the idol) sounded, with many smaller drums, and shells, whistles, and a kind of small trumpets, the combined sounds of which were most sad and frightful; and when we looked above at the lofty idol temple whence the sounds came, we saw them pushing and buffeting our companions whom they had made prisoners when they defeated Cortez, as they were carrying them to be sacrificed; and when they had arrived at the top of this temple where their accursed idols were kept, they put plumes on the heads of some of the prisoners and made them dance before Huicholobos (their idol), and immediately after they had finished dancing they laid them on their backs on the stones, which had been made for such sacrifices, and with knives made of flint they cut open their breasts and took out their hearts. The bodies they threw down the steps to the Indian butchers who were waiting below to receive them, who cut off the arms and legs and skinned the faces, which, with the beards on, they dressed as skins are dressed to make gloves. These they exhibited at their feasts. And in this manner they were all sacrificed. They ate the arms and legs, the hearts and blood were offered to their idols, and the other parts of their bodies were thrown to the lions, tigers, and serpents which were kept in the menageries. All these cruelties were seen from our tent by Pedro Alvarado and Sandoval, and all our other captains. The curious readers of this narrative will imagine what our grief must have been, and we said among ourselves, Oh, thanks to God that they have not also sacrificed me! And let it also be considered that, although we were not far off, we could not prevent it, but could only pray to God that He would save us from so cruel a death."

There are many other interesting things in this museum also, among them the "Goddess of War" and the portraits of all the viceroys, beginning with Cortez. It contains upward of two hundred historical manuscripts, some in hieroglyphical character anterior to the conquest, and many in the different ancient languages of the country. Of ancient sculpture, it possesses two colossal statues and many smaller ones, besides a variety of busts, heads, figures of animals, masks, and instruments of music or of war, curiously engraved, and indicating the different degrees of civilization of the different nations to whom they belonged. A great many of the vases of tecal, and of the candlesticks in clay, curiously worked, were taken from excavations in the Isle of Sacrifices, near Vera Cruz, Oaxaca, etc., and from the suburbs of Mexico. There are also a collection of very ancient medals,—to the number of six hundred,—a bronze bust of Philip the Fifth, and about two hundred Mexican paintings,—comprehending two collections of the portraits of the Spanish viceroys, many of the celebrated Cabreras,—and various dresses, arms, and utensils from both the Californias. In the cabinet of natural history there is a good collection of minerals, together with some very fine specimens of gold and silver.

The Minería, or School of Mines, is another interesting place to visit. This magnificent building is a palace whose fine proportions compare well with those of any famous edifice in Europe. This was the work of Tolsa, Mexico's famous architect and sculptor. All is on a grand scale, its noble rows of pillars, great staircases, lofty roofs, and spacious apartments witnessing to the munificence of the rich Spaniards who contributed to its construction.

I should not omit to notice the great national pawnshop of Mexico, El Monte de Piedad, the funds of which are supplied by the government, an institution under the superintendence of a distinguished and virtuous man. Persons who are pressed for money and have anything to pawn take the article there and have it valued, receiving in money two-thirds of the sum at which it is valued.

El Monte de Piedad was founded by Señor Don Pedro Romero de Terreros, who was born in Spain in 1710, and educated at the University of Salamanca. His father came to Mexico on business, and while returning died in Vera Cruz. His son, Don Pedro, came to arrange his father's business matters, and afterward established himself in Querétaro with an uncle, who placed him at the head of his business, where he showed great business talent and rapidly acquired wealth. Upon the death of his uncle he invested in mines and became fabulously rich, but at the same time gave generously to the poor and to charitable institutions. The King of Spain, hearing of this, conferred upon him the titles of Caballero de la Orden de Calatrava and Count of Regla.

STATUE OF CUAUTEMOC, ON THE PASEO.

Although he had aided so many, he wished to establish an institution which should be a perennial fountain from which the needy could derive succor, and thus he conceived the idea of this institution,—El Monte de Piedad Nacional.

The building fronts upon the plaza, opposite the cathedral. The staircases are cut from blocks of lava from Popocatepetl, and the horrible heads which Cortez had placed over the doors and windows are still there, while in the patio are the flag-stones trodden by "the grandest filibuster and most pious and heroic butcher of all time."

There are employed two appraisers, a mean of whose estimates is adopted. On diamonds and articles of unchanging value they lend up to seven-eighths of the value. The interest ranges from three per cent. to nine and three-fourths per cent. per annum. If the interest fails to be paid, the article is placed in the vault for seven months; a value is then placed upon it by appraisers, and it is sold. If more is received for the article than covers expenses, the balance is placed to the credit of the depositor or his heirs, and is subject to his or their orders for one hundred years. If not called for in that time, it reverts to the bank. Amounts loaned vary from one dollar up to several thousand. For seventy-five years the profits went to pay for masses for the repose of the soul of the founder, but since then they have been devoted to establishing branch institutions; but, as one connected with the institution remarked, after seventy-five years of prayer his soul would probably be out of hot water, if ever.

Of all the spots in Mexico, the Alameda is the most beautiful. It is a public square on the western border of the city, containing about forty acres, enclosed by a stone wall. It is covered with a thick growth of poplar trees, whence the name. The whole square is intersected with walks paved with flagstones. All these walks unite in the centre, where there is a beautiful *jet d'eau*, and from this point they diverge in every direction, to unite again in four or five smaller circles. There is a carriage-way inside of the wall entirely surrounding the square.

A short distance from the Alameda is the Paseo,—the fashionable ride. The people drive every day, from five to seven, along the Paseo, which was planned from the walls of the city to the castle of Chapultepec. This boulevard, three miles in length and two hundred feet in width, with double avenues of fine trees shading stone sidewalks, with seven great circles, each three hundred feet in diameter, breaking its long, level straightness, makes a fit setting for the brilliant display it holds. The centre of each circle is to be filled with a monument or statue, surrounded by a garden with fountains and flowers, around which, on either side, the avenue sweeps superbly. Through this magnificent drive-way hundreds and hundreds of brilliant equipages pass and repass in the late afternoon,—the

THE NOCHE TRISTE TREE.

carriages full of brightly dressed ladies, the servants in splendid and showy livery, and gilded youth in fine array dashing on small fiery steeds through the central space; the young girls with flowers in their dark hair, the elders with head and shoulders draped in soft black lace, which lends grace to even a homely woman; the cavalier, valiant in picturesque bravery; all these meet there with nods and smiles and that fascinating little Mexican greeting which is spoken with the fingers. Sometimes, I may venture to say, one may see a thousand carriages on the Paseo. When I return to Mexico I shall go to the Paseo, the Bois de Boulogne of that city, with the utmost confidence of meeting all my acquaintances, and, indeed, everybody else, there. It is a habit of their lives to ride on the Paseo in the evening and to go to the theatre at night.

The Zócalo forms a centre from which radiate many of the principal streets, making the Plaza Mayor one of the best known localities in the city. In the centre of the plaza is the Zócalo, screened with groups of orange-trees, choice shrubbery, and flowers. There are also a fountain and a music-stand, where out-of-door concerts are given by military bands in the evening.

The principal market-place in the city, until a few years ago, was situated at the southwest end of the Zócalo. In the plaza is a curious monument to Enrico Martinez, the famous engineer by whom the drainage of the valley was effected by the cut of Nochistongo. On a base surrounded by an iron railing having bronze lamps at its angles is raised a square pedestal of marble supporting a female figure in bronze, emblematic of the city of Mexico, modelled by the sculptor Noresa.

What stories the Zócalo might tell of human sacrifices and stern Aztec priests, mad fights of Spaniards and fierce natives, brilliant processions of Castilian viceroys, enthusiastic patriots, clerical bigots, and red-handed revolutionists!

The Zócalo is in a lively and beautiful plaza, both by day and by night, and, whether in the sun's blaze or in the mellow rays of the moon, it is always a scene of varied and engrossing enchantment. The walks are as smooth as marble, the flowers are grouped in exquisite designs, snowy statuary gleams through the veiling foliage, and from the centre of this grand park issue delicious strains of music. There is no place on earth that compares with this in the gayety and variety of the types it presents. It is a living, moving, breathing kaleidoscope of all nations, colors, types, and costumes, from ladies and gentlemen of the most exalted rank to groups of bull-fighters, poor peons, and ragged Indians. So fairy-like and bewildering is the scene that one can scarcely realize that it is a nineteenth century reality and not a dream of the time of the Arabian Nights.

CHAPTER VIII

THE MARKETS AND CHAPULTEPEC

VISITORS to Mexico are always attracted by the markets, and writers invariably devote many pages to their description. In the markets may be found all the flowers, fruits, and vegetables of a tropical climate. Most of them are raised near the city or on the floating gardens of La Viga, and on the canals may be seen hundreds of boatmen paddling along with their crafts filled with gay blossoms.

In the markets are many characteristic types. Each class of the population wears a garb which is the uniform of its occupation. The water-carrier, in armor of leather, bears his heavy jar suspended from a band around the forehead; the ochre-man, stained like a terra-cotta image from head to foot, carries his package of brick-colored clay above his matted locks; the fruit-vender, crying his luscious wares in sudden shrill monotone, balances his enormous pannier on his head, and steps as airily as if he were beginning a fandango. Under the open arches of the portales the crockery-merchant sits before his pile of Guadalajara jars and brightly glazed pottery; Indian women carry their double load of baskets and babies with the superb indifference to fatigue which marks their race; dealers in "frozen waters" call their sherbets in prolonged piercing notes like those of a midsummer locust; sidewalk cooks squat on their haunches beside small fires of mesquite, over which bubble earthen dishes of stewed vegetables, frijoles, or crisp tortillas; and flower-

THE ARCADES.

girls sit in the midst of piles of glowing poppies, pyramids of heliotrope and pansies, baskets of scarlet cactus blossoms, and tangled heaps of superb roses magnificent in color and perfume, which fill the atmosphere with fragrant beauty.

In every direction the roads running out from the city of Mexico are broad, well-kept avenues, and there are none of the squalid mean districts so characteristic of the suburbs of Northern cities. These roads wind between massive cottonwood-trees, through flourishing fields carefully cultivated. Velvety green meadows form the fringe to Mexico, rather than the mean hovels too often seen in other cities. Bridges and aqueducts, rivulets and ditches, distribute the sparkling water through these, and consequently the fields teem with rich harvests in their season.

Everywhere are the signs of fertility and bounteousness, and over all, shining in the clear life-giving air, are the summits of Popocatepetl and Ixtaccihuatl, rising in supreme and stately beauty. The spires and domes of the great city glow with varied color, and there is withal an Oriental mingling of white walls and arches, trees, gardens, and fountains against a magnificent background.

THE GATEWAY TO CHAPULTEPEC.

The streets of Mexico are, in a measure, unlike those of any other city we have so far visited. Straight, wide, and lined with handsome houses, built of stone and two or three stories in height, the city lacks that Eastern aspect which narrow lanes of blank adobe walls give to the lesser Mexican towns. The large windows of the handsomer houses open on to small stone balconies, and these latter, ornamented often by carvings, and always by balustrades of wrought iron, brightened by gilding and color, and shaded by linen awnings, make a feature in themselves. Here, on Sunday and fête-day, as well as toward evening, the youth of the city gathers, in the full dress of private life; and the stolen glances which form the only intercourse allowed between the sexes flash back and forth between youth and maiden. Even though deprived of the opportunity for interchange of vows, for hand clasping and tender greeting, it is self-evident that a young Mexican girl, true to the traditions of her Castilian forebears, can make as much havoc with her languishing dark eyes and the softly fluttering fan which supplements them as any girl arrayed in the more modern outfit of courtship. The pretty girls are exquisite; the slender oval of the face, the rich olive of the cheek, the long sweeping dark lashes over superb eyes glowing at once with passion and tenderness, the low forehead with its rippling mass of dusky hair, the slender neck, the lithe form, the springing step, and the dainty foot, make these girls like a poet's dream of darkly brilliant loveliness, not to be measured by any type with which we have been heretofore familiar.

The large and well-paved avenues cross the city at right angles, overflowing with shops of every description, well stocked, and for the most part conducted by French and Germans. Native traders offer their wares under the portales and in the open market-places which are to be found in every quarter. Nothing in the city is of greater interest than these crowded and

THE CASTLE OF CHARLEVILLE.

seemingly disordered piles of merchandise, attended by groups of swarthy merchants, men and women. The bright foreign air gives to even the smallest lane an interest and novelty. Every occupation has its distinctive mark in dress; and this, with the varying costumes of Indian, Spaniard, Mexican, Frenchman, and American filling the narrow pavements, gives constant variety to the swaying crowd. Anywhere along the curb-stone native men or women sit down to rest with basket or bundle; and some of the groups thus made are exceedingly picturesque. Each long vista, gay with color and life, is closed at last by some towering mountain height, which frowns or smiles as sun or shadow rests upon it.

The best hotel is the Iturbide, a good specimen of the best Mexican hotel,— larger and finer than most, on account of its original use as the palace of the old emperor, but following the same general plan. Entered from the street by a large archway, the house rises around a fine court-yard, upon which each of the four stories opens in a succession of galleries supported by arches and pillars of stone. Every room has a hinged window opening to the floor and entering directly on these airy, shaded balconies. Over the casements and corridors leading to the state apartments elaborate carvings ornament the heavy stone trimmings, and projecting from the flat roof, with long gutter-pipes of metal protruding from their grinning mouths, a line of grotesque gargoyles, of great size and striking artistic effect, surrounds the four sides. Other arches open in three directions on other courts, and broad stone stairways lead to the upper stories. The rooms, opening usually by one great balconied window on the street as well as on the inner courts, are large, charmingly cool, well furnished, and scrupulously clean.

ONE OF THE LARGE CYPRESS-TREES IN THE GROVE OF CHAPULTEPEC.

The Paseo runs now quite out to the hill and palace of Chapultepec, the favorite pleasure-garden and resting-place of Montezuma. The hill is a solid mass of rock nearly two hundred feet higher than the surrounding country. At its foot are semi-tropical gardens and the famous cypress groves, while all around among the great towering trees are noble avenues and beautiful drives. The cypress forest is not surpassed in magnificence anywhere on this continent. The grand old trees, most of which must date back for many centuries, tower up to a tremendous height, and stand in sombre majesty the solemn guardians of the treasures of animal and vegetable life below them.

From their lower branches festoons and soft draperies of long, gray moss sway lightly over the dim aisles below, and here the wood in its twilight indistinctness is like some vast cathedral or a dream of paradise. The largest of these trees have a girth of over forty feet, and are as stately and graceful and straight as any Northern pine.

The view after one has emerged from these shaded avenues and come out onto the hill of Chapultepec is beyond description. The foreground of majestic cypresses ; the broad bright fields beyond ; emerald patches edged with cactus-hedges ; the country roads fading into the blue distance ; the glowing city shining in the sun, with its myriad towers and domes and minarets ; the sparkling lake ; the villages dotted here and there throughout the valley ; the

SALA IN THE PALACE OF CHAPULTEPEC.

wonderfully clear atmosphere ; and around all, guarding it as the "mountains round about Jerusalem," the amethystine mountains, crowned by those always marvellous white luminous summits, Popocatepetl and Ixtaccihuatl,—what artist could transcribe the scene to canvas, what pen reproduce it on common paper? Well may it be called the "Valley Beautiful."

The marble castle of Chapultepec was first built under the direction of Maximilian, and has since been restored for the occupancy of the presidents.

The castle itself, modern though it may be, seems like a tradition. The Viceroy Galvez, who built it, was of a by-gone race. But Chapultepec should be visited in the morning, when the dew is on the grass, or in the evening, when the last rays of the sun are gilding with rosy light the snowy summits of the volcanoes. Here for centuries has stood "Montezuma's Cypress," a stupendous tree, dark, solemn, and stately, of majestic height, and forty-one feet in circumference. A second cypress standing near, of almost equal size, is even more graceful, and they and all the noble trees which adorn these speaking solitudes are covered with a creeping plant resembling gray moss, hanging over every branch like long gray hair, giving them a venerable and druidical look. Here one may wander through the noble avenues and rest under the trees, walk through the tangled shrubberies, bright with flowers and colored berries, or enter the cave and stand by the large clear tank, and then climb the precipitous ascent on which stands the castle.

From the terrace that runs around the castle the view forms the most magnificent panorama that can be imagined. The whole valley of Mexico lies stretched out as in a map:—the city itself, with its innumerable churches and convents; the great aqueducts which cross the plain; the avenues of elms and poplars which lead to the city; the villages, lakes, and plains which surround it; to the north, the magnificent cathedral of Our Lady of Guadalupe; to the south, the villages of San Augustin, San Angel, and Tacubaya, which are embowered in trees and look like an immense garden. And though in the plains below there are many uncultivated fields and many buildings falling to ruin, yet with its glorious enclosure of lofty mountains, off whose giant sides great volumes of misty clouds are ever rolling, and with its turquoise sky forever smiling on the scene, the whole landscape, as viewed from this height, is one of unparalleled beauty.

Chapultepec, only a short league from Mexico, is perhaps the most haunted by recollections of all the traditionary sites of which Mexico can boast. Could these hoary cypresses speak, what tales might they not disclose, standing there with their long gray beards and outstretched, venerable arms, century after century, already old when Montezuma was a boy, and still vigorous in the days of Bustamente! There the last of the Aztec emperors wandered with his dark-eyed ladies. Under the shade of these gigantic trees he rested, perhaps smoked his "tobacco mingled with amber," and slept, his dreams unhaunted by visions of the stern traveller from the far East, whose sails even then were perhaps within sight of the shore. In these tanks he bathed. Here were his gardens and his aviaries and his fish ponds. Through these woods he may have been carried by his young nobles in his open litter, under a splendid dais, stepping out upon the rich stuffs which his slaves spread before him on that green and velvet turf.

And from the very rock where the castle stands he may have looked out upon his fertile valley and great capital, with its canoe-covered lakes and outspreading villages and temples and gardens of flowers, no care for the future darkening the bright vision.

Tradition says that now these caves and pools and woods are haunted by the shade of the conqueror's Indian love, the far-famed Doña Marina.

The castle is indeed a beautiful building. A double row of light and elegant arches in white and pale-tinted marbles marks the broad colonnades, from which the main body of the palace springs into the air with an effect of great delicacy and beauty. All the rooms open on these marble balconies; and on the uppermost flight, reached by an exquisite stairway with gilded balustrades, have been built fountains and terraced gardens, enchanting as the hanging gardens of Babylon. Around under the arches the walls have been painted in fine copies of Pompeian frescos and Greek designs, executed with great purity both of color and of form. This flowery arbor, perfumed and beautiful, forms the centre around which cluster the rooms of the palace. These are convenient for the purpose of summer residence, and contain some marvellous ceilings, wherein Cupids play among tangled flower-wreaths or blow on conch-shells to waken sleeping Love. And over all the wonderful outlook makes it ideal.

Adjoining the palace, the military academy gives a passing opportunity to note the system of instruction provided by the government to prepare its future soldiers and scientists.

CHAPTER IX

THE MEXICAN INDEPENDENCE DAY

INDEPENDENCE DAY in Mexico means the same thing from the Mexican standpoint as the Fourth of July means in the United States; and on that day Mexico celebrates two events of national importance: President Diaz was born at eleven o'clock P.M., September 15, 1830, and one hour later, at twelve o'clock of the 16th, was first inaugurated the birthday of Mexican independence. After General Diaz became president of the republic the custom was changed to inaugurate Independence Day and the president's birthday at the same time. On the night of September 15, 1896, for instance, at exactly eleven o'clock, there went up from the plazas of the great cities, from plain and valley and mountain top, one mighty shout from tens of thousands of freemen's throats, " Viva México!" " Viva el Presidente!"

Congress held its reunion and adjourned at eleven o'clock to participate in the celebration. At that moment a salute of twenty-one guns was fired by the national guard, and there followed an uninterrupted hour of festivities. A banquet was given at Chapultepec to President Diaz by the Mexican army, when the secretary of war congratulated the president in the name of the army on reaching his sixty-fifth birthday and on being so firmly intrenched in the hearts of his people. Besides the army, the diplomatic corps, the Mexican cabinet, and many of the prominent people were present at this brilliant occasion.

On the 14th it is customary for the people of the city of Mexico to celebrate President Diaz's birthday with their unrivalled "Battle of Flowers." The sixty-fifth anniversary of his birth was celebrated in the city of Mexico by nearly a quarter of a million of people. It was a great day, and when "fair Tenochtitlan" arrays herself for a *fiesta* the display rivals anything ever seen elsewhere on the continent. It was on this occasion a continued rivalry between the beauty and loveliness of the brilliantly-robed ladies and the masses of gorgeous, many-hued flowers. This celebration is observed with the utmost informality. It is one of the days when everybody has full license. The rich and the poor mingle and pelt one another with flowers in the most democratic manner. It is an occasion on which the rich prepare splendid spectacles and brilliant displays, which the poor are allowed to witness and enjoy in the freest manner. The day is intended as an object-lesson, teaching loyalty to the republic through the faithful observation of the birthday of its president. On the occasion in question there could have been seen before sunrise large numbers of Indians coming from every section, down the mountains, through the thoroughfares and byways, across the valley, and through every gateway, into the city, bearing large supplies of the choicest and rarest flowers. These early comers hastened through the streets to the humble homes or shops of their relatives or friends, and before ten o'clock every building of note in the city was profusely decorated in honor of the occasion. Numerous fine bands were brought from barracks and from the capitals of other

Independence Day, 16th of September.

provinces or states. These were stationed along San Francisco Street at the crossings between the Alameda and the palace.

Shortly after ten o'clock the president and Mrs. Diaz took position on one of the balconies of the Jockey Club building, and the long procession was soon in motion. The scene presented was striking in beauty. There were countless fine carriages, barouches, four- and six-in-hands, tandems, all bedecked with flowers in artistic taste. There was raging a continuous battle, even the president taking a lively part. The streets were strewn with flowers. They showered from balconies and house-tops.

Visitors, especially Americans, were delighted with the inexhaustible supply of flowers and the innate taste of the Mexican people. The passing pageant was in harmony with the prevailing architecture. Graven house-fronts, statuary, escutcheons, fantastic ironwork of balconies, the tiles of the porcelain palace, all helped to frame a picture the like of which no other city on the continent can hope to rival. Such is the wonderful spectacle of Mexico's floral carnival.

The story of Mexico's Liberty Bell is most interesting. In September, 1810, when Hidalgo and his little band of patriots were secretly consulting how they could best effect the freedom of Mexico, this bell was rung to sound the first note of Mexican liberty. It hung in a little church in the hamlet of Dolores Hidalgo, near the city of Querétaro. On the 15th of September, as the little band of patriots were counselling together, a special courier came hastening thither with a message from the Corregidora Señora Dominguez to the effect that their plot for freedom had been discovered by the Spaniards. This lady's memory is revered to-day throughout Mexico, and the key-hole in Querétaro where she listened to the Spanish councils is one of the sights of that city. On the Mexican Independence Day her picture is exhibited in the city side by side with that of Hidalgo. When Hidalgo received the news at Dolores he had this bell rung to summon all the patriots in the vicinity, and made a stirring speech, which resulted in their starting out together to strike the first blow in the revolution. The bell weighs 982 kilogrammes; its height is .78 of a metre; its circumference at the base is 3.298 metres. The following inscription is on the bell:

THE LIBERTY BELL.—1810.

DE S. S. JOSEPH
22 DE JULIO DE 1768.

It is made of copper and silver, with enough of the latter metal to give it the silvery ring for which it was so famous.

The celebration September 14, 1896, was marked by the transportation of Mexico's Liberty Bell to the National Palace. It was mounted on a car handsomely decorated for the occasion with red and white flowers and with gilded wheels. At the front was a Mexican eagle with wings outstretched. Immediately behind was an old brass cannon cast by Hidalgo in 1811, and behind the cannon was a group of trumpets, arms, gun-sponges, picks, and shovels. Next was the bell itself, which is inscribed with the date of its founding, July 22, 1768, and with its name. Over it was an artificial wreath of laurel and oak, and behind was another military trophy. At the end of the car was a gilded star with a crimson oval centre inscribed with the word "Independencia" in gilt letters, and above it "1810."

The procession included all the prominent officials of the state and country, and awoke the enthusiasm of thousands of people on the route to the palace. Flowers, serpentines, and

RURALES ON THE 16TH OF SEPTEMBER.

confetti were showered upon them as the dignitaries followed the car to the lively strains of the band. At the Plaza Major every foot of space was crowded by sight-seers. When this magnificent pageant reached the front of the palace several speeches were made.

The bell had been brought from the village church of Dolores Hidalgo in Guanajuato, and General Rocha made the first speech, praising the achievements of General Diaz in establishing order and good government throughout Mexico. He said the notes of this bell would be a perpetual reminder to the people of the exploits of their favorite heroes, and implored all Mexicans to swear that they would rather die than submit to foreign dictation. The bell which in Dolores awakened patriotism may be again the tocsin to summon the Mexican people to die in defence of their country.

General Diaz replied in an inspiring speech full of patriotism, declaring that the notes of the bell would seem to the people like the voice of Hidalgo embalmed in metal. Every year, he promised, this bell shall be rung to recall the heroes of the past, to encourage the people to defend Mexican independence and to continue the work of national regeneration, of which the struggle for independence was only the preface. After this the band struck up the national anthem, the cathedral bells were set ringing, a thousand doves, with neck-bands of the Mexican tricolor, were let loose, and, amid acclamations from thousands of throats, the bell was raised to its place at the front of the palace. The troops then marched past, saluting the bell, and the ceremony came to an end.

The capital of Mexico is changing perhaps more rapidly and radically than any other city of the country. Many of the residences are lighted with electricity. It goes without saying that they are handsomely furnished. Streets in the city of Mexico are paved and kept clean and in good repair. The street-car lines extend into the country for miles beyond the city limits, and run in all directions out from Cathedral Square. These cars are drawn by mules, and are by no means slow. Indeed, the way these little animals throw up their hind legs, as if afraid the cars will catch up with their heels, is very amusing. The drivers are mostly Indians.

A very pleasant thing in connection with the car service is that you can hire a car by the day, going how and where you please. In this way you can visit all parts of the city and suburbs, switching off at different points and connecting with different lines, taking out a party of friends with you, and being left, when evening comes, at your own door. Where else can this pleasure be indulged in?

Another custom in Mexico City is to use these cars for funeral purposes. When a funeral is to take place, the corpse is placed in a car with wheels so arranged that they will run either on or off the car-tracks. Mourners follow in a special car with white linen curtains at the windows. The drivers are in black, and the funeral cortége passes in a solemn and decorous manner to the cemetery.

The big drainage canal, leading to and through the mountains thirty miles distant, is practically finished. This is one of the greatest engineering works of the century. The city of Mexico stands in the centre of a valley hemmed in on all sides by high mountains. The distance across it is from forty to sixty miles.

The canal starts at San Lázaro, running twenty-nine miles along the eastern side of the Guadalupe range, crossing lakes San Cristobal, Xaltocano, and Zumpango, and arriving at the mouth of the tunnel near the town of Zumpango.

CHAPTER X

GENERAL PORFIRIO DIAZ

THE personality of General Porfirio Diaz is widely known as the President of Mexico, and the greater nations of Europe and America have all come to realize his superior statesmanship. He is to-day one of the great men of his century. The history of his remarkable career, military as well as political and administrative, has occupied the pens of many intelligent writers, but none have yet been able to do him justice.

He was born September 15, 1830, in the city of Oaxaca, in the state of the same name,— the evening before the glorious anniversary of national independence. His parents were Don José Faustino Diaz and Doña Petrona Mory. Oaxaca has been styled "the dwelling-place of heroes in the garden of the gods," "the Eden of America," "tomb of the conquerors and the cradle of patriots." The state, although mountainous, is rich in agricultural and mineral productions. The scenery is grand, and the spot is well adapted to be the cradle of sons who should be the hope of the nation and who should raise aloft the standard of liberty.

The ancestors of Porfirio Diaz were Spaniards who left their mother-country in the first years of the conquest. His father possessed in a high degree all the natural qualities necessary to make him a patriot, a soldier, or a statesman. He was tall, symmetrical, muscular, and active, and carried himself in a manner indicating him to be a man of great resolution. While we find that he was, like his son, most affable in his manners, of a good heart, and extremely generous, yet if an injury or injustice was done him, he resented it with the greatest determination and energy. This quality exists in all great men, who, while ever ready to have justice done, are also prompt to punish evil. One who enters into combat, whether physical or moral, will never come off conqueror unless possessed of force and perseverance.

President Diaz's mother, of the family of Morys, came from Asturias, whose strong and valiant sons were noted for their independent spirit and their ancient lineage, possessing the impetuosity of the Celts and the frankness and integrity of the Goths. Señorita Mory's grandfather, a Spaniard, married in the Mixteca an Indian woman, who was General Diaz's great-grandmother, so that in the veins of Don Porfirio is mixed the blood of the proudest provinces of Spain with that of the highest nations of America, as the Mixtecas were fully as advanced in civilization as the Aztecs.

His father rented in Oaxaca the property known as the Mesón de la Soledad, where Don Porfirio was born. There were six other children, two of whom died in infancy. In 1833 the Asiatic cholera invaded Mexico, and among its victims was Captain Diaz. This was a great blow to the family, as the mother's health was delicate and the children were young; but she had all the energy of her race, and after her husband's death she continued to manage the inn (*mesón*), and showed in every way great firmness and intelligence, maintaining with vigor in all her acts her integrity as wife and mother. She possessed fine feelings, was industrious and hospitable, courteous and dignified. With all her modesty and delicate instincts, she was brave, and in those tumultuous times, if necessary, could use arms in defence of herself and children. Her great desire was that her children should receive such intellectual development as should fit them for any place which they should be called to occupy.

Don Porfirio was in a primary school until he was seven years old. At fourteen he entered the seminary directed by Roman Catholic ecclesiastics. There were several reasons for his entering this seminary rather than the government Institute of Arts and Sciences. First, business matters had not been prosperous with his mother, and little by little she had been obliged to sell portions of houses, etc., to maintain and educate her family. In the seminary aid was rendered by bright students (although he was not a boarder in the institute), besides which, the father had desired that his sons be educated for the Church. The clergy used all their influence to augment the number of their pupils from good families, seeing that they were losing ground among the principal classes, especially since independence had been established.

After studying for a time to prepare himself, our hero felt that he should do something to aid his mother, whose means had become exhausted, and he commenced to give lessons in his leisure hours. While doing this he came in contact with Don Marcos Perez, judge of the Supreme Court of the state and professor in the Government Institute of Arts and Sciences. Señor Perez became very fond of young Porfirio, whom he often took to the Institute, discussing with him the tendency of extending civil and religious liberty.

One day Perez invited him to be present at the distribution of prizes in the Civil College of the state. The governor, Benito Juarez, was present, and Porfirio was presented to him. Juarez knew Porfirio's father slightly, and had heard of the manly efforts Porfirio was making to get an education in order to be his mother's staff and comfort. The governor spoke encouragingly, and young Diaz found therein the fountain of ambition and source of desires, hopes, and aspirations such as he had never dreamed of before, and he could hardly sleep that night as he thought of the wonderful words, the magnetism, the intellect, and the influence of the great man. As he looked about upon his country he saw nothing but perdition, the curse of Spain and the pernicious results of ill-directed efforts to force upon the Mexican people a foreign religion and civilization, and he resolved to consecrate his life to his country. As a little boy in his play he had ever been a soldier, and had always been made a leader or general by the other boys, so that his inclinations toward and capacity for a military life were early recognized by his friends.

When the war with the United States commenced, in 1846, Porfirio's heart was filled with enthusiasm to fight for his country, and he and several of his college mates petitioned the governor to send them to the front that they might help fight the enemy. Governor Guerque smiled, but placed their names on his list, and the youths were inscribed upon the roll of the national guard, consisting of one battalion, which, by reason of the extreme youth of those composing it, received the epithet " Better than nothing."

When Porfirio was nineteen and had finished his preparatory studies, the bishop offered to confer on him in the following year the lesser orders and to give him a scholarship; but Diaz then declared his intention of studying jurisprudence in the Institute. The prelate was surprised at a young man in needy circumstances disregarding such valuable aid. It was considered a crazy decision. His uncle, the bishop, withdrew his help and forbade him his house, which made the young man's mother inconsolable.

Maternal tears affected the heart of the affectionate son, and, although insensible to the counsels of the bishop, as also to his threats, he promised to do as his mother desired. But, although a pious and devoted churchwoman, with great desires for his spiritual and temporal prosperity, she did not wish to go contrary to his will and to oblige or persuade him to follow a calling that would be disagreeable to him: so she left him free to follow his inclinations.

She lived long enough to see the practical wisdom of her son's determination, as after a few years came that blow which destroyed the power of the Church and placed a limit upon its influence, while men of intelligence and position found free scope in the profession of the law.

Porfirio Diaz entered the Institute and commenced in a systematic manner the study of jurisprudence, helping himself by teaching. Juarez, who had not forgotten him, gave him—unsought, as Diaz never asked favors—the position of librarian. After four years of study, having been elected assistant professor of Roman law even before graduating, he had, in compliance with the law, to enter a law office and practise two years, as the course of study required. Benito Juarez was now practising law, his term of governor having expired.

During this time—1853—Santa Anna, who had been made dictator, improved every opportunity to destroy his enemies, and Juarez was arrested and taken to Vera Cruz, whence, after having received most cruel treatment in prison, he embarked for Havana, going eventually to New Orleans to live. His business affairs were passed over to his associate, Señor Perez; but, the latter having been imprisoned shortly after for holding correspondence with some of the enemies of Santa Anna, Porfirio Diaz took sole charge. Here he gave proof of his honesty and activity, and showed great skill in the exercise of his profession.

Seeing the injustice exercised in voting for the dictator, he and other students were indignant at the unwarrantable exercise of power. However, when he saw the frauds committed, the young patriot could endure it no longer, and he and one other went to the table where the negative list was to be voted. An order was soon issued for their arrest, and they were obliged to flee.

Shortly after Diaz was called to put into practice what he had learned in his military drill; and, although only twenty-five, he was found fully competent to direct soldiers, and in the mountains of the Mixteca joined a small company of patriots, two or three hundred in number, commanded by Captain Herrera, who opposed the dictator. Herrera recognized his competency and took his advice. Soon after, though few in number, having but few arms, and being but poorly disciplined, they gained a victory at Scotongo over the large and well-disciplined forces of Santa Anna.

When Santa Anna was overthrown and the liberal government was established, Porfirio returned, and was rewarded by being made chief of police in the district of Ixtlan. Shortly after, when the national guard was formally organized, he was elected captain of the fourth company of the second battalion, and, yielding to his military inclinations, resigned his position as chief of police, with its salary of one hundred and forty dollars a month, to accept that of captain at sixty dollars.

In 1857 he went out under Lieutenant-Colonel Velasco to put down an uprising in Jamiltepec. At Ixcapax he was badly wounded, but, seeing that one of his lines was in great danger, without heeding the blood streaming from his wounds he went forward, and with rare military courage so diverted the enemy as to defeat them.

His mother died about the end of 1858, while he was in Tehuantepec. Through all his vicissitudes he had ever been an affectionate and obedient son, and her death caused him great sorrow.

It was in that year that he went to Tehuantepec under General Ignacio Mejia to fight Cabos, who was defeated at Jalapa, and while there he was made military commander of that district. He maintained the government in that region, contending against an enemy superior in strength, without aid from the general government, and counting only upon the resources which he alone knew how to obtain. He remained in Tehuantepec two years, fighting almost every day against large odds. Again he was wounded, but the victory was complete, and he was advanced from the rank of major to that of lieutenant-colonel. Discretion and prudence united to patriotism and noble aspirations have ever been the base of his military character.

The extraction by a surgeon from the United States of a ball that he had carried in his body for months relieved him from the acute physical suffering that he had long endured. Soon after he received his commission as lieutenant-colonel for a victory obtained in June, 1859, in Mixtequilla. For another one gained in Tehuantepec in November, 1859, the government rewarded

NATIONAL LIBRARY.

him with the rank of colonel. On the 5th of August Diaz won another victory over Cabos in Oaxaca. He had only seven hundred men and three pieces of artillery, while Cabos had two thousand men and twelve pieces. Diaz, although wounded in the foot, remained in the saddle, and, while weak and faint from the loss of blood, continued to give orders and inspire his soldiers, until he saw his enemy put to flight and the victory won. Shortly after he was attacked with typhoid fever, but was much encouraged during his sickness by the knowledge that his fellow-citizens had honored him by his appointment as deputy to the General Congress in recognition of the great services he had rendered his country.

Diaz ever loved above all other things a military life, and he could not bear the thought of separating himself from the army. On the battle-field, surrounded by his faithful companions, he experienced more than anywhere else the pleasure of satisfied ambition. There he could open up for himself a way without contending against the jealousies and envy which were to be encountered in legislative halls. The hardships of war had been until now his sweets of life, and the noise of battle still resounded in his ears like sweet and harmonious music. But he had to submit to his lot and repair to the capital of the republic, there to work as a legislator, having gained another step on the ladder of success. Although virtually the Conservative forces were destroyed, some chiefs, who could find no better occupation than to live by war, were aided by the Church and the prospect of booty. Leonardo Marquez, one of the most prominent of these revolutionary chiefs, on June 24, 1861, attempted an attack on the capital. Congress was in session when the unexpected news reached them of his arrival. Diaz, being, as he said, "a soldier above all things," asked permission to retire, and hastened to the scene of danger. The forces from Oaxaca, which were quartered in the convent of San Fernando under General Mejia, resisted Marquez's attack, and Colonel Diaz's arrival was celebrated with cheers from his old companions in arms, whose enthusiasm he served to revive. Mejia gladly accepted his aid, and the victory was theirs. The importance of the aid that Diaz here gave can be better understood from the reward that the government conferred on him by giving the command of the brigade of Oaxaca to him,—General Mejia being then ill,—with the order to join Ortega's division and to march on and destroy the rest of the Conservative forces. Suffice it to say that on the 13th of August, 1861, the fourth anniversary of one of his first triumphs, Diaz, with a few soldiers, gained another victory over Marquez and his four thousand men. In his attack upon Marquez he had disobeyed General Ortega, and it was not pleasant to the latter to feel that all the glory of that campaign belonged to a subordinate. But Ortega hastened to recommend him. The entrance of Diaz into the capital was one triumphal march, and the government had awarded him the rank of brigadier-general.

Shortly afterward Benito Juarez was elected president of the republic, and the French invaded the country. On the 5th of May, 1862, General Diaz gained a notable victory over the invaders at Puebla de los Angeles. General Zaragoza was the commander-in-chief in this engagement, General Diaz commanding a division.

The writer is under obligations to General Hinojosa, late secretary of war, for the following:

"In the report rendered to the secretary of war by Ignacio Zaragoza, the general commanding the Liberal forces of the constitutional government of President Juarez, giving the detail of the battle of Puebla, of the 5th of May, 1862, in which the invading army of France was defeated, is found the following:

"'On the 4th I ordered the brigades under command of Generals Berriozabal, Diaz, and Lamadrid to form three columns of attack, the first being composed of one thousand and eighty-two men, the second of one thousand, and the third of one thousand and twenty. General Diaz with two sections of his brigade and one from that of Lamadrid, with two field-pieces, and the remaining one from Abzarer, not only held the enemy in check but repulsed the column that made a bold attack on our position. Thus repulsed, they fell back upon the hacienda of San José Rentaria, where they united with the force repulsed from the hill, which, having reorganized, was preparing for the defensive, having already made loop-holes in the heavy walls of the buildings.

"'Although they had been routed, I could not attack them in that position, their numerical force being so much superior to mine; consequently I recalled General Diaz, who, with great ardor and gallantry, was following them up, and ordered that simply a menacing attitude be maintained.'"

On the 16th of March, 1863, the French General Forey marched upon Puebla with twenty-six thousand men, and, after a brave defence, General Ortega wisely surrendered, having refused to capitulate. On the 17th of May the white flag invited the French to enter and receive as prisoners eleven thousand soldiers and fifteen hundred officials. It was difficult to guard so many prisoners, and Diaz and Berriozabal took the first opportunity of escaping, as others afterward did; and the two generals, especially Diaz, were received in Mexico with enthusiastic demonstrations. Again he was given the command of a division when Juarez evacuated the city of Mexico. He left his command to General Comonfort and went to Oaxaca to organize the Army of the East. Marshal Bazaine went in command of eighteen thousand men and forty-eight pieces of artillery to attack Diaz in Oaxaca. Diaz surrendered, and was sent a prisoner to Puebla, but escaped. Ten thousand dollars was offered for his capture or proof of his death. He gathered together a small force, and here and there would have engagements, with varying success. But the brilliant triumphs of Miahuatlan and La Carbonera over the French brought back to General Diaz all the lustre and fame that he had gained as the most prominent general of the country. While the battles themselves were eclipsed by many of his previous victories, they were most notable for the indisputable establishment of republican supremacy in all the vast region of the south,—the result of more than a year of vigorous and persevering efforts.

He again organized new troops, and defeated Visoza at Julingo, state of Puebla, on the 1st of October, 1865. He then went to La Providencia, where General Juan Alvarez gave him some two hundred arms, and he again defeated Visoza at Comitlipa, state of Guerrero, on the 4th of December, 1865. He fought successfully against General Ortega at Pinotepo and Jametepec, state of Oaxaca, in March, 1866. He again defeated the Imperialists, under Major Cevallos, at Puebla, state of Oaxaca, on the 14th of the same month. At Nochistan, in the same state, Diaz fought Hungarian cavalry under the Count of Gauz, who was killed on the field.

At Miahuatlan General Diaz captured over one thousand muskets and two pieces of artillery, with all the ammunition of the enemy. A battalion of chasseurs under French officers was captured; the colonel, Hourie Icolart, was killed.

From Miahuatlan he marched to the city of Oaxaca, and while besieging that capital he learned that the Imperial government had sent a column under command of Baron Luker, an Austrian officer, to relieve the besieged garrison of Oaxaca. General Diaz decided at once to march on the approaching relief column, which he met at La Carbonera on the 18th of October, 1866; and, after routing it completely, he returned to Oaxaca, when the garrison surrendered on the 31st of the same month. He thus obtained forty-two pieces of artillery, twenty-five hundred muskets, and all the garrison provision and stores.

The 1st of November, 1866, General Diaz entered his natal city to be crowned with laurel as its liberator. On April 2 he won at Puebla another glorious victory, which made the walls of the empire totter, as Puebla was one of the invader's three strongholds. Among the prisoners were eleven generals and three bishops. By law all the officers taken prisoner were to be shot as traitors, and even foreigners were to suffer the same fate after the French armies had been withdrawn. Presenting himself before the eleven generals, Diaz politely invited them to follow him, without being guarded, to the episcopal palace, where were six hundred officials, many of them occupied with confession and making their final arrangements, as they knew the fate that had befallen other prisoners.

"Gentlemen," said Diaz, "it is very painful to me,—it is impossible for me to execute the punishment which the law imposes, and there is no alternative for me but to make you prisoners; but I remember well my own sufferings while a prisoner in this same place, and I wish to prevent your being put to such straits. Go, then; you are free. All I ask of you is that you promise me to put yourselves at the disposition of the supreme government if you are so ordered. The nation will pronounce its sentence upon the empire, but it will be indulgent to its misguided sons."

This general amnesty, which only found its parallel at Appomattox, caused on all sides a great deal of satisfaction. Men who had before been enemies pledged themselves hereafter to be friends. Many turned away to hide their tears. General Diaz himself was profoundly moved. Among the prisoners was a colonel who was ashamed and fearful at the same time, and could not believe that he was free; for when Count von Thun had fixed the price of ten thousand dollars upon the head of General Diaz when he escaped from Puebla, this Colonel Escamilla (then chief of police of Izucar) had offered another thousand from his own pocket. The general understood well his captive's feelings, and said, "Colonel, that imprudent action was suggested by blind duty; let us forget it." From that time Escamilla was one of his most loyal partisans.

After the occupation of the city of Oaxaca, General Diaz marched to Tehuantepec, but the enemy overtook him at Lachitova, under command of Colonel Toledo, and on the 19th of December, 1866, General Diaz defeated him, driving him back. On the 26th of the same month he again defeated Colonel Toledo's forces at Tequisisitan.

General Diaz then returned to Oaxaca, where he reorganized his army and marched his forces to Puebla, which city was invested on the 3d of March, 1867, and was taken by assault on the 2d of April following.

His tempering with magnanimity the rigor of the law, avoiding the baptism of blood, had its influence on the fall of the city of Mexico, winning for Diaz great praise among friends and enemies. General Tamariz, who died shortly afterward, said, with emotion, "Twice Diaz has conquered me by his military talent and once by his generosity. With pleasure I would serve such a man, although it were as a common soldier."

After the capture of Puebla, General Diaz went to meet the Imperial General Marques, who had left Querétaro to relieve Mexico, and who was marching against Puebla. On the 5th of April General Diaz overtook Marques at San Diego Notario, where a battle was fought, ending in the defeat of Marques. General Diaz followed up his victory, and met Marques again at San Lorenzo on the 10th of April, defeating him completely. Marques came to the city of Mexico with a small force of Hungarian cavalrymen.

General Diaz then came on to Mexico, establishing himself in Tacubaya, and commenced operations to put the city in a state of siege. On the 14th of May General Escobedo took Querétaro. Maximilian was tried by court-martial, and was condemned to death in accordance with his own decree of the 3d of October, 1865, that all officers taken prisoner should be shot. As General Arteaga and all the republican generals had been, so was he put to death.

Maximilian, the ex-emperor, with Miramon and Mejia, his principal generals, were shot on the 19th of June, 1867, victims of Napoleon the Little.

Diaz had continued with great vigor the siege of the capital, and on the 20th of June the Conservatives yielded, and he entered the city quietly and took a small house in the suburbs, having his office in the School of Mines. No banner of any sort was raised on the palace until the 15th of July, when Juarez himself hoisted the flag, for which occasion our loyal general had reserved twenty thousand dollars, with the object of making a celebration worthy of the occasion. The contrast between this spectacle and the modest asylum of the victorious leader impressed the people in favor of one who, with utter forgetfulness of self, had thought only of the welfare of his fellow-citizens. On rendering his accounts, he delivered to the treasury one hundred and forty thousand dollars,—an act which caused great astonishment, as the expenses of the war had been so enormous compared with the resources at command.

The day following the surrender of Mexico Diaz presented his resignation as commander of the line and Army of the East, and after a few months returned to his native city, Oaxaca, which with open arms welcomed the hero home again. His was one triumphal march from the capital to his home. He was given by the legislature of Oaxaca the Hacienda de la Noria, to which he retired, living there quietly for two years, resting from his labors and fatiguing marches.

He had formed, even when quite young, an attachment for Delfina Ortega y Reyes, and on the day of the surrender of Puebla, the 2d of April, that memorable day in which he gave liberty to the captives, he was joined in matrimony to the woman of his choice. Señora de Diaz possessed great sweetness of character and kindness of heart, and her greatest pleasure was in works of charity and in aiding the elevation and education of her sex, taking upon herself the care of a college for girls which her husband had founded. She was naturally timid, which, combined with her inborn graces, made her a most attractive woman.

Benito Juarez was now president, and Diaz was elected as deputy to Congress for his state. The country continued in a state of revolution, and great judgment and tact were needed to keep the peace. On July 18, 1872, Juarez died, and Sebastian Lerdo de Tejada succeeded him. Lerdo was afterward elected to the presidency, but, there being much dissatisfaction by reason of his attitude against the Church party, and of a feeling among the soldiers that General Diaz should be the president, the revolutions continued throughout the country. General Diaz, on December 5, 1875, took steamer at Vera Cruz and went to the United States. Later, in company with others in whom he had confidence, he gathered an army in the states of Tamaulipas and Coahuila, and returned to Mexico. But he was overcome and obliged to make his escape. He embarked on the steamer City of Havana, having taken precautions to change his name and, as much as possible, his appearance. He knew many on board, but they did not recognize him, and all went well until their arrival at Tampico, where a company embarked for Vera Cruz, and he was recognized by them. Seeing that he was suspected and that the officers were making preparations to take him prisoner, at dusk he let himself down over the steamer's side into the water, hoping to escape the sharks and swim to the shore. But his enemies had been watching, and cried out, "Man overboard!" Soon the oars were plying; and, although he made good time swimming, he was overtaken and carried back to the steamer. As they were about to make him a prisoner, Diaz called the captain and asked protection under the United States flag. The captain acceded to his request until arriving at Vera Cruz. Although there had been a guard at his state-room, he went to the purser's room with a life-preserver, desiring to make his escape again, but the purser, Mr. Coney, persuaded him to hide himself in his sofa and let the life-preserver down into the sea, in order that they might think he had really escaped thereby. This was done, and the life-preserver was afterward picked up on shore, where many testified that there were blood-stains on it and signs that it had been bitten by a shark. An examination afterward proved the stains to be iron-rust.

Great was the commotion when it was discovered early the following morning that General Diaz had escaped. The troops and crew united in searching the steamer, and frequently were in very close proximity to him in his hiding-place. Finally an official report announcing his disappearance was sent out, making it appear that the general had been drowned. For one week he remained in his place of torture, as it was the custom of the Mexican officials to gather in the purser's room and drink and play until morning, and he did not wish to have a stop put to that pastime, so that there should be no suspicion in regard to the stateroom.

Although in Vera Cruz the steamer was surrounded by soldiers, Diaz escaped them, in the dress of a seaman, with some workmen in a cotton lighter. He passed through many vicissitudes, and at last, on November 16, 1876, with an armed force gained a victory over the Lerdists at Tecoac.

Lerdo, hearing of the loss to his party and of the brilliant victory of Diaz, started, with some of the faithful members of his cabinet and with what money he could lay his hands on, on November 20, 1876, for Acapulco, there taking passage for the United States. General Diaz

THE PALACE OF MINES.

entered Mexico on the 23d of the same month, and five days afterward assumed the executive power. He formed his cabinet, raised a loan of five hundred thousand dollars to commence the new administration, and, leaving General Mendez as president *ad interim*, went out to finish up with the revolutionary element.

There were then really three presidents of Mexico,—Lerdo, who, however, had abandoned the country; Iglesias, who had been chief justice, or vice-president, under the Lerdo government; and Diaz. Iglesias, realizing the desperate condition in which he was placed, followed Lerdo's example, embarking at Manzanillo for San Francisco, California, on the 17th of January, 1877. For two months General Diaz marched from the central states toward Guadalajara, capturing all the Lerdist troops without firing a single shot. At the end of the two months he relieved General Mendez and took his seat as the actual president of the republic.

Many radical improvements were made in all lines, and, with the exception of a few revolutionary movements, the country again began to enjoy peace and quiet. Friendly relations were established with foreign powers, and confidence was at last inspired in the new government. After having served his term as president, General Manuel Gonzalez, who had distinguished himself as a military man by the side of General Diaz, was elected to succeed him.

The popularity of President Diaz was heightened by the influence of his wife, Doña Delfina, whose mission on earth was love and charity, as was shown by her interest in hospitals and schools. She had one son, and on April 2, 1880, the anniversary of the famous victory of General Diaz in Puebla, a daughter was born, to whom was given, in commemoration of the event, the name of Victoria. The whole country united in the double congratulations; but the child lived only a few days, and the mother followed immediately afterward, on April 8, being the first wife of a president to die in the National Palace. Her remains were deposited in the Guadalupe Cemetery with appropriate ceremonies. So that year of Diaz's presidency, so happy for the country and so glorious for him, was covered with a dark cloud of personal sorrow.

For a time under President Gonzalez General Diaz was Ministro de Fomento, but retired in May, 1881. Soon after he was elected senator from the state of Morelos, and governor of Oaxaca, which latter position he took November 30, 1881. Two years after the death of his wife he married Carmen, a notably beautiful brunette, eldest daughter of Señor Romero Rubio. They harmonized well,—he the personification of strength, she of beauty and purity. Simple, without affectation, she unites to a kindly heart a most admirable presence of mind and dignity. She speaks with facility English and French; every one is delighted with her affability and the sweetness and melody of her voice. They spent part of their honeymoon in the United States, where they were everywhere received with honors, special trains being put at their disposal and great courtesy shown them by all.

On December 1, 1884, the second presidential period of General Diaz was inaugurated. The ceremony took place in Congress Hall, formerly the Iturbide Theatre. The diplomatic corps were in full dress, while General Diaz had on a simple black suit. In five minutes after he appeared he had taken the oath of office and retired as quietly as he came to the palace, there to receive the congratulations of General Gonzalez and to appoint his cabinet.

Under President Diaz's administration many reforms in the constitution and laws of the country have been made, and the result is that there exists under him a security which was never before known in the republic. His liberal ideas, his enthusiasm for the development of the country, and his previous honest administration enabled him to begin his second term under much better conditions than existed during his first; and again the confidence of the public was not misplaced, since during his second administration Mexico progressed more than ever before.

Diaz's life has been identified with that of the Mexican republic for the last forty years. The life of this really wonderful man presents many points and lessons for future generations to study. He is to-day, as he has been for many years, the first soldier of the republic, and, what is better, its first citizen. From the very bottom of the ladder, from a young lieutenant at the age of twenty-three to the highest commission in the army, as its general-in-chief, his career has been spotless and brilliant.

But it is not most as a soldier that he has won the admiration and fame which he enjoys to-day, at home as well as abroad. It is as a statesman, in his civil duties, in the many political, financial, and diplomatic questions which he has so successfully solved, that the greatness of Porfirio Diaz must be considered.

It is a well-known fact that when he assumed the presidency the country was bankrupt and disorder reigned supreme throughout the republic. From the beginning he started to work with a will and check all the evils with which his country was afflicted.

All Mexico regarded him as the first soldier of the nation, but few, if any, thought that he possessed the quality of a statesman. Happily, he proved to be as good a statesman as he had been a soldier. He pacified the country. The public treasury, instead of being plundered, as in former times, was devoted only to the services of the nation, and at the end of his first presidential term, in 1880, the country began to observe the change which, like a magician, he had effected in so few years. Every industry had been helped by the government. Mining and agriculture had received a vigorous impulse. The national credit, which for many years had been an unknown quantity, was re-established, and the monetary centres in Europe, which a few years before would not lend Mexico a single dollar, were willing to lend millions to a country governed by so upright, honest, and iron-handed a president.

His countrymen regarded him as a soldier, but not as a statesman, yet this soldier has made the great pacific revolution of the century. Through his iron will and energy the most revolutionary country in the world has been changed to the most pacific, and those who regarded him as not possessing the qualities that go to make a statesman of the first order have seen their mistake, and to-day look upon him no longer as merely the first soldier but as the first statesman. To-day, as yesterday, no man is so popular as he; to-day, as yesterday, his whole aim, his great ambition, is to see his beloved country developed and respected and occupying among nations that place to which she is entitled by reason of her wonderful natural resources.

When Diaz was elected president in 1877 the country was in turmoil and revolution. The primitive roads and many of the towns to which they led were at the mercy of revolutionists and raiders, and there was but one railway, that from Vera Cruz to Mexico. Since the beginning of Diaz's *régime* railways have been reaching out into all parts of the country and new lines proposed and built. In 1876 Mexico had no means of constructing railways, and, having been regarded for so many years as incapable of paying its debts, it would have been impossible to raise money to build the desired roads. Business stagnation and financial disrepute were the conditions of the Mexico of that day. Thanks to the administration of General Diaz, the country is not only solvent but prosperous, its people are profoundly peaceful and contented, the foreign residents are in hearty co-operation with the Mexican citizens in promoting the well-being of the country, and both foreigners and natives see in the re-election of Diaz a guarantee of continued protection and encouragement and advancement in all forms of legitimate and useful enterprises.

In his daily life President Diaz is a remarkable man. He is a human dynamo, and infuses life and vigor into every department of his administration. To-day, although in the sixties, he is as alert and active as he was at forty. Take him all in all, he is one of the greatest men of the century. Whether he is at his city house, in Cadena Street, or in his summer home, in the castle of Chapultepec, occupying the apartments where Maximilian resided, his routine of life goes on with clock-like regularity. Everything is systematized in the daily life of the Mexican president. He gives from one to two hours every morning to a conference with his able and energetic minister of finance, Señor José Ives Limantour, one of the youngest cabinet ministers in America. General Diaz is determined to maintain the credit of the nation, and is as much interested in all the details of financial administration as he is in military administration. He is an early riser, and his accomplished private secretary, Señor Rafael Chausal, who opens the voluminous daily mail of the chief magistrate, by eight o'clock in the morning must be ready to sit down with him to receive instructions for the immediate answering of even the most insignificant note. At half-past one he stops work and is driven in his coupé, unattended by military escort, to his home, where he dines at leisure. He is a simple liver, preferring a soup and a plain roast to the most elaborate *menu*, and drinking very sparingly. He cares little for tobacco, only occasionally indulging in the mildest cigars.

The private life and domestic relations of public men do not fairly belong to the public, but I may say that the family life of General Diaz is a happy one, and that his wife, Señora Doña Carmen Romero Rubio de Diaz, is the crown and solace of his home, where the Mexican president becomes the man of family and allows his social side full scope. He knows how to relax, as all great men do. The fun-loving side of his character, his sense of humor, his genuine kindliness of nature, have free vent in the social circle.

In the afternoon, at half-past three, the president is again at the palace, where he receives the public railway managers, great lawyers, contractors of public works, and properly accredited representatives of the native and foreign press. He is a man of business, and every one whom he receives is treated with politeness. He is always dignified, and his manner is that of a soldier, softened by a sense of what is due to those who have business with him.

As is necessary with successful great men, he has a remarkable memory. He knows by name every man of consequence, even in the remotest villages; he knows the alcaldes, the judges of the minor courts, the planters, and every old soldier. His judgment of people is clear and precise. He knows how to be magnanimous to ancient foes; men who served Maximilian well he has all around him in close relations. As they served their imperial master faithfully, he reasons that they will serve him with equal loyalty. He likes a frank, opinionated, honest man.

In short, if a man is doing anything to help on the progress of Mexico, he will find General Diaz cordial and ready to aid; but if he is merely a selfish schemer, he will be found out and treated accordingly. No man or woman deceives him. He may indulgently play with a cunning, artful person, and that person may go away thinking he has got the best of him; but let that individual wait a week or a month, and he will find out that the president has sifted his schemes, and has already taken measures to outwit him. He communicates with politicians, governors of states, military men, by wire, and often in cipher. His book of ciphers—some eight hundred—is in the hands of his trusted secretary, and by means of it the president is able to consult on the same topic with a great many people. Among his confidential friends are many private individuals, with whom he communicates in case of necessity by cipher. Thus the Mexican president knows all that is going on all over the broad domain which he governs so wisely and so forcefully. He likes bright, active, enterprising foreigners, and would be glad to have them naturalized, so that he could utilize them in public office. The whole bent of his work is to build up modern Mexico, which is already taking its place among the progressive, solvent, and busy nations of the world.

He is the idol of the Mexican army, for the men who served under him are aware that he won his position and his fame by military genius and personal valor. General Diaz's object has been to develop Mexico's resources at home, to bring her into touch with foreign countries, to strengthen her not only materially, but in every other way that will give her a respectable standing before the nations. History will place him among the nation-builders.

CHAPTER XI

THE MINISTERS OF THE CABINET

THE government of Mexico is conducted very much after the plan of that of the United States. The president is elected for a term of four years, and he appoints the ministers of his cabinet, which is composed of seven members. Following is the list of these offices, with their present incumbents:

Secretario de Relaciones (Foreign Affairs), Lic. Don Ignacio Mariscal.

Secretario de Gobernación (Interior), General Don Manuel Gonzalez Cosio.

Secretario de Hacienda (Treasury), Lic. Don José Ives Limantour.

Secretario de Guerra y Marino (War and Navy), General Don Felipe Berriozabal.

Secretario de Justicia y Instrucción Pública (Public Instruction), Lic. Don Joaquin Baranda.

Secretario de Fomento (Encouragement), Iñigo Don Manuel Fernandez Leal.

Secretario de Comunicaciones y Obras Públicas (Public Works), General Don Francisco Z. Mena.

When the president is re-elected to another term of office it is the custom of the Mexican cabinet to resign in a body, thus leaving the president free to form a new bureau, if he chooses,—a custom to be commended to older and larger republics. This custom is but another sign of the universal courtesy and instinctive politeness of the Mexicans, which would thus relieve the head of the nation from any embarrassing position that might arise. Thus far, however, the president has seen fit to request his ministers to remain in charge of their respective offices, and by this means a continuity of good government is insured, while the dangers of change and disruption are avoided.

The minister of foreign affairs sends in his resignation through the sub-secretary of his

LIC. DON IGNACIO MARISCAL,
SECRETARY OF FOREIGN AFFAIRS.

department. All the other ministers tender theirs through the secretary of foreign affairs. The president replies to the resignation of the latter as follows:

"Let the minister of foreign affairs be informed that his resignation is not to be accepted; inasmuch as the president of the republic considers his re-election for another constitutional period as an implicit approval of his acts as chief executive, and as Señor Mariscal is one of his associates, he looks to his patriotism that he will continue to co-operate in the labors of the public administration." And to all the other ministers he sends an answer couched in similar terms, requesting them to remain in office.

This course of action on the president's part is but another proof of his wise statesmanship, as each of his ministers was carefully chosen in the first place with a view to his fitness for the work to be intrusted to his judgment and abilities; and in no case has the choice proved a wrong one.

Perhaps the best known of these ministers, from his connection with other nations, is Señor Lic. Don Ignacio Mariscal, a man as universally beloved as he is admired and respected for his truly great qualities of heart and head.

SALON OF THE SECRETARY OF FOREIGN AFFAIRS.

He was born in Oaxaca on the 5th of July, 1829. His parents, who belonged to an honorable family, endeavored to educate their son according to his aspirations. When quite a youth he showed that he had political talent. At twenty years of age, after sustaining brilliant examinations, he received his title as a lawyer, and at once took a high position. He affiliated himself with the Liberal party, for which he has at all times been ready to make every sacrifice. He became a member of the Constitutional Congress—representing Oaxaca—and distinguished himself as one of the most active in giving Mexico its Magna Charta. He was ever one of Juarez's most ardent friends. In 1861 and 1862 he occupied a seat in Congress, after which he was magistrate of the Supreme Court, and later was appointed secretary of foreign relations. During the war of intervention he went to Washington as secretary and legal counsel of the Mexican legation, together with Señor Juan Antonio de la Fuente, minister plenipotentiary from Mexico. Then it was that Mariscal revealed great talent as an expert diplomat, aiding Señor Matias Romero in influencing the American government to take an active stand against Napoleon.

When Mexico became conqueror, Mariscal was appointed chargé d'affaires in Washington, where he won public appreciation and sympathy. Desiring to return to his native country, he resigned this high position, and was appointed president of the Supreme Court of Justice of the federal district, was next elected to Congress, and afterward was chosen justice of the National Supreme Court.

In 1866 he was a member of Juarez's cabinet as secretary of justice and public instruction.

He is the author of "Reforms in Criminal Law," a work which reflects upon him great honor. His services were once more needed as minister plenipotentiary from Mexico to the United States of North America, which position he held for six years.

During Lerdo's administration he represented Mexico in the United States, and afterward returned to Mexico to private life; but President Diaz, knowing how useful and talented a man he was, appointed him as judge of the Supreme Court of Justice of the district, and in December, 1879, made him secretary of justice and public instruction. In 1880, under his direction and supervision, there was published the Code of Civil Proceeding,—the law and regulations governing the new organization of tribunals and penal proceedings,—which was of great importance to legislation. Afterward he was appointed secretary of foreign relations; and when President Diaz finished his term, and General Manuel Gonzalez succeeded him, the latter kept Señor Mariscal in this position on account of his vast knowledge of international law.

During President Gonzalez's administration Señor Mariscal filled several difficult and high positions, among others that of minister plenipotentiary to Great Britain.

On General Diaz's return to the presidency he again called Señor Mariscal to his side and appointed him secretary of foreign affairs, which position he still holds. In this delicate position he has justified the confidence deservedly placed in him, and has amicably arranged differences which had arisen, and re-established friendly relations with France, England, and the other nations of Europe.

As a diplomat Señor Mariscal has an enviable reputation, and as a lawyer he is one of the notabilities of the Mexican forum. His opinion on any question of public, private, or international rights has great weight. As a speaker he uses with great facility, elegance, and correctness of style the rich language of Cervantes. He speaks several languages, English among others, and has translated into Spanish some of the choicest poems of Longfellow, Poe, Bryant, and other American writers.

GENERAL DON MANUEL GONZALEZ COSIO,
SECRETARY OF THE INTERIOR.

In his home he is an affectionate father and an excellent husband, and is a type of the perfect gentleman. His wife is an American lady of high standing.

For his important services he has won high consideration from the governments of France, Portugal, Venezuela, and others, which are unanimous in greatly honoring him.

Señor General Manuel G. Cosio is the secretary of the interior, one of the most important positions in the cabinet.

Few men in Mexico are so enthusiastic for the development of the country as General Cosio, and few have the ability, push, and energy that he has developed in the many offices which he has occupied.

Señor Cosio was born in the state of Zacatecas, and, besides having occupied the position of governor of that state and that of congressman and senator, he displayed great ability as mayor of the city of Mexico. He is one of the most popular men of the cabinet.

There is quite a romantic episode in the life of General Cosio. During the civil war of the United States he was in New York in company with two other young officers, destitute, but anxious to return to Mexico to fight for his country against the French. None of the three had enough money to take him back, so they decided that one of them should be selected by lot and enlist in the army of the United States, obtain the eight hundred dollars in greenbacks which were given as bounty to each enlisting man at that time, and give the money to the other two to go back to Mexico and fight for their country.

The lot fell to Cosio, who was on the point of presenting himself at head-quarters in New York and enlisting in the army so that his two companions could go back to Mexico with the money thus obtained, when General Mejia arrived in New York. He was visited by the three young officers and acquainted with their intention, and he gave them all passage-money and sent them back to Mexico as commissioned officers. Thus it was that instead of fighting for the American Union, as Cosio came very near doing, he battled for his own country until the French were banished from Mexico. The popularity of General Cosio is unquestioned. He is a man of large intelligence, long experience in civil affairs, and proved capacity. A man who has fought in revolutions, won distinction for gallantry in the war against the empire, suffered imprisonment in France as an incident of that conflict, served twice as governor of Zacatecas, been

Señor Don José Ives Limantour,
Secretary of the Treasury.

a deputy and a senator in the Federal Congress, and for ten years held the most conspicuous place in the municipal council of the city of Mexico, is surely qualified to hold an important ministry in a great country.

The charities of Mexico City are wonderfully abundant. These are both public and private. There are at least half a dozen institutions maintained by private enterprise and Christian philanthropy. The public charities of Mexico are organized and conducted under the auspices of the federal department of the interior, of which General Manuel Gonzalez Cosio is chief. Many sick and dying, hungry and homeless, have had reason for gratitude to a government so considerate. Minister Cosio is especially interested in these charities, and often makes personal inspection of these institutions in his department. One of these is the Proveeduria de la Beneficencia Pública, or Storehouse of the Bureau of Public Charities. This immense storehouse supplies provisions for several public establishments, where the poor are provided for without money and without price.

The system of the hospicios is exceedingly beneficent and worthy of a much more extended description than can be given in these pages. Mexico takes good care of its sick and unfortunate ones, and some of her benevolent institutions are very old. The Hospital of San Andres, for instance, was founded in 1626 by private donations. It was converted into the Jesuit College and the Church of Santa Ana in 1642, but Captain Andres Tapia Carbajal reconstructed it in 1676 and called it San Andres. After the Jesuits were expatriated it was abandoned until 1779, when Archbishop Alonzo Nuñez de Hara y Peralta turned it into a pest-house for smallpox. In 1861, under the Reform Laws, it was secularized, and now, under the Secretaria de Gobernación, it is a large and spacious institution, with fine wards for the sick and infirm, who are all well cared for by the protecting government.

Away back in 1575 the Augustinian fathers founded a college in the city of Mexico which flourished for some years but was finally abandoned. Later on, a cuartel was built from its decayed ruins, which was fortified and occupied until 1847, when it was converted into a "Hospital Provisional." The founder of this project was Urbano Fonseca, who placed therein forty beds for men and twenty for women. The first to occupy these beds were the wounded from the battle of Padurna, August 23, 1847. Later this building was converted into a municipal hospital and named "Hospital Juarez," under which title it has been the source of relief for many unfortunates. The same period of war was the occasion of founding another of Mexico's great charities. In 1850 a committee rented the Tecpan de Santiago, in order to provide a suitable retreat for the young prisoners who were then in the national prison. It was called at first a branch of the prison, but later it became necessary to place there many children who were not criminals. Señor Azcarate established there, for all these children, in 1853 some excellent schools and workshops, and put them under the direction of Señor Licenciado Antonio Diaz de Bonillo. As first conducted, the school partook of a correctional nature, but some years ago it was renamed the Industrial Orphan School, and the character of it somewhat changed. This school was protected by the late Hon. Manuel Romero Rubio, but it is now in the direct charge of General Cosio.

GENERAL DON FRANCISCO Z. MENA,
SECRETARY OF COMMUNICATIONS AND PUBLIC WORKS.

Other institutions under his efficient care are the Hospicio de Pobres, founded in 1765 by Fernando Ortiz Cortez, who obtained a license to establish a local hospital for the poor of the city,—the place was recognized and formally opened in 1774,—and the Casa de Maternidad, founded by Carlotta in June, 1865, with an annex for hospital purposes.

The departamento de hacienda, which is the treasury of Mexico, is without doubt the most important of public departments. This is at present under the able, well-organized management of Señor Lic. Don José Ives Limantour, one of the most notable financiers of Mexico, whose superior intellectual faculties have placed him in this office, where he has shown remarkable executive ability.

In "La Aduana," a building situated in the Antigua Plazuela de Santiago Tlaltelolco, are located all the offices, store-rooms, deposits, etc., that come under the direction of the minister of the treasury. It also serves as a wareroom for the railroads that belong to the republic.

The Casa de Moneda (Mint) was established in 1526, and then occupied a department of the Municipal Palace. In 1640 the mint was built on Calle de Moneda, which was afterward taken for the National Museum (which up to date has cost more than a million dollars). On account of unpaid contracts, the department came under the charge of the government afterward, and later became entirely government property. It now occupies a large and handsome building on Calle del Apartado. The bureau of engraving is situated in the National Palace, and the Loteria Nacional is in the first Calle del Reloj. The latter is a spacious building, with fine offices and a grand saloon, where the drawings take place. The Loteria is under charge of the secretario de hacienda.

Señor Don José Ives Limantour was born of French parents in the city of Mexico in 1853. His parents being wealthy, he had the opportunity of the best schools in the city. In 1866 his parents took him to France to complete his education. Some two years later he returned to Mexico to study law in the School of Jurisprudence. The term for graduation, as fixed by the faculty of this school, is six years, but Mr. Limantour, being an unusually bright and studious scholar, completed his graduation in four years, becoming distinguished for his intelligence and his energy.

GENERAL DON FELIPE BERRIOZABAL,
SECRETARY OF WAR AND THE NAVY.

Mr. Limantour is especially versed in political economy, and during his college course excited considerable comment from the politicians of the day by his views on political economy. After his graduation he was appointed by the faculty professor of that branch in the School of Jurisprudence. Later he was sent by the government to Europe to settle several difficult financial questions. Owing to his extreme modesty, Mr. Limantour kept out of public life until the year 1893, when Mr. Matias Romero tendered him the office of sub-secretary of the treasury, which he accepted. Although he was an entirely new man in the department, he soon won the confidence of Secretary Romero; and in the same year, when Mr. Romero was appointed minister to Washington, Mr. Limantour was appointed secretary of the treasury, which place he fills to-day with ability and honor, returning his salary each month to the treasury of the republic. He has a sufficient income from his individual property to satisfy his every want. Although the depression of silver during the administration of Mr. Limantour has been very great, yet through his ability as a financier he has paid every obligation of the government that is due and has sustained the credit of the country, even though the bankers of Europe have attempted to depress the values of Mexican securities; and now the balance on the ledger is on the credit side, where it had always been on the debit side until his administration.

The Department of Communications and Public Works is under the wise and statesmanlike management of General Don Francisco Z. Mena; and under his charge are the railroads, the post-office, and the telegraph systems of the republic. No more acceptable man for the onerous duties of his position could possibly be chosen. General Mena has lived many years in European capitals, and was acting in the capacity of minister to Germany when he was called to the president's cabinet. During his life abroad he had exceptional opportunities to study social conditions as well as financial questions, and the results of his knowledge of modern methods of transportation and intercommunication are plainly visible in the administration of the affairs of his present office. At one time he was governor of Guanajuato, and under his administration that state made rapid advancement in all modern progress and was greatly benefited. As a soldier, too, General Mena has a fine record, beginning as sub-lieutenant of the Batallón de Zapadores and rapidly ascending the rigorous military scale until he was finally made general.

LIEUTENANT-COLONEL DON MANUEL MONDRAGON, INVENTOR OF THE FAMOUS GUN, WHICH HE PRESENTED TO THE MEXICAN GOVERNMENT.

The offices of General Mena and his assistants are located in the old custom-house, a building which was founded in 1731, and still stands, mighty and commanding, in elegant and substantial style. The Administración de Correos occupies the building intended formerly for one of the mints. Here are all the offices of postal authorities and the general post-office. The latter is finely conducted under a very rigid administration, and the income from it grows larger every year. General Mena has instituted many substantial reforms which react strongly for the benefit of the whole republic. The same is true of the telegraph systems and all the public works.

General Pedro Hinojosa was for years the secretary of war and of the navy. He is an old soldier who has been in the service of his country for the past fifty years. Born in Matamoras during the troublesome period of the almost unbroken series of wars which Mexico had to sustain, General Hinojosa early enlisted, and by his strict attention to duty, by his bravery in the thick of battle, and by his thorough knowledge of the tactics and science of war, reached the highest grade in the army, that of general of division, and was finally appointed by General Diaz to his present position. In future years General Hinojosa will be honorably remembered as the secretary under whose administration the beginning of the new Mexican navy was started and who introduced many desirable reforms in the army.

In 1884 President Diaz appointed him secretary of war and the navy, a position which he held in the cabinet until March, 1896, when he resigned. He is now the president of the military court, and one of the most popular and beloved military men of the country; and, having lived for many years on the United States frontier, he has among "Uncle Sam's" soldiers many warm friends, who will cherish his memory throughout life.

General Hinojosa resigned on account of his advancing years and consequent infirmities, and President Diaz appointed in his place General Don Felipe Berriozabal.

The present minister of war was born in Zacatecas on the 23d of August, 1827. He was still continuing his studies when the invasion of the republic by the armies of the United States filled him with patriotic ardor and with the desire of fighting in behalf of his country. Consequently he entered the army as lieutenant of a company of engineers, and served throughout the campaign in the valley of Mexico. On the occupation of the capital by the American forces, Berriozabal went to Toluca to aid the acting president, Don Manuel Pena y Pena. When the latter went to Querétaro he left the young engineer in charge of a very delicate matter.

When the war was over, he retired to the capital, where he completed his studies and graduated as an engineer, April 26, 1849. He at once began exercising his profession, and for the next few years he held many important offices. Among others, he was appointed by the government to examine, amplify, and complete the plans of the lands of the states of Mexico and Tlaxcala, and to estimate the value of their rural and city properties.

In the city of Toluca he became successively a member of the ayuntamiento, jefe politico of the most important district of the state, diputado, adviser to the governor, and finally governor of the state. Later he was elected to the federal parliament. He has successively been governor of the states of Guanajuato, Querétaro, Vera Cruz, and Michoacán. In 1876 he became minister of the interior.

LIC. DON JOAQUIN BARANDA,
SECRETARY OF PUBLIC INSTRUCTION.

By a decree of October 21, 1872, the government of the state of Mexico, in recognition of his many services, honored him by placing him upon the list of the illustrious men of the country. Many scientific societies have also recognized his worth by electing him an honorary member.

It is interesting to follow his career as a soldier. In his twentieth year, he commenced his services on the 2d of July, 1847. In 1856 he was raised to the rank of lieutenant-colonel

NATIONAL PREPARATORY SCHOOL.

on account of his gallant conduct in the Plaza de Toluca. In 1858 he became colonel of Tacubaya. As a result of his bravery in the attack upon Mexico in 1859 he was made colonel of horse. The following year he was appointed general of brigade. He distinguished himself in the battle of the 5th of May and in the defence of the city of Puebla in 1863, and as a reward was given the high post of general of division. Since then he has filled a long list of important posts and commissions. The list of battles and engagements in which General Berriozabal took part would fill more than a page. He has the right to wear on his breast thirteen medals of honor given only for special and distinguished services.

In addition to this, General Porfirio Diaz has presented him with a certificate of honor, which alone would be recognition enough to satisfy the pride of the most ambitious soldier.

Under his charge are the excellent military schools of the country. El Colegio Militar was established in 1821, but experienced a series of changes and *contre-temps* until it was finally removed to the castle of Chapultepec, where it is now in a flourishing condition. During the North American war many brave young cadets lost their lives in defending this noble old castle against the invaders, September 13, 1847. The college is now a fine military institution, under charge of experienced generals in military tactics and learned professors in all branches. It is remarkably well organized, with fine observatories, and scientific cabinets full of instruments and apparatus of all descriptions. The course of instruction, as may be judged, is very complete.

The Fabrica de Armas was established in 1873, and is constantly being improved and enlarged. It is in charge of Lieutenant-Colonel de la Plaza Mayor Facultativa de Artilleria Don Manuel Mondragon, the

ACADEMY OF SAN CARLOS.

inventor of the famous gun which bears his name and which is used entirely by the Mexican army. In this factory, where all classes of arms are made, most of the work is done by young girls. The National Powder Factory is situated in Las Lomas de Santa Fé, and is also under the supervision of Lieutenant-Colonel Mondragon, who has for some time devoted his efforts to perfecting smokeless powder.

The Fundición de Artilleria is an immense building, in which are manufactured all the necessaries for artillery purposes, serving also as a warehouse for the costly machinery imported from Europe. The Cuartels de Ingenieros, de Artilleria, and de Infanteria are all well appointed and in remarkably good condition.

The most ancient fort of Mexico was probably that of Chapultepec. It occupied the most beautiful spot of the valley of Mexico, and with its many historical reminiscences still towers there, a grand old castle. When the Aztecs reached Mexico and saw this valley, they chose this as the site of a fortification that should effectually protect them from their innumerable enemies. Until Cortez occupied it, it served their purpose. During the reign of the Marquis de Galves it was turned into a palace for the viceroys, and for three centuries of varying fortunes for Mexico it served in that capacity. During the occupancy of Maximilian the old castle experienced a marvellous transformation. It was then that the palace was gorgeously fitted with rich Gobelin tapestries, inlaid floors, magnificent furniture, and priceless bronzes, while the gardens and observatory were turned into dreams of beauty and splendor of vegetation and brilliant coloring.

PATIO OF THE CONSERVATORY OF MUSIC.

Señor Don Joaquin Baranda is the secretary of justice and education. He was born at Campeche on May 7, 1840. He comes of a distinguished family, his father having been one of the most prominent men in the state of Yucatan. Señor Baranda received a complete and brilliant education, and adopted the law as his profession. He was admitted to the bar when scarcely twenty years old. At the beginning of his political career he joined the Liberal party, and, having a strong inclination for newspaper work, he commenced spreading his Liberal principles through the press.

The first important office which Señor Baranda occupied in his native state was that of civil and criminal judge. He served in this office up to the time of the war with France, when he resigned to fight for the liberties of his country. He did more than any other, through the press, to arouse public spirit against the invading soldiers of Napoleon III. When the republic was re-established, Señor Baranda was appointed judge for the district of Campeche, but soon after was elected representative to the Fourth and Fifth National Congresses.

In 1880 President Diaz appointed Señor Baranda judge of tribunal for the circuit which comprises the states of Yucatan, Campeche, Tabasco, and Chiapas, which office he occupied until he was elected senator in 1881. In September of the following year he was called to the cabinet of President Gonzalez and was given the portfolio of justice. From the first he displayed great talent and eminent qualifications for the office, so that General Diaz, on assuming the presidency for a second time, kept Señor Baranda in the same high office that he had occupied under President Gonzalez.

Don Ignio Manuel Fernandez Leal,
Secretary of Encouragement

It is hardly necessary to enumerate the many reforms which Señor Baranda has introduced in the department of justice, but it may be noted that he was the author and the champion of the free will law, which during his incumbency was passed by the Mexican Congress. He has co-operated in the establishment everywhere of graded schools for the education of the people, and convened a pedagogic congress, with the object of introducing a uniform system of teaching, which has revolutionized the old methods. For his labors in behalf of the education of the people, and for his achievements in that course, Señor Baranda has been decorated by several foreign governments, among them those of France and Venezuela. He is yet in the full enjoyment of manhood, and, great and valuable as are the services he has rendered his country in the past, even greater things are expected from him in the near future.

It is needless to say that Señor Baranda has the utmost confidence of his chief, and that he enjoys very great popularity, especially among the younger generation of Mexico, for whom he has provided hundreds upon hundreds of public schools, in which every branch of learning is taught free of charge, even books and other necessities being supplied through the generosity of the Mexican government. A man of high attainments intellectually, he is considered one of the finest orators of the nation. His enthusiastic spirit has been of great benefit to the department of public works. Under his fostering care, while the cause of public education is in a most flourishing condition, the higher schools and colleges have come to be unsurpassed in any country. Among the more prominent of the latter is La Escuela de Medicina (the school of medicine), which was founded in 1768, although not until 1833 was it actually under scientific direction. Now, however, it is thoroughly equipped with necessary apparatus, and all the scientific accessories needful to bring it up to the standard of modern requirements and place it on a level with similar institutions in other countries.

The church of San Augustin was converted by Maximilian into the Biblioteca de San Augustin, or public library, with a large collection of valuable books of all kinds. Among the schools one of the most interesting is the normal school, or La Escuela Normal para Profesores.

This recently established institution occupies the ancient convent of Santa Teresa, which was constructed by Estebán Molina de Mosquera in 1678. It is a modern school, fitted up with every equipment that can in any way serve to instruct and assist the teacher who comes here to perfect herself in her profession. The Escuela Nacional Preparatoria is an ancient but well-preserved building, which cost when it was built four hundred thousand dollars. It is admirably fitted as a large college, with spacious rooms for every department, superior apparatus, and a fine library.

Other important institutions in Señor Baranda's department are La Escuela de Jurisprudencia, which occupies the ex-convent of the Encarnación and was founded in 1868; La Escuela de Agricultura, founded under the careful oversight of the government in 1854; and La Escuela Nacional de Ingenieros, which occupies one of the finest buildings in Mexico.

The fine arts are not neglected in Mexico. There are well-equipped art-schools for both boys and girls, with superior teachers, foreign and native. The ancient Academy of San Carlos was founded in 1847, and its galleries contain a fine collection of ancient paintings, costing hundreds of thousands of dollars. Foreign masters are brought here to teach *las bellas artes*. The Conservatorio de Música Nacional was founded in 1867, and occupies a building that served as a university in the reign of Charles III, and for many years afterward. It is conducted on a liberal scale as a conservatory of both music and oratory.

GENERAL PEDRO HINOJOSA,
PRESIDENT OF MILITARY COURT.

The Museo Nacional is under the direct care of Secretary Baranda, and is more particularly described in a chapter on Mexico City. It has cost more than a million dollars, and it is here that the scientific congresses are held. Its magnificent departments of archæology, natural history, etc., have long been the admiration of travellers as well as of the people of Mexico.

Under the administration of the department of Fomento come the branches of boundaries, colonization, agriculture, mines, industrial pursuits, statistics, observatories, institutes, and scientific commissions.

The government has established, by means of colonization companies, some two-score colonies in different parts of the country, the majority of which are in a very flourishing condition. The colonists are given certain concessions, covering definite amounts of land to be cultivated under certain easy conditions.

Under these laws new facilities are constantly offered for the opening of rural estates and the enlarging and strengthening of old ones.

This department, too, has charge of boundary-lines and geographical explorations, the apportioning of lands to the Indians, and the general standard of weights and measures. One of the most important achievements of the present secretary, Iñigo Don Manuel Fernandez Leal, was the re-marking of the boundaries between the republic of Mexico and the United States, which was effected in December, 1896. Almost as important, too, was the work of the boundary commission which defined the lines of separation from Guatemala.

Señor Iñigo Manuel Fernandez Leal came to his work with a long training which fits him admirably for the responsibilities of his position. He is a native of Jalapa, in Vera Cruz, and was born in 1831. While he was still very young his people moved to Puebla for a few years, afterward going to Mexico. In the capital he developed a marked aptitude for engineering pursuits, and took a course at the National College for Engineers. When he was only twenty-three he was appointed commissioner to settle the boundaries between the United States and Mexico, and for two years he was on the border engaged in that work. In 1856, having negotiated the treaty of La Mesilla, he went back to Mexico City, and was soon after placed at the head of the topographical department of the valley of Mexico as governor-in-chief. Two years were passed in this position, and then came the revolution, which sent Juarez to Vera Cruz and obliged Leal to stop work. When Juarez returned, in 1861, he was placed at the head of one of the sub-departments of public works. This did not last long, however, and, during Maximilian's occupancy, he accompanied Juarez throughout his wanderings until the latter's return to Mexico. Then came his appointment by Juarez to the post of first assistant secretary of public works. Since that time he has been almost constantly connected with the department, except during those years when he was heading special commissions for the public benefit. He was a commissioner to confer with the United States in regard to the proposed ship railway across the Isthmus of Tehuantepec. He was sent to Japan in 1874 with the famous Mexican astronomer Señor Don Francisco Diaz Vovarenvias, to make certain astronomical observations, and went round the world before returning to Mexico. Since 1878 he has been minister of public works, a post for which he seems to have had special training, and in which he has distinguished himself over and over again. All the colonization improvements, geographical explorations, irrigation schemes, and similar experiments have been made under him for the last twenty years.

SEÑOR DON MANUEL ROMERO RUBIO.

Owing to his thorough training, long service, and true patriotism, he is regarded by the people of Mexico as exactly the man for his place; and he furnishes one more example of the wisdom of President Diaz in choosing the men to conduct such affairs as he intrusts to his cabinet.

Señor Manuel Romero Rubio, the father of Señora Diaz, was for many years the distinguished secretary of the department of the interior, one of the most important positions in the Mexican cabinet. This eminent statesman and politician was one of the best lawyers in Mexico. His career from the day that he was admitted to the bar until his death, October, 1895, was a series of triumphs, and his eloquence as one of the greatest orators in Mexico gave him great fame. Whether in the exercise of his profession, in the halls of Congress, or in political discussions, Romero Rubio was always at the front. He was one of the framers of the Mexican constitution of to-day, and the author of many important bills which have helped to build up the country and to develop its manifold resources.

Although not now a member of the cabinet, Señor Don Matías de Romero, like General Hinojosa, has been so closely connected with it in times past that it seems especially fitting to speak of him here.

Señor Matías Romero, minister of Mexico at Washington, was born at Oaxaca, the birthplace of so many of the noted men of Mexico. He entered the School of Arts and Sciences in his native town when quite young; there he studied philosophy and law, displaying rare talent in all his studies. He has held many honorable positions in his own country. In 1892 he was in the cabinet of General Diaz as secretary of the treasury. At Washington he is universally respected and admired by the citizens and by the members of the diplomatic corps. Mr. Romero is a prolific writer. His articles in the "North American Review" have called frequent attention to Mexico. As a distinguished statesman he is much respected among the foremost men of the United States. He is beloved by the people of his native land, and considered one of the mighty pillars on which is solidly built the great Mexican republic.

CHAPTER XII

THE LADIES OF THE CABINET

SEÑORA DOÑA CARMEN ROMERO RUBIO DE DIAZ, besides being one of the most beautiful women in Mexico, is the best loved. Added to her natural endowment of beauty, she has a thorough knowledge of various languages. She is twenty-nine years old, and the president is about forty years her senior. She became *la Presidenta* at the age of eighteen, their love and courtship alike being as romantic as her daily life at the castle of Chapultepec.

She has filled this position with the grace and elegance of a queen, her salons being quite famous. She dresses with exquisite taste. Her gowns are made in Mexico, for she feels that as the wife of the president she should have her toilettes made by native workers. She has been seen at balls of magnificent splendor beautiful and radiant in a dainty white gown of silk garnished in point applique; a cord of pearls hung from her waist, and in her lovely black hair a solitary red rose nestled, as if proud to be worn by the first lady of the land. While the Mexican women are all inclined to displays of colors and jewels, "Carmelita," as every one loves to call her, sets a worthy example of good taste and refinement. She is not fond of society, and only a few friends are admitted into the intimacy of the home circle.

SEÑORA DOÑA CARMEN ROMERO RUBIO DE DIAZ,
THE WIFE OF THE PRESIDENT OF MEXICO.

On *fiesta* days Señora Diaz is found standing in the shadow of the massive doors of the cathedral, tossing pennies to the poor, who gather there to receive her gifts. In an hour thousands of *centavitos* are given from her hands to the grateful wretches, who deem it an honor and privilege to kiss the hem of her gown as she stands there, all simplicity, distributing her favors, occasionally recognizing a friend, and bowing and smiling to those who tip their hats in recognition of the president's wife. In fact, Señora Diaz is probably the most popular woman in Mexico, occupying a very warm place in the hearts of the Mexican people. She goes about from street to street and from house to house in the poorest suburbs and districts of the city of Mexico every day, distributing alms and alleviating the sufferings of the poor. For her many charitable acts and her social qualifications, her virtues and amiability, it is safe to say that one of the sources of the popularity of General Diaz comes from his wife.

The president has a charming family. The eldest daughter married, a few years ago, Señor Don Ignacio de la Torre, who belongs to one of the old and distinguished families of Mexico. She is as beautiful as she is gracious, and is a great favorite in society at the Mexican capital on account of her many endearing personal qualities, as well as her accomplishments and position. Captain Porfirio Diaz, the only son, gives great promise of a distinguished military career.

SEÑORA IGNACIO DE LA TORRE,
DAUGHTER OF THE PRESIDENT.

He is at present studying in Europe. One young daughter, Señorita Luz, is a lovely and gentle girl, whom every one loves. She may be seen almost every morning on the Paseo, where she goes for a constitutional on horseback, with her distinguished father as her escort.

There are a number of beautiful American women who have married prominent Mexicans and have settled down into good señoras. This land of romance and enchantment has waved a beckoning hand to these beautiful and distinguished American women, and they have obeyed her summons. The life of the ladies of the public service in any land calls for rare intelligence, unerring tact, and exquisite affability, and these qualities are of special value in the Spanish-American countries, where the blood runs hotly, revolutions are of quick growth, and sudden changes of leaders not infrequent. To all these require-

SEÑORITA LUZ DIAZ,
DAUGHTER OF THE PRESIDENT.

CAPTAIN PORFIRIO DIAZ.

ments the American women who have graced the court circles of Mexico have responded with a record that has proclaimed them born diplomats and queens of society.

Señora Ignacio Mariscal is a rarely enchanting woman. Every feature is perfect, and her countenance is lighted by eyes of softest splendor. She was Miss Laura Smith, of Maryland, U.S.A. Her family at one time resided in Washington, and she was one of the most noted belles of the city. It was while Señor Mariscal was secretary of the Mexican legation that his life's happiness in this beautiful form came to him. Their marriage was a notable social event. Señor Don Ignacio Mariscal has occupied many posts of honor, and in every position Señora Mariscal has shown charming adaptability and unusual force.

Mrs. Limantour and Mrs. Moran, both of whom are members of *la alta sociedad* in the city of Mexico, are daughters of Señora Mariscal, who is a grandmother, but still fresh and beautiful. Her official position gives her the seat of honor at the right hand of the wife of the president.

Señora Manuel Cosio is the distinguished wife of the Secretario de Gobernación. She devotes her time to charities, and her name is connected most prominently with many of the worthy charitable institutions of Mexico. She is a beautiful woman, and an ornament to any society.

Señora José Ives Limantour is the youngest lady in the cabinet, and is a typical Mexican, with large and beautiful dark eyes. Her home in Avenue Juarez is one of the most beautiful in Mexico. She loves society, and entertains a great deal during the season.

Señora Joaquin Baranda has a sweet and sympathetic personality, and is very gracious in manner. She is an accomplished linguist, speaking English perfectly, as well as several other languages. She lives with her children in Campeche.

SEÑORA MARISCAL.

Most Mexican ladies speak more than one language. In addition to their native Spanish, Mexican señoritas are taught English and French. One charming trait about them, too, is

Señora Limantour.   Señora Cosio.

their extreme kindliness of manner. One never hears rough words or unkind sentiments among them, nor even in the Mexican family circle. As a consequence, the people are universally polite, and the women especially have exquisite manners.

CHAPTER XIII

THE JOCKEY CLUB

ONE of the most prominent buildings in the city of Mexico is the handsome club house of the Mexican Jockey Club. It is unique, and there is an air of old Spain all through it, with Moorish architecture and Venetian oddities. It was formerly the palace of the Count del Valle, and the main floor of the curious little chapel which served for family orisons is now used for games of *tresillo*. One feature about this building that impresses itself alike upon the tourist and upon the older inhabitants is its massiveness of outline.

The façade of the Jockey Club building is entirely encrusted with porcelain tiles of blue and white, which have been so firmly fastened into the walls that even the fingers of old Time have failed to dislodge them. The entrance is massive and elegant, and the varnished cedar doors with copper ornaments, with interior sweep of open courts, are suggestive of some palace old and deserted. Superb cylindrical columns sustain the first floor. The first impression on entering is that one has wandered into a deserted Andalusian palace.

To the left is the Jockey Club library, and at its door-way stand two bronze warriors, whose lances are tipped with light. Gilded lamps with snowy crystal globes, afire with the witchery of electricity, turn their light upon the tables and book-shelves, devoted to the literature of the club. This includes every legitimate sporting paper of note published in the world, also novels and books devoted to horse-racing, horse culture, and like topics. There are tables, willow chairs, and an exquisite cabinet of rosewood, carved in relief.

There is in the open court-way a relic of the old days of Count del Valle and millionaire Martinez de la Torre; it is a fountain, curious and delicate, a chef-d'œuvre of sculpture from the magic chisel of the sixteenth century, and looks like a bit of the Alhambra in Mexico.

GENERAL PEDRO RINCON GALLARDO,
PRESIDENT OF THE JOCKEY CLUB.

In the two patios are rare flowers, hortensias, camellias, azaleas, gardenias, and roses, with palms and precious plants.

The grand stairway and its surroundings are practically unchanged from the olden times. A large lamp with alabaster globes is at the turn of the landing; it was under its shadow that the Count del Valle met his death at the hands of an assassin. Venetian mirrors hang high up on the vestibule walls, and octagonal windows with curiously designed panes of stained glass are set deep into the granite walls. The ceiling over the stairway is of cedar and porcelain tiles in alternate rows.

On the main floor the corridor is tiled in white and blue, and around it sweeps a splendid railing made of the old-time "tumbago," a bronze composite brought from China in Spanish galleons. This composite was considered worth its weight in silver, and is of the same material as the railings in the cathedral. The balconies of the Jockey Club facing San Francisco Street

PATIO OF THE JOCKEY CLUB.

and Callejon Condesa are of this material. On this corridor and on the landing of the grand staircase, surrounded by porcelain lights, is the coat of arms of the Count del Valle, with his motto.

"Fuerza agena ni le toca ni le prende
Solo su virtud le ofende."

The surroundings of the grand staircase are unique, and the finest in Mexico. The porcelain tiles cost at the time of their use more than silver, for the reason that silver was superabundant. Among these unique relics are the quaintly carved cedar door-way and the sculptured arch of the old oratorio or chapel of the Count del Valle, which is on the main floor adjoining the reception-room; this chapel once held the sacred relics and paintings of the noble family and served as a place of retreat and prayer.

The Jockey Club was started in the year 1881. General Pedro Rincon Gallardo and

CORRIDOR OF THE JOCKEY CLUB.

Francisco Somera were the initiators. The club was established under the auspices of the municipal council of the city of Mexico on the 8th of June, 1881. At that meeting Francisco Somera was elected president of the club. Later, the Honorable Manuel Romero Rubio, secretary of the interior, was elected president of the club, and remained in that capacity until his death in October, 1895, when he was succeeded by General Pedro Rincon Gallardo, then governor of the federal district.[a]

There are two seasons for the races, spring and fall respectively, beginning generally on Easter Sunday and on the first Sunday in October. The club pays stakes and purses each

SALA IN THE JOCKEY CLUB.

year. The city council also has a standing prize (premio de ayuntamiento), and the Department of Encouragement of the federal government puts up two annual prizes. Horses can be entered from the stud-books of England and the United States, the Bruce stud-book being a much-consulted authority of the club.

On these occasions all the wealth and beauty of Mexico are out in full force. All the "four hundred," in their best finery (and nowhere in the world can be found more beautifully dressed women), are there; in short, the Jockey Club races form the grand gala-days of the year.

[a] To the secretary, Señor Manuel Nicholin y Echanova, I am indebted for many handsome photographs and interesting data.

CHAPTER XIV

LA VIGA AND THE SUBURBS

LA VIGA and the floating gardens or markets form another diverting and intensely interesting phase of life in this unique and poetic land. They are easily reached by car from the Plaza. The canal makes a circle of over eight miles, and presents a scene of unequalled activity and unusual features. One need not look for gardens, as the name suggests, but rather for an aquatic market-place. The gardens are made up of countless boats in motion, filled with every imaginable growth of farm, orchard, and vineyard, with garden flowers, fruits, chickens, birds, and all other living and growing things that can be sold. As soon as you leave the car the crowd surges around you, imploring you to hire their boats.

At first they are high in their ideas of the return desired, but they are apt to reduce their prices to less than one-third if the new-comer exhibits the proper amount of patience and reserve. These boats are low, long, and flat on the bottom, with an awning overhead, and gayly decked with flags and streamers. The boatmen use only one long oar, with which they pole or scull the craft along. In no other way can one gain so accurate an idea of the varied population of Mexico; in no other way can so many charming effects in costume and personal ornamentation be studied; and certainly nowhere else can such a marvellous array of products of this most marvellous of all countries be seen.

One might almost go blindfold through Mexico, uncovering his eyes for two or three hours only at La Viga, and be able to give a fair account of the almost incredible resources that are the heritage of this nation.

Santa Anita is a peculiar little spot, Mexican in every detail, and a favorite pleasure-resort for the people of Mexico City. Hither come in shoals the lower and middle classes on Sundays and feast-days. It is a town of reed-thatched houses, and everywhere there is a tempting odor of Mexican culinary dainties. Excellent specimens of Mexican dishes may be had here, which are wonderfully toothsome even if they are served in rude fashion.

Pulque may be had in various wonderful and insidious styles in which the original flavor is merged in something far more agreeable. There are swings and lively games with typical Mexican music, and flower-stands where the merry people buy garlands of bright-hued poppies. Surrounding the town are the chinampas, the so-called floating gardens. Perhaps they did float once, but they are now simply gardens separated by narrow canals. Here are grown vegetables for the city market and flowers for the Sundays and saints' days at home.

The church of Santa Anita is a quaint old building, with a fine tower, and a little plaza in front, where all the world and its wife take pleasure at holiday times.

At Ixtacalco are more chinampas, with less gayety, a little market, and a very handsome church. A fine old stone bridge crosses the canal at this point, with a ruinous old chapel at the water's edge, where in the old days the passing boatman muttered an *ave* and deposited an offering to the patron saint, in the hope that good luck would follow him on his voyage and that his vegetables would sell for a few more *tlacos* than usual. In front of the church, which is dedicated to San Matias and which has a Franciscan foundation more than three hundred years old, is the customary little plaza with a fountain of running water.

Beyond Ixtacalco the surrounding scenery changes and the country is less populous, although possessing a peculiarly pastoral charm.

Mexicalcingo is about seven miles from the city. Although it now has only about three hundred inhabitants, it was a place of importance before the conquest. A small monastery founded by the Franciscans at a very early period is in a ruinous condition, but the church of San Marco is in tolerably good repair. The road to Ixtapalapan crosses the canal at this point, and a very picturesque view is the high old bridge, with bright green maize-fields on one side and the grim old ecclesiastical buildings on the other, embowered in masses of dark foliage from great trees growing to the water's edge. This is a good place to tie up and have breakfast (provision for which must be carried along) in a leisurely fashion, preparatory to starting on the return trip.

THE VIGA CANAL.

Culhuacan is the last hamlet on the Viga. It is a picturesque old town, lying partly on a hill-side, with a fine church and monastery in ruins. Here the Viga begins to broaden into the lake.

San Angel, Coyohuacan, San Augustin, and Miscauque are extremely pretty villages in the vicinity of the lake. San Angel is surrounded by fields of maguey, its scattered houses, its market-place, and its monastery and church of El Carmen making up a characteristic and pretty Mexican village; its narrow lanes and high-walled gardens, its Indian huts and profusion of pink roses, its clusters of trees, its little bridge and avenue, forming a picturesque whole. Here are the Indian with his blanket, the ranchero with rebozo and broad-brimmed hat, the old leporo in rags basking on the sunny seat by a door-way, the portly padre sauntering up the lane, with all the little boys smiling and taking off their hats to him, and all brightened and made light and gay by the purest atmosphere and bluest sky and softest breeze that ever blew or shone or sparkled above a workaday world; and there is always a fine view of Mexico, with her cathedral towers, the volcanoes, the lofty mountains, the surrounding landscape.

Coyohuacan is almost a continuation of San Angel, but there are more trees in it, and every house has its garden or its inner court filled with orange-trees. Both villages serve as a popular summer resort for the rich dwellers in the city of Mexico. It was at Coyohuacan that Cortez took up his residence for several months after the total destruction of the ancient Tenochtitlan. Here he founded a convent, too; and in his last will and testament he expressed a desire to be buried in this convent, in whatever part of the world he might finish his days,—a wish that was not complied with.

At the time of the conquest Coyohuacan, with Tacubaya, Tacuba, etc., stood on the margin of Lake Tezcuco; most of the houses were built upon stakes, as they had to be entered by means of canoes. But now, like Tezcuco, they are back two or three miles from the lake.

It is thought that Coyohuacan was always Cortez's favorite village, and it is even now one of the prettiest in Mexico, having one of the handsomest village churches in that country.

San Augustin is another of the fascinating villages of the territory of Mexico, and one where life seems to be almost one continual gala-day, so numerous are the festivals throughout the year.

In short, it is difficult to enumerate the charms of this wonderful valley. A delightful way to reach it, if one has time enough in these modern, hurrying days, is to approach by the carriage-way from the Tlaxcala side. The road enters the basin of the lake some sixteen or eighteen miles from Mexico. On the right hand is the salt lake of Tezcuco, on the left the fresh-water lake of Chalco.

INDIAN WAY OF CARRYING CHILDREN

The city does not stand in the centre of the valley, but near the northeastern part of it, not more than three miles from the mountains, in the direction of Guadalupe. Cortez gives to the valley a circumference of two hundred miles, meaning, no doubt, at the crest of the mountains. Clavigero, a much later—and, on this subject, more reliable—authority, fixes it at one hundred and twenty miles at the lowest point of elevation. The latitude is 19°26′ N. and the longitude 99°5′ W., and its elevation above the level of the sea is seven thousand four hundred and seventy feet. The appearance of the valley is that of an oval basin surrounded on all sides by mountains of every degree of elevation and every variety of appearance, from the Pinolis (little rugged promontories) to Popocate-petl, the highest mountain in Mexico, and the highest upon this continent, and covered with perpetual snow, ten thousand four hundred feet higher than the city itself. No description can convey to the reader any adequate idea of the effect upon one who for the first time beholds that magnificent prospect. With what feelings must Cortez have regarded it when he first saw it from the top of the mountain between the snow-covered volcanoes of Popocatepetl and Ixtaccihuatl, a short distance to the left of where the road now runs! The valley was studded all over with the homes of men, containing more than forty cities, besides towns and villages without number. Never has such a vision burst upon the eyes of mortal man since that upon which the seer of old looked down from Pisgah.

Near Mexico City, embowered in the stately cedars and cypress groves of Tacubaya, is the National Astronomical and Meteorological Observatory of Mexico. It is located on Observatory Hill, and the site was formerly occupied by the palace of the Archbishop of Mexico, and at one time by the Military Academy. Tacubaya is the most fashionable suburb of Mexico City, containing the summer residences of many of the prominent people of the capital, and being a most beautiful place.

The observatory stands on the highest point within the limits of Tacubaya. The view from the roof of the new observatory is remarkable, taking in as it does the salient features of the historic valley of Mexico.

In the not far-distant future the Penon baths will be one of the great attractions of Mexico. For some reason Mexicans generally have never bestowed much attention on mineral waters. Their character is brought out in bold relief by the history of the Penon spring or baths, the existence of which seems to have attracted some attention more than a century ago, as in 1792 Mr. Gabriel D. Ocampo, doctor of medicine of the Royal Pontifical University, expressed himself as follows:

"The large quantity of mephitic gases by which, as experience proves, candles are extinguished and small birds suffocated or otherwise killed is, in my opinion, the active cause which restores as if by magic the lost activity of paralyzed or semi-paralyzed limbs. This is the gas which restores the necessary equilibrium in the circulation of the liquids and the muscular action of the solid parts of the body, and not only of those parts generally, but of the small fibres of which they are composed; causing thereby if not a total extirpation of gout and rheumatism, a notable and beneficial relief of the same, a restoration of appetite, of the digestive powers, and the vital force."

These boiling springs are said to contain sulphate of lime, carbonic acid, and muriate of soda, and the Indians make salt in their neighborhood much as they did in the time of Montezuma, with the difference, as Humboldt informs us, that they use copper caldrons, while their ancestors used vessels of clay. The solitary-looking baths are ornamented with odd-looking heads of cats and monkeys, which grin upon you with a mixture of the sinister and facetious that is rather appalling.

On one of the sites where these mineral springs are to be found still stands a little church or chapel which dates back to the beginning of the colonial period, and suggests that, like the Pocito de Guadalupe, the Penon waters may have been used, with prayer and supplication, for effecting miraculous cures. But the baths have been in a state of almost total disuse as far back as those now living can remember, having been destitute of every accommodation until the present beautiful and commodious buildings were erected a few years since by Mr. Manuel Romero Rubio, who has transformed not only the old-time baths but also the surrounding country, over which flowed the waters of Lake Tezcuco. These waters still neutralize to a certain extent the herculean efforts that are being made to convert what was a short time ago only a swamp into a beautiful park or garden, for, as the waters are saline, the atmosphere is destructive to a greater or lesser extent of vegetation. Wonders have been accomplished, however, and Penon is already one of the prettiest and most interesting as well as most health-giving spots in or near the city of Mexico.

Among other attractions to be found at Penon is the manufacture of flooring-tiles, as beautiful in design and finish as those used by the Moors in the historic halls of Spain. There are patterns of every description and color. Then there are roofing-tiles, thin as slate but hard as iron, plain and glazed; there are also street-paving blocks and artificial stone, blocked for finishing work without further need of sculptor's or mason's chisel. There is a lime-kiln with four furnaces; there is a factory for making Portland cement; there are salt-pans for the manufacture of salt and sal soda by the process of evaporation. The hill of Penon is encircled by a railroad track, on which tramway cars as well as freight cars run, and the hill is a quarry from which enormous supplies of stone are daily shipped.

CHAPTER XV

THE STATE OF MEXICO

IN considering the state of Mexico we must remember that it is not mere acreage or population, public institutions or temples or monuments of any kind, however imposing, however venerable, however historic, however beautiful, that constitute a state.

It has been the men of thought and action who have brought Mexico from under the yoke of the Spaniard (who in three hundred years wrung so many million dollars in treasure from her suffering people) and made of the down-trodden province a free and independent country among the nations of the globe.

There are many delightful spots and interesting places in the state of Mexico. Here are found lofty peaks and deep barrancas, broad meadows and narrow vales, inaccessible heights and cultivated fields, succeeding one another in delightful variety. Porphyry, basalt, and lava are common, and "firm as the everlasting hills" could find nowhere a more fitting application.

Molino de Flores is a charming country-place belonging to the family of Cervantez which lies off the line of the railway, about three miles west of Tezcuco. Its chief beauty is a rocky ravine, plentifully shaded, in which, beside a rustic chapel, is a waterfall. The gardens watered by the stream are laid out with

SEÑOR GOBERNADOR-GENERAL JOSÉ VICENTE VILLADA.

much taste and filled with flowers. In their midst stands the large and handsome residence, and a short distance below the waterfall is the mill. At times when the residence is not occupied strangers are admitted to the grounds by the steward.

The beauty of the scenery is indescribable. The path winds ascending through a wilderness of trees and flowering shrubs, bathed by a clear and rapid rivulet; every now and then, through the arched forest-trees, we catch glimpses of the snowy volcanoes and of the distant domes and lakes of Mexico.

The ruins of the old Carmelite convent, standing on the slope of a hill, are surrounded by noble forests of pine and oak and cedar,—long and lofty forest-aisles, where the monks of former days wandered in peaceful meditation. But they removed from this beautiful site to another equally beautiful and wilder, also called the Desierto, but much farther from Mexico; so this fertile region belongs to no one, and lies here deserted in solitary beauty. Some poor Indians live among the ruins of the old cloisters, and the wild deer possess the undisputed sovereignty of the woods. It is said that a benighted traveller who had lost his way in these solitudes, and was miraculously saved from dying of cold, founded this rich convent of Carmelite monks in gratitude to Heaven for his deliverance, expressing his desire that all travellers who passed that way should receive hospitality from the convent. Certainly no place more fitted for devotion could have been selected than this mountain retreat; and when the convent bell tolled at evening, calling the monks to prayer, and awakening the echoes of the silent hills, its deep notes must have been all in unison with the solemn scene.

An old chronicler, Thomas Gage, an English monk of the Dominican order, who was smuggled into Mexico about the middle of the seventeenth century, thus describes, in his "New Survey of the West Indies," Desierto in its palmy days:

"Northwestward three leagues from Mexico is the pleasantest place of all that are about Mexico, called La Soledad, or by others *el desierto*, the solitary or desert place, and wildernesse; were all wildernesses like it, to live in a wildernesse would be better than to live in a city. This has been a device of poor Fryers named discalced or barefooted Carmelites, who to make show of their hypocritical and apparent godliness, and that whilst they would be thought to live like Eremites, retired from the world, they may draw the world unto them, they have built there a stately cloister, which being upon a hill and among rocks, makes it the more admired. About the cloister they have fashioned out many holes and caves in, under, and among the rocks like Eremite lodgings, with a room to lie in, and an oratory to pray in, with pictures, and images, and rare devices for mortification, as disciplines of wyar, rods of iron, hair-cloth girdles with sharp wyar points to girdle about their bare flesh and many such like toys, which hang about their oratories, to make people admire their mortification and holy lives. All these Eremetical holes and caves (which are some ten in all) are within the bounds and compass of the cloister and among orchards and gardens full of fruits and flowers, which may take up two miles of compasse, and here among the rocks and springs of water, with the shade of the plantains and other trees, are most cool and pleasant to the Eremites: they have also the sweet smell of the roze and jazmin, which is a little flower but the sweetest of all others; there is not any other flower to be found that is rare and exquisite in that country which is not in that wildernesse to delight the senses of these mortified Eremites. All this lovely place is really a solitary place, a wildernesse now, but even in its ruin it is one of the most beautiful spots to be found near the city, while the remains of the cloister and the 'Eremetical holes and caves' make it one of the most curious and interesting."

The way to Lerma is through a massive stone gateway, from which the gates were removed very long ago. The streets are broad but straggling, the houses comfortable rather than grand or even elegant, and the many eucalyptus-trees planted around the picturesque adobe and stone church go back probably to the time of Maximilian. Across the way from the church is the old graveyard which all tourists in Mexico soon hear about. There are indisputable records in the convent in the city of Mexico to prove its age. The graves of the Spanish *conquistadores* are nine in number, and were marked with limestone slabs over two centuries ago. It is a custom among the Mexicans, who sell pebbles and cobble-stones from these graves to tourists, to throw on a fresh handful on the occasion of each visit hither. As a result, each grave is surmounted by a heap of small white stones a yard high.

Tetzcotzinco, about three miles east of Tezcuco, is the laughing hill (*risueña colina*) of Tetzcotzinco. Here is an enduring monument to the engineering skill and good taste of Netzahualcoyotl, in the shape of the wonderful pleasaunce that he caused to be built for his amusement and recreation. The remains of terraced walks and stairways wind around the hill from the base to the summit; seats are hollowed in shady nooks among the rocks, and every-

VILLAGE OF TLAPACOZO.

where traces are found of ingenious contrivances by which the natural beauty and cool comfort of the situation are enhanced. The most important and most curious of these remains, at an elevation of eighty or one hundred feet, is that to which has been given the purely fanciful title of "Montezuma's bath,"—a circular reservoir about five feet in diameter and three feet deep, whence water was distributed through many channels to the hanging gardens below. In order to supply the little reservoir stupendous works were executed. Near the laughing hill, distant one-half or three-quarters of a mile, is another small hill, and beyond this, twelve or fifteen miles, is the mountain-chain that encircles the valley.

From the side of the reservoir, the side of the hill in which it is hollowed is cut down and levelled, as though graded for a railroad, for about half a mile; thence the grade is carried across a ravine to the adjacent hill on an embankment fully sixty feet high; thence the side of the second hill is graded for a distance of a mile and a half, and thence the grade is carried on an embankment across the plain to the distant mountains. Along the top of the level thus formed was built an aqueduct, much of which still remains in excellent preservation and testifies to the skill of its builders. It is formed of very hard plaster, made of lime and small portions of soft red stone, is about two feet wide, and has a conduit about ten inches in diameter,—a concave trough covered by convex sections of plaster, forming a tube. A part of this pleasuring place, though some distance from it, is the Bosque del Contador, a magnificent grove of *ahuehuetes*, enclosing a great quadrangle that probably in ancient times was a lake.

The great causeway to Ixtapalapan was that by which Cortez twice entered the city across the waters of Tezcuco, the first time hailed with demonstrations of welcome by myriads of Aztecs, the second, the occasion of Tenochtitlan's final conquest, greeted by the fiercest and most desperate resistance.

Here were the famous gardens of Cuitlahua, Montezuma's brother, where he feasted the visiting Spaniards. Here, also, was the home of Guatemozin, the last great Aztec emperor. Now gardens and palaces have disappeared, and only a dusty, scantily populated village remains.

High in mid-air, as it were, the climate of the state of Mexico, while it has a pleasant variety, leaves nothing to be desired by those to whom pure air without keen cutting winds, bright sun that does not scorch, and abundance of pure and running water melted from the eternal glistening snows are indispensable. The climate, be it said in a word, is such as to bring contentment and peace the year around, without undue lassitude at any time.

And yet this is the country of the sweetest, happiest *dolce far niente* on the globe. Here man can be rich without being fatigued, and be happy without being either.

The value of rural property here is estimated at nineteen million seven hundred and seventy-six thousand and thirty-two dollars, and that of city possessions at five million three hundred and seven thousand seven hundred and seventy-one dollars; it is therefore evident that the people here are sufficiently well-to-do, as a whole, to satisfy the average demand. Yet those who bring here the feverish thirst for riches may find in her fertile plains and in the rocky veins of her grand and silent mountains "riches beyond the dreams of avarice," with surroundings permitting the mere money-grabber to live happily among the sources of his wealth.

The variety of climate permits the production of all classes of crops. There are abundant harvests of wheat, Indian corn, and other cereals in the valleys of Toluca, Iztlahuaca, Tenango, and Tezcuco, and of sugar cane, coffee, and other tropical products in the districts of Temascaltepec, Tenancingo, and others. The forest products are remarkable not only for their diversity but for their richness.

The raising of cattle is one of the principal resources of this state, and is increasing rapidly each year, the annual product already reaching eight hundred and fifty thousand head.

But pastoral life is giving way to more modern methods of existence and livelihood-winning. The iron horse is shrieking his way along over these vast plains and around and among these lofty mountains.

Toluca, the capital of the state, is united, since 1882, to the capital of the republic by the Mexican National Railway, which traverses a most picturesque country all the way to San Luis Potosi. All the railways which centre in the metropolis cross this state, giving it ready exportation for all its products.

The Mexican Central runs north and south through the state, from the borders of the

Federal District, through Lecheria, Cuautitlan, Teoloyucan, Huehuetoca, and Nochistongo; at Tula, just over the line in the state of Hidalgo, having a branch to Pachuca. This splendid railway gives direct and rapid communication, through Juarez and El Paso, with New York by the Santa Fé route to Chicago, thence over the picturesque Pennsylvania system, while branches from the main line give outlet on the Gulf of Tampico and on the Pacific at San Blas.

The National Mexican road, or Laredo route, also gives free communication northward with the rest of the world. What will make the railways pay best are, perhaps, the mineral treasures that abound on every hand.

The mining industry is as yet little developed, although it is certain that with proper developing facilities it will be a most important factor in the state's material progress. In the mines of Temascaltepec and Zacualpam, as in those of Oro, the profits are large, gold, silver, lead, iron, and copper being obtained in large quantities. The supply of sulphur from the great snow-capped mountain, the volcano Popocatepetl, is enormous. There is in this district coal of excellent quality, and zinc is found in the form of blendes accompanied by silver ore. There is, however, greatly increased activity in mining in this state. The Quebradillas mines, in Temascaltepec, are limiting the amount of their dividends in order that they may continue indefinitely. The Tejupilco district is being steadily developed, and in the Sultepec district the Hidalgo Company is running a custom smelter, for which there is plenty of ore obtainable in the neighborhood.

The good citizens of Mexico are by no means ignorant. If any of them were, it would be their individual fault, for there are in the state one thousand and twenty-four public and seventy-nine private schools, in which are taught fifty-six thousand five hundred and fifty-two pupils, or more than fifty per cent. of those of proper age. There are eight hundred and forty-five boys' schools, with forty-one thousand nine hundred and fifty-eight pupils, and one hundred and seventy-six for girls, with eleven thousand four hundred and eighty-nine pupils. The amount expended on public institutions by the state of Mexico is two hundred and eleven thousand one hundred and four dollars per year.

In Toluca there is a splendid Girls' Normal School of Arts and Trades, established by Governor Villada. These schools are largely for the purpose of elevating the ignorant and inferior classes. In those for both sexes in Toluca are many of the Mazahuatl, Otomi, and Aztec indigenes, whose ambition is to return to their villages as primary teachers. The spread of the Spanish language, thus accomplished, will do much toward the unification of the republic and the inculcation of patriotic ideas.

The venerable Literary Institute of Toluca was reorganized in 1886 as the Scientific and Literary Institute of the State of Mexico.

Public charities are also well organized. There are an asylum for boys and one for girls, a general hospital in the city, and a local hospital in each of the cities of Sultepec, Jilotepec, Tlalnepantla, Tezcuco, and Valle de Bravo.

The capital of the state of Mexico has a penitentiary, with spacious quarters, where machinery is run by steam-power, and the establishment is lighted by electricity. The object of this institution is the reformation of the criminal and the abolition of the death penalty. Humanitarian ideas of the most advanced character are evident at all stages of one's progress through this model institution. Education is compulsory, each prisoner being given sufficient instruction to enable him to earn his own living honestly by handicraft when he is liberated.

There is a woollen-mill at Toluca which produces handsome cloths. In this country manufactures have made such rapid strides, and have become so important, that it will not be long before it can be called a manufacturing centre.

A trip over the westward division of the Mexican National Railway is full of pleasure. The swift ride up the Madre Mountains, playing hide-and-seek with the volcanoes on the way along as the train enters the cañon on the mountain's crest, and the passing under the aqueduct hundreds of feet above the village of Ocoyoac, are exciting and interesting in the extreme. Leaving the city of Mexico from the Colonia station, the train passes under an old aqueduct,— this is a country of aqueducts,—Chapultepec is seen to the left, the bell of Noche Triste and the churches of San Estebán and Los Remedios to the right; then through the valley and the Hondo, and over the hill to the Lerma and the valley of Toluca, there are fine views.

GARDEN AND PALACE IN TOLUCA.

The soft-named and beautiful capital of this interesting state nestles at the foot of snow-crowned mountains, one of them the extinct volcano from which it is named, whose white top looks silently down with the calm of centuries upon the city with its hum and movement and restless progress, as the still ages might look down upon the onrushing to-day. Her wide and well-paved streets, her spacious plazas and shady squares, her imposing buildings, some gray with centuries, some new with the spirit of the nineteenth century, combined with the delightful situation and the grandeur of the surrounding scenery, succeed in making this city of the upper air one of surpassing interest and beauty. Its modern institutions devoted to education, progress, and humanity deserve special mention in this brief record.

Toluca lies in the centre of the fertile plains west of the Sierra Madre. It is one of the cleanest cities in the country. Its parks and plazas are beautiful. From the summit of the volcano named one may look at once on the waters both of the Gulf of Mexico and of the Pacific Ocean.

In this, as in every other Mexican town, there is a plaza, which is a place of recreation for the people. Usually the cathedral and the government buildings are found on this public square.

The beautiful Alameda, the rendezvous for the *élite* of the city on fête-days and Sundays, is one of the most perfect parks in the republic. It is the result of the strenuous efforts of Governor Villada, a man wedded to his work in making the state of Mexico famous for its advancement and improvement. In this gorgeous display of verdure, drives, and lakelets he has succeeded in adding another feature to the already acknowledged beauty of Toluca. Entering this lovely park by wide arched gateways, we are confronted by a masterpiece of art and industry. Swans gracefully curve their long necks to greet the visitor; deer, already tamed by the young children, come forward sniffing a glad welcome; and if it is the good fortune to visit this plaza on a *fiesta* day, there are lovely señoritas, clad in delicate gowns, gay parasols, colors,—everything pertaining to gladness and beauty. There we have an opportunity of studying a phase of life among the young folks in this vast country of relics.

A lovely girl passes, gayly decked in her own becoming color, her dark beauty enhanced by the blossom of youth. She is accompanied by some friend or chaperon, perhaps her mother, and behind her follows her *novio*, or sweetheart. It is in these parks and under the balcony of the young woman in question that all the love-making is done. Not a word alone are they permitted to utter, and the language of their eyes has brought their hearts to communion long ago. They are happy, for they know no other method of love-making. One could scarce imagine a girl in the United States subjecting herself to this custom, but she who has long since tired of the soulless flirtation is first to appreciate the utter sincerity in the rapid exchanged glances. The women of this country are gentle, womanly, beautiful, devoted to their husbands; tender, loving mothers, gracious, and gifted.

When Cortez and his hosts came to Mexico in 1519, the conqueror found the people in Toluca the most prosperous of the subjects of Montezuma. The Spanish had a revenue of five millions of dollars in one year from the deposits of precious stones alone in Toluca, and big baskets of emeralds, sapphires, and garnets were taken from the mountain-sides of Toluca for sale in Europe. Cortez began the erection of a home near Toluca for the comfort of his old and wounded soldiers. To this day may be seen the stone foundations laid for that structure, which went no further because of the sudden change in the fortunes of the conqueror. Comparatively few tourists in the old republic visit Toluca.

In going there from Mexico City the way leads down the beautiful Paseo de la Reforma, which united Mexico with Chapultepec, and takes one through Tacubaya and over a great mountain wall. Up above the last pueblo the climbing gets pretty steep, especially after leaving the pine belt. The fir-trees in this region resemble the hemlock-spruce, but have a different arrangement of the needles. Polypodium ferns grow in tufts on every hand, and cardinal flowers, but very long and straggling and by no means so beautiful as the same plant elsewhere. Scarlet tanagers and blue tanagers fly about everywhere. There are also sparrow-hawks even more beautiful in plumage than the tanagers, and doves unusually brilliant in color, not to mention hundreds of parrots of every hue and variety. On the crest of the mountains that divide the country of the Tolucans from the city of Mexico the character of the vegetation suddenly and marvellously changes. Here in the same altitude, but facing a warmer sun and milder winds, are forests of tropical chestnuts. Mahogany and tangerine-orange-trees are seen, and the ground is green with the grazing plant known as *alfilerea*. About half-way down the mountain-range is a wide plateau, and about half a mile from it is the historic glen of Las Cruces,—the Bunker Hill of Mexico. The spot is marked by an obelisk, some thirty feet high, of limestone set upon a heavy foundation of concrete. This is the scene of the first real victory of the Mexicans over the Spaniards in the war of 1810. It was in the glen of Las Cruces that Hidalgo, with the mountaineers of the place, drove back the royalist troops with heavy loss. The engagement gave the Mexicans self-confidence, proving to them that under favorable conditions they might defeat the well-trained and completely armed soldiers of the Spanish viceroys.

Half a mile to the north, on the same plateau, is the old pueblo of Las Cruces. The population of the town is about twelve hundred, and its livelihood is derived entirely from the sale of the beautifully polished woods of the mountain forests and all manner of gewgaws, toys, and silver filigree work, which have a large sale among tourists who visit the city of Mexico. Leaving Las Cruces, the soil becomes well watered and very fertile. One sees hundreds of farmers at work in their fields of alfalfa, barley, onions, and maguey, and in orchards of olives, prunes, and almonds, that cover hundreds of acres.

The peak of Toluca was made famous by the historian Prescott. It is more than sixteen thousand feet high, but not snow-covered. The peak of Toluca has probably an extensive snow-field on its summit, but this is hidden by irregular ridges, which compare ill with the symmetrical cone of Popocatepetl or the battlemented crest of the White Lady (Ixtaccihuatl). The wind blows snow in fine jets from the hidden snow-field, and this makes the mountain appear to be smoking. The folk-lore of the Aztecs in the days of Montezuma was redolent with legends about the smoking Toluca and its supernatural power.

On the plains of Toluca one sees the river Lerma like a ribbon of silver. This is one of the great rivers of Mexico. It flows northwest to Lake Chapala, the largest lake in the republic. From this it runs north, and under the name of Rio Grande de Santiago rolls a navigable stream to the Pacific Ocean, which it enters near San Blas. The city of Lerma is on the rocky eminence, and the bell-tower and dome of its famous church are very conspicuous. The whole plain rises gently from the marsh land at the foot of the hills and sweeps up to the base of the great mountain-range of which the peak of Toluca is the culmination. Far as the eye can reach the soil is cultivated and gives evidence of lavish care. The variegated coloring of the fields, planted in different varieties of grains, gives it the appearance of a mammoth checkerboard. Everywhere are big villages or imposing haciendas. One of these, perched upon the last slope of the hill-side, might have been taken bodily from one of the Italian cantons of Switzerland.

At the outskirts of Toluca are two elaborate shrines, where one may often see a group of farmers and laborers who have stopped on their way home to offer prayer. Near by is a queer old stone one-arched bridge over a little stream. It is a very crude, massive affair, unlike anything in the United States. Not a half-mile away is an American steel bridge, and the contrast between them is striking. One is inadequate, expensive, unscientific, and yet picturesque; the other is plain, cheap, perfectly sufficient, but utilitarian. These two bridges represent early Mexico contrasted with to-day under the enlightened rule of President Porfirio Diaz.

The little village of Otumba, about twenty-five miles from Mexico, was the scene of one of Cortez's greatest battles. From these plains, stretching far away to the territory of Tlaxcala, can be seen the venerable pyramids of Teotihuacan, which, next to the pyramid of Cholula, are the most remarkable remnants of ancient American civilization in North America. They were found by the Aztecs, according to their traditions, on their entrance into the country, when Teotihuacan, the habitation of the gods, now a paltry village, was a flourishing city, the rival of Tula, the great Toltec capital. The two principal pyramids were dedicated to Tonatiuh, the sun, and Mextli, the moon. The former, which is considerably the larger, has been found by recent measurements to be six hundred and eighty-two feet long at the base and one hundred and eighty feet high, dimensions not inferior to those of some of the kindred monuments of Egypt. They were divided into four stories, of which three are now discernible. The interior is composed of clay mixed with pebbles, encrusted on the surface with the light, porous stone tetzontli, so abundant in the neighboring quarries. Over this was a thick coating of stucco, resembling in its reddish color that found in the ruins of Palenque. According to tradition, the pyramids are hollow, but hitherto the attempt to discover the cavity in that dedicated to the sun has been unsuccessful. In the smaller mound an aperture has been found on the southern side at two-thirds of the elevation. It is formed by a narrow gallery, which, after penetrating to the distance of several yards, terminates in two pits or wells. The largest of these is about fifteen feet deep, and the sides are faced with unbaked bricks ; but to what purpose it was devoted nothing is left to show. It may have been to hold the ashes of some powerful chief, like the solitary apartment discovered in the great Egyptian pyramid. That these monuments were dedicated

CUMBRE DE LAS CRUCES,
THE PLACE WHERE A GREAT BATTLE WAS FOUGHT.

to religious uses there is no doubt, and it would be only conformable to the practice of antiquity in the Eastern continent that they should have served for tombs as well as temples. Prescott, who gives the best description of them, says, '' Distinct traces of the latter destination are said to be visible on the summit of the smaller pyramid, consisting of the remains of stone walls showing a building of considerable size and strength. There are no remains on the top of the pyramid of the Sun, but the traveller who will take the trouble to ascend its bald summit will be amply compensated by the glorious view it will open to him : toward the southeast the hills of Tlaxcala, surrounded by their green plantations and cultivated cornfields, in the midst of which stands the little village, once the proud capital of the republic ; somewhat farther to the south the eye passes across the beautiful plains lying around the city of Puebla de los Angeles, founded by the old Spaniards, and still rivalling, in the splendor of its churches, the most brilliant capitals of Europe ; and far in the west he may behold the valley of Mexico spread out like a map, with its diminished lakes, its princely capital rising in still greater glory from its ruins, and its rugged hills gathering darkly around it as in the days of Montezuma.''

The summit of this larger mound is said to have been crowned by a temple in which was a colossal statue of its presiding deity, the Sun, made of one entire block of stone, and facing the east. Its breast was protected by a plate of burnished gold and silver, on which the first rays of the rising luminary rested. An antiquary in the early part of the last century speaks of having seen some fragments of the statue. It was still standing, according to report, on the invasion of the Spaniards, and was demolished by the indefatigable Bishop Zumarraga, whose hand fell more heavily than that of Time itself on the Aztec monuments.

Around the principal pyramids are a great number of smaller ones, rarely exceeding thirty feet in height, which, according to tradition, were dedicated to the stars, and served as sepulchres for the great men of the nation. They are ranged symmetrically in avenues terminating at the sides of the great pyramids, which face the cardinal points. The plain on which they stand was called Micoatl, or "Path of the Dead." The laborer, as he turns up the ground, still finds there numerous arrow-heads and blades of obsidian, attesting the warlike character of its primitive population.

"What thoughts must crowd on the mind of the traveller as he wanders amidst these memorials of the past," says Prescott; "as he treads over the ashes of the generations who reared these colossal fabrics which take us from the present into the very depths of time! But who were their builders? Was it the shadowy Olmecs, whose history, like that of the ancient Titans, is lost in the mists of fable? or, as commonly reported, the peaceful and industrious Toltecs, of whom all we can glean rests on traditions hardly more secure? What has become of the races who built them? Did they remain on the soil and mingle and become incorporated with the fierce Aztecs who succeeded them? or did they pass on to the south and find a wider field for the expansion of their civilization, as shown by the higher character of the architectural remains in the distant regions of Central America and Yucatan? It is all a mystery, over which time has thrown an impenetrable veil that no mortal hand may raise. A nation has passed away, powerful, populous, and well advanced in refinement, as attested by their monuments; but it has perished without a name; it has died and made no sign."

A few hundred yards from the pyramids, in a secluded spot shut closely in by two small hillocks, is a very remarkable stone, no doubt a sacrificial stone. It is about ten feet long, five or six feet broad, and as many feet in height. It is very handsomely hewn, with a well-cut cornice, but has none of the human or other figures in relief which are so well cut on other sacrificial stones in Mexico. The whole weight of this huge mass of porphyritic stone cannot be less than twenty-five tons.

From these pyramids a broad street leads off in a southern direction for six or eight hundred yards, and terminates in the ruins of the old city Teotihuacan. These ruins cover an area very nearly as large as that of the present city of Mexico, and the streets are distinctly marked by the ruins of the houses. There is one large public square of twenty acres, with the ruin of a stone building in the centre of it, with many more smaller squares in different places, each having the same ruin in the centre, which is proportionately as much smaller than the ruin in the large square as the difference in the size of the squares themselves. If it was desired to build a new city on the same spot one could not be laid out in any respect better than by adopting the plan of this one which is in ruins. The streets and public squares are designated by the large piles of rock in close juxtaposition on the sides of each, but each pile separate, and having exactly the appearance, only larger, of a long row of potato hills. These stones have manifestly not been placed one upon another, but have exactly the appearance of a brick or stone house which has tumbled down. On the western side of this ruined city is a ravine some forty feet wide, the sides of which are for the greater portion of its extent of a soft rock. On each bank of this ravine there are niches eighteen inches or two feet in diameter, and of a circular form; these are said by the natives of the country to have been places of sepulture.

The ancient city of Tezcuco, which at the period of the conquest was second only to the city of Mexico, is also a place famous in history as the spot where Cortez launched his thirteen brigantines, which were used with so much effect in his second and successful attack upon the city of Mexico. They were built in Tlaxcala, sixty miles distant, and were carried to Tezcuco by the Tlaxcalans and put together and launched there. The city of Tezcuco was at that time on the eastern shore of the lake, but the waters have receded and left it three miles distant. The site of Mexico is the same now as then, but it was then surrounded by water and connected with the mainland by three causeways. The same receding of the waters of the lake at Tezcuco leaves the city of Mexico the same distance from the western shore. The lake is daily crossed by Indians from the neighborhood of Tezcuco carrying vegetables, coal, and other articles to Mexico for sale.

CHAPTER XVI

HIDALGO

LET us now leave the state of Mexico and journey through this fascinating republic, which combines so much of the old and the new, the romantic and the historic, the traditions of the past and the spirit of modern progress.

Closely adjacent on the northeast lies the state of Hidalgo. The word *hidalgo* is applied in Spain to every noble man and woman, though strictly belonging only to the lowest orders of nobility, constituting the *hidalguia*.

This state bears the name of Mexico's Washington, the priest Miguel Hidalgo y Costilla, who was the first to proclaim the independence of his country (September 16, 1810), and who gave his life for the nation that was to be. Touching the state of Mexico (its southern boundary), and enclosed by that and the states of Querétaro to the west, San Luis to the north, and Vera Cruz and Pueblo on the side of the rising sun, it has a cluster of delightful and prosperous cities and towns along the lines of the Mexican Central Railway. El Salto, Tula, San Antonio, Marquez, Nopala, Cazadero, are strung, like jewels, along the thread of steel rails forming the main line, while Pachuca, the capital, Tlaxcoapan, Rosal, Temoaya, and Concepcion are on the branch which leaves the main line at Tula.

SEÑOR GOBERNADOR-GENERAL RAFAEL CRAVIOTO.

Pachuca, the capital city, has a population of forty thousand, which rejoices in the fact that the city is eight thousand feet—a good mile and a half—above sea-level. It is the seat of government, and is entirely devoted to mining and metallurgical reduction and the business growing out of these twin industries. Pachuca is surrounded by high mountains veined with silver, which the Spaniards mined three hundred and seventy-five years ago, and the Aztecs before them. North of the city is the deepest shaft in the country, sixteen hundred and forty-five feet deep, with fortress-like walls. Real del Monte has one of the largest water-wheels on earth, fifty feet in diameter.

Hacienda de la Purísima, in Pachuca.

The largest pump in the world may be found at the Dificultad mine in Real del Monte, the road to which from Pachuca is very fine, and was built by the originators of the Real del Monte Mining Company at their own expense.

The city of Pachuca is considered one of the most prosperous in the republic in proportion to its population. While it has no artificial drainage system, a natural sewer in the shape of a river supplies this deficiency.

The plantation of Santiago Tuxtla once belonged to Cortez, and is said to be the one on which he first planted sugar-cane in Mexico; in fact, the remains of old sugar-mills said to have been built by him are still to be found, overgrown with cedars some of which are over two feet in diameter, which certainly shows that the ruins are very old.

HACIENDA OF SAN BUENAVENTURA.

Pachuca is a shell of porphyry with its open edge toward the northeast and its curves lost in the lofty Sabanillas and San Cristobal range. The Pachuca skies are a lovely blue and the mountains brown. Only now and then a bit of green shows among the deep gullies. The river is of a muddy color, but the bridges of stone between east and west Pachuca are quite picturesque. Her streets spread out like the stems of a lady's fan, bearing the names of Guerrero, Allende, Bravo, and other Mexican heroes. The *patio* of one house is often on a level with the roof of a neighbor, and the streets climb up the sides of the mountains like so many flights of stairs. The boulevard to the Cuesco hacienda and the road to the Santa Gertrudis mine are each very pleasant. Prosperous has been its career in the past, but with the swamping of the three greatest mines in December, 1895, the growth of the place received a short check. It was in the year 1557 that Bartolomé de Medina, a monk, initiated the "patio" process for reduction of silver ores. The Pachuca mines were then twenty years old, and, although millions of silver *pesos* have been taken from the heart of the mountains, the silver skin of Pachuca has as yet only been scratched. Previous to the accident in December, 1895, when the three great mines of San Rafael, Maravillas, and Camelia were flooded, the district had an output in silver of five hundred thousand dollars per week.

The mines have already started up, however, and have installed new electrical plants, so that the future of Pachuca mines is definitely settled to be greater than anything the past has ever known. These electrical plants were put in with twelve hundred horse-power, so that, with the growth of the future, Pachuca is destined to be, as it has been, one of the most celebrated mining centres in the world.

The transmutation of the hoary past into the aggressive future is nowhere better illustrated than by the growth and prospects of Tula. It is true beyond question that in the near future

Tula will be a resort like Orizaba and Cuernavaca, although it is not quite seven thousand feet high. The city is built upon a series of terraces that go down to the bottom lands of emerald green. The broad, well-paved streets and fine sidewalks are arranged along these terraces. Half-way down to the river is an old church which looks more like a fortress than a house of worship. It stands on an enormous square artificially raised and perfectly level; a battlemented wall around it is a modification of those known in Europe as *redaus*, which were common in Mexico prior to the Spanish conquest. The towering massive church has its roof battlemented in the same way. At regular intervals along the walls are solid buttresses with stone sentry-boxes. This square and its outer wall are ascribed to the ancient Toltecs.

There are three ancient bridges in the vicinity, one of which at least is Toltec. Various Toltec traditions have come down about this locality, flavored with all the musty romance of the past. There is good reason to suppose that one of these bridges was built in 210 A.D. and fell in the middle of the eleventh century, the remains still forming a picturesque bit of Tula. In this vicinity, too, are other antiquities, summed up in what the citizens call "The Treasury of Montezuma."

On the same hill are some ancient Chichimec fortresses,—circular heaps of loose stone with earth thrown over them to keep them in place. They resemble the funnel which the ant-lion makes for the destruction of the wandering ant. From their summit there is a most exquisite view of the valley of the Tula River and of the city with its lower terraces embosomed in verdant ash-trees. The church looks like a mediæval fortress, and the valley is an emerald patch of waving wheat-fields. "The Treasury of Montezuma," now in ruins, is on the top of the hill. There are two distinct kinds of fragmentary walls, eight feet thick. There is one large room thirty-two feet long, with the chunam flooring nearly perfect. The people of Tula visit these ruins continually, believing many treasures to be concealed there. They dream dreams, and then go out and sink pits in the flooring, hoping to enrich themselves with wonderful treasures of Montezuma's time. It is probable that at one time these ruins were the abode of the patriarchal chief, when the whole slope was covered with fruit-trees and the summit a beautiful garden.

STATUE OF HIDALGO.

There are other strange relics of ancient times on another hill near Tula. These are carved rocks resting upon a stratum of adobe, below which the hill slopes down to the river precipitously. The carvings are symbolical, and are supposed to have been made about 1160 A.D., in the Chichimec era. There is a great wealth of carving, although the details are not so distinct as they might be, because some clerical vandal has covered it with paper, fragments of which still cling there. There are seven of these rocks,—a magical number,—and it is thought they were objects of adoration previous to the conquest. Indeed, it is believed that certain Indians worship these rocks to-day. It is a deplorable thing that the Spaniards disturbed the rock-carving at Chapultepec or that vandals meddled with these at Tula.

The beautiful valley in which Tula is situated teems with tropical flowers and foliage, and is noted for the Toltec ruins and relics which have been found and are still found there. The old church, which was built three hundred years ago, has walls seven feet thick, which seems enough for all practical purposes of construction, and the tower is one hundred and twenty-five feet high. It lies in the valley which the Toltecs entered when they came southward in 648, nearly twelve hundred and fifty years ago. What can we say definitely of the happenings in our own country more than eight hundred years before Columbus landed, and about four hundred years before Leif the Red set foot upon our shores? Tula was an important town more than a thousand years ago, and in fact was the capital of Mexico until A.D. 1325. The proof of all this lies everywhere around,—the casas grandes, the broken columns, the quaint images all about the present town.

MINE OF REAL DEL MONTE.

The queer old church—although built in 1553 it is new in Tula—was evidently both fortress and church, as its seven-foot walls attest. Modern lime-kilns in this neighborhood, older than Egypt, mar in some measure the æsthetic beauty of the scenery around about.

When I crossed the little market-place near the plaza and turned into the high-road to the city of Mexico—which commences in a rude causeway over which immense trees cast a grateful shade—I came to an old stone bridge over the Tula River, and at once there opened before my enraptured eyes one of the finest landscapes on the American continent, the flowing river, the far-reaching meadows, the wide-branching trees, the clambering vines, the brilliant and contrasting flowers, the blue and cloudless sky, all combining to make a perfect picture that the artist might search for a lifetime to improve upon. When the now long-departed Toltecs after long wanderings saw this lovely country spread out before them, "fair as the garden of the Lord," no wonder they halted there and set up their homes and altars. Nowhere in Mexico does one feel more strongly the impression of ancient Mexico than at Tula. Here is the witchery of an old, old world,—shadowy people, vague and mystical rites and ceremonies, and dreams of ancient Toltec civilization. In the small plaza stand the remains of old gods in the blazing sunshine of to-day; and down yonder, crumbling into dust, is the old Toltec pyramid, built how many centuries ago? One may, by a little searching, find broken pieces of obsidian razor-blades and flint arrow-heads that were bathed in human blood before American civilization was even dreamed of; one may read in the old church venerable hieroglyphics pertaining to the idolatrous worship of the Aztecs and Toltecs; one may see on every side evidences or traces of the romance and traditions of the long-forgotten past; or one may take note of modern ideas and progress creeping in on every hand, of new ideas, of little children worshipping in the old church in the purer religion of to-day, of charming, cordial people; in short, the most curious admixture of yesterday, to-day, and to-morrow imaginable.

When at Tula, fifty miles from the national capital, we must not forget the canal of Nochistongo, a piece of work to which the Suez Canal is nothing. It is an open cut twelve miles long, with an average depth of one hundred and eighty feet and an average width of four hundred feet, built, at the cost of many thousand lives and eighteen million dollars, to save the city of Mexico from inundation from Lake Tezcuco.

This cut, or *tajo*, of Nochistongo was commenced in 1607. In its greatest width it is six hundred and thirty feet across. It may be seen very well from the line of the Mexican Central Railway, the trains passing along one side of the cut.

At Cazadero, more than eleven hundred feet above the last principal station (San Juan del Rio), the scenery is very fine, embracing three varieties,— broad plain, deep-reaching valley, and cloud-piercing moun-

THE GOVERNOR'S PALACE.

tains. It was here, three and a half centuries ago, that the natives honored the first Spanish viceroy, Mendoza, by a grand hunt, as was their custom, in token of good will and welcome.

The western part of the state is generally flat, or broken by mountains of but slight elevation; the centre and north, however, are quite mountainous, the principal chain being that of Metztitlan (some of whose peaks are two thousand feet above the sea), noted for its magnificent basaltic columns. There are beautiful lakes, one of them, Metztitlan, being about twenty miles long and ten wide; then there are others, also beautiful,—Tecomulco, Apam, and Zupitlan.

In some parts, as Pachuca and Apam (the celebrated pulque district), the climate is very variable. It is hot in Huejutla and other parts, and cold in other portions of the state.

The principal riches of the state of Hidalgo are its innumerable mineral deposits, especially those of silver, gold, copper, lead, iron, and coal. There are three hundred and seventeen mines in operation, and of these one hundred and ten are yielding metal. The more noted mineral districts are Pachuca, Real del Norte, El Chico, Zimapan, Zacualtipan, Ixmiquilpan, and Actopan. Pachuca, Real del Norte, and El Chico are the most prosperous, having forty mines in yield, some of which, as Santa Gertrudis, San Rafael, La Luz, Pabellon, El Barón, La Blanca and Dificultad, San Antonio, and El Rico, are very rich in silver. The mines of the Zimapan district yield silver and lead. The district of Actopan, although known to and worked by the Spaniards, was comparatively neglected until recently, but will prove, when further developed, a valuable district, as much rich ore has been found there which carries a larger quantity of gold than that of Pachuca. The most notable mines there are the San Eugenio and the property of the Baron de Humboldt Company, whose drainage adit has now almost reached the main vein; when this is done, the company intends to establish a reduction works at the mine, thus avoiding the heavy cost of carriage. These mines are on the eastern slope of the "Frailes" mountains, six leagues, or twenty-four kilometres, west of Pachuca.

Pachuca is in the rich metal-bearing zone, which extends from northwest to southeast from Sonora to Oaxaca. The state of Hidalgo produces nearly six million dollars of silver per year from its two mineral centres. There is considerable gold in its beautiful mountains, but so far it has not been worked properly. The richness of these mines has been known throughout the world for three hundred years, and all of them seem inexhaustible.

In Pachuca, where the "patio" process of silver reduction was invented by Bartolomé de Medina, his old hacienda is still worked.

The noble metal platinum, the use of which is increasing in the useful and decorative arts, is found in the state, but is not yet worked. It is certain that with foreign capital and methods fortunes could be made from this source alone.

There are large deposits of coal, which are as yet unworked; and ere very long Americans will go down and make money developing the "black diamonds" for local use, as well as for export.

Pachuca has twelve reduction works, El Chico nine, Real del Monte eight, and Zimapan eight. Pachuca exported in 1892 silver in bars to the value of nearly five and a half millions of dollars, besides nearly nine and a half millions in ore.

There are in the state six iron-works; and in the districts of Zacualtipan and Huejutla are deposits of coal, which are to be developed by a powerful English company. In Molango are graphite deposits.

The mines in Pachuca were worked by the Spaniards in 1523, only two years after the conquest. Think of the untold millions that have been withdrawn from the inexhaustible deposits of the precious metal, where busy men of to-day still delve with the same eagerness as of old, but with increased interests and wants.

This is one of the few districts in the world where that wonderful plant vanilla grows, the beans of which are worth in New York from ten dollars to twelve dollars a pound. In some years as high as three hundred per cent. profit has been made from this crop. This is one of the explanations of the enormous, almost fabulous, riches of some of the Mexican planters.

In this state we find the same maguey as in Mexico,—*la planta de las maravillas*, or the marvel plant, as it was called by Father Acosta,—being here of the very highest quality and largest yield.

In Apam, Pachuca, Tula, and elsewhere we find all the cereals produced; and Apam and Pachuca are the greatest centres for the production of pulque. In the rest of the hotter districts there are cultivated with great success coffee, cotton, sugar, tobacco, vanilla, and india-rubber; and there is an abundant supply of naturally produced medicinal plants and valuable cabinet woods.

I cannot speak of Hidalgo without mentioning its pulque, the yield of which is about a gallon and a half a day for three months for each plant. This industry yields eight million dollars a year to Hidalgo. Nor must I forget mescal, a highly intoxicating liquor, so fiery that

Zócalo in Real del Monte.

when one takes his first drink the sensation is that of swallowing a torchlight procession. The best brand of this comes from the Tequila hacienda, and from this all mescal is ordinarily called tequila, just as all brandy is often called cognac.

The conditions of the state, especially under the present governor, Rafael Cravioto, lend themselves very favorably to the establishment of new enterprises, only a few of which I may name. One of them is irrigation, there being in every part of the state large tracts under almost every condition of climate which would yield enormous returns by the establishment of systems of irrigation. *Per contra*, there are also extensive tracts where there is too much water, which, while now subject to inundation and not suitable for agriculture, would yield excellent returns if properly drained. There is room for a large extension of textile industries, the raw material for wool and silk manufacture being abundant. In the northern part of the state there is opportunity to develop at great profit the cabinet woods and deposits of marble, pitch, petroleum, and coal.

In the capital there is a scientific and industrial literary institute, in which are prosecuted the studies necessary for the occupations of assaying and topographic, hydrographic, and mining engineering. There is also a practical mining school belonging to the federal government, in which pupils sent from Mexico City acquire practical training under the direction of a professor of metallurgy and one of mining exploitation.

OMITLAN.

In this state I have added to my already large and varied collection of aboriginal names such beauties as Tlaxcoapan and Polotitlan, on the Central road, and Zimapan, Zacualtipan, Metztitlan, Yahualica, Huejutla, Jacala, Molango, and Ixmiquilpan, to which the railway has not yet penetrated.

And now, having noted within the limited space at my disposal my impressions of the material part of the noted state of Hidalgo, I can only add a word concerning its distinguished chief magistrate, General Rafael Cravioto, a brave and patriotic soldier and statesman, whose every heart-beat is for his state and his country. Hidalgo and her people are fortunate in their noble governor. One of his chief efforts has been in the promotion of public instruction, compulsory education in this state having been decreed years before it was in the capital of the republic. Another testimony to his zeal in this direction is the establishment of the State Literary and Scientific Institute, where the methods of education are based on lines similar to those adopted in the city of Mexico.

CHAPTER XVII

TLAXCALA

SOUTH of Hidalgo lies the historic state o Tlaxcala, the scene of so much human tragedy during Cortez's conquest. Tlaxcala is one of the oldest places in all Mexico, and was founded by the Chichimees. For many years before the conquest this gallant little republic had maintained its independence against the Aztecs, of whose great family it was a branch. According to Prescott, "they came on the grand plateau about the same time with the kindred races, at the close of the twelfth century, and planted themselves on the western borders of the lake of Tezcuco. Here they remained many years, engaged in the usual pursuits of a bold and partially civilized people. From some cause or other, perhaps their turbulent temper, they incurred the enmity of surrounding tribes. A coalition was formed against them, and a bloody battle was fought on the plains of Poyauhtlan, in which the Tlascalans were completely victorious. Disgusted, however, with their residence among nations with whom they found so little favor, the conquering people resolved to migrate. They separated into three divisions, the largest of which, taking a southern course by the great volcano of Mexico, wound around the ancient city of Cholula, and finally settled in the district of country overshadowed by the sierra of Tlascala.

"The warm and fruitful valleys locked up in the embraces of this rugged brotherhood of mountains afforded means of subsistence for an agricultural people, while the bold eminences of the sierra presented secure positions for their towns."

Tlaxcala signifies "land of bread," and the name was indicative of the fruitfulness of the soil then as now. Yellow harvests of maize and the bountiful maguey covered the rocky hill-sides, just as they do now, and contributed to the wealth of the little republic. Their geographical position was encompassed with mountains, and their warlike bravery gave them

SEÑOR GOBERNADOR CORONEL PROSPERO COHORANTZI.

a great reputation as soldiers, and excited the wonder and admiration of Cortez and his army. Nowhere else did the Spaniards encounter such troops or meet with such determined resistance ; and the great Spaniard was quick to see that the Tlaxcalans would serve him much better as friends than as enemies.

Says Prescott, "Nothing could be more picturesque than the aspect of these Indian battalions, with the naked bodies of the common soldiers gaudily painted, the fantastic helmets of the chiefs glittering with gold and precious stones, and the glowing panoplies of feather-work which decorated their persons. Innumerable darts and spears, tipped with points of transparent itztli or fiery copper, sparkled bright in the morning sun, like the phosphoric gleams playing on the surface of a troubled sea, while the rear of the mighty host was dark with the shadows of

GOVERNOR'S PALACE IN TLAXCALA.

banners on which were emblazoned the armorial bearings of the great Tlascalan and Otomi chieftains. Among these, the white heron on the rock, the cognizance of the house of Xicotencatl, was conspicuous, and still more, the golden eagle with outspread wings, in the fashion of a Roman signum, richly ornamented with emeralds and silver-work, the great standard of the republic of Tlascala.

"The common file wore no covering except a girdle round the loins. Their bodies were painted with appropriate colors of the chieftain whose banner they followed. The feather-mail of the higher class of warriors exhibited also a similar selection of colors for the like object, in the same manner as the colors of the tartan indicate the peculiar clan of the Highlander. The caciques and principal warriors were clothed in quilted cotton tunics, two inches thick, which, fitting close to the body, protected also the thighs and the shoulders. Over these the wealthier Indians wore cuirasses of thin gold plate or silver. Their legs were defended by leathern boots or sandals trimmed with gold. But the most brilliant part of their costume was a rich mantle of the *plumaje*, or feather-work, embroidered with curious art, and furnishing some resemblance to the gorgeous surcoat worn by the European knight over his armor in the Middle Ages. This graceful and picturesque dress was surmounted by a fantastic head-piece, made of wood or leather, representing the head of some wild animal, and frequently displaying a formidable array of teeth. With this covering the warrior's head was enveloped, producing a most grotesque and hideous effect. From the crown floated a splendid panache of the richly variegated plumage of the tropics, indicating by its form and colors the rank and family of the wearer. To complete this defensive armor, they carried shields or targets made sometimes of wood covered with leather, but more usually of a light frame of reed quilted with cotton, which were preferred as tougher and less liable to fracture than the former. They had other bucklers in which the cotton was covered with an elastic substance, enabling them to be shut up in a more compact form, like a fan or umbrella. These shields were decorated with showy ornaments, according to the taste or wealth of the wearer, and fringed with a beautiful pendant of feather-work.

La Parroquia.

"Their weapons were slings, bows and arrows, javelins, and darts. They were accomplished archers, and would discharge two, or even three, arrows at a time. But they most excelled in throwing the javelin. One species of this, with a thong attached to it, which remained in the slinger's hand that he might recall the weapon, was especially dreaded by the Spaniards. These various weapons were pointed with bone or the mineral itztli (obsidian), the hard substance already noticed as capable of taking an edge like a razor, though easily blunted. Their spears and arrows were also frequently headed with copper. Instead of a sword they bore a two-handed staff about three feet and a half long, in which at regular distances were inserted transversely sharp blades of itztli,— a formidable weapon, which, as an eye-witness assures us, he had seen fell a horse at a blow.

"Such was the costume of the Tlascalan warrior, and indeed of that great family of nations generally who occupied the plateau of Anahuac."

Their weapons, however, even with their bravery, were no match for the military science of the Spaniards; and after four terrible battles, preceded by a good deal of sharp skirmishing, the Tlaxcalans were defeated. After some politic delays they were completely subdued and became the faithful allies of the Spanish. Had this not been effected, it is doubtful if Cortez's name would have descended as "the great conqueror," at least in Mexico.

Tlaxcala City is the capital of the state, and dates far back of Cortez's arrival in the place.

where he fought and subdued them with such excellent effect. This historic town has now less than six thousand inhabitants, but the very air is alive with romance and tradition. Age, hoary and musty, is stamped everywhere, although the people are as wide awake and prosperous as could be required. There are many relics of Cortez's visit in the picturesque old town, among them a grant from Charles the Fifth, with his signature, and a silken flag which the great conqueror presented to the Tlaxcalans. The latter is in a fair state of preservation, and is handsomely embroidered in silk with a curious battle-scene between the Spaniards and Tlaxcalans. Then there are idols from neighboring mounds, the city charter from Philip II. in book form, bound in vellum and dated May 10, 1585, with the royal signature, baptismal robes of chiefs, and their ancient genealogical trees.

In this city, too, which at the time of the conquest was compared favorably by Cortez with Granada, but which is now the mere shadow of its former self, a half-deserted, decaying village, is found the most interesting collection of Cortez relics in all Mexico. One sees here the banner which accompanied Cortez in his memorable march, the standard which Cortez presented to the Tlaxcalan chiefs who befriended him, portraits in oil of the latter, the robes which they wore at their baptism, the font in which they were baptized, and a silken embroidery on which is pictured the first battle between the Spaniards and Tlaxcalans; and one can visit the house occupied by Cortez.

Cortez declared in all his accounts that the city had then thirty thousand souls, and that it was larger than Granada, then the capital of Spain. But one feels it necessary to take this statement "with a grain of salt."

The houses were built, for the most part, of mud or earth, the better sort of stone and lime, or of bricks dried in the sun. They were unprovided with doors or windows, but in the apertures for the former hung mats fringed with pieces of copper or something which by its tinkling sound would give notice of any one's entrance.

AN ARCHWAY IN TLAXCALA.

The streets were narrow and dark. Cortez asserts that thirty thousand people were often gathered in the market on a public day. These meetings were fairs, held, in all great towns, every fifth day, and attended by the inhabitants of the adjacent country, who brought there for sale every description of domestic produce and manufacture with which they were acquainted. They peculiarly excelled in pottery, which was considered equal to the best in Europe. It is a further proof of civilized habits that the Spaniards found barbers' shops, and baths, both of vapor and of hot water, familiarly used by the inhabitants. A still higher proof of refinement may be discerned in the existence of a vigilant police which repressed everything like disorder.

TLAXCALA

The ancient capital, through one quarter of which flowed the rapid current of the Zahuatl, stretched along the summits and sides of hills at whose base are now gathered the remnant of its once flourishing population. Far beyond, to the southeast, extended the bold sierra of Tlaxcala, and the huge Malinche, crowned with the usual silver diadem of the highest Andes, its shaggy sides clothed with dark-green forests of firs, gigantic sycamores, and oaks whose towering stems rose to the height of forty or fifty feet unencumbered by a branch. The clouds which sailed over from the distant Atlantic gathered around the lofty peaks of the sierra, and, settling into torrents, poured over the plains in the neighborhood of the city, converting them, at such seasons, into swamps. Thunder-storms, more frequent and terrible here than in other parts of the table-land, swept down the sides of the mountains and shook the frail tenements of the capital to their foundations. But, although the bleak winds of the sierra gave an austerity to the climate unlike the sunny skies and genial temperature of the lower regions, it was far more favorable to the development of both the physical and the moral energies. A bold and hardy peasantry was nurtured among the recesses of the hills, fit equally to cultivate the land in peace and to defend it in war. Unlike the spoiled child of Nature, who derives such facilities of subsistence from her too prodigal hand as supersede the necessity of exertion on his part, the Tlaxcalan earned his bread—from a soil not ungrateful, it is true—by the sweat of his brow. He led a life of temperance and toil. Cut off by his long wars with the Aztecs from commercial intercourse, he was driven chiefly to agricultural labor, the occupation most propitious to purity of morals and sinewy strength of constitution. His honest breast glowed with patriotism, or local attachment to the soil, which is the fruit of its diligent culture, while he was elevated by a proud consciousness of independence, the natural birthright of the child of the mountains. Such, says Prescott, was the race with whom Cortez was now associated for the achievement of his great work.

SACRED WELL OF OCOTLAN.

What of the Tlaxcala of to-day? Situated in the centre of so beautiful a country, it has illimitable advantages. Tlaxcala has the oldest church in North America, with its cedar ceiling and beams brought from Spain, Cortez's church of San Francisco, constructed in 1521. In this church, too, is the pulpit from which the gospel was first preached in the New World. There is artistic wood-carving by Indian artists of power and taste in the church of Ocotlan, perched on a hill in the same city of Tlaxcala; indeed, almost every leading church of every considerable town has a treasure of some sort, a Murillo, an alleged Titian, or some other exhibit to interest the sight-seer. The pastor of the famous shrine of Ocotlan, Father Angelo Morales Rodriguez, gave a dinner October 18, 1895, at his home to the American bishops who had come to Mexico to celebrate the ceremony of the coronation of Our Lady of Guadalupe.

The governor of Tlaxcala, who is a full-blooded native Indian, was unable to be present, but several distinguished Indians were there, as well as prominent Mexicans. Tlaxcala is noted for the number of Indians who have entered the legal profession, and it was one of these, Mr. Francisco Zempoalteca, who made the speech of welcome in his native language. To a stranger the number of these educated and active native Indians is something of a surprise.

The following is the address of welcome of the eloquent Tlaxcalan, with a faithful translation:

"Teopixcatlahtoanime; pipiltsitzi:

"In Altepetl Tlaxcalan ipan i nin cahuitl aencapaqui ihuan tlazohcamachilistica non mech mo zelilia i tlalpan, no mech mo ixpantilia in i mahuiso in i chan in i yolo. Zenca tic ilehuia non quimoyu zehlisque i nin icnomahuisotl no mech mo neltoltilia in Motlacuitlahuihcatiopixcatzintli Calixto del Refugio Orhelas i Tocaipan ihuan in zentetl Altepetl Tlaxcalan. Fehhuan tic mo tlatlahtilia in ilhuicae tonantzi zemihcae ichpochtli Ocotlan Chaneheatzintli ma no mech mo yec pili ica zentetl chicahualistl ica zentetl pahpaquilistli iepan non metstiesque icxitlantzinco huan tonahuae Za nolhqui tic temachia ihcuae non qui mo cahuilisque in Mexihcahueyaltepeti huan mahxitisque non mo chautzinco, non huchca tlalpan campa o non hual mo hehuitihque, ze tlatlatlahtilistl non qui mo titlanilisque ixpantzinco in zenca huel neli Tzotl to panpa, huan yehhuatrin itech in i tlazohmahuistic Flamamanilitzi qui mo chihuilis ma mo zohzoa ic ahcopa ic tlani ic tonal i quizayan huan ic i calaquia in tlamelahca tlaneltoquilistli i huiepa zentetl zamanahuae ti mixmatisque ti monahuahtequisque huan ihcuacon i teoixpantzinco tic chihuasque san ze Flanechicol huan ti caquisque san ze nemachtilistli tic piasque san ze Tlaneltoquilistli huan tic zelisque san ze necuatequilistli. Nehhuatl ica zentetl no yolo nic motlatlahtilia in Yehhuatzi ma nel quimi axcan ó no mech mo nechicalhuili tonahuae icxitlantzinco in to chipahuae mazehualnantzi Malintzi Tecuapanope i nic o non qui motilico, quenin in to tlahtohcateopixcatzintli Pili Tenetli Prospero Maria Alarcon o qui mo yeyantili ipan in i zenquisca tzontecontzi in neca mahuistic cuayehual i nesca i machio in zentetl tlahtohcayotl ma ihcon tech mo nechicalhuiliti nochtin ompa i tlahtocachantzinco campazehmihcae pahpaquilo.

"Ipanpa in i weltilis in to tlanequilis, ipanpa in i chicahualis in to tlahtoheatzi mahuistic tlacatzintli teotetahtzi Leon XIII. metstica ompa huei altepepan Roma, ipanpa in to tetlahpalohcatzitzi nican tech mahuizotia ma tic mahzehuacan in nin atzintli ma huel tepitzi xocoe saman tzopelic huan tic hueliemati i zepan in to tetlasohtlacatzitzi.

"TLASCALA, Octubre 18 de 1895." "WANCISCO ZEMPOALTECA."

TRANSLATION.

"YOUR GRACE:

"The people of Tlaxcala on this occasion are greatly honored by your presence in their midst, and cordially tender to you their sincere respects, the hospitality of their home, and the warmest affection of their hearts.

"We wish exceedingly that you deign to accept this little present which Father Calixto del R. Orhelas, in his name, and also in the name of all the Tlascalteca people, present to you. We fervently pray that the Celestial Queen of Heaven, Our Lady of Ocotlan, may preserve your health and strength during your stay among us.

"We hope also that when you leave our territory and return to your magnificent city, you will pray for us to the God of Truth, that our Holy Religion may be as widely propagated in the North as in the South, and in the West as well as in the East, so that we will all be members of the one only Church, we will hear only one teaching, and we will be all baptized in the one faith. With all my heart I pray to God, that as now we are all gathered together before our National Mother of Guadalupe to see His Grace Monsignor Prospero Maria Alarcon, Archbishop of Mexico, place the beautiful crown, which is the symbol of power, on the head of our Lady, so we may be all united in heaven before the throne of God.

"That these earnest wishes may be fully realized; that the life of the beloved and illustrious head of the Church, Leo XIII., may long be preserved; and that our distinguished guests may return in safety to their respective homes, is the heart-felt prayer of all present."

Tlaxcala abounds in interesting relics of ancient times. Among them are some very old portraits of the heroes of former days, a cloak which belonged to a noble Indian of that time who was the first to receive Christian baptism, and the wonderful standard which once belonged to Cortez. Then there are the city titles given by Philip II. of Spain, old plans and maps, and some genuine idols. The church of San Francisco was the first Catholic church erected in the

New World. Its architecture is very original inside and out, and dates from 1524. The pulpit has a very peculiar form and exquisite filigraned work full of gilt carvings; and the sacred vestments, beautifully embroidered in silver and gold, were brought over from Spain and used in the first Roman Catholic service in this country. These vestments are shown to-day, with the first baptismal fountain. The sanctuary is dedicated to the miraculous virgin of Ocotlan, and is situated on the summit of a little hill close to the city. One curious thing about the temple is that one half of it is of an architecture of several centuries ago, the walls being covered with the finest chiselled workmanship possible to imagine and richly gilt, while the other half is entirely of modern style, splendidly sculptured by modern artists. On the walls are hundreds of wax reproductions of human limbs, left there by patients who have been miraculously cured of various diseases, and who celebrated these cures by giving the church these symbols.

Around Tlaxcala the scenery is the grandest in Mexico. On one side, like two grim sentinels guarding the valley, stand the giant mountains Popocatepetl and Ixtaccihuatl, at whose feet lies the valley of San Martin. On the opposite side lies the long low ridge of the Malinche, which the declining sun lights up with all the brightness of the tropical sunset. Watching the varying shades of light playing tenderly around the top, one can

THE FIRST PULPIT IN MEXICO.

readily understand whence came the soul of poetry that makes the beautiful Tlaxcalan legend of the Malinche the most poetical of all the Mexican legends; and one can easily believe at such times the old legend that Tlaxcala was the garden of the great spirit of war, and that the sun-carpeted top of the Malinche was his home.

Through this fruitful and enchanting valley will run a new railway that is shortly to prove a boon to the grain-growers of the valley. It will not only be an outlet for many rich properties, and drain the most fertile valley in Mexico, but will be the most picturesque in the republic.

Wherever the railroads have gone the Indians are beginning to forsake their native speech. In Tlaxcala one realizes that the Aztec is not yet a dead language. The governor of Tlaxcala, Prospero Cahuantzi, has done much to develop and perpetuate Indian traditions and institutions. He has published books to that end, and also an ancient Tlaxcalan record, which gives a curious history of the conquest told in pictures.

Few people, perhaps none except scientists, know that in the heart of this ancient state is a race of pygmies. They are small of stature, with dark-brown skin, broad faces, and shocks of black tangled hair. They are very shy and wild-looking, and wear serapes made of coarse sacking. We naturally expected from what we had heard of them to find them hidden among the rocks in some rude shelter, living a precarious life from hand to mouth. What we really found was this: fine clearings on the hill-slopes extending almost to the crest of the mountains, flourishing fields of grain, cattle grazing in the pastures, fowls and turkeys being fattened, and log houses of substantial construction surrounded by neat little enclosures and occupied by peaceful little men and women. Clearing after clearing repeated this story of industry, thrift, and prosperity.

Finally, our appearance in the market town caused quite a sensation. They crowded around us on all sides. Some gazed suspiciously from the outside, but others were quite friendly, and regarded us with childlike curiosity. They examined our saddles and our baggage

PRINCIPAL STREET, TLAXCALA.

with great interest, and even felt of our clothes; but when we presented our letters from the governor and the good president they became our admiring servants.

Up in that region, between Ajutla and Juquila, is a marvellous lake of clouds. A deep blue sky and the brilliant southern sun, without a suggestion of mist in the still air, make the place wonderful on a grand scale. Clad with foliage clear to the summit, the great ridge forms half of a mighty amphitheatre whose sides are furrowed by mountain torrents. Five distant mountains form the wall of an oval valley, with lower peaks running parallel. At one side a spur juts out, making the only notable break in the enclosing rim. The great lake seems to approach this edge like a mighty river and pour over the great precipice like a dozen Niagaras combined in one. It is a cloud-lake, mighty, mysterious, and noiseless, making one of the greatest wonders in the region of wonders.

CHAPTER XVIII

PUEBLA

TLAXCALA is nearly surrounded by the fertile state of Puebla. The latter is bounded north and east by Vera Cruz, south by Oaxaca and Guerrero, and west by Mexico, Tlaxcala, and Hidalgo. The Cordillera of Anahuac crosses it and gives rise to many small streams, but Puebla has no large rivers. The mountains form a water-shed, and the state is drained partly into the Gulf of Mexico and partly into the Pacific. The average elevation is about six thousand feet, and the soil is generally fertile. Silver, marble, and alabaster abound, and plentiful crops of grain, fruit, sugar, and cotton are raised. Many remarkable remains are found of ancient Mexican civilization.

The city of Puebla, capital of the state, was founded soon after the Spanish conquest, the soldiers of Cortez laying it out six miles from the ancient sacred city of Mexico,—Cholula. The Puebla of to-day is a finely laid-out city with handsome squares. The city contains over sixty churches, twenty-one collegiate or theological schools, charity schools, hospitals, and other benevolent institutions. Some of the handsomely ornamented churches were injured in the French siege of 1863, when the city withstood General Forey and his French army during a siege of two months.

Within sight of Puebla are Popocatepetl, twenty-five miles away, Ixtaccihuatl, thirty miles northwest, Malinche, twenty miles northeast, and Orizaba, sixty miles east. The climate is delightfully mild and agreeable, and the country all around exceedingly fertile. Seen at sunrise from Puebla, the view of the great volcano is unrivalled. The clouds roll away as a curtain is drawn from a high altar. The snowy top and sides appear shining in the sun like a grand dome of pure alabaster. One thinks of Sinai; of Moses on the mount when the glory of the Lord was revealed; of the

SEÑOR GENERAL DON MUCIO P. MARTINEZ,
GOVERNOR OF PUEBLA.

mountain of the Transfiguration ; and then the sun rising higher and higher from the radiant brow of Popocatepetl sheds its glory on all below, and ushers in another day of Mexican sunshine.

Orizaba, which forms a boundary between the departments of Puebla and Vera Cruz, is said to be the most beautiful of mountains on a near approach, as it is the most magnificent at a distance ; for, while its summit is crowned with snow, its central part is girded by thick forests of cedar and pine, and its base is adorned with woods and sloping fields covered with flocks, and dotted with white ranches and small scattered villages, forming the most agreeable and varied landscape imaginable. Ixtaccihuatl means white woman ; Popocatepetl, the mountain that throws out smoke. They are thus celebrated by the poet Heredia :

Nieve eternal coróna las cabezas
De Ixtaccihuatl purísimo, Orizaba
Y Popocatepec : sin que el invierno
Toque jamas con destructiva mano
Los campos fertilísimos do ledo
Los mira el indio en purpura ligera
Y oro tenirse, reflejando el brillo
Del sol en occidente, que sereno
En hielo eterno y perennal verdura
A torrentes vertió su luz dorada,
Y vió á naturaleza, conmovida
Con su dulce calor, hervir en vida.

TRANSLATION.

Eternal snow crowns the majestic heads
Of Orizaba, Popocatepetl,
And of Ixtaccihuatl the most pure.
Never does winter with destructive hand
Lay waste the fertile fields where from afar
The Indian views them bathed in purple light
And dyed in gold, reflecting the last rays
Of the bright sun, which, sinking in the west,
Poured forth his flood of golden light, serene
'Midst ice eternal, and perennial green,
And saw all nature warming into life,
Moved by the gentle radiance of his fires.

SEÑOR LICENCIADO DON AGUSTIN FERNANDEZ,
SECRETARY OF STATE, PUEBLA.

As you approach the city of Puebla, there are farms of considerable extent on both sides of the road. The grains chiefly cultivated are wheat, barley, and Indian corn. The wheat is used for bread by the better classes, and I have never seen better bread anywhere. The Indian corn is used chiefly, I believe entirely, by the Mexicans in making tortillas. The tortilla is the bread of the great mass of the people. The grain is softened by soaking it in water ; it is then ground on a smooth stone, with a long roller made also of stone, and after mixing the due proportion, which is always a very large proportion, of chile and some wine, it is spread out in a thin layer and cooked as negroes do the hoe-cake.

Puebla is a beautiful city, with lofty houses built in the purest style of architecture, and broad and remarkably clean streets. The cathedral of Puebla is a magnificent edifice, which has been said, though hardly with justice, to rival the cathedral in Mexico.

PUEBLA

The cathedral is noble and inspiring. It is said that the rapid progress of building was owing to the assistance of two angels, who nightly descended and added to its height, so that each morning the astonished workmen found their labor incredibly advanced. It is not so large as the cathedral of Mexico, but it is elegant, simple, and in excellent taste. Sixteen columns of exquisite marble, adorned with silver and gold, form the tabernacle (in Mexico called *el Ciprés*). This native marble, called Puebla marble, is brought from the quarries of Totimehuacan and Tecali, respectively at two and seven leagues from the city. Everything there is interesting or historic; of especial interest are the tombs where the

INTERIOR OF CATHEDRAL IN PUEBLA.

bishops are buried, and a vault in which lies a martyr, whose body, enclosed in wax and loaded with paste emeralds and diamonds, is supposed to have been miraculously preserved for centuries.

The towers are three hundred feet high, and it would scarcely be possible to find a more beautiful building in Mexico.

The cathedral, with its floor of colored marbles, its rich and artistically attractive high altar of different varieties of Puebla onyx, and the beautiful iron work and wood carving about the choir, boasts an interior which equals that of the cathedral of Toledo, of Burgos, of Leon, or of any other town in Spain. The music at Puebla is good. An organ, a piano, a violoncello, and other stringed instruments, and men and boys in vestments, combine with excellent results.

There are three theatres in Puebla, the Guerrero, the Principal, and the Casino. The Guerrero theatre was built in 1868, and stands on the site of the old city prison. The interior is built entirely of wood taken from an old bull-ring, and has a capacity of about fifteen hundred people. It is owned by the city, and has been greatly improved with modern scenery and stage fittings. This theatre attracts the attention of all visitors on account of its beauty of proportion and its artistic decorations. The prevailing colors are white and gold, while the interior of the boxes and the galleries are finished in deep red.

CATHEDRAL OF PUEBLA.

It is thought that the "Teatro Principal" of Puebla is the oldest theatre on the western continent. It was inaugurated in 1790, by the Viceroy Ahumada. It used to be known as the "Teatro de los Arrieros," being the favorite amusement place of the *arrieros*, or mule-drivers. To-day, however, it is patronized by the best classes of society. It is unusually interesting on account of its old Spanish architecture, with solid masonry boxes and galleries. If, as is asserted, this really is the first theatre built in the New World, it should be of more than local interest.

The Casino was built as a private theatre for a local society, but has now passed into the hands of the Administrador del Timbre, who leases it to travelling companies.

There is also a bull-ring in Puebla, with seats for three thousand people. It is an uncommonly large ring, but for that reason is not popular with bull-fighters. Another place of popular amusements is the Puebla athletic grounds, or "Velodromo," from which there is a very fine view. It may be of interest to state that Puebla has a playwright of considerable reputation. Francisco Neve, whose "La Llorona" is a very fine tragedy.

Puebla, the "City of Angels," with its hundred domes and spires gleaming in the sun, makes the same impression upon the traveller of to-day as ancient Cholula, the "City of the Gods," made upon Cortez and his army when they entered it in the course of their march against the kingdom of the Montezumas; that is, Puebla, which is only six miles from Cholula, is in some ways the representative of the older city. The tradition goes that the ancient Aztecs used to see the sun-lit forms of angels and fair spirits hovering over the sacred city of Cholula. These, they believed, were reinforced by hosts of guardian spirits behind the fleecy clouds, placed there by the gods to watch over the sacred city which they loved so well. When the ancient city had fallen into decay, and Puebla began its growth, the good people believed that the spot for the "City of the Angels" was indicated to them by these spirits of the air, and that while they slept these angels spread protecting wings over it. It is certainly a pretty idea this, that the spirits deserted the shattered idols and ruins of Cholula to raise up a new city unto a new faith. Cholula of old was the Aztec city of churches and shrines; Puebla of to-day is the great Christian city of modern Mexico.

As of old, too, when the people of ancient Cholula were further advanced in the arts and sciences than those around them, so to-day the people of Puebla have made their city in many respects the most beautiful in the land. It is a model of cleanliness and good taste; while the people unite the push and thrift and ingenuity of their Indian ancestors with the ambitions and demands of modern enterprise.

In Puebla one appreciates the real beauty of the climate. The houses are bright and cheerful, the streets are beautiful, and the city has the best system of sewerage in the republic.

PANORAMA OF PUEBLA.

The common people are gifted with imagination, which throws a halo of romance over all their lives. Surrounded as they are by magnificent scenery, the spirit of poetry is developed even among the poorest of them. Among these neglected descendants of mighty nations one comes across legends older than the dead races, yet perfectly poetic in thought, form, and language. In travelling through Mexico, not according to guide-books, but off the beaten tracks and among the middle classes, one comes to realize a spirit that the modern tourist knows not of, and finds that the Mexican people have plenty of poetry in their souls.

There are persons who can witness the view from Cholula or the light of the setting sun on the Malinche without the slightest stir of emotion in their souls. These are not the ones, however, to know and feel the romance and poetry of the common people in Mexico.

The tradition of Quetzalcoatl and his life up among these great purple sun-lit hills is

PICTURESQUE MEXICO

A COUNTRY ROAD IN PUEBLA, SHOWING POPOCATEPETL.

a most beautiful story. Never was there a more tender spirit than Quetzalcoatl, who loved all living creatures and could not bear that any should suffer or live in sin and ignorance. But, alas, the people, while they loved the "fair god," feared the other powerful gods who were devoted to bloodshed and battle. They built temples to the latter and daily offered human sacrifices to the gods of war on these altars. This grovelling fear filled the great heart of Quetzalcoatl with pity and deep sorrow, and so he left his beautiful, peaceful home to teach these people, with a wonderful eloquence, the gospel of love and charity. Such was his influence that at last they deserted the altars of the cruel gods, and instead of offering human holocausts, whose quivering hearts had burned upon the sacred fires, they climbed the hills to lay upon the altar of Quetzalcoatl heaps of flowers and fruits; and war ceased and prosperity reigned.

But the cruel gods, so the tradition runs, when they found that the people had deserted them, combined against this beneficent spirit of the air. One bright spring day they came down in a body and drove Quetzalcoatl out from among the people into the great plains, where he wandered many days over the hot, sun-parched sands. At last he lay down on the burning waste, flushed with fever and perishing with a terrible thirst, seemingly deserted of gods and men. But hither came the spirits of the air which so long had hovered over Cholula, and now descended to his relief.

Lifting him from the earth, they gave him to drink a wondrous liquid like the wine of the gods; then they led him to a great maguey plant, whose fresh green leaves laughed at the dust and the sand and the heat. One of them made a hole in the trunk where the great leaves

PENITENTIARY OF PUEBLA.

branch out, and inserted a long reed. Through this he sucked up the sap of the plant and emptied it into a gourd, which he gave to Quetzalcoatl, who drank until he forgot the desert and the burning sun, and lay down to sleep. When he awoke it was night and the spirits had left him; but he arose and continued his journey. Here and there were scattered the great maguey plants, and when he grew tired or faint he slept under their green leaves, and drank from their hidden sources whenever he became thirsty.

And so he wandered for months until he came to the little village of Cholula. The people received him kindly, and he began teaching them much that was civilizing and uplifting. He taught them to build stone houses, to cultivate the land, to work beautiful designs in gold and silver and feather work, to weave the fibres of maguey into cloth, and to write their histories on

CHOLULA PYRAMID.

the leaves of the maguey. He made them understand that the greatest gift of the gods to man was the ability to work with intelligence and steady application; and he changed them from wandering savages into a people with a steady habitation and a city of their own. And then he imparted the secret of the maguey plant, and gave to the people of ancient Cholula the first knowledge of their favorite pulque.

After he had been with them for years, and had made them an intelligent people, he felt that he must return to his native land, far away. Toward sunset he ascended a little hill that stood alone on the plains and bade them farewell. As he stood against the rays of the declining sun, his face lit up with strength and purpose, the multitude of people below, looking upon the glory of his godlike head, realized for the first time that it was a god who had lived and worked among them. When he had finished his loving words of farewell, a wonderful spirit of peace descended upon the people, and they followed him a long distance across the plains and up the mountains. Only at the very top did he turn again toward them and spread out his hands in blessing. Then he turned and disappeared.

Then the people returned to Cholula and began the construction of the great pyramid in memory of Quetzalcoatl. On the top of it they built the temple of Cholula, and dedicated it to the worship of the "fair god." For generations they toiled and builded, until more than a century afterward the pyramid was completed, standing bold and distinct on the dust-blown plain, the everlasting token of a nation's faith. They believed, these people, that this pyramid

LA MATERNIDAD, IN PUEBLA.

would stand until Quetzalcoatl should come back to them. And there it stands to-day, almost as indestructible as time itself.

The view from the top of the great pyramid toward evening is almost beyond description. With the softened light of the setting sun upon the plains and the hills, one can easily understand why it was that the gods and the angels loved this region, and why the great heart of Quetzalcoatl wept when he bade farewell to it. Back from the soft, tender light in the valleys the great mountains stretch up bold and distinct against a background of the palest aerial blue, that contrasts wonderfully with the varying lights on the mountain-side. Towering over all stand Orizaba, Popocatepetl, and Ixtaccihuatl, each in the whitest of snow-caps, while just below stretches the Malinche.

Cholula probably numbers now some five thousand people. But there is no doubt that at the time of the conquest it was one of the largest towns in Mexico.

The perpendicular height of the pyramid is one hundred and seventy-seven feet. Its base is one thousand four hundred and twenty-three feet long,—twice as long as that of the great pyramid of Cheops. It may give some idea of its dimensions to state that its base, which is square, covers about forty-four acres, and the platform on its truncated summit embraces more than one acre. It reminds us of those colossal monuments of brickwork which are still seen in ruins on the banks of the Euphrates and, in much higher preservation, on those of the Nile.

"Nothing could be more grand," says Prescott, "than the view which met the eye from the area on the truncated summit of the pyramid. Toward the west stretched that bold barrier of

ZÓCALO OF PUEBLA.

porphyritic rock which nature had reared around the valley of Mexico, with the huge Popocatepetl and Ixtaccihuatl standing like two colossal sentinels to guard the entrance to the enchanted region. Far away to the east was seen the conical head of Orizaba soaring high into the clouds, and nearer, the barren though beautifully-shaped Sierra de la Malinche, throwing its broad shadows over the plains of Tlascala. Three of these are volcanoes, higher than the highest mountain peak in Europe, and shrouded in snows which never melt under the fierce sun of the tropics. At the foot of the spectator lay the sacred city of Cholula, with its bright towers and pinnacles sparkling in the sun, reposing amidst gardens and verdant groves, which then thickly studded the cultivated environs of the capital. Such was the magnificent prospect which met the gaze of the conquerors, and may still, with slight change, meet that of the modern traveller, as from the platform of the great pyramid his eye wanders over the fairest portion of the beautiful plateau of Puebla."

This great temple was afterward purified by Cortez's orders, and the standard of the cross solemnly planted in its midst. From this pyramid, it is interesting to know, Baron Humboldt made many of his valuable astronomical calculations early in the present century.

The church now standing there is dedicated to the Virgin de los Remedios. The popular tradition among the native Indians is that the pyramid was erected by a family of giants who had escaped inundation, and intended to raise it into the clouds had not the gods become angry and sent down fire from heaven to stop them where it is truncated.

Cholula was the scene of a great massacre during the time of Cortez, and his otherwise wonderful character suffers a deep stain from the terrible slaughter which he instituted here, although it must be remembered that he was in the midst of a powerful, warlike, and hostile people, and accompanied by only five hundred of his own warriors. According to Bernal Diaz,

SCENE IN PUEBLA.

he was obliged to resort to this massacre to save himself and his army. The old Spanish chronicler says that Montezuma had arranged that twenty thousand Indians should attack the Spaniards, capture them, and deliver them to death by torture.

But what a land of romance! How can busy nineteenth-century people realize that in 1519 such things were making Mexican history, and that even then the wonderful pyramid dated far back of legend or tradition?

Without exaggeration, and from an unbiassed view, it is easy to see that few localities in tropical Mexico equal the privileged section of northern Puebla. Here nature has lavished its profuseness ungrudgingly, and for the man of energy, industry, and capital to locate here means success and prosperity. The natural products are many and diversified. This is the home of the rubber, *chicle*, or chewing-gum tree, orange, lemon, lime, allspice, vanilla vine, and ginger, jalapa, and sarsaparilla roots. Among the building woods cedar, jobo, ceiba, or silk-cotton tree, chaca, quiebra-hacha, romerillo, palo de gato, chijol, jaovin, pipin, ojite, and tlacuilo are found in quantities. The fine woods suitable for furniture, existing mostly in the unexplored forests, are cedar, mahogany, rosewood, ebony, caobilla, and chico zapote; there are also several dye woods and plants, logwood, fustic, dragon's blood, and a species of wild indigo. Various fibres, such as pinada, pita (*Bromelia sylvestris*), ixtle (*Agave heterocantha*), and mala mujer, a gigantic species of nettle, also higuerilla (castor-oil plant), zacatona, fibrous grass root largely used by the Mexicans for the manufacture of brooms and brushes, and the guava, the fruit of which produces the finest kind of jelly, abound amidst forest, meadow, and hill. Several gum trees exist, among which copal and liquidambar may be mentioned. There is also plenty of wild game, including the jabali (a wild boar), cojolite (a wild turkey), chacalaca (a wild hen), deer, parrot, quail, heron, crocodile, and rabbit; likewise large quantities of fish of various kinds are found in the limpid streams. Along the western section there are long stretches of natural grass, well adapted for pasture, and the products of stock-raising here would bring very satisfactory returns. Sheep- and hog-breeding can be recommended also, as the high prices of wool and lard and the great demand for mutton and pork in the plateaux of Hidalgo, Puebla, and Vera Cruz would insure a good income.

The cultivated products of the district are coffee, corn, beans, rice, peas, sugar-cane, tobacco, cotton, starch plant, vanilla, pineapple, banana, and rubber. Corn yields here four hundred bushels for one; cane produces without irrigation, in a plot six by six metres square, twenty-five pounds of sugar each year, for eight or ten years, at a cost of one dollar a hundred pounds, and without the use of modern appliances; the product of beans and rice is sixty to eighty for one; tobacco yields more than two thousand pounds to the hectare; a rubber plantation of two hundred trees to the hectare produces two and a half to three pounds per tree when six years old; and the coffee-tree, three or four years from transplanting, gives to the industrious planter as a reward for his care and work one and a quarter to two pounds of merchantable coffee.

There is a good future for the successful growth of the coffee and rubber plants. June, July, and August are wet months, but September and October are fine, with occasional showers. In November, December, January, and February there are frequent rains from the north; still, they occur more often from the middle of December to the end of January. There is usually fine weather in March; April and May are the two hottest months. Likewise, the district is well watered by streams. The Pantepec River, carrying a large body of water (about four or five feet in depth and twenty-five to thirty yards across in the dry season), runs through the middle of the district in a north and northeasterly direction and empties into the Tuxpan River, which is navigable for thirty-five or forty miles. Flat-bottomed boats have been floated down the Pantepec during the rainy season; and by the outlay of a little effort and expense low-draught boats of any kind might ply between the port of Tuxpan and this well-favored district at all seasons of the year. Besides the large Colotla and Beltran streams, several smaller ones add to the moisture of the district.

Fruit-growing, especially oranges, lemons, bananas, pineapples, and mangoes, would prove one of the most profitable occupations. Bee-culture in connection with vanilla would also be a source of wealth.

The district of Aztlan lies at the base of the Sierra Madre range in the state of Puebla, and comprises the extreme north end of the rich and fertile county of Huauchinango. It forms a portion of the famous "Huasteca Veracruzana," and is located at a distance of eighty miles southwest of the port of Tuxpan, and one hundred and forty miles northeast of Mexico City.

The district takes in an area of over one hundred and sixty square miles of the most excellent lands of tropical Huauchinango.

The towns of Pantepec, Mecapalapa, Ixthuatlan, San Pedro Petocotla, Coapetatlan, and several ranches supply the district with necessary labor. There is now a considerable English-speaking population in the district.

The soil is a rich dark loam of a vegetable nature, invariably having a porous subsoil of considerable depth, finely adapted to the cultivation of coffee, rubber, vanilla, tobacco, and sugar-cane, and capable of yielding prolific crops of semi-tropical and tropical products.

The temperature in summer, although hot in the daytime, is cool and pleasant in the evenings and mornings. The winter months are generally delightful.

Four-fifths of the lands are undulating slopes abounding with fine forests and inviting streams; the remaining one-fifth consists of well-drained plains covered with perennial grass.

STREET IN PUEBLA.

Every square foot of this country is tillable except along the river-beds. Every section of these lands is of easy access. More than one road connects the district with the outside world. There is a wagon-road from Tuxpan that taps the north end of it, and two good mule-roads connect it with the county seat, Huauchinango, which communicates with Tulancingo, the present eastern terminus of the Hidalgo Railroad, by an easy-riding stage-road. By slow walking, the distance from Tuxpan can be made in forty-eight hours, and by moderate driving or riding in the dry season, in from twelve to fourteen hours. The Ward Line steamers call at Tuxpan from Vera Cruz or Tampico every week, and the Mexican mail boats once every ten days. The distance from Mexico City can be travelled in two and one-half days.

There are many charming places in the state of Puebla. Atlisco is a large town, with a high mountain behind it crowned by a white chapel, and with a magnificent church at the base; the whole city is full of fine churches and convents, with a plaza and many good houses. Here, too, is the famous cypress mentioned by Humboldt, which is seventy-three feet in circumference.

This valley of Atlisco, as, indeed, the whole department of Puebla, is noted for its fertility and its abundant crops of maguey, wheat, maize, frijoles, garbanzos, barley, and other vegetables, as well as for the fineness of its fruit. There is a Spanish proverb which says, "If you go to live in the Indias, let it be within sight of the volcanoes," for it appears that all the lands surrounding the different volcanoes are fertile and enjoy a pleasant climate. The great Cordillera of Anahuac crosses this territory, and among its peaks are the mountain of the Ma-

IXTACCIHUATL.

linche, Ixtaccihuatl, Popocatepetl, and the Peak of Orizaba. The Malinche, a corruption by the Spaniards of the Indian name Malintzin, signifying Doña Maria or Marina, is supposed to be called after Cortez's Indian Egeria, the first Christian woman of the Mexican empire.

Though given to Cortez by the Tabascan Indians, it seems clear that she was of noble birth, and that her father was the lord of many cities. It is pretended that she fell into a tributary situation through the treachery of her mother, who remarried after the death of her first husband, and who, bestowing all her affection on the son born of this second marriage, determined, in concert with her husband, that all their wealth should pass to him. It happened, in furtherance of their views, that the daughter of one of their slaves died, upon which they gave out that they had lost their own daughter, affected to mourn for her, and at the same time privately sold her, after the fashion of Joseph's brethren, to some merchants of Cicalanco, who in turn disposed of her to their neighbors the Tabascans, who presented her to Cortez. That she was beautiful and of great talent, versed in different Indian dialects, the devoted friend of the Spaniards, and served as their interpreter in their negotiations with the various Indian tribes, there seems no doubt. She accompanied Cortez in all his expeditions. He followed her advice; and in the whole history of the conquest Doña Marina (the name given to the beautiful slave at her Christian baptism) played an important part. Her son, Martin Cortez, a knight of the order of Santiago, was put to the torture in the time of Philip the Second on some unfounded suspicion of rebellion. It is said that when Cortez, accompanied by Doña Marina, went to Honduras, she met her guilty relatives, who, bathed in tears, threw themselves at her feet, fearful lest she might avenge herself for their cruel treatment, but that she calmed their

SCENE NEAR PUEBLA, STATE OF PUEBLA.

fears and received them with much kindness. The name of her birthplace was Painala, a village in the province of Coatzacoalcos. After the conquest she was married to a Spaniard, Juan de Jaramillo.

Quite important are the Metlaltoyuca colonization lands, which lie along the gulf slope on the Mesa de los Coroneles, a beautiful table-land nestling among the foot-hills toward the Gulf of Mexico. The journey there from Mexico City is most interesting, leading across deep chasms and beautiful valleys. Sometimes the road clings to the shoulder of the great mountain, with deep-mouthed chasms below and rough overhanging crags; sometimes it rushes suddenly into a lovely valley carpeted with Mexican flowers or gay with ruby coffee or tasselled corn. Wide fields of grain and coffee spread for miles along the sides of the road leading to the colony lands. Here and there are great forests with cedar, mahogany, ebony, rosewood, and rubber trees, and interlaced with rich tropical foliage and clinging parasites. Bright-winged birds and orchids of wonderful color light up the recesses of the forest, and groves of luscious oranges and lemons perfume the air. Shortly before the road reaches the outskirts of the Metlaltoyuca lands it crosses the Pantepec River, swiftly making its way to the gulf. The crystal waters reveal a pebbly bottom about sixty feet wide; and the entire stream forms one of the most beautiful rivers in Mexico.

On the outskirts of the Metlaltoyuca lands are some intensely interesting ruins, which offer a new field to the student of archæology. These are immense stone mounds, evidently built in a past so dim as to be beyond human record. In fact, tremendous forest-trees are deeply rooted in the ruins, showing that thousands of years may have elapsed since they were abandoned by a once mighty people. One wall, still in good preservation, bears witness to wonderful architecture and mechanical ability, as the stones hang together by the remarkable cement employed in those bygone times. Learned scientists have examined these ruins, and decided

PORTAL DE FLORES, PUEBLA.

them to be probably coeval with Egyptian if not Phœnician times. A curious thing is the fact that Indians may be seen even to-day offering worship around these mounds to their idols, and in some unfrequented spots may be found a little shrine to the Virgin Mary side by side with a hideous Aztec idol.

The prospects of this colony—American, by the way—are very bright. Extensive fields of grain may be seen here, the warm, moist climate being particularly well adapted to the raising of cereals. Coffee and rubber are also wonderfully productive, while the place is unusually healthy. Nature has been lavish in gifts to this region; the climate is delicious, the thermometer seldom going above ninety in the daytime, while double blankets are needed at night. The houses are of bamboo, comfortable and cool, although there is plenty of stone for more substantial buildings. Some of the houses have rosewood floors, and lovely gardens help to make the region home-like and pleasant. There is a spirit of association and friendship throughout the place, and in the centre of the colony is a small village of about three hundred inhabitants.

The raising of sugar-cane on Puebla plantations also offers great opportunities to the planters. Already some plantations turn out a sugar crop valued at one hundred thousand dollars per annum in refined white sugar. Of course, however, these plantations are equipped with modern machinery. Great profit is made also on the muscovado, or unrefined sugar. The Mexican cane is much richer than that of Cuba or Louisiana. Eighteen sugar refineries have been established in the following districts: six in Atlisco, six in Matamoras, two in Chiatla, and four in Tehuacan. There are many flour-mills, and eighteen cotton and wool factories. Thus it will be seen that the state of Puebla is full of the present-day enterprise.

Industry is animated in various branches and is being actively developed, particularly the textile manufactures; since the products of the numerous and well-equipped mills for weaving and spinning cotton and wool, scattered through the state, rival the foreign products, and are worthy of attention through their variety and excellence.

Commerce is very active, involving in its processes a value of fourteen million dollars, and the culmination of its operations is guaranteed by the complete abolition of duties, since there are no more domestic custom-houses. Merchandise circulates freely through the state, and the industrial establishments and mercantile houses are subject only to the payment of taxes, which has been advantageously substituted for the odious system of excise.

There are good hotels; the Jardin, in Puebla, is especially fine. The noted sulphur baths are in the suburbs. They are thronged with visitors from all parts of Mexico, who bathe in their health-giving waters.

It is in this city that we find the exquisite onyx carved and painted in the most artistic manner. The mines are situated in this state. Puebla is the "Lowell" of Mexico; the principal cotton factories are located here, all in successful operation.

The state of Puebla is noted for its system of public instruction. I have never seen finer schools in any country than those in the city of Puebla, where the German system of instruction is employed. To their democratic governor, General Mucio P. Martinez, Puebla owes one of its most important reforms,—the new law of elementary instruction, the wise provisions of which are perfecting primary education and elevating higher instruction to a plane commensurate with the latest achievements of science and the greatest educational attainments of the century. The result of this system of education will inevitably make the state of Puebla an invincible stronghold of liberty.

General Martinez was one of the ablest generals of the French war. His popularity has been proved by his having already served two terms as governor of the state, and under his enterprising and progressive administration Puebla has been raised to the rank of the second city in importance in the republic. Licenciado Agustin Fernandez, the Secretary of State, is an important factor in this administration. He is a man of great ability. The total number of inhabitants in the state is nine hundred and sixty-nine thousand one hundred and forty-three.

CHAPTER XIX

OAXACA

"THE STATE OF PATRIOTS" is the name by which Oaxaca is known to the hearts of those who love this beautiful part of Mexico. Pastoral scenes, stupendous mountains, riven cañons, swift dashing rivers, magnificent views, tropical foliage, and a range of temperature that rises from cool and bracing to hot and stifling, and settles back over the gradients again; a people not too much changed by contact with railroad civilization, which has disturbed their ancient repose but a few years; a city quaint and charming; ruins of races that vanished and left little behind, and an insight into the industry of coffee-raising that is attractive to the practical mind, are a few of the attractions of this wonderful state.

Everybody knows the influence which Oaxaca has exerted throughout the republic under the name of Diaz; just as great was that of Juarez, the inflexible native president, who led the resistance to Europe at the head of an army of patriots from Oaxaca and conquered in the struggle. From this state also came Señor Ignacio Mariscal, secretary of state, besides many others who have risen to prominent public positions throughout the country, so distinguished is Oaxaca for her talented scholars, her able financiers, her brave soldiers, and her wise politicians.

The hospitality of Oaxacans is well known. It is sufficient even now to knock at any door in that charming state to have it opened with offers of shelter, food, and friendliness, and all without money and without price. Until within a few years inns and hotels were unknown, the hospitality among the private houses doing away with the need of such accommodations. The friendship and affection of the Oaxacans for one another are proverbial. Social reunions are constantly held, and there is much gayety and light-heartedness in consequence.

SEÑOR GENERAL DON MARTIN GONZALEZ,
GOVERNOR OF OAXACA.

From its geographical position, geological formation, fuel and water, means of communication, and climate, the state of Oaxaca is a veritable paradise for the prospector and capitalist seeking investment in mining properties. Two vast mountain ranges traverse the state from north to south, whose peaks in many cases rise to an altitude of from ten to twelve thousand feet.

These mountain ranges, which are the culmination of the Rocky Mountains of the United States and the Sierra Madre of Southern Mexico, are highly mineralized throughout their length and breadth, the veins in some portions breaking through chlorite or argillaceous, and in others through a formation carrying gangue quartz or spar, with here and there a tremendous dike of igneous rock.

The principal metals found in these veins are gold, silver, copper, lead, and iron, either free or in various combinations with one another. The veins carrying free gold are those most extensively worked, and, although comparatively few mines have been opened up, those that have been are producing large quantities of exceedingly rich mineral. The Indians are working out the gold by hand in many districts, and are bringing into the city of Oaxaca monthly hundreds of ounces for sale. Gold in combination with other metals cannot be extracted by these Indians, and, as they are the only prospectors in the country, little attention is paid to copper, lead, and iron, and some classes of silver ores. A few small companies are working silver properties, the mineral from which, however, carries a fair percentage of gold, and the larger part of the ore from these properties is being shipped to Monterey smelters, a distance of eight hundred miles, or to Europe, for treatment. The whole state is practically an unexplored field, only a few districts having been superficially prospected. Within a few years we may expect to see Oaxaca one of the first metal-producing districts of the republic.

There are already located in the city of Oaxaca two agencies representing large ore-purchasing companies, which are taxed to their utmost capacity in sampling, assaying, and shipping. The finest Mexican onyx also comes from this state.

Oaxaca is a maritime state, lying between the Pacific Ocean and the states of Puebla and Vera Cruz, and, with Chiapas, extends farther south than any other in Mexico. Oaxaca has an area of twenty-seven thousand three hundred and eighty-nine square miles, with a fast increasing population. The great chain of the Mexican Andes crosses the state, giving it some of the most magnificent scenery in the entire republic. The mountains are divided into chains and ridges that give a surprisingly picturesque and beautiful variety to the country. The most remarkable summit is that of Zempoaltepec, in the district of Villalta, which rises to an elevation of ten thousand five hundred and forty-two feet, and from the top of which may be had magnificent views of the entire state, with broad glimpses of both the Atlantic and the Pacific Ocean. Other important peaks are the sierra of San Juan de Ozolotepec; Chicahaustla, in Teposcolula; Colcoyan, in Hanjanpam; Jilotepec, in Tlacolula; and Mijes, in Quetzaltepec. The three principal rivers are the Quiotepec, which rises north of Oaxaca City and, uniting with the Cosamaloapam, runs a course of one hundred and twenty miles; the Villalta, descending from the Zempoaltepec and emptying into the Pacific,

A BEAUTY OF TEHUANTEPEC.

THE BIG TREE AT TULA.

after running its course of one hundred miles; and the Atoyac, which rises near the capital and winds for one hundred and seventy miles before reaching its mouth.

The climate of Oaxaca is in general very salubrious, for, although it is nearer the equator than some other states, its high mountainous altitudes give it healthy breezes.

Besides her vast mining resources, the agricultural resources of Oaxaca are practically limitless. All the products of the temperate zone are raised in great abundance, while the more profitable ones of the torrid zone abound. The cacao raised here is equal to the best from Caraccas, while the annual yield of cochineal is over five hundred thousand pounds.

One of the chief products of the land is maize, which produces at the rate of four hundred to one. There are always two crops, and sometimes there are three, a year, the produce being sold on the spot at good prices, for it is one of the staple food-stuffs of the country; therefore there is no fear of over-production. The same may be said of beans, which are also a staple article of food. With the maize crop and the beans are planted bananas. They grow quickly, require little care, and bear in the first year. All these are very valuable products, and will support the colonists for the first few years, while the other crops are coffee, tobacco, cocoa, and oranges; but most of these, except tobacco, take a few years before they begin to yield. Cocoa is even more productive than coffee. The cultivation of fruit is a most profitable enterprise in Oaxaca. Since the destruction of the orange-groves in Florida by severe frost a few years ago, Oaxaca oranges have found an illimitable market in New York and other chief cities of the United States. Then there is the cultivation of various fibrous plants, such as the ramie and the sisal hemp. These products have raised the province of Yucatan from one of the poorest states to one of the richest. These plants require little or no care. Many, indeed, use them as hedges to divide the fields.

The Mexican government is anxious to encourage English colonists and English enterprise, and has given proof of its good will by granting several important favors and exemptions to colonists. Among these are exemption from taxation, whether federal or local, for a period of ten years; freedom from import duties for all goods, machinery, building material, clothing, and cattle coming into the country for the use of the colonists; and exemption for the same period from all military and municipal services.

An English colony in that part of Oaxaca cornering on Chiapas and Vera Cruz owns fifteen thousand acres of the finest land, selected on a spur of the Sierra Madre, near the important town of Suchil, close to the Tehuantepec Railway. The importance of this fact can scarcely be over-estimated. The railway, one hundred and thirty miles long, and connecting the Atlantic with the Pacific coast, was opened in 1894. Its traffic receipts, according to the British consul's reports, have already doubled. The Mexican government has determined to assist in developing this district by deepening and enlarging the port of Salina Cruz, on the Pacific side, and the port of Coatzacoalcos, the terminal point on the Mexican gulf. This property is well timbered, and is divided into lots of one hundred acres each, suitable for the cultivation of fruits, coffee, and tobacco. A new railroad has been surveyed, which will cross the rich coffee regions of Teutila, Jalapa de Diaz, and Textepec, and will be a great advantage to Villa Alta and Coapan, which undoubtedly are destined to become the richest coffee regions in the world, as they are superior to those of Uruapam. By this road the exportations from the state of Oaxaca to the Gulf of Mexico and any point on the Atlantic will be made three hundred kilometres shorter than by any other route. Several points of the state of Puebla will also be greatly benefited by the new railroad. From this it can readily be seen that the people of Oaxaca are waking up to the spirit of modern enterprise.

Although Oaxaca is practically an agricultural state, there are a great many manufactories, the more important being of soap, sugars, aguardiente, or cane-rum, beer, gunpowder, and palm-leaf hats. There are also flour-mills, salt-mills, tanneries, and cloth-factories. By the way, Mexican cotton-mills declare large dividends. It has been amply demonstrated that Mexican cotton prints can drive out European goods on the Pacific coast. Mexico on a silver basis and with cheap labor will parallel the manufacturing achievements of Japan.

The state of Oaxaca, and especially the valley of Oaxaca and its tributaries, are especially rich in subjects for research, and have never had the attention their importance demands. The city of Oaxaca is situated at the junction of three valleys, with high mountains surrounding it: the Etta valley extends to the northwest, the Flacololula valley lies nearly due east, while the

THE CATHEDRAL OF OAXACA.

principal or Oaxaca valley extends to the south. These valleys to-day support a population of nearly two hundred thousand people, which is probably not one-third of that which they had supported prior to the time of the conquest and for ages before, for here was the seat of the great Zapoteca empire, that had successfully defended itself against all invasions, and had never paid tribute or acknowledged allegiance to the great power of the Montezumas.

While its artisans were famous throughout Mexico at the time of the conquest, they had allowed many magnificent structures to fall to ruin, and even the traditions of some of their greatest works to be forgotten, or to be found only in the picture-records which had been preserved for centuries, but which were all destroyed during the Spanish conquest. Had these been preserved they would undoubtedly have been of inestimable value at the present day.

Six hours' ride from Oaxaca behind galloping mules brings one to the ruins of Mitla. There, as firmly and securely in place as they were on the day in which they were put in position, can be seen great stones eighteen feet long, six feet wide, and five feet thick. When the visitor has seen these walls, which have stood for centuries, and has witnessed the awkward efforts of the Indians of this generation as they pull and tug at a top block of onyx to get it on the cars, he is prepared to believe that these brown-skinned people of to-day have no knowledge of the ancients who built Mitla. There are no arches in this wonderful architecture of Mitla. Everything is square. In one of the courts of what is supposed to have been the temple is a row of columns. Each column is a single stone seven feet in circumference and twelve feet high.

At Oaxaca are collections of idols, grotesque and quaint, and strikingly similar to those which come from Egypt and India. These idols are dug from what appear to have been burial-places in the country round about Oaxaca. The Indians of the present find them and bring them into the city to sell. The places where these idols are found are walled with sun-dried brick. Presumably there were bodies of people buried there, but nothing remains but the little soapstone and limestone images, carved from blocks with the same straight lines that characterize the architecture of the ruined temple and the hieroglyphs. The ancient Mexicans left ruins of temples to astonish latter-day civilization. The modern Mexicans are giving demonstrations in a more practical direction.

RUINS OF THE TEMPLE OF MITLA.

The ruins of Mitla may be fairly classed with those of Yucatan and Honduras, the best in Central America. They cover many acres of ground, and are in every stage of destruction and decay. The hand of the vandal has done more to destroy them than the tooth of time.

Where vandalism has not disturbed them, the walls are perfect as when erected. Not in all the wall now remaining is there the slightest settling crack or mar from faulty construction. The thing that most attracts attention on coming in range is the perfect design of fretwork or moulding running through the whole structure, all formed by geometrical lines, the pattern being known as Grecian the world over. Some writers have called this work mosaic, but, while each and every member of this moulding or fretwork is cut from stone, and cut to fit the adjoining stone, all are set in the wall, fitting as perfectly as paper in a tablet, without mortar or cement. So well has the work been done that, after the lapse of centuries, it requires a close inspection to find the joints. The ruins contain a few columns of the most primitive order, with a slight diminish, but no sign of base or cap.

The buildings are very extensive, and are magnificent in the skill and art shown in their construction. They were so designed as to face a central square. They were not connected at the corners, but the centre court was protected by a wall of rock and mortar which filled the spaces. Each building had only three openings, all facing the court. There were no windows or other means of lighting the interior. The walls were made of a very tenacious adobe, veneered both within and without with finely cut stone laid in regular courses and interspersed with panels which are filled in with what may be denominated herring-bone work, in a profusion of patterns, each cut to fit its particular place, whether a square or a scroll, and the joints are so perfect that only the thinnest kind of cement could be used, if indeed any were used ; and to-day, after centuries of earthquakes, these joints are so perfect as to call forth the admiration of all who behold them. The lintels over the door-ways are each of one solid stone, and, with all our modern appliances and engineering skill, it would be considered a great triumph to

PALACE OF THE GOVERNOR.

place them in their position. It is therefore marvellous when we consider that the quarry from which these immense rocks were cut is on a mountain fifteen hundred feet above the valley and distant some five miles. They were brought this distance and elevated to their position by means unknown to us. Without doubt many underground rooms and passages exist. There is what appears to be a passage-way leading down to these subterranean chambers, and tradition says they extend for miles. At the west of these buildings there is a large adobe mound having a broad flight of cut-stone steps leading to the top. About half-way up is a platform. These steps are on the east side of the mound and face the principal buildings. Just across the creek to the south are the remains of several mounds, in the midst of which is a teocalli, which at one time had a broad walk winding around its sides until it reached the top. The walk is still to be seen in several places, although the greater part has fallen down.

Small mounds abound in the vicinity. Few works of art, such as vases, fragments of statues, and the like, have been found in this vicinity. Inside the ruins no iron is found, and no iron tools. Granite utensils, red copper axes and chisels, and fragments of pillars and architraves, have been found near Mitla.

Some two or three miles to the east, in the Hacienda de Zaaga, under a part of the house, an ancient tomb was discovered. We do not know what was found in it. In form it is a Latin cross. The arms of the cross are about nine feet long, the head eleven feet, and the entrance about nineteen feet. The width is four feet four inches, and the height five feet six inches. The

THE GREAT COTTON-MILLS OF OAXACA.

roof is formed of a large dressed stone, and the interior was at one time covered with cement. The walls are of finely dressed stone, and are ornamented with panels, like the buildings at Mitla. The Greek cross is used in ornamenting some of the panels.

Still farther east, and commanding the only pass through the mountain in this direction, is what seems to have been a fortification, with walls from twelve to twenty feet thick and about ten feet high. There seems to have been a terrace around the inside, of such height that a person standing upon it could see over the top. A little farther up the mountain is a magnificent tomb in the form of a perfect Greek cross, built of immense rocks, different from any other that I have ever seen. The whole interior is carved in relief, resembling the letter T. This tomb was probably never finished, as the roof is lacking, although several large stones lying near were evidently intended for this purpose; also, great stones are encountered in the direction of the quarry, which is on the opposite side of the mountain and over a mile distant.

The pretty town of Oaxaca, with straight, well-built streets, is two hundred and eighty-eight miles southeast of the capital of the republic, and nearly a mile above sea-level. It was founded in 1486, under the name of Huaxyacac, and fell under the Spanish rule in 1528. It has a rapidly increasing population of thirty thousand. The state library is there, and contains thirteen thousand volumes. The streets are regularly laid out, wide and spacious, and the houses are for the most part handsome and substantial, though largely of adobe. The principal buildings are the cathedral, the Santuario de la Soledad, and other churches and convents gorgeously decorated. There are, also, the *cabildo*, or city hall, the episcopal palace, the government buildings, and several handsome plazas embellished with flowers, trees, and fountains.

ANCIENT PILLARS AT MITLA.

The surrounding country is exceedingly picturesque, being literally covered with gardens and cochineal groves. The hospital at Oaxaca is one of the best in Mexico, and education is zealously promoted.

Oaxaca, old as it is, is extremely pleasant. Its houses are white, and on the balconies every day may be seen groups of young people, well dressed and cheerful, giving a festive air to the whole city. The government building is exceedingly beautiful, recalling those of the time of the viceroys. In the Plaza de Armas is a beautiful monument to the patriot Juarez, which is one of the most elegant in Mexico. The park of Guadalupe is very delightful, large and stately, with flowers and groves of beautiful trees, while the cathedral is one of the most striking features of the town. There are a great many schools in Oaxaca, including a scientific institute and a fine seminary. There are also an historical museum, a public library, and a branch of the National Bank of Mexico.

Probably the present condition of no Mexican city illustrates the early condition of all of them better than that of Oaxaca. It has been easily accessible for so short a period that its circumstances are essentially what they were before the railway was built. Through three centuries of its history it has grown as an interior town in the fullest sense of that term. It lies in one of the most beautiful and fertile valleys of Mexico, or rather at the meeting-point of three valleys. It is shut off from the ocean on the south by a solid range of mountains; it is separated from the cities of Central Mexico on the north by a mass of rough and broken country. The region of which it is the centre is a part of the world by itself, and the community which occupies it is practically a self-sufficing body of people. The population has grown so slowly through its long existence that it has learned to satisfy its wants as they have appeared by its own products. The hand-looms which have been used for generations are still in use.

TEMPLE OF LA SOLEDAD.

The pottery which the inhabitants of this region must have learned to make centuries ago is still made and turned to all conceivable uses, from cooking-stoves to children's toys. Articles made from the potter's clay serve most of the purposes of our articles of iron or tin or wood or brass. If you wish a bell, you will buy it of the potter. If you wish a whistle, you will buy it of the potter. If you wish tiles to cover the dome of the cathedral, you will buy them of the potter. Apparently simple materials are also made to serve a large number of ends. The maguey plant is a familiar instance of a single kind of material put to a multitude of uses. So skilfully, under the pressure of necessity, have the resources of this region been utilized, that if a wall of absolute exclusion were built along the ridge of the encircling mountains the life of the community would go on without noteworthy inconvenience to the bulk of the inhabitants. The well-cultivated cornfields would produce, as they do now, an abundant supply of the staple food. The flocks and herds would multiply as they do now, and their skins would be turned into sandals, shoes, and other articles of clothing. On the physical side there would be few wants unsatisfied. As now, few would be rich, and each would have something.

The condition of Oaxaca is typical of the condition of all Mexican towns that have grown up where they are by reason of their rich agricultural neighborhood. This condition of things is the basis of the remark by an engineer who has had great experience in locating railways in Mexico, that it is never worth while to go out of the way to reach a Mexican town, but quite worth a special effort to reach the great plantations. This would be permanently true if the towns were to remain as the railways find them. But they do not so remain. The coming of the railway means for the town a transformation of its life. And so the city of Oaxaca is rapidly growing and developing by contact with the outer world.

The Isthmus of Tehuantepec is that narrow neck of land in tropical Mexico which lies between parallels 18° and 16° N., dividing the Atlantic and Pacific waters. The shortest transcontinental railroad on this hemisphere (already referred to) is built there, and its trains run across in about six hours. It is the verdict of all who have been there that it is not only a magnificent and beautiful country, but has also the most delightful tropical climate they have ever been in. The railroad is destined in a very short time to be the most important little road in America. Twice the United States government spent a great deal of time and money making a survey across that neck of land with a view of cutting a canal, once in 1852, and again in 1871, when Captain Shufeldt, of the United States Navy, was sent with a large expedition to make surveys. Again, Captain Eads spent a great deal of time there on his plan to build a ship-railway. Now that the isthmus is opened up by a railway, which will soon be followed by steamship communication, that portion of Mexico, more than any other, will participate in the wonderful progress Mexico is now making.

The mountain scenery in the Isthmus of Tehuantepec, and the numerous beautiful rivers fringed with the perpetual green foliage of the tropical plants, with the interesting variety of birds and other game found there, the delightful climate all the year round, and the perpetual fresh breezes from the two oceans, will make that part of Mexico the most delightful section on this continent to live in. Besides the rich coffee plantations dotted all over the isthmus, you will see hundreds of elegant homes surrounded by magnificent flower-gardens, owned by people in this part of the country, who spend their winters here every year.

The Mexican Coffee Trading and Planting Company's plantation, so far, promises to be one of the largest and most important on the isthmus. The company own twenty thousand acres of land, situated on the banks of the now famous Coatzacoalcos River, and only about four miles from the Tehuantepec Railroad. They have already begun planting, and have one million five hundred thousand plants started in the nurseries.

The distance from Oaxaca to Tehuantepec is considerably less than from Puebla to Oaxaca. The railway connection when made will give this southern half of Mexico an outlet to the Pacific which is badly needed. It will also complete, with the link building beyond the isthmus, through rail connection between North and Central America. Down the cañons of the Rio Salado and De los Cues and up the cañon of Tornellin the builders pushed their way, solving some of the most difficult problems ever encountered in railroad construction. They not only tunnelled to get passage for the trains, but they bored the spurs of the mountains in three places to give the rivers new channels. The bare gray and brown and red cliffs tower two thousand feet above the track. Tourists journey across the United States for brief halfhours in cañon scenery; on this Mexican Southern the traveller rides half a day through awe-inspiring gorges. The train reels down and then staggers up grades which are only a fraction below the legal limit of four per cent. The route is through masses of rock; in some places the boulders are so poised that it seems as if slight jarring would dislodge them. The traveller, when the train starts down these curves, can look ahead and see the route and the stations an hour in advance of the schedule time.

The completion of the Tehuantepec Railway and its opening to traffic have not attracted as much attention as they deserve. The construction of the railway was a matter of national importance. It was carried out by the Mexican government at its own cost, by the advice of President Diaz, who recognized its strategic value.

President Diaz has distinguished himself as much in the council-chamber as upon the battle-field. After restoring peace and security to his country, he has especially studied its

STONE CARVING AT MITLA.

agricultural and industrial development. With this object he has encouraged the construction of railways in all parts of the country, by means of which produce may be carried to the best market.

Travel throughout the state is remarkably free from danger, and the officials, as well as the indigent natives, are uniformly kind and considerate in their treatment of strangers, gladly welcoming the investor, who, they know, in seeking to better his own condition cannot fail to better the condition of those with whom he is thrown in contact.

The state of Oaxaca is notable for having been the stronghold of the Mixtecas, a race of Indians who emigrated many centuries ago from the north and, displacing the Chochones, occupied the state, together with Puebla and Guerrero. They were an intelligent and progressive race, and were governed by independent chiefs. The Aztecs afterward subdued some of the Mixtecas, but those of Oaxaca remained independent, and many of them still are found in parts of the state. Their chief towns are Huajuapan, Yanhuistlan, Tlaxiaco, and Tepascolula. Remains of their former cities, temples, and fortresses show that they had considerable cultivation. They believed in a heaven, called Sosola, and had sacred caves in the mountains. Probably they had something to do with the original Mitla. They had a distinct language, with several dialects. A Mixtecan grammar was published in 1593, and there are still existing religious treatises printed in Mixtecan in the sixteenth and seventeenth centuries. The Mixtecans of to-day are intelligent, quiet citizens.

Not far from the city of Oaxaca is the big tree of Tula. It is one hundred and fifty-four and a half feet around six feet from the ground; at least I know it takes forty men to reach around it.

THE JUAREZ GARDEN.

It is of the cypress family, and must have been here long before Columbus touched Western shores. On the tree is a wooden tablet, placed there by Humboldt, the great German traveller.

My first visit to the city of Oaxaca was made when the journey had to be performed on horseback. While compiling the material for this book, I was taken there in a special car over the fine new track, and noted the most astonishing changes. Everywhere villages were springing up, and manufacturing industries showed the spread of modern enterprise. Besides the generous assistance of President Diaz, much of this progress is due to Governor Gonzalez. This official, General Martin Gonzalez, who is almost like a member of the president's family, is a gentleman of distinguished ability, competent in every way to lead Oaxaca toward the highest social, economical, and industrial plane.

CHAPTER XX

VERA CRUZ

ONE of the most important states of Mexico is Vera Cruz, which lies stretched along the eastern coast. It is traversed by the Sierra Madre, and is generally mountainous, except the sandy region, which is about thirty miles wide. The highest peak is Orizaba, seventeen thousand one hundred and seventy-six feet high, on the border of Puebla. The Cofre de Perote, near Jalapa, is fourteen thousand three hundred and nine feet high, and San Martin, or Tuxtla, nine thousand seven hundred and eight feet. All of these are volcanoes, and Orizaba is perpetually snow-capped. The principal rivers are the Panuco, Alvarado, and Coatzacoalcos, the mouths of which are obstructed by sand-bars. There are several large lagoons on the coast, of which Tamiagua is about sixty miles long and twenty miles broad. Alvarado, the largest in the south, is divided into smaller lagoons by many islands. The climate is hot on the coast, where yellow fever prevails from May to November, but in Jalapa, Córdoba, Orizaba, and other elevated places it is agreeable and healthful. The soil of the interior is very fertile, and produces, according to elevation, a vegetation ranging from tropical almost to arctic. Sugar is cultivated in all the eighteen cantons, coffee in fifteen, tobacco in fourteen, cacao in eleven, and vanilla in five. Cotton also is extensively cultivated, as well as the cereals and fruits. The coffee is very fine, and the tobacco is said to equal the Cuban. Cattle are raised in great numbers. Among the mineral products are gold, copper, lead, and iron.

Vera Cruz is divided into eighteen cantons,—Acayucan, Chicontepec, Coatepec, Córdoba, Cosamaloapan, Huatusco, Jalapa, Jalacingo, Minatitlan, Mizantla, Orizaba, Papantla, Tampico, Tantoyuca, Tuxpan, Tuxtla, Vera Cruz, and Zonzolica.

The city of Vera Cruz was built in a semicircle fronting the sea, and was formerly enclosed by a wall six feet high and three feet thick, and defended by two redoubts on shore and by the castle of San Juan de Ulua or Ulloa, which stands on an island of the same name about half a mile from the shore. The streets are regular and wide and form many squares, and some of those running east and west have a stream in the middle. The houses are strongly built of coral limestone in the old Spanish style, enclosing a square court with covered galleries. Most of the windows are furnished with iron gratings, and window-glass is not common. Among the principal buildings are the municipal palace, built in 1609, the custom-house, the provincial treasury, the commandant-general's office, and the old convent of San Francisco, the tower of which was fitted up as a light-house in 1872. In the same building is the public library, founded in 1870. There are also several churches, a theatre, a bull-ring, an exchange, a casino, three hospitals, and an artillery school. The harbor is an open roadstead between the city and the castle. A new mole was finished in 1873, but it is unapproachable during northers by any but small boats. On one of the bastions of San Juan de Ulua is a light-house, and on another a watch-tower. There are also a chapel and a cemetery on the island. Besides this island there are in the roadstead a small island called Verde and the Sacrificios and Blanquilla isles. Vera Cruz is the most important port of the republic. Its exports amount annually to about twenty-five million dollars, and its imports to twenty-six million dollars; of the latter, about two million dollars are from the United States. The chief exports are coffee, vanilla beans, hides, tobacco, cochineal, caoutchouc, jalap, fustic, and indigo. Vera Cruz is connected by railway with Mexico, with Medellin, and with Jalapa and Boca del Potrero, and by steamers with New York, New Orleans, the West Indies, and Europe.

The city of Villa Rica de Vera Cruz was founded by Cortez in 1519, a short distance north from the present site, but was abandoned in a few years for a position near the mouth of the Antigua, which was called Antigua Vera Cruz. About 1590 it was again removed to the present site and named Nueva Vera Cruz. Philip III. conferred on it the title and privileges of a city in 1615.

The castle of San Juan de Ulua, which was the last foothold of the Spaniards in Mexico, was surrendered by them to the patriots in 1825. In 1838 Vera Cruz was bombarded and taken by the French, and in 1847 by the Americans under General Scott. It was surrendered to the allied British, French, and Spanish squadron in December, 1861, and was restored to Mexico in 1867.

The name Villa Rica de Vera Cruz means "the rich town of the true cross," and Cortez chose it as signifying the union of spiritual and temporal interests. The sudden growth of the town under Cortez's direction reads almost like the marvellous upspringing of some of the "boom towns" in the Western United States to-day, except that the buildings were much more substantial. Cortez selected a "wide and fruitful plain" and pressed all his Indian allies into the building of Vera Cruz or Villa Rica. He laid out the circuit of its walls, the sites of fort, granary, town-house, temple, and other buildings.

SEÑOR GOBERNADOR DON TEODORO DEHESA.

The friendly Indians brought stone, wood, lime, and sun-dried bricks; and every man, including the great conqueror himself, labored with his own hands to construct this town, which was to be a magazine for stores, a retreat for the disabled, and the head-quarters in Mexico of the Spanish army. And so Vera Cruz was the first colony of New Spain.

The present city of Vera Cruz is not the same that was built by Cortez, known as the first European settlement ever made upon this continent,—that is to say, in the year 1519. The Villa Rica de Vera Cruz—the "rich town of the true cross"—which was settled by Cortez is distant about six miles from the present city. Vera Cruz is a pretty town, with broad and reasonably clean streets.

The present city of Vera Cruz is two hundred and sixty-three miles distant from the city of Mexico. The twenty-four thousand inhabitants are renowned for their culture, their frank and simple manners, and their patriotism, of the latter of which they have given many proofs during the various sieges which the town has sustained against foreign foes, thus justifying the appellation of "heroic" given to the town.

The cathedral in Vera Cruz is a Gothic building, with the same profusion of paintings and statuary that is to be found in all Mexican churches. There may be seen a wax figure of the Saviour in the tomb, life-size and singularly beautiful. There are three representations of the crucifixion, as large as life and of different shades of color, each retaining all the features and lineaments to which we are accustomed in the portraits of Christ, somewhat strangely combined

THE PORT OF VERA CRUZ.

with the peculiarities of the physiognomy of two of the three races that constitute the inhabitants of Vera Cruz. A very handsome custom-house has been erected on the mole at Vera Cruz. The material of which it is built was brought from Quincy, in Massachusetts, although there is stone equally good within ten miles of Vera Cruz.

Once Vera Cruz was encircled by a wall and was considered a strong place, but now it is defenceless. The grim old castle of San Juan de Ulua, just across the roadstead, is of no utility for defence or offence. It cost a vast sum, this island fortress, and it is said that Charles the Fifth, coming down once to the shore in distant Spain, stood with hand over his eyes to shade them and gazed across the ocean steadfastly for some moments. "What is your majesty looking at?" asked a courtier. And the king replied, "I am looking for San Juan de Ulua; it has cost me so many millions that it must needs be big enough to be discerned across the sea."

VERA CRUZ

The experience of three Mexican revolutions makes it easier to conceive the extent to which this unfortunate city must have suffered in the struggle made by the Spaniards to preserve the castle, their last bulwark on this continent. San Juan de Ulua remains a lasting memorial of the great works which, almost immediately after their arrival on these shores, were undertaken by the Spanish conquerors.

In 1582, sixty-one years after they had set foot on Aztec soil, they began this fortress in order to confirm their power. The centre of the space which it occupies is a small island, where the Spaniards under Juan de Grijalva arrived one year before Cortez reached the Mexican continent. Having found the remains of two human victims there, they asked the natives why they sacrificed men to their idols, and, receiving for answer that it was by order of the kings of Acolhua, the Spaniards gave the island the name of Ulua, by a natural corruption of that word. It is said that the fortress cost four millions; and though this statement is, no doubt, an exaggeration, the expense must have been very great, when we consider that its foundations are below the water, and that for nearly three centuries it has resisted all the force of the stormy waves that continually beat against it. Many improvements and additions were gradually made to the castle. In 1603, however, Vera Cruz was sacked by the roving corsair Nicholas Agramont, incited by one Lorencillo, who had been condemned to death for murder in Vera Cruz and had escaped to Jamaica. Seven millions of dollars were carried off, besides three hundred persons of both sexes, whom the pirates abandoned in the island of Sacrificios when they re-embarked.

In 1771 the viceroy, then the Marquis de la Croix, remitted a million and a half of dollars to the governor, in order that he might put the castle in a state of defence; and the strong bulwarks which still remain attest the

WATERFALL, BARRIO NUEVO.

labor that has been bestowed upon it. The outer polygon, which looks toward Vera Cruz, is three hundred yards in extent; to the north it is defended by another of two hundred yards; whilst a low battery is situated as a rear-guard in the bastion of Santiago, and on the opposite front is the battery of San Miguel. The whole fortress is composed of a stone which abounds in the neighboring island, a species of coral, excellent for building, *piedra mucara*.

In 1822 no stronghold of Spanish power remained but this castle, whose garrison was frequently reinforced by troops from Havana. Vera Cruz was then inhabited by wealthy and influential Spaniards. Santa Anna commanded in the province, under the orders of Echavarri, the captain-general, and with instructions from Iturbide relative to the taking of the castle. The commandant was the Spanish General Don José Davila. It was not, however, till the following year, when Lemaur succeeded Davila in the command of the citadel, that hostilities were begun by bombarding Vera Cruz. Men, women, and children then abandoned the city. The merchants went to Alvarado, twelve leagues off, whilst those who were driven from their houses by a shower of balls sought an asylum among the burning plains and miserable huts in the environs. Some made their way to Jalapa, thirty leagues off; others to Córdoba and Orizaba. With some interruptions, hostilities lasted two years, during which there was nearly

GOVERNOR'S PALACE AT JALAPA.

a constant firing from the city upon the castle and from the castle upon the city. On the 15th of September, 1824, the brave General Copinger, with the few troops that remained to him, marched out of the fortress, terminating the final struggle against the progress of revolution.

The castle is now a prison, and the most desperate offenders in Mexico are confined in the prison fortress: "twenty years at Ulua" is justly regarded as a death-sentence, as it seals the murderer's fate.

Vera Cruz changes but slowly, and one notes from year to year the disappearance of old landmarks. The wall of defence has mostly gone, and only one of the "spit-fire" batteries is left. Vera Cruz is doing a deal of business, however. It is a great port, and there is much rumbling to and fro of laden carts, much bustle on the piers, and all the enterprise and "hustle" of a modern progressive city.

The working people of Vera Cruz are a clean, well-fed lot. They earn far better pay than the workers of the table-land cities. The common laborer gets a dollar and a quarter a day, and a stevedore three dollars.

In coming down from Mexico—and many residents of the capital do come down between November and May—the passenger makes a descent of seven thousand three hundred feet in eleven hours, and finds the most picturesque scenery in the world, besides meeting a most sudden and absolute change in temperature. The train leaves Mexico in the morning; at Esperanza the wonderful scenery is seen about noon; this grows more and more picturesque until Paso del Machio is reached, forty-seven miles from Vera Cruz, and five hundred feet above the sea. Soon after leaving Esperanza you near the edge of the plateau, and the marvellous panoramas begin to pass before the delighted vision. The train turns and twists and crawls down a serpentine track along a terrace cut into the mountain-side. Thousands of feet below is the luxuriant valley of La Joya, and across are the encircling mountains, seemingly of green velvet cut into a ragged line against the blue and white horizon. As you speed along, the Scripture verse comes unbidden to the mind, "The mountains skipped like rams, and the little hills like lambs," so swiftly do they glide and disappear behind. Between Bota and the little village of Maltrata, which at first lies down below you, spread out in the lap of the valley like a checker-board, the train passes through an appalling number of curves and reverse curves, going a distance of five or six kilometres to make one. By and by you leave the valley of La Joya and enter the "Barranca del Infernillo," or "Little Hell." Here the road clings to a precipitous cliff hundreds of feet high, and over yawning chasms, across bridges above bottomless depths, or through tunnels that pierce rocky promontories and mountains. There are specially constructed engines to do all this, however, and they can climb this ascent on the way back at the rate of two thousand five hundred feet an hour, while they descend in perfect safety. This ravine opens into the valley of Orizaba and leads to the city of the same name. Its low, squatty dwellings, quaint churches, and picturesque mills, its wealth of orchards and brilliant foliage, and the noted cascades of the Rincon Grande and Barrio Nuevo, all help to make this one of the most beautiful spots in the world. The remainder of the distance is a veritable paradise. The air is perfumed with sweet-scented blossoms and enlivened by song-birds of brilliant hue, while the scenery and foliage keep the traveller dazzled with the richest tropical views,—with reds and yellows, blues and greens, lichens and mosses, ferns and orchids, each outdoing the other in vivid color-glory. Coffee plantations speckled with scarlet hibiscus succeed the sugar groves, and over all the glistening silver peak of Orizaba keeps watch and ward.

Throughout the city of Vera Cruz the stranger finds something enchanting and unreal in the different streets, with their innumerable balconies and fluttering awnings. During the hot afternoon one looks in vain for any sign of life in the great stone houses with their many windows and with their heavy draperies lazily waving in the soft breeze. Behind those walls the women are sleeping the long after-dinner siesta, and the black eyes that will flash in the plaza at evening are closed beneath long languorous lashes. The city is still; no hum of traffic greets the ear. The long rest-time has cast its spell over everybody, and there is nothing to do but go and lie down to dream of the ships, the bearded captains, and the grim castle; of the far-distant days of romance when Cortez and his men in armor first saw this strange land; and even farther back than that, when the Toltecs and Aztecs had things all their own way; and then Vera Cruz seems hoary with antiquity, and the creatures of to-day naught but mere incidents in the great scroll of history.

CASCADE OF RINCON GRANDE.

The surface of the state rises gradually from the Gulf coast to the Cordilleras, forming a series of delightfully terraced hills, whose scenery is everywhere picturesque and exuberant, while the vegetation is luxuriant in the extreme. The mountain streams, especially, are enchantingly picturesque as they rush down to the valleys, there to become peaceful gliding rivers.

One of the finest pieces of engineering work in this country is the Metlac bridge, across the river of the same name, and erected by the Mexican Railway.

Nowhere in Mexico is there a more beautiful spot than the city of Jalapa. When the atmosphere is clear, one can see the shipping in the harbor of Vera Cruz with an ordinary spy-glass and the white caps of the waves with the naked eye. The elevation of Jalapa above the sea is a little more than four thousand feet. It is situated on a shelf of the mountain, the summit of which at Perote, a distance in a direct line of about twenty miles, is four thousand five hundred feet higher than Jalapa.

HACIENDA OF SAN ANTONIO, IN VERA CRUZ.

The whole horizon, except in the direction of Vera Cruz, is bounded by mountains,—among them Orizaba, which is distant from Jalapa about twenty-five miles, though, owing to the remarkable clearness of the atmosphere and the sun shining upon the snow with which it is always covered, it does not seem to be five miles. All the tropical fruits grow there, and are cultivated with great care and skill. It is not exaggeration to say that it is impossible for one who has not been on the table-land of Mexico to conceive of a climate so elysian. There is not a day, and scarcely an hour, in the year when one could say, "I wish it were a little warmer, or a little cooler." It is never warm enough to make you pull off your coat, and rarely cool enough to button it.

Perote is thirty-five miles from Jalapa, and is eight thousand five hundred feet above the sea-level. This name was made familiar to American readers as the place of confinement of the Texan prisoners and of General Santa Anna himself. Its great elevation and the vicinity of the mountain of Orizaba make the climate uncomfortably cold at night. It has a very large and strong military fortress.

English merchants and other inhabitants of Vera Cruz go to live in or near Jalapa during the reign of the *vómito*. There are some old churches, a very old convent of Franciscan monks, and a well-supplied market-place. Everywhere there are flowers,—roses creeping over the old walls, Indian girls making green garlands for the Virgin and saints, flowers in the shops, flowers at the windows; and, above all, everywhere there is one of the most splendid mountain views in the world.

The Cofre de Perote, with its dark pine forests and its gigantic chest (a rock of porphyry which takes that form), and the still loftier snow-white peak of Orizaba, tower above all the others, seeming like the colossal guardians of the land. The intervening mountains, the dark cliffs and fertile plains, the thick woods of lofty trees clothing the hills and the valleys, a glimpse of the distant ocean, the surrounding lanes shaded by fruit-trees, aloes, bananas, and chirimoyas, mingled with the green liquidambar, the flowering myrtle, and hundreds of plants and shrubs and flowers of every color and of delicious fragrance, all combine to form one of the most varied and beautiful scenes that the eye can behold.

Then Jalapa itself, so old and gray and rose-covered, with echoes of music issuing from every door and window, and its soft and agreeable temperature, presents, even in a few hours, a series of agreeable impressions not easily effaced.

Jalapa is indeed a rare old place. It seems to be built on edge, with streets like stairs climbing the hills, while terraced houses cling to the hill-sides. Nevertheless, Jalapa with her twenty thousand people has acquired considerable importance as a market for coffee, cotton, and other staples. Indeed, this is so true that the railway line between Puebla and Jalapa and Vera Cruz is not sufficient as a means of communication with the outside world, and an electric railway is being put in.

In the Jalapa canton are some of the most picturesque places in the republic. The Actopan River in its volcanic bed, the crystal Jalancingo, and the Znacinco wind along under arches of noble forest-trees toward the Gulf. The cascades of Orduna and Calichal hang like

PARK AND THEATRE IN ORIZABA.

curtains of light against a great cañon, and the quaint towns of Coatepec and Misantla, with reminiscences of Victoria, are some of the salient features of the landscape. The ride from Coatepec, over a narrow mountain pathway up to Jalapa, curtained in clouds, is a wild one, and almost persuades the traveller that an electric road would be a modern miracle. Electricity in this oldest and quaintest of regions seems like the wand of amber with which the ancient Greeks used to perform feats of magic.

Jalapa itself is a curious place, very ancient and yet very modern. It is like an old man who has found the elixir of life and imbibed the strength of youth with all the ambitions and force of manhood. Tradition makes it a town away back before the period of the Aztec. It is certain that Cortez stayed there the second night of his famous march from the sea.

After this the Franciscans built a great monastery and established a new religious life. In those days the market at Jalapa was known throughout Mexico. When the republic was formed Jalapa was raised to a new dignity, and was made the capital of Vera Cruz; but as the activity increased along the sea-coast the industries of Jalapa declined, until it became merely a picturesque village among the hills. With the railroad and modern speculators Jalapa underwent another change. New factories sprang up, stores and markets were opened, and agricultural interests assumed a new phase of activity. Quaint, old-fashioned Jalapa has awakened from a two hundred years' sleep and become suddenly a city of manufacturing importance. The factories give employment to more than a thousand people, and old-time thrift has mingled with modern prosperity.

MUNICIPAL PALACE AT CORDOBA.

Jalapa became the seat of a fair in the eighteenth century, which was intended to hold the same relation to the trade between Spain and Mexico that the great fair at Porto Bello, on the isthmus, held to the trade between Spain and South America. In order to avoid the effects of the unwholesome climate of the coast, goods arriving at Vera Cruz were transported to Jalapa, to be there exchanged for Mexican products destined to be exported to Spain. Jalapa was chosen for this purpose, although an inland town, because of its agreeableness and healthfulness as a place of residence. It is sufficiently warm to permit many tropical plants to thrive, and, as it is favored with rain at all seasons, the neighboring valleys and hillsides are perpetually fresh and green. From the plaza, where one has the higher part of the town above him and overlooks the lower part and the broken country in the distance, the world appears a very beautiful place. Although great wealth is produced on the coffee plantations not far away, Jalapa still figures as a resort for pleasure and a place of waiting till the ships go out. And in this character it is becoming more conspicuous since the completion of the Interoceanic Railway from Mexico to Vera Cruz, which, in descending from the table-land to the coast, passes through Jalapa.

Orizaba is another charming city, which claims to have been admired by Cortez. At least, he stopped here on his march to the city of Mexico, leaving a small force behind him. Lucky was it for them that Sandoval came along with more soldiers soon after, or Cortez's garrison would have been murdered. It was not a new town even then. The old church of Santa Teresa dates back to 1564. This church still stands, but is unused, a new one having supplanted it; but it forms a most picturesque old ruin, such as Mexico abounds in. Maximilian, too, favored Orizaba, and used often to resort here. It is still a favorite watering-place for inhabitants of Puebla, Jalapa, Vera Cruz, and Mexico.

It is a flourishing city, too, numbering over fifty thousand inhabitants. From several points within its limits may be seen the snowy glistening peak of Orizaba; and the Orizaba River runs through the town, its rocky banks gay with tropical flowers and fruits. The city is surrounded with mountains, the chief of which, next to its patron saint, is Cerro de la Escamela. The city is set like a jewel in a charming valley in the midst of these mountains, and is everywhere surrounded with coffee and sugar plantations and other luxuriant tropical vegetation. With its exceptional situation and delightful climate, no more desirable place can be found in Mexico.

Orizaba, like Jalapa, lies about midway between the two extremes of the coast and the plateau, but in most other respects the two towns stand in sharp contrast with each other. At Jalapa the view ranges over a wide extent of hills and valleys; at Orizaba it is limited by the closely surrounding mountains. Jalapa has a number of important industries, but Orizaba is one of the busiest manufacturing towns of Mexico. Its cotton- and jute-mills employ a large number of laborers. Lying on the line of the oldest railway in the country, not far from Vera Cruz, and with easy access to the interior cities, it has unusual facilities for obtaining imported raw material and for reaching markets for its finished products. The rapid stream which passes through the valley furnishes adequate water-power, and in this lies one of its special advantages as a manufacturing town.

DRYING COFFEE.

The town of Coatzacoalcos, at the mouth of the Coatzacoalcos River, is one of the few places that look like an American town. The port of Coatzacoalcos is destined to be the principal one on the Gulf coast. It is a natural and safe harbor for vessels of large tonnage; the water is from four to seven fathoms, with plenty of room for large vessels. The place is growing rapidly, especially since the Tehuantepec Railroad has been built across the isthmus.

The large dry-dock to accommodate vessels of fifteen hundred tons' capacity, for the Mexican government, at Tlacotalpan, is located on the Papaloapan River, in the southern part of the state. This river is of sufficient depth to permit of large ocean vessels navigating its waters, and a steamship line has been inaugurated to carry freight and passengers to Tlacotalpan. This city is picturesquely located, and is the general distributing point for a surrounding country of many miles in radius.

Heretofore the war-ships of Mexico have been obliged to go into dry-dock for cleaning, scraping, and general repairs in some foreign port. But the Mexican government decided to have this done in the future within its own jurisdiction. The dry-dock will possess all modern and latest devices for both convenience and safety of vessels. The foundation is to be of concrete, while every stick of timber and piece of iron or steel used in its construction will possess durability and utility fully proved by tests.

COFFEE RANCH IN VERA CRUZ.

Tuxpam is beautifully situated on the river a few miles above the coast. The vegetation all around is of the most luxuriant sort, and the city has a growing population of several thousand.

The state of Vera Cruz possesses a sufficient diversity of climate and scenery to suit every taste except that which inclines to the wholly frigid. It has ample resources to meet every reasonable want of mankind of high or low degree. It affords the widest scope for the energy and skill of the manufacturer and the merchant, the stockman, the planter, and the navigator. It is a most inviting field for the lumberman, the fisherman, the fruit-grower, the market-gardener, and the dairyman. It is easy to realize, after the study of the unique physical characteristics of this section, that the true lover of that which is grand and beautiful in nature will here find much to admire.

In Tuxtla's woods and waters are game and fish resources adequate to the wants of a nation of sportsmen and epicures. That eminent American naturalist Professor Nelson says, "The most unexpected and striking impression received by a stranger visiting Tuxtla is that produced by the remarkable varied beauties of the scenery." He next notes the richness of the soil and the great agricultural possibilities of the district, and wonders at the vast amount of uncultivated land lying in a state of virgin freshness awaiting the coming of tillers to yield an abundant harvest. Going to and from any of these places one is constantly passing through landscapes worthy of the painter's brush, so full are they of charming interest.

The state of Vera Cruz is rapidly gaining fame for the variety, beauty, and sublimity of its scenic attractions, as well as for the fertility of its soil. Few regions present greater attractions to tourists, pleasure-seekers, and lovers of the picturesque and sublime in nature. Capitalists can hardly make a mistake by investing their money either in real estate, transportation lines, or manufactories. Tobacco has been for many years the king crop in Tuxtla County, while coffee, sugar, vanilla, cacao, bananas, cocoanuts, rice, rubber, corn, pineapples, and beans have been successfully cultivated for generations, large quantities of coffee being exported yearly. One cannot ride in any direction without seeing forests of valuable timber, composed principally of fine cabinet woods, such as cedar, mahogany, laurel, rosewood, ebony, chicozapote, chagani, jonote, gateado, lignum-vitæ, etc.

In the county of Tuxtla alone there are many villages ranging in population from one thousand to eight thousand souls. Good business houses are to be found. Schools in which English is taught, churches, two telegraph lines, post-offices and daily mail service to the larger towns, also telephone service to the smaller ones and to private haciendas, are among the many advantages of this county. Thousands of acres of land are cut up into small tracts and owned by the poor people or Indians of the county.

A greater combination of natural advantages, suitable either for the capitalist or for the sportsman or the angler coming from the frozen northern regions to pass the dreary winter months, does not exist on the American continent. The altitude and the salt breezes from the Gulf combined prevent malaria and produce a remarkably cool and health-giving air.

Rubber-trees produce, in Tuxtla County, in seven years after planting the seed. Cacao and vanilla, pineapples and bananas, grow in profusion. Cocoanut-trees have a vigorous growth, and attain a great age, up to an altitude of twelve hundred feet above sea-level. In the plaza of San Andres there is a tree seventy-five feet high that is said to be one hundred years old. Cocoanut-trees produce in six years from the time of planting.

The group of mountains in Tuxtla County constitute the only high headland bordering the Gulf from Florida to Yucatan; hence its healthful conditions over any Gulf region.

The connecting of Tampico and Tuxpam by the lagoon of Tamiahua also opens up a great section of fertile country. The country around the lagoon and around Tuxpam has a population of many thousands, and they would cultivate large areas of land and produce many things for export if there were regular facilities for shipment. Bananas, oranges, lemons, limes, pineapples, and many other things that require certain, regular, and rapid transportation, can be produced as easily, surely, and profitably there as in any other part of the world. Coffee, sugar, tobacco, and corn grow to perfection. Coffee-trees are as easily raised as peach- or apple-trees, and the crop is sure every year when bearing age is attained, at four or five years from planting, and will give an annual average profit of fifty dollars per acre.

ALAMEDA IN VERA CRUZ.

No irrigation is required; the rainfall is sufficient, together with the humidity of the sea-breezes, to keep vegetation green and growing constantly. Bananas and pineapples grow as well about Tuxpam as they do in Jamaica and Honduras. Tuxpam has the advantage over those places of being three days nearer the United States markets by sea, via Tampico, while from Tampico there is a direct rail line to the northern cities, thus insuring quick transit.

Vera Cruz will always be a port of consequence and a great gateway of commerce. It is the natural outlet of a fertile agricultural region, and must share in the prosperity of the export trade. The competition of Tampico is already felt in tonnage, and it is likely that the more northern port is already abreast in that particular of the City of the True Cross, for the growth of Tampico has been very rapid during the past few years. A friendly rivalry between the two ports, which are chief among the trading points of the Gulf coast, and between the railways using them as termini, will do no harm, for there is business enough in modern Mexico for both.

Physicians continue to send anæmic and debilitated patients to the coast, and for one who has too long lived in the dry and over-stimulating table-land climate a change to the sea-shore is most beneficial. There one breathes easily and the denser air is more heavily charged with oxygen. The change observable in a nervous invalid is immediate, for color comes back at once to the pale cheeks and whitened lips of the anæmic. The sea-breeze is nature's own tonic, never improved upon by the art of the drug compounder. There is so much to see and enjoy in Vera Cruz that for the table-land-dweller it is a complete novelty; and the invalid from the sea plateau finds in the sight of the sea and the ships a novel distraction, contributing to the restoration of nervous poise.

The state of Vera Cruz has an accomplished and popular executive head in Señor Don Teodoro A. Dehesa, to whose ability is owing much of the present progress of the place.

CHAPTER XXI

TAMAULIPAS

AT the extreme northeast of the state of Vera Cruz one crosses the Panuco River to Tampico, a rival port of Vera Cruz City. This is a convenient port for handling heavy tonnage, and, consequently, Tampico is fast becoming one of the most important towns in Mexico. It is in the state of Tamaulipas, and was originally named "Santa Ana de Tamaulipas." This state has several ports, but they are mostly encumbered with bars that hinder navigation.

Tamaulipas extends from Vera Cruz to the Rio Grande del Norte, which divides it from Texas. It has an area of twenty-eight thousand six hundred and fifty-nine square miles and a population considerably above one hundred thousand. The coast is low and sandy, and there are several lagoons along the shore, the largest of which—Laguna Madre—is over one hundred miles long, and in some parts over twenty miles wide.

The principal rivers of this state are the Fernando, or Tigre, Borbón, Santander, and Tampico. In the northern part the flat coastlands extend inward for many miles and then rise to elevated plains; in the south the country is diversified by many mountains and valleys, and the scenery is very picturesque. There are rich silver- and copper-mines, which promise great and undiscovered wealth, in these directions. Valuable timber abounds on the mountains, and, as the soil is very fertile, all the fruits, grains, and vegetables of the temperate and torrid zones are easily raised. This is also an excellent state for stock-raising of all kinds.

The chief towns are Ciudad Victoria, the capital of Tamaulipas, Matamoras, and Tampico. The latter town is built on rising ground, with wide streets crossing at right angles. The houses are mostly of stone. There are several churches, a custom-house, hospitals, a prison, good schools, and a number of monuments.

SEÑOR LIC. GUADALUPE MAINERO,
GOVERNOR OF TAMAULIPAS.

It was at Tampico that Americus Vespucius, the Italian navigator, first landed on this continent; and it was probably the harbor afforded by the mouth of the Rio Panuco that attracted the Spaniards who were cruising around the Gulf of Mexico in 1497, seeking for new worlds to conquer. Vespucius left a record of a famous game dinner which he enjoyed at Lariab, as the port was then called. This was four hundred years ago, and still the country around Tampico is a sportsman's paradise. When this queer ship landed and the first Europeans stood on American shores, the bold navigator at the head of the little group of men could hardly have expected that so great a country would commemorate his name.

Tampico is built upon a rocky bluff forty feet high, surrounded by lagoons of salt water. The town has about six thousand inhabitants, and connects with the various boat-landings by means of stone steps, in true Venetian style. The architecture of Tampico is more American than most Mexican towns display, owing, doubtless, to its ready communication with New Orleans and other northern ports. The houses are built of both wood and stone, with sloping roofs and outer verandas. Color prevails everywhere, the houses being painted in blues and yellows, each street looking fresh, bright, and clean, and especially so the brilliant façades clustering about the plaza. The latter is a densely shaded park paved with granite and provided with seats free to rich and poor, traveller and home-keeper alike. No flowers grow in this plaza, but the householders around it seem to vie with one another in window and veranda gardening. One house will have balconies on the street front with rows of blossoming orchids and amaryllis along the walls; another house will be covered with vines; and so on around the brilliant façade. Just out of Tampico may be found thousands of orchids growing wild, hanging thick on the seaward side of the rocks, where the tropical sun and perpetual moisture give them a most luxurious growth.

The market-place forms one of the most interesting features of Tampico. The pavement of the square is provided with holes, into which are thrust the long handles of the odd-looking umbrellas made by the natives. Under their shadows on market-days may be seen men, women, and children squatting beside plaited palm mats, upon which their wares are spread. These include, besides chile, the universal Mexican condiment, tiny earthenware jugs of honey neatly covered with a bit of corn-husk tied with maguey fibre, fans and beads, birds and onions, artistically carved wooden implements for household purposes, and everywhere bunches and heaps of marigolds.

Then there is a wonderful old church, with ancient wood-carving and frescoes by Spanish artists. It is a strange mixture of old and new that the traveller meets at every turn in Tampico; but the wonderful jetties built out from the mouth of the Panuco seven thousand feet into the Gulf are perhaps the most interesting of all. These jetties have great banks of stone with easy slopes and rounded tops, like those at the mouth of the Maas in Holland. The sand-bar which once obstructed this harbor has entirely disappeared, and now the inland harbor of Tampico is one of the most important on the American continent. The cost of these improvements was over three millions of dollars, borne largely by the federal government and the Mexican Central Railway.

Thus there has been opened to Mexican shipping an inland harbor on the eastern coast, free from the storms which make the roadstead of Vera Cruz sometimes inconvenient and dangerous. And the new port of Tampico has already regular lines of steamers connecting it with New York, Mobile, Havana, and European ports. While this is the first inland port that has been opened on the eastern coast of Mexico, the western shore has good harbors; and by the Mexican Gulf Railway running northwestward to Monterey, and the branch of the Mexican

Central which runs through San Luis Potosi, the port of Tampico is brought into immediate communication with the great internal system of Mexican railways.

Tampico is the strong rival of Vera Cruz, which long had a practical monopoly of Mexico's external trade toward the east. The New York and Cuba Mail Steamship Company's line of steamers make direct weekly sailings between New York and Tampico.

The lands in the neighborhood of Tampico for a distance of several hundred miles are unsurpassed in fertility. A few hours' ride from the city brings the traveller into a great plain covered with a dense wood. All over this plain are scattered hundreds of flat-topped mounds, some moated and some with sides of stone slabs. It is supposed that these mounds were once

MARKET AT TAMPICO.

the foundations of houses of reeds or bark, of which all traces have utterly disappeared. Small vestiges of pottery and a few pieces of stone carving have been found in this wilderness, leading archæologists to locate here a prehistoric race allied to the Mayas.

Aside from the commercial importance of Tampico, it is a popular beach-resort. The Gulf beach, several miles in extent, affords an opportunity for surf-bathing second to none on the Atlantic coast, and this, too, for every day in the year. As a resort this place offers special inducement for the erection of a modern American sea-side hotel, with the particular advantage that such a hotel would be remunerative all the year round.

Aside from the surf-bathing, Tampico is an ideal hunting and fishing resort. This is the home of the tarpon, as well as of almost all varieties of salt- and fresh-water fish. Seven miles out on the Gulf are the banks of the red snapper. The lakes and rivers in the vicinity are, during the winter months, literally covered with ducks, geese, swans, flamingoes, etc. In the mountains, thirteen miles back from Tampico, are found deer, turkeys, pheasants, and wild hogs in abundance. Mountain lions and tigers also exist. Tampico offers exceptional inducements to the health- and pleasure-seeker.

Between Villar and Tampico the mountains, foot-hills, and plains along the coast are teeming with game. Alligators and manati may be seen on the river banks, and, in fact, this section is a paradise for the canoeist or the camper-out.

The wharf and custom-house facilities at Tampico have assumed large proportions. Tampico has the most modern conveniences for the handling and discharge of cargoes, making the port second to none on the North American continent in economic handling and quick despatch of merchandise.

The regions whose outlet to tide-water is through the port of Tampico are among the most pleasant sections on the face of the globe. Here coffee does better than in any other part of Mexico, and better, some contend, than anywhere else in the world. There are navigable rivers to Tampico, land transportation, and the railroad. Here, besides, are a beautiful climate, plenty of rainfall, an abundance of good labor at low prices, and all the conditions which make successful and profitable agricultural ventures.

LANDING AT TAMPICO.

There is not a more favored section on the American continent for the successful cultivation of sugar-cane than that along the railroad between Monterey and Tampico. The acreage in sugar-cane is being constantly increased, and extensive sugar-refineries are springing up at all principal points, in which are used the latest improved sugar machinery and the most modern methods. Primitive methods of refining are still in use extensively, but it will not be many years before the great bulk of the business will be done at the modern refineries.

The ribbon cane is the most profitable crop now grown in this district. From Tampico to Monterey, whenever a hacienda comes in view, may be seen the fields of graceful cane. In the lower country it grows to a gigantic size, often fifteen feet high ; everywhere it averages eight or nine feet in height and an inch and a half through. For cane culture the perennial summer of Tamaulipas is auspicious. The plant becomes also perennial. It is common, however, to replant once in seven years, as better results are secured. One crop is harvested annually. It matures in the fall, when the peons strip off the leaves, and, cutting the stalks with *machetes*, or heavy knives, carry them on two-wheel ox-carts to the plantation mill. This consists of cast-iron rollers geared together and driven by a mule. The juice pressed by the rollers escapes into shallow open vats or pans, where it is neutralized with lime-water and evaporated in the air. The thick black syrup is poured into earthenware moulds and permitted to cool. The sugar thus made is known as *piloncillo*. For market, the tapering cylinders, each some six inches long and three inches in the larger diameter, are wrapped in dried cane leaves and packed, one hundred and fifty pounds together, in a square sack of coarse matting. The great bulk of the sugar of Tamaulipas is this dark pilon sugar and molasses. The refinery at Linares makes one hundred and ninety tons or so of excellent white, granulated sugar in a year, so that it is no longer necessary for each farmer to put in his own mill and evaporator.

During the civil war in the United States, 1861–1865, Tamaulipas made a handsome income by raising cotton and exporting it to that country. Many farmers became rich in that way; but when the war was over, and cotton fell in price with the return of peace and the revival of the Southern States, the production declined. There is no reason, how-

THE LIBERTY SQUARE, TAMPICO.

ever, why Tamaulipas should not grow cotton as abundantly as the state of Vera Cruz, which has an annual production approximating twenty-five million pounds, with prospects of extension.

Matamoras is a frontier city of Tamaulipas, being only forty miles from the mouth of the Rio Grande, and directly opposite the city of Brownsville, Texas. It has a population of over twelve thousand, made up mostly of Americans and people of Spanish descent. English is commonly spoken. The city is finely situated on a bend of the river. Its wide streets cross at right angles, and the houses are mostly of brick and built in modern style. There is a beautiful cathedral, as well as numerous churches and convents. There is a good public school system, besides plenty of private schools. The climate is hot from April to September, and cool from December to March. Matamoras was founded early in the present century, and was named after the great patriot, Mariano Matamoros, whose bones lie with those of Hidalgo and Morelos in the cathedral at Mexico City.

Laredo is a name by which a line of *condes* of Spain was called. One figured under the Duke of Bexar in his campaign on the Levant, proving himself an able and gallant general, and it is probable the town was named in honor of him, whether on account of the Sanchez family, one of whom founded it, being descended from this gallant general, *conde* and grandee of Spain, or directly in memory of the *conde*, is not certainly known.

Captain Sanchez came from the Alamo on the Salado River with a number of families in search of a place to settle, and, being dissatisfied with the place on the Nueces, he obtained permission to locate, and remained several years before his little settlement was formally recognized as a town, in 1767.

PLAZA, TAMPICO.

The royal commission, called "Visita General," in that year laid out the town, giving it four leagues of land,—two on each side of the Rio Grande,—and laid off above and below the town tract, on both sides, the tracts now called *porciones*, distributing them to the settlers. Since that time Laredo has been recognized as a town with municipal powers. In the earlier days of its existence, savage Indians continually committed depredations on the surrounding country, and robbed the people of their horses and cattle; but the citizens, inured to such hardships, often chastised the savages and killed many of them in battle, always maintaining a justly merited reputation for skill, courage, and gallantry. Laredo was a kind of supply station during the Texas revolution, but took no very active part in the war. It remained under the control of Mexico, as a part of Tamaulipas, until 1846, when it was divided into two towns. Nuevo Laredo, on the Mexican side, remaining a quiet, progressive town, whose principal industry has been stock-raising, horses, cattle, and sheep; and several handsome fortunes have been made in it.

While we were in Tamaulipas, Señor Don Alejandro Prieto was the governor, and extended to us many courtesies. To his wisdom and activity the state owes a fine penitentiary, a beautiful government palace, and many other substantial improvements. His term having expired since then, Señor Guadalupe Mainero is now governor of Tamaulipas, and is carrying on with great ability the excellent system of government to which he has succeeded.

The Tamaulipan Mexicans are brave, daring patriots, who are zealous to a man for the integrity and independence of their country. This state was the nucleus of the heroic army of the north during the French campaign, and the stoic bravery of the Tamaulipan soldiers will never be forgotten in the history of the siege and fall of Querétaro; many of their illustrious names will ever stand for the bravest and most inflexible of patriots.

CHAPTER XXII

NUEVO LEÓN

NUEVO LEÓN is an inland state, bordering on Tamaulipas, Coahuila, and San Luis Potosí. It has an area of about fifteen thousand square miles, and a population of about three hundred thousand. Its surface is irregular, as several branches of the Sierra Madre range come into it, and about one-fourth of the state forms a part of the great central table-land of Mexico. Its extensive and beautiful valleys are divided between forest, pasture-land, and cultivated fields, which are intersected by numerous and precipitous rivers and streams. Among the larger of the rivers are the Salado, forming a boundary between Nuevo León and Coahuila, the Sabinas, Salinas, Santa Catalina, San Juan, Ramos, Pilon, Linares, and Blanco, besides which are numberless mountain streams and several small lakes, so that the state is exceedingly well watered.

Mineral productions abound in the mountains, and include gold, silver, copper, lead, iron, and cinnabar. Sulphur, nitrate of potash, several varieties of sulphate of lime, alabaster, and marble are also found, while salt is very abundant. Sulphur and thermal springs abound, especially near Monterey and Morelos.

The climate is hot and humid in the lowlands and some of the valleys, temperate in the elevated regions, and varied in the hill-regions. The soil is fertile, and yields three crops a year of maize, sugar-cane, and beans (*frijoles*). Wheat and barley are raised to advantage, although not so thoroughly and extensively as they might be. Manufacturing is carried on quite extensively, cotton cloths, hats, furniture, and shoes, all of excellent quality and style, being the principal results. Steam-power is used in many manufactories, and in the weaving establishments several thousand workers are employed.

SEÑOR GENERAL BERNARDO REYES,
GOVERNOR OF NUEVO LEÓN.

There are good public and private schools, a civil college, a female college, and a seminary.

SADDLE MOUNTAIN.

In colonial times this state was called the Kingdom of Nuevo León, and divided into nine *partidos*, or districts,—Monterey, Cadereita, Villaldama, Salinas, Victoria, Doctor Arroyo, Garcia, Morelos, Cerralvo, and Linares. The capital is Monterey. Other chief towns are Cadereita, Linares, and Morelos.

Every one has heard of Monterey, the Chicago of Mexico. The city has attracted unusual attention both in Mexico and in the United States, and interest in it is increasing. Prior to 1890 it was the nearest point to the frontier that afforded the traveller from the United States an opportunity to peep into the life of a strange and interesting people; so that Monterey became more widely known than any other point in the Mexican republic. In 1889 the present governor, General Bernardo Reyes, assumed office, and from that date its progress has been rapid and striking. He has been re-elected several times, and has so well gained the confidence of the people that his failure or refusal to continue to serve as executive of the state would be regarded as a calamity.

The climate is perfect. The atmosphere is never chilled with frost, unless when it steals in at long intervals like a thief in the night, to disappear in the darkness ere the sun has risen. Such a thing as snow is unknown in the valley of Monterey, and is seen only rarely on the peaks of the mountains which surround the city; neither, from the rising to the setting of the sun, does the thermometer ever descend to the freezing-point, and it is rarely that the condition of the atmosphere prevents the weakest and most delicate consumptive from sitting or promenading in the plazas and inhaling the fragrance exhaled by the flowers which always grow out-doors in profusion and gladden and cheer and exhilarate the invalid.

Monterey is indeed charming beyond description. Nature

SAN PEDRO MINES, DIENTE CAÑON, NEAR MONTEREY.

is vested in gladness, expressed by beauty and wealth of color over which flows the mellow radiance of a semi-tropical sunshine. And when to such conditions are added the music which draws the populace to the public promenades on Thursdays and Sundays—supplied without expense to the citizens, as is the delightful custom—and the outpouring of the fair and the brave, is it surprising that all should find contentment, even those who as strangers turn their thoughts sometimes to their homes in the chilly and frozen north?

Monterey is rich in mountain treasures, and in time will be the city in which the wealth from the mountains will be invested. It will grow in population and become a city of beautiful homes, homes into which the warm sunshine and the fragrance of flowers will penetrate in winter as well as in summer.

It was a quaint old city, but has been made over, and now has all sorts of modern improvements; and it is surrounded by some of the most beautiful mountain scenery in the world.

Monterey is fifteen hundred feet above sea-level. The streets are regular, well kept, and well lighted; the houses are well built and tasteful both in architecture and in interior decora-

STATUE OF HIDALGO.

tion. The principal square has a marble fountain by native artisans. Among notable edifices are the cathedral, the handsomest church in the republic, and the municipal and government palaces. There are also a fine hospital, a good prison, an abattoir, a seminary, two colleges, and plenty of public and private schools.

New vitrified brick pavements, a complete water-system, electric railways, and modern hotels are but parts of the grand plan which will make Monterey an important centre of "the coming country."

Monterey is still a Mexican city, however, and its government is still distinctly Mexican; but I am happy to add that its government, and indeed the government of the whole state of Nuevo León, of which it is the capital, is liberal as well as Mexican, or Mexican plus American enterprise. This is seen even in superficial things and national customs. One of the customs of the country seen in every Mexican city is for the men and women to parade the wide walks surrounding its central plazas twice or three times per week to the music of a military band, the men marching together upon one side of the walk and the women marching in an opposite direction on the other. This is an old custom, but the men are dressed to-day as the same class of men would be in New York City, and the silent pantomime of incipient courtship is conducted beneath the electric light of modern days casting its lights and shades through ancient orange-trees and oaks, and glistening in every drip of the playing fountains. It is the old and the new combined. But the change is seen in more than these superficial aspects. The old Mexican business of silver mining has been modernized. Where but a few years ago there stood smelters handling daily two or three tons of earth brought on ox-carts and carried out of the mines on the backs of men, now is heard the puff of the locomotive bringing the ores to the new smelters that can absorb twenty car-loads per day.

SWAN-POND IN THE ALAMEDA PORFIRIO DIAZ, MONTEREY.

One should not visit Monterey without taking a bath in the famous Topo Chico hot springs. These are situated about a half-hour's ride on the street-car from Monterey, and are noted in Mexico and Texas as the Hot Springs in Arkansas are noted in the United States. The large spring rises in the centre of one of the hotels of Topo Chico, and fills the stone tank, which is twenty by thirty feet square and ten feet in depth. The water is said to be of great medicinal value in rheumatism and kindred diseases.

The Casino, Monterey's social club, is one of the finest club-buildings in the world.

Again, do not leave Monterey without visiting places of historic interest. Of these, there stands prominently before one the bishop's palace on the foot-hills of the mountains west of the city. On these hills were placed the Mexican cannon that were to protect the city from the attack of General Taylor in 1846. Ten of the cannon are there yet, spiked and dismounted, and the deserted bishop's palace shows the marks of thousands of Taylor's bullets.

Morelos, or Monte Morelos, is about seventy miles southwest of Monterey, and is two thousand feet above sea-level. The original name of the city was San Mateo del Pilón. The old portion is in ruins, but the modern part has wide, regular streets, substantial buildings, and court-yards tastefully laid out with trees and flowers. Streams of purest water abound in the city. There are several churches, public schools, and manufacturing establishments.

Southward from Monterey, on the Mexican National Road, the scenery begins in earnest. The track follows the narrow valley of the San Juan, deep cut as if hewn from the towering rocks for a Titan roadway, now reduced to the uses of the modern railway, whose pigmy trains are insignificant as compared with the gigantic surrounding rocks; and the cuts seem a misfit for even the ponderous locomotives that awaken the echoes as they, toiling, climb the resisting grade. The noisy little Rio San Juan foams and frets, first on this side, then on the other, as the track crosses from one side of

STREET SCENE IN MONTEREY.

the cañon to the other to find easier ways to get over the hills. The little hamlet of Garcia, sometimes called Pesqueria, is just below Santa Catarina, both places being objects of excursions by rail and carriage from Monterey. There are two caves at Garcia, and from the left windows of the cars a careful look will find a curious hole through the crest of the mountains, as if made by a monster cannon-shot. The wildness of scenery grows as the train rolls on through the ever-narrowing cañon, and each turn brings some new picture grander and more beautiful than that other just back around the curve.

The town or village of Mexico that has not its legend is unworthy of its name. Wherever the train stops, during the few minutes it stays at the station a bit of legend is hurriedly told, and if the starting-bell interrupts the story the conductor or trainmen will tell the rest. The legends are of history, sacred and profane, not confined to earth, but reaching the heavens above and the waters beneath it; and from the vasty deep the spirits have been called. If you doubt it, evidences are shown in the bridge at Monterey, where the Virgin stood and held at bay the invading Americans in '47, or the stone cases at Guadalupe that encase the sails and foremast that the sailors carried

ALAMEDA, MONTEREY.

from Vera Cruz and erected in front of the Virgin's holiest shrine, as they had vowed to do if she would save them from shipwreck. The rocks are shown whence Juan Medina leaped, and the Mexican National cars run over the spot where he fell; and the famous Titian at Tzintzuntzan, near Patzcuaro, has its legend as well as authenticated history. And thus, at this station or that, all along the line, some new story is told.

A visit to the San Pedro mine in Diente Cañon, which nets about one thousand dollars per day, is a delightful experience. The mouth of the mine is four thousand feet above Monterey City and within one thousand feet of the top of the mountain. What a valley! What scraggy heights. What millions on millions of tons of ore in the depths of the mountains! Through a long tunnel dug in solid rock, lighted by electricity, we turn into side chambers, and there the

TOPO CHICO HOT SPRINGS, MONTEREY.

ore surrounds us. But what do we see? Here also is modern Mexico. Here is the electric dynamo hoisting the ore from the chambers one hundred and fifty feet in depth. The old mine three hundred years old and originally worked by the Spanish conquerors is now lighted by an American-made machine, while the former conqueror has not the power to-day to hold the last of her possessions on the American continent. Up the mountain cañon there are massive structures of wood and stone to support the cable for carrying the ore from the mouth of the mine and depositing it in the cars below. The cable is seven thousand two hundred feet in length, and swings its cars in many places two hundred or two hundred and fifty feet above the rocks below. The cable cost eighty-five thousand dollars.

Our visit to the San Pedro mines in company with Mr. Horace Gibson forms one of the pleasantest memories of our trip through Mexico. We had gone to Monterey to visit Governor

Reyes, arriving there early in the morning. The governor was at the San Pedro mine, hundreds of feet above us. We could see the governor's cottage from the railway station perched high up on the mountain, and were soon on our way thither in a special train. It was ten o'clock when we reached the mines and received a royal welcome from Nuevo León's noble governor. After a pleasant trip through the mines, we were given one of the finest dinners, up among those clouds, that we ever enjoyed in all our travels in the United States or in European capitals. And after a charming visit of several hours with the governor's most interesting family, we mounted our horses and descended the mountain, while the slanting rays of the westering sun threw a charm of romance over this wonderful scene.

General Don Bernardo Reyes, the governor of Nuevo León, is loved and respected throughout the Mexican republic. To him is owing not only the wonderful growth of Monterey but also a great part of the progress of the state of Nuevo León. Some of the developments of his administration are the public schools and the buildings for the study of medicine and jurisprudence. He it was too who added the extensive iron galleries around the market; through

CANAL IN MONTEREY.

his influence the Alameda was improved and beautified with a kiosk and two artistic fountains, new pavements, and iron seats; under his administration the Juarez bridge and the penitentiary were built, with the aqueducts providing drinking-water for the park and the penitentiary; and under him the plazas of Zaragoza and Hidalgo were paved with artificial stone and the two great promenades constructed at the north of the capital.

Public instruction, especially, has been greatly developed under Governor Reyes. Large sums of money are yearly spent by the state government for educational purposes. There are some three hundred primary schools under the charge of the cities of Nuevo León, with high schools and professional schools superintended by the state. The law regulates the courses of study, and, in fact, all matters connected with the schools. In this connection may be mentioned a state public library, which is constantly enriched and kept up to the times. It is readily inferred that Nuevo León is one of the most advanced states in the Mexican republic. Its history has many brilliant pages, and on its soil many notable men have drawn the first breath of life.

CHAPTER XXIII

COAHUILA

COAHUILA lies just west of Nuevo León and east of the state of Chihuahua, having an area of fifty-eight thousand nine hundred and twenty square miles. It is the third largest state in the Mexican republic. The main line of the Mexican International Railway traverses the entire state. The population of this state is about one million and a quarter, and its resources are unbounded. Some of the richest mines in the republic are found within its limits; the Sierra Mojada mines, for instance, having an output of over twenty thousand tons a month, while in the Mula range there are mines yielding thousands of tons per month. The location of smelters within the republic has given an impetus to the mining of lower grades of ore, and thousands of tons are shipped monthly to the San Luis Potosi and Monterey plants. The location of large smelters on the line of the Mexican International Railroad and the opening of the Durango extension have opened mines of fabulous wealth. Sixty miles from Torreon is the famous Cuencame mining range.

A Belgian syndicate, under the name of the Compañia Carbón de Piedras Negras, is working the Fuente coal-mines. It has one hundred and thirty thousand acres of coal land, and has a tap line of two miles connecting the mines with the Mexican International Railroad.

Along the line of the Mexican International Railroad are some of the finest health and pleasure resorts in the world. Health-seekers should try Mexico's famous hot springs at Hermanas. The town nestles among the hills, and the location of the springs—some two hundred yards from the railroad track—is ideal. They are the largest springs of hot mineral water on the continent, and, flowing out of the hill-side, form a river of hot, clear water, which passes through the finest grove of guisache-trees in Northern Mexico. The natural temperature of the water is 110° F. Physicians recommend these waters in preference to those of the Arkansas springs. They "cure all," affording relief to all those who are afflicted by blood-poisoning, scrofula, rheumatism, etc. San Antonio's leading physicians recommend the water for cancer, as well as for the diseases just mentioned. Hermanas has other attractions. With unexcelled scenery, the climate is invigorating; there are no dews at night, and the dry but not hot atmosphere renders the place a consumptive's elysium. The mountains rising to the east and west, with their deep ravines, have plenty of game, and the pellucid waters of the Rio Salado repay the angler his casting there.

The surface of Coahuila is rough, several ranges of mountains crossing it from northwest to southeast. The only plain of any extent is on the western side, and is called the Bolsón de Mapimi, from its peculiar formation, having no opening except on the north. Several tribes of savage Indians live in this vicinity, and formerly interfered seriously with farming and mining interests. A large part of the state consists of rough, mountainous country, with much good grazing land.

In the Bolsón de Mapimi are the lakes Caiman and Parras. The river Mapimi flows into Caiman, and the Rio Grande del Parras into Parras. Other rivers tributary to the Rio Grande are the Salado, Sabinas, Toya, and Meteros; none of them are large. Silver-mines exist in the mountains, and offer great opportunities for development. The tillage lands yield abundantly of wheat, maize, and barley. In the southern part of the state are large maguey plantations, and the vicinity of Parras is famous for its vineyards and the excellent quality of their wine. Brandy of remarkably good quality is made there also. These, with coarse cloths and potteries, are as yet the principal products of Coahuila.

Saltillo, the capital of Coahuila, is reached by the Mexican National Railroad. It is a well-built city on the Rio Tigre, four hundred and thirty-five miles from the city of Mexico. The town, which now numbers some twenty thousand inhabitants, was founded in 1586, and incorporated as a city by Leon Vicario in 1827. The government house and the parish church are the chief edifices of interest. The annual fair held in Saltillo, lasting eight days, is largely attended from all parts of the state, and makes a general *fiesta* most popular with all. Saltillo is celebrated for its good wine and the many and brightly colored serapes, the pride of the Mexican's wardrobe, prized more highly than the overcoat of the American or the top-coat of the Englishman. To own a serape of Saltillo is to possess the best and most artistically woven in intricate

SEÑOR LIC. MIGUEL CARDENAS,
GOVERNOR OF COAHUILA.

colors that can be produced, with all the factories of Mexico striving to imitate those hand-woven in Saltillo. The climate of Saltillo is fine. The town is at its best in summer, and has claims as a resort at all seasons. There are an especially fine plaza and a cathedral. These and the long stone aqueduct which brings the city's water-supply from the mountains, the old French fort, the gardens, and the orchard, are objects of interest to the tourist.

A few miles south of Saltillo is the battle-field of Buena Vista. Still on the up-grade, the railway train reaches the summit at Carneros, where the company has a coaling station. At Carneros the descent to the plain commences. Just before leaving the hills the village of Gomez Farias is pointed out on the right, once the home of a noted brigand, and now inhabited by his better-behaved descendants.

In quest of a quiet, recreative spot yielding health and pleasure, where the days are bright and warm without being oppressive and the nights delightfully cool, one may well try the Mexican Alpine city of Parras. Flanked on the southwest by the magnificent mass of the Sierra Mojada, five thousand feet from base to summit, and on the other sides by mountain-chains of lower elevation, the upland valley in which Parras, like a "sleeping beauty," lies is one of the most charming in all Mexico. Its height above sea-level is five thousand and thirty-three feet; its mountain air is dry and invigorating; its temperature during the hottest month of the year 1889 was at the highest 88 degrees, and at the lowest 55 degrees—the very atmosphere to breathe after the somewhat relaxing summer heat of Southwest Texas. Parras has many attractions. Shady lanes, with rose clad hedges, by running streams afford pleasant drives and walks; *tajos*, long and deep, tap the inexhaustible reservoirs of water underneath the adjacent hills, and a net-work of ditches irrigates the entire valley below. Extensive bodegas may be visited, where about six hundred thousand gallons of Parras wine are annually sold;

CITY OF SALTILLO.

and pure, undoctored wine can be had in the city at five cents per tumbler. But it is in July, August, September, and October that Parras is most attractive, for then its vineyards are laden with ripening grapes.

Parras is not vainly called the "Garden of Coahuila." It is a picturesque little paradise, an oasis in the desert, a rose in the crown of Mexico.

From Tescalco there is a full view of the beautiful valley of Parras. In front is the road from Paila winding through the hills. To the right lies the Hacienda del Rosario, with its cotton-mill, one of the largest in the republic, its immense vineyards, and its extensive bodega, in which every year are stored from twenty thousand to thirty thousand gallons of excellent wine. To the left is a range of the Sierra Madre, the highest peak of which boasts an elevation of ten thousand feet. Below lies Parras, the quaint little old Mexican town; it has about ten thousand inhabitants, and looks rather queer to American eyes. Its better houses are all built in Moorish style, the court-yard generally a flower-garden in the middle of the house, the rooms built around it, windows and doors opening into it, and very few out upon the street. This is very characteristic of Mexican life, where you seldom see the ladies outside of the house, and where it is very difficult for a stranger to gain admittance into the family circle. The flat roofs are made of hard, stamped soil, and give generally sufficient protection, as there is very little rain here. The rainy season is in July, August, and September, with a nice shower in the afternoon which makes the air delightfully cool and bracing. Soon after the rain is over one can go everywhere, as mud is almost unknown. There is a cave with a wooden cross on it, where on the 15th of August, 1594, the first mass in this region was celebrated. Inside the cave there was

PLAZA DE SAN FRANCISCO, SALTILLO.

only room for the priest, his dusky congregation, consisting of Indians of different tribes, kneeling or standing outside among the rocks, some looking at the image of the Christian God with loving devotion, others with ill-concealed mistrust, comparing it mentally with fierce Huitzilopochtli, their god of war, to whom, every spring, were sacrificed thousands of human beings.

Tescaleo is situated on the south side of the Plaza de Armas, a pretty square with evergreen trees and a sparkling fountain in the middle. The flower-beds are surrounded by rosehedges, the broad walks between them paved with slate, just as it is brought from the quarry, in all manner of shapes. Even the floors of the houses are mostly made in this fashion. Nearly every house has its vineyard, and these, the wealth of Parras, stretch far out to the foot-hills. Many of these vineyards are hedged in by centifolia roses and elderberry, forming the lovely little lanes in which we so delight to ramble. A little white chapel on the top of a hill is the first sign of Parras, in whatever direction you approach. To reach it one must ascend a steep, rocky path, and pass through the strangely-shaped rock that crowns the hill, by a flight of steps roughly cut out of it. On reaching the small plateau in front of the chapel there is a magnificent view, which fully repays one for the fatiguing ascent. In the chapel there is a large, old cross, which stood on the summit of the hill long before the chapel was built. Every spring about fifteen men dressed in Indian style, colored feathers on their heads, small mirrors on their chests, bring this cross, decorated with garlands of fresh flowers, down to the parroquia (principal church). Here it is newly consecrated, and then taken up again to the chapel. In descending and ascending with the cross the men, called Matachines, perform an Indian dance to the rhythm of a drum and flute. After having replaced the cross, the Matachines dance the remainder of the day under an arbor made of fresh boughs of trees. Nearly half the population of Parras assist at this ceremony or are spectators of it.

One thing Parras can really be proud of, and that is its unsurpassed climate. The winters are mild and dry. In December and January there may be a little cold spell, which lasts two or three days, but the cold is hardly felt during the day in the warm bright sunshine which seldom fails. Perhaps three or four times every winter the quicksilver falls below freezing-point, but, as a rule, this happens only at sunrise. *Aguacates*, bananas, lemons, and oranges grow, although the summer sun is not fiery enough to make them sweet. All these trees, as well as the oleander, bloom during the winter; so do roses, violets, and geraniums in the gardens. Grape-vines covered with fresh young leaves and peach-trees in bloom at Christmas-time are not uncommon. The stranger wonders how everything can look so fresh and green when

PORTALES, SALTILLO.

there is so little rain,—sometimes in nine months hardly a good shower. Although the soil is exceedingly fertile, the people would not be able to raise anything without irrigation. There are in the southeast some springs which, if left alone, would form quite a river; as it is, they are put into leading-strings and made to do duty from their earliest infancy. A part of the water is led through ditches to the vineyards for irrigation; the other, by far the larger part, is gathered in a large tank back of a cotton-mill, to which it furnishes power and then irrigates the lower portion of the vineyards and fields. This water, however, is not sufficient to irrigate the whole valley, and to supply this want enterprising men have built *tajos*,—*i.e.*, tunnels opened at the foot of these rocky hills and driven into them horizontally. Although labor is very cheap (an ordinary laborer not earning more than thirty-seven cents per day), these tajos cost immense sums of money, as they have to be worked often for years before they produce a sufficient flow.

The construction of the Mexican International Railroad was a very important event in the state of Coahuila. It penetrated a country that is rich in mineral and agricultural resources.

The state affords splendid inducements to the miner, manufacturer, and agriculturist, as well as to the home-seeker, the pleasure-seeker, or the health-seeker. The prosperous condition of the various enterprises situated on and adjacent to the line of this road testifies beyond question to the practicability of profitable investment.

Ciudad Porfirio Diaz, named in honor of the president of the republic of Mexico, is the northern terminus of the road, and one of the most enterprising cities on the Mexican border. The custom-house and post-office buildings, including other federal offices, are splendid specimens of modern architecture, and perhaps the finest public buildings in the republic. The International Club, a handsome and substantial building, equipped with a modern gymnasium, an elaborate reading-room constantly supplied with the leading periodicals and dailies of Mexico, the United States, and England, a bowling-alley, a billiard-room, and a tennis-court, furnishes pleasant and profitable diversion for the *habitués*. The Mexican International Reservation is one of the most attractive features of the city. It abounds in beautiful homes, which are rented exclusively to the railroad employees at minimum rates.

Fuente, four miles from Ciudad Porfirio Diaz, is a quaint and attractive village, located on the picturesque Rio Escondido in the fertile Rio Grande valley, which is so well adapted to agriculture. Cotton, corn, and wheat are raised in great abundance and find ready and profitable markets. The famous Fuente coal-mines, which contain an almost inexhaustible supply of coal, are located at this point.

Nava, twenty-five miles, and Allende, thirty-two miles, from Ciudad Porfirio Diaz, are situ-

PENITENTIARY, SALTILLO.

ated in a rich agricultural region, susceptible of the highest cultivation, by virtue of the ample supply of water which, at a minimum cost, may be utilized for irrigation. This section is particularly adapted to the raising of cotton, corn, and wheat. The enterprising agriculturist could scarcely find a more desirable section for investment.

Sabinas, seventy-two miles from Ciudad Porfirio Diaz, is situated on the Sabinas River in the Sabinas valley, noted for its fine grazing lands, especially the great Hacienda Soledad, its rich vegetation, and its abundant water-supply. A branch road extends from Sabinas to Hondo and Felipe, a distance of twelve or thirteen miles, where are the prolific Sabinas valley coal-mines, from which coal is shipped to all parts of the republic, and also exported, to some extent, to the United States. The production is now twenty thousand tons per month. At Hondo, the Coahuila Coal Company manufacture about one hundred tons of coke per day.

Monclova, one hundred and forty-eight miles from Ciudad Porfirio Diaz, formerly the capital of Coahuila and Texas when they formed one state, is an attractive city of about fifteen thousand inhabitants. It is the centre of an extensive and paying mining region. A railway line from this point to the rich mining region of the Sierra Mojada, one hundred and fifty-nine miles distant, will pass through Cuatro Cienegas, forty-seven miles from Monclova, and the centre of a section splendidly adapted to the purpose of colonization,—land rich and cheap, water plentiful, and climate unsurpassed. It is, perhaps, the best wheat region in Mexico; and, there being only a few wheat-producing districts in the republic, no industry guarantees a quicker, surer, and more profitable return for the amount invested. Grapes of many varieties and of the best quality are raised in great abundance with very little labor. Several colonization companies have this section in view, and it is only a question of time when it will become one of the most popular and desirable in the republic.

Trevino is the junction of the Mexican International and Monterey and Mexican Gulf Railroads. The former has located a line from or near this point to Monterey, which will be completed in the near future. This line, in connection with the branch from Monclova to Sierra Mojada, will bring that inexhaustible mining camp in direct connection with Monterey, the great smelting centre of Mexico.

Jaral is noted for its spicy and exhilarating air. At this point connection is made by stage with Saltillo, the capital of Coahuila, forty-five miles distant.

From Paila there is a stage line which passes through the rich haciendas of San Carlos and Lorenzo. Parras, by virtue of its almost perfect climate, its abundance of fruit of every variety, its pure water, picturesque mountain scenery, and magnificent foliage, is destined to become one of the most popular winter and summer resorts on the American continent. A branch line will no doubt be constructed from Paila to Parras at no distant day. Contiguous to this point are some of the largest and most productive haciendas and vineyards in Mexico. A feature of this place is the excellence and cheapness of its wines and brandy. The best quality of grape brandy, which is equal (being absolutely pure), if not superior, to French cognac, may be purchased at three cents per drink.

From Hornos a branch line extends to San Pedro, fourteen miles north. This latter point is in the great Laguna district, famous for its large production of cotton. The plant produces from five to ten years without renewal. Many thousand bales are annually shipped from this point. The famous Viesca salt-mines, which are well-nigh inexhaustible, and which supply salt to points all over the republic, are only a few miles south of Hornos.

Torreón, three hundred and eighty-five miles from Ciudad Porfirio Diaz, is the junction of the Mexican International and Mexican Central Railways. This point has experienced a phenomenal commercial growth in the last few years. Torreón is a city of about eleven thousand

PARK ZARAGOZA, SALTILLO.

inhabitants, with wide streets and sidewalks, and with a fine prospect for the future, being the youngest city of its size in the republic. The surrounding country is one of the great cotton belts of the south, and is thoroughly irrigated and cultivated. A large cotton-factory, oil-mills, soap-factory, flouring-mill, and ice-factory are in successful operation here, together with the other manufacturing and mercantile establishments usually found in cities of this size.

Not many miles from Torreón is Tlahualilo, which has been made famous as the place of an experiment to utilize negroes as farm-laborers. A fuller account of the growth of this successful colonization company, with its wonderful cotton-fields and factories, will be found in another part of this volume.

The state of Coahuila has attained commendable progress under the statesman-like guardianship of Governor Lic. Don Miguel Cardenas. His excellency is a member of the Mexican bar, has been a member of the legislature, and has had careful political training for his high office. He is a man of wealth and education, and always wins an enviable reputation among visiting foreigners. He found the public treasury nearly empty, but under his administration a handsome balance is now always on hand. Public instruction has made rapid strides under his fostering care; every town in the state has now one or more good primary schools, with several in Saltillo. The State Normal School in the latter place is also a great aid to the cause of education in Coahuila.

Mining interests have been developed extensively during the Cardenas administration. The projection of new railroads into mining regions and the lowering of state contributions are doing much to further the success of mining interests in Coahuila. Land business is rapidly increasing, and great stock lands in the northern portion are being developed by American and English capital.

CHAPTER XXIV

CHIHUAHUA

CHIHUAHUA is the largest state in the republic of Mexico, having an area of one hundred and five thousand two hundred and ninety-five square miles. It is bounded on the east by Coahuila, south by Durango, and west by Sinaloa and Sonora. The Rio Grande separates it from the United States on the north. A prolongation of the Sierra Madre range of mountains covers the western part of the state, and is rich in mineral deposits; these mountains in some parts are one hundred and seventy-five miles in breadth. The plains average four thousand to five thousand feet above the sea-level, while the mountain-tops rarely rise more than a thousand feet higher, except in instances where some of the peaks reach an altitude of eight thousand feet. The Conchos and the Verde are the most important rivers. The valleys are very fertile and support large herds of cattle; in fact, stock-raising is the greatest industry in the state, rivalled only by its mining interests. The soil especially in the region bordering the eastern slope of the Sierra Madre is reputed the richest in the state. The vine is successfully cultivated; cotton is raised also; but the chief agricultural resources lie in the enormous herds of cattle, sheep, horses, and mules.

SEÑOR CORONEL DON MIGUEL AHUMADA,
GOVERNOR OF CHIHUAHUA.

Chihuahua mines have been celebrated for centuries, and contain gold, silver, copper, iron, tin, and lead; but the most noted are the silver-mines of Batopilas, Jesus Maria, and El Parral in the Sierra Madre, and those of Santa Eulalia in the plain just out of Chihuahua City. In fact, Chihuahua is one of the richest states in deposits of every kind. Numerous and important exploitations of silver ore have been made. The principal ones are those of Parral, worked by several companies, and which produce annually more than one million dollars' worth of silver; Batopilas, where an American company produces about one million dollars a year from seventy mines in silver; Cosihuiriachic, where another American company produces six hundred thousand dollars a year; Pinos Altos, where an English company produces six hundred thousand to seven hundred thousand dollars in silver and gold, and numbers of others.

A very important gold deposit at Orro Colorado, near Batopilas, consists of a mass of porphyry in which the gold is disseminated very irregularly throughout its entire body, the average yield of metal being about one ounce per ton. The mountain, which is about fifteen hundred metres long, more than one thousand wide, and five hundred high, is penetrated in every direction by veins of soapstone, and everywhere in this neighborhood gold is in the greatest abundance. By crude hand processes rich ores are worked which give eleven to fourteen pounds per ton; and these are the only ores which are treated, the poor ones being reserved to be worked by a large establishment in course of construction, power for which is to be furnished by the river Batopilas, about a mile from the mine.

The ride over the Mexican Central route from El Paso down through Chihuahua furnishes picturesque scenery not to be out-rivalled anywhere in the world. The table-lands, with their long parallel mountain-ranges, make an ever-changing series of infinitely beautiful views. The distant heights are rich in mineral dyes and exquisite in outline. Close at hand one may see a hacienda divided up into hamlets, with corrals and sheepfolds, with luxuriant gardens and upspringing wheat and sparkling streams of pure water. Across the distance the dome of a church peers out among the foliage; a shepherd drives white flocks of silken-fleeced Angora goats or sturdy cattle; an Indian guards his group of burros and horses; and the massive stone buildings which form the centre of the estate stand in the centre of all. Through some break in the hills one catches a glimpse of an exquisite valley with the slanting sunlight streaming across it and a glint of shining water at the bottom. Silent far-away cities, forests of cactus and yucca, palms, and hosts of bril-

THE ARCH OF THE ALAMEDA, CHIHUAHUA.

liant flowers are always fleeting backward, until the approach to Chihuahua brings one to the first distinctly Mexican city. Below are purpled mountains in the distance. Two tall campaniles of the cathedral dominate the landscape, and low flat-roofed houses lie along the reddish horizon with a truly Oriental effect. Across the plain, as one rides to the town, the serapes of the horsemen recall the burnous of the Arab, as does also the magnificent horsemanship. Inside the city streets, long colonnades, Moorish arches outside the houses, offer shelter from the mid-day sun, and the outer walls are frescoed in bright blue, yellow, or red. Broad stone seats with high backs line the principal streets under flickering shadows, while clumps of Mexican aloes and prickly cactus hedge the roadways. There is a barbaric richness of ornamentation about the façade of the principal church, carved in solid stone by the native artists. From its flat roof a beautiful prospect opens on all sides. A row of gray stone arches marks the aqueduct built more than two hundred years ago to convey water from the mountains. A bird's-eye view into the inner portion of the adobe houses near adds strange interest to the scene. A courtyard below has a tiled floor, surrounding a garden bright with peach-bloom and century plants. Shaggy burros and picturesque children play in and out among the heavy stone arches of the galleries; shadowy forms lounge against the pillars of the wall; a woman's voice comes singing from the rooms beyond; and perhaps a flock of doves rises and falls like a soft cloud above the roof. Down the long cottonwood-fringed street horsemen in white or deep red, with flying parti-colored sashes, shine like blotches of color against the pale sky.

Chihuahua was founded in 1691, and erected into a town in 1718, when it is said to have had over seventy thousand inhabitants. The most noteworthy of its public edifices are the magnificent cathedral in the Plaza Mayor, built of hewn stone at a cost of eight hundred thousand dollars, which was raised by a special tax upon the Santa Eulalia mines mint, the prison, formerly a Jesuit convent, and the handsome aqueduct supplying the city with water. In the Plazuela de San Felipe is a monument commemorating the execution on the spot of the first

THE PALACE, CHIHUAHUA.

heroes of Mexican independence. There are two hospitals, a house of correction, a military school, and several other schools.

The state-house at Chihuahua is a stone building covering a square, with the regulation patio and wide balconies. The legislative hall is elegantly frescoed and handsomely furnished, and would be a credit to any state. The governor's reception-room, which is about seventy by thirty feet in dimensions, is carpeted with heavy velvet carpeting, and the black-walnut furniture is upholstered in silk velvet. The executive mansion is not only a handsome building in outside appearance, but inside it is furnished with an elegance commensurate with the refinement one finds in all the Mexican houses where wealth predominates.

Chihuahua has a population of forty thousand, and an elevation of four thousand six hundred and forty-five feet. The view from the cathedral and the Plaza Mayor is a beautiful picture. In the background the purple hills; to right and left the dark, gray, flat-roofed houses spread out on a brown plain; in the foreground the gray foliage of the plaza; these, with the great dome and the two high, graceful towers rising against the sky, combine to make a picture which once seen can never be forgotten. Novelty may add to its charm, but its real beauty is what makes a lasting impression; after you have seen all the great landscape views of this land of beauties you remember this as one of the finest of them all.

As the city is built upon an elevated plain, it can be seen a long time before the station is reached; and as the train does not come within a mile of the town, the passenger has a long look at this charming picture, which grows in beauty as the distance lessens.

Shortly after leaving Chihuahua one approaches the smelting-works of the famous Santa Eulalia mine, and not far away is a great hacienda, comprising more than sixty thousand acres of fine land. On that estate is an adobe palace two hundred feet long and one hundred and twenty-five feet wide. The gates and pillars are of cut stone, finely carved by natives. It has beautiful towers at the angles, and a patio within that is as large as the plaza of some towns, and much more attractive. It has a yearly crop of seventy-five thousand bushels of wheat and of twenty-five thousand bushels of corn. A little farther on are two more haciendas, one of sixty thousand acres and another of one hundred and twenty-five thousand acres.

Santa Rosalia is famous for its hot springs, which in wonderful curative properties are claimed by those who have used these waters to excel any known springs in America. These springs are especially noted for their wonderful curative properties in cases of inflammatory rheumatism and all blood and skin diseases.

Jimenez is a city of about eight thousand inhabitants, and is the railway shipping-point for the rich silver-mines of the Parral and Guanacevi districts. A daily stage line connects these points with Jimenez.

There are two thousand people or more living within the precincts of the pueblo of Morris. This place is situated about six leagues northwest of Jesus Maria, at the junction of the Santa Maria and Morris Rivers. The town being located in a lovely valley, well watered and with

THE CATHEDRAL, CHIHUAHUA.

lands extremely fertile, the farms produce with little or no labor abundant crops of corn, wheat, etc., to say nothing of oranges, sugar-cane, bananas, figs, grapes, etc. It is one of the best located towns in the sierras. The residents are kind-hearted and hospitable in the extreme, as many an American can testify. They are about two hours' journey from the Santa Maria mines, where they are taking out and milling some good gold ore, and about three hours' ride (mule-back) from El Socorro mines.

About one day's journey away are situated the celebrated Carmen mines, also La Cruz, both producing good ores. On the river Carichic, about one and a half days' journey away, is situated the mill of an American company, that is taking out and milling with good results some good silver ores.

Escalón is the junction-point with the Mexican Northern Railway, running to the great mining district of Sierra Mojada, seventy-eight miles east, one of the largest carbonate camps in the world.

General Miguel Ahumada, governor of Chihuahua, is a prominent figure and much talked about by railroad men and stockmen, as he who made the large shipments of cattle into the United States possible by the appointment of a state sanitary board and live-stock inspector, guaranteeing the good health of all cattle passing through his domain. Governor Ahumada assumed the responsible duties of governor of the great state of Chihuahua in 1892. At that time the affairs of the state were in a most deplorable condition. The treasury was empty, the pay of the state employees was overdue several months, and a floating debt hampered the state government.

INTERIOR OF THE PALACE, CHIHUAHUA.

The war with the Tomochis, also, was unsettled, and involved an additional and heavy outlay, to meet which no provision had been made. So strained were the state finances, in fact, that the ill influence hung over the business world as a depressing cloud, checking enterprise and exciting general uneasiness. Under such inauspicious circumstances General Ahumada, a soldier only, and that by life-long training, assumed charge of the administration of the state. No sooner had he taken hold of the reins of power than his sagacity and energy in his new rôle began to tell in the quickened and healthful movement throughout the organism of the state, and within six months a complete change had been effected in the aspect of affairs at Chihuahua. The Tomochis were subdued, and the authority of the government was re-established throughout its territory.

Since 1894 the governor has been conserving the state finances, fostering education, and maintaining the public peace; so that the entire state, having regained confidence in its future, has progressed as never before in all branches of trade and material development.

In addition to the new water-system, a commodious and modernly appointed public hospital has just been completed, while a building for the accommodation of the art school is under construction; and a technical or industrial school for young ladies, which cannot fail to be of great benefit to young women who are called upon to support themselves by their own efforts, has just been inaugurated.

The prison in which Hidalgo was kept after his capture here in 1811 is opposite the national palace. Another point of interest in Chihuahua is an ordinary-looking building known as the temple of San Francisco. In a modest chapel at its right, and on the side of the great altar, is a black marble slab with the following inscription:

> ON THIS SPOT WAS DEPOSITED
> THE DECAPITATED BODY
> OF THE FATHER OF MEXICAN INDEPENDENCE,
> DON MIGUEL HIDALGO Y COSTILLA,
> SHOT IN CHIHUAHUA, JULY 31, 1811.
> HIS REMAINS WERE EXHUMED IN THE YEAR 1827,
> TO BE CARRIED TO THE CITY OF MEXICO.

Here it was that the great Father of his Country, Hidalgo, suffered martyrdom for Mexico, and on the remote northern border of this state the beloved Juarez kept alive the fire of national independence during the time of the empire.

The people of Paso del Norte—of Ciudad Juarez, as it is called to-day—have always stood foremost and served as an example for their patriotism and loyalty, as history has demonstrated in several instances.

After the revolution between the Partido Liberal and the Partido Conservador had reached its culminating point, and Maximilian, assisted by the French army, was endeavoring to usurp the government, Benito Juarez, who was then the constitutional president of the Liberal party, was driven from one place to another until he reached the remote refuge of Paso del Norte, to which place he came, with his cabinet and civil employees, in August, 1865. He came without any protection, firmly believing that in the midst of the patriots of Paso del Norte neither precaution nor protection was needed.

President Juarez left Paso del Norte in November, 1865, for Chihuahua, believing he could

THE BRIDGE OF SAN FRANCISCO, CHIHUAHUA.

establish his head-quarters there; but he had to return again in December of that year with his cabinet, accompanied by Colonel Yepes, commanding some one hundred and fifty men, who formed the remnant of the famous "Batallón de los Supremos Poderes." From August, 1865, the time of the arrival of Benito Juarez, to April, 1866, when he departed for the interior, the citizens of Paso del Norte assisted him not only with money but also with rations and forage. After General Terrazas had defeated the French forces in April, 1866, at Tavalaopa, near Chihuahua, President Juarez left with his cabinet and staff for Chihuahua, taking with him eighteen thousand dollars in money which the people of Paso del Norte had collected under extreme difficulties to aid his cause. President Juarez, knowing the sacrifices the people had made to raise this money, returned the eighteen thousand dollars to the inhabitants of Paso del Norte as soon as he

PART OF THE ARCHWAY OF AN OLD AQUEDUCT, CHIHUAHUA.

could get the money at Chihuahua. In addition to paying the loan, and desiring to make known to the people of Paso del Norte his appreciation of their patriotism and devotion to his cause, which he considered the beginning of his rising star, he passed a law exempting the people of Paso del Norte from paying any duties on salt, a gift from the poor to the poor; and, in fact, duties were not collected on salt at Paso del Norte until the year 1885, while the article paid import duties at all other places in the republic. He furthermore assured the citizens of Paso del Norte that when the government should be better established and again in possession of its resources they might always rely upon steady help as a just reward for the great and patriotic assistance they rendered the Liberal cause during the dark and uncertain time when its adherents made their head-quarters in the city. In the year 1866, when the Rio Bravo overflowed its banks and destroyed the farms, washing away the irrigation canals and inundating the place. President Juarez, upon learning of the calamity, setting all other urgent requirements aside, donated twelve thousand dollars toward repairing the damage done, which was given as a proof of his esteem for the town of his former refuge. The people so love his memory to this day that they have changed the name of their town from Paso del Norte to Ciudad Juarez.

To the historian and antiquary, probably the most interesting spot in the state of Chihuahua is Casas Grandes (Great Houses), a town of four or five thousand inhabitants, on the San Miguel River and near the Sonora line. This place is noted for its ruined houses, which are apparently the relics of some aboriginal metropolis, and seem to have been owned or constructed by the same race or tribe whose traces are so plentiful in Arizona. It is difficult to form a correct idea of the original arrangement of such an edifice, but its main features seem to have been three large structures connected by ranges of corridors or low apartments and enclosing several courtyards of various dimensions. The extent from north to south must have been eight hundred feet, and from east to west about two hundred and fifty feet. A range of narrow

HIDALGO'S PRISON, CHIHUAHUA.

rooms, lighted by circular openings near the top, and having pens or enclosures three or four feet high in one corner, supposed to be granaries, extends along one of the main walls. Many of the apartments are very large, and some of the enclosures are too vast ever to have been covered by a roof. About two hundred feet west of the main building are three mounds of loose stone, which may have been burial-places, and two hundred feet west of these are the remains of a building one story high and one hundred and fifty feet square, consisting of a number of apartments ranged around a square court. For some distance south the plain is covered with traces of similar buildings, the nature of which cannot now be determined; and for twenty leagues along the Casas Grandes and Llanos Rivers are found artificial mounds from which have been dug up stone axes, corn-grinders, and various articles of pottery, such as pipes, jars, pitchers, etc., of a texture far superior to that made by the Mexicans of the present day, and generally ornamented with angular figures of blue, red, brown, and black, on a red or white ground. The best specimens command a high price in Chihuahua and neighboring towns. On the summit of a mountain about ten miles from Casas Grandes are the remains of an ancient stone fortress, attributed to the same people that built the Casas Grandes, which may have been intended as a lookout.

Mr. Alexander R. Shepherd, formerly a prominent citizen of Washington, D.C., has become a large owner in the great Batopilas mines, and has settled there for life. He has served as governor of the district.

Batopilas is on the west slope of the Sierra Madre, and many miles from any railroad. The town of Batopilas itself, near which the hacienda is situated, has only about four thousand inhabitants, and is located on a river of the same name,—a mountain stream, low and quiet during nine months in the year, but sometimes rising to a mighty torrent in the rainy season. And yet, owing to the steady work in the mines, Batopilas is more advanced and has many more advantages than other towns in the vicinity.

"San Miguel," the home of the Shepherds in Batopilas, is an old Spanish hacienda, large and roomy, with many windows opening to the ground. All the houses have only one floor or story, the house and ground being enclosed by a wall. The climate of Batopilas is delightful, and the winters are charming; frost and snow are things unknown, and wraps are a useless acquisition to one's wardrobe. The country is rocky and mountainous, leaving but little land for agricultural purposes; hence the American family living in the valley must import canned goods, butter, and such staples. The surrounding Indians (Taharumari) are quiet and friendly, and raise a few cattle and sheep for a living. The Batopilas mines are among the richest in the world, although Chihuahua has several others which rank almost equally well. Humboldt predicted, ninety years ago, that this region, lying in the western half of the state of Chihuahua and on the eastern side of Sonora, would prove to be the richest area of precious mineral deposits on the face of the globe; and the constant discoveries and developments of to-day prove him to have been correct. For instance, the convoy which set out from Batopilas for Chihuahua in September, 1895, was composed of one ingot of gold valued at three thousand eight hundred and eight dollars, and silver to the value of eighty-five thousand five hundred and sixteen dollars. Near Urique a very rich vein exists, which becomes more regular in formation and the ore of which proves of a better quality the farther the excavation progresses.

Leaving Juarez in a southwesterly direction, and crossing rolling prairies for a distance of one hundred and twenty miles, you reach the great mining districts of Corralitos, Sabinal, Bismarck, and many other developed and undeveloped mines. As the products of operated mines in that district are now daily about three hundred tons of ore, varying in value from fifty to two hundred and fifty ounces per ton, and as there is a railroad projected through this district, with prospects of its being built in the near future, this wonderful ore-producing region will exceed the present output beyond any computation which may now be ventured, even by the most sanguine. The building of this railroad will open up a section five hundred miles longitudinally and one hundred miles latitudinally of the great Sierra Madre range, with its unlimited resources in precious metals; timber-growth as varied as it is immense; unequalled grazing for live stock; numerous living springs and running currents of pure water, teeming with the finny tribe of every variety; game of all kinds; natural scenery in comparison with which all other mountain regions pale into insignificance; and at the foot-hills of which are valleys, such as those of the Rio Casas Grandes and Rio Santa Maria, as fertile as ever yielded to the labors of the agriculturist. With all these advantages, what might not be calculated upon as the result of railroad connection to this section, with the natural development which would follow?

The workings of the great mines of Batopilas, those in the districts of Jesus Maria, Pinos Altos, Cusiguriache, Guerrera, Corralitos, Sabinal, and many others, give constant and abundant testimony to the forecast of the greatest of travellers and scientists. Owing to the fact that the Sierra Madre range was an impenetrable fortress of hostile Apaches until about five years ago, when they were driven out by the combined military forces of Mexico and the United States, this great and wonderfully rich section had been practically unknown. It was from this stronghold that the Apache made his periodical forays upon the villages and haciendas in the contiguous valleys, both on the Sonora and the Chihuahua side of the Sierra Madre. Massacres, thefts of stock, and destruction designated the trail of these savages. The large majority of stock-raisers, farmers, and miners were compelled to flee their homes and leave their property to destruction. Only in rare instances did civilization maintain its foothold in this beautiful and immensely rich country, until within the last eight or nine years. Since then civilization and prosperity have begun to dawn upon that section.

Many capitalists are being attracted to the flourishing mining districts of Santa Barbara. This is one of the oldest mining districts in the country, the Spaniards having found it here at the beginning of the conquest. The early miners had but one object,—to extract all the ore possible of a high grade and at the least possible cost. The Santa Barbara mines, however,

MONTE DE PIEDAD, CHIHUAHUA.

were rich enough to stand even this drain upon their resources. The native miners firmly believe that the "Nopal" contains a hidden treasure of rich ores in untold quantities. In the auriferous district of Uruapa are located the "Gold Fields of Mexico," owned principally by an English company. Their object is the handling of high-grade gold ores in large quantities. There are twenty-six mines in various stages of development on this property, and a conservative estimate places their value at several million dollars. The Los Hundidos gold-mines at the northwest corner of the Uruapa district are within a mile of the railroad and within easy distance of the new crushing-mills and reduction-works at Zapote. This makes the Los Hundidos particularly valuable for investment purposes, as indeed are all these mines on the Uruapa.

An interesting feature of Chihuahua is the Mormon colonization movement. At the present writing there are ten colonies of Mormons, comprising five thousand inhabitants, in Chihuahua. Mr. Andrew J. Stewart is the *concessionnaire* and manager of the colony in Hidalgo, which owns a large tract of land in the Santa Maria valley. The colony has a dam which irrigates fifty thousand acres of what is already proving grand farming land for ordinary grains and vegetables and for dairy purposes. These colonies are not sectarian, however, although the majority of the colonists are Mormons. Governor Ahumada has been a friend to these colonies and has helped them in many ways.

It is recorded that when Joseph Smith originally started the Mormon movement in America he desired to found his first settlement in Mexico; and now this first idea of the great Mormon apostle is being carried out.

The foreigner who goes to Mexico, invests capital, and gives due respect to the laws of the country can have no just cause of complaint. "It is only the tramp American who goes to Mexico with the expectation of making a fortune within a brief period, and who, failing in this, expends his spleen in deriding the government, the people, and the laws of the country. It is this class of people who go through the land disseminating their spite against Mexico and her people."

CHAPTER XXV

DURANGO

DURANGO lies south of Chihuahua, and has an area of forty-two thousand six hundred and twenty-three square miles. The western portion of the state is broken up by the range of the Sierra Madre, but the east is very fertile, with wide plains and beautiful scenery. On the western slopes of the mountains, too, are rich valleys, where sugar-cane and the tropical fruits and plants are raised. Flax and potatoes grow wild in Durango, and cotton is raised in large quantities. The climate is cold on the mountains, hot on the western slopes, and temperate in other portions. Wheat and all vegetables peculiar to the temperate zone are produced in large quantities; in fact, Durango offers excellent opportunities to the Northern agriculturist, especially in the eastern and central districts. Gold is abundant near Santa Maria del Oro.

Durango, besides many silver-mines, contains inexhaustible iron-beds. It is often called the "State of the Iron Mountain." Less than two miles from the capital city, Durango, is the largest mass of iron in the world, being a solid mountain of iron, called Cerro del Mercado. It is estimated that this mountain contains more than one hundred and twenty-five million tons of iron, the larger portion of which is magnetic. This entire property now belongs to a company known as the Durango Steel and Iron Company. Governor Flores owns a section of this wonderful mountain. An explorer has said that the Cerro del Mercado could supply with iron for three hundred and thirty years all the foundries of Great Britain, the value of the iron consumed in that time reaching the enormous figure of nine billion nine hundred million dollars; that is to say, seven times more than the value of all the gold and silver coined at the mint of Mexico from 1690 to 1803. Widner's calculation

SEÑOR GENERAL DON JUAN M. FLORES,
GOVERNOR OF DURANGO.

TUNAL, THE GREAT COTTON-MILLS OF DURANGO, DURANGO.

reports the Cerro del Mercado a mile long, three hundred and eighty-eight yards wide, and six hundred and forty feet high, representing one billion two hundred and forty-six million nine hundred and eighty-four thousand two hundred and twenty-four cubic feet.

The capital is Durango, which is beautifully situated some seven thousand feet above the sea. It was founded in 1560 by Alonzo Pacheco as a military station, and soon after was made an episcopal see. It was originally called Guadiana, and is still sometimes called Victoria. The most noteworthy buildings are the government house, the cathedral, a number of parish churches, a spacious hospital, a penitentiary, a state prison, a coliseum, an arena for bull-fights, and a sumptuous-looking cockpit. There are attractive public gardens, public squares, and public baths. Thermal springs supply the city with water, and the place is remarkable for cleanliness. There are cotton and woollen manufactories, also leather-, iron-, glass-, and tobacco-factories. The mint at Durango coined twenty-seven million nine hundred and sixty-two thousand six hundred and sixty-eight dollars between 1811 and 1845. There is an institute in which law, languages, and the sciences are taught, with several very good public and private schools.

Durango is a very peculiar town. It is very rich; some thirty-five thousand people, the owners of lands, timber, mines, etc., have to be coaxed to sell. At the same time, there are large mineral districts not yet explored, and Americans have found good gold-bearing properties. There is no mining exchange, board of trade, or other business organization. The people are rich and contented, and the resident merchants do not care to have any more

PUBLIC WASHING-PLACE FOR THE INDIAN WOMEN, STATE OF DURANGO.

competition. The fact that there has not been one failure here in sixteen years is a good indication of solidity. The developed mining district is very rich, and the cattle industry is large. Cotton-, woollen-, and print-mills represent large capital. The climate is perfect all the year; never lower than twenty degrees above zero nor higher than eighty. The people are getting more enterprising now, after three years of railroad communication, but the town is a solid, slow business place, entirely able to exist independently of the world.

Durango is, in fact, literally covered with mines. Among the important mining centres are El Oro, Indi, and Coñito ; some of these have yielded from sixteen hundred to four thousand six hundred dollars per ton. There are plenty of other mines in the state, the estimated average yield amounting to six hundred thousand dollars weekly. Large beds of tin have also been

A MOUNTAIN OF SOLID IRON, DURANGO.

discovered, and promise great profits. The mines of Guanacevi, San Juan de Guadalupe, Mapimi, Metates, Topia, Indi, Papasquiaro, Santiago, San Dimas, and El Carmen are all of importance, but one of the largest is that of Peñoles, whose estimated annual value is about half a million dollars.

The agricultural interests in the state have not been neglected, the situation being especially favorable for the cultivation of cotton, as well as of other profitable crops. That cotton is profitably raised is proved by the fact that there are several mills in the state for weaving, spinning, and printing cotton, besides two or three for the manufacture of woollen goods. These facilities, and the fact that a ready market is found in the city of Mexico for all its products, give excellent promise for the future.

The rich agricultural district surrounding Lerdo is under irrigation, and from eighty to one hundred thousand bales of cotton are raised there yearly, in addition to the corn, cane, beans, and fruits which are produced in great abundance. This is part of the Laguna district (which lies partly in Coahuila), which is traversed by the river Nazas throughout its entire valley. Among the chief tributaries of this river are the Castine and the Santiago, which unite to form the Ramos. A strange feature about this river is the fact that it furnishes a large volume of water which never reaches the river Nazas, the disappearance of which has never been fully accounted for. Consequently, during the summer months the Nazas dwindles to a very small stream, and this has been utilized to irrigate the Laguna lands. Corn, wheat, and *frijoles* are raised there, but the most important crop is the cotton for which the Laguna district is famous. The cotton-fields at this point are immense. The broad irrigating ditches take the places of

CASA OF MAXIMILIAN DAMM, DURANGO.

fences or hedges, so that the view covers one broad sweep, miles in extent. These fields are often two miles square, white as snow when the bolls are open, and they are repeated as far as the eye can reach along these river banks.

A few miles out from Durango is the Fábrica del Tunal, one of the oldest cotton-factories in the country, having been established by the father of the present owner, Señor Emilio Stahlknecht, in 1837. This establishment has eighty looms, which will probably be increased in the near future to two hundred and fifty looms, as there is a water-power of nearly three hundred horse-power. The establishment includes bleaching and print works, and its products of fine cloths are known everywhere as among the finest cotton goods of Mexican manufacture.

The city of Lerdo was founded in 1867, but has already ten thousand inhabitants, with a surrounding territory containing a population of fifty thousand more. Lerdo occupies a beautiful site, surrounded on three sides by low mountains. It has wide streets and a beautiful plaza with plenty of trees and flowers. Here is one of the finest hospitals in the republic, the Hospital Francisco Garza. The building is two stories in height, with a large area, and has in connection an orphan asylum and a poor-house. Governor Flores has contributed largely to the support of this magnificent structure, which would do credit to a city ten times the size of Lerdo. There are a large number of manufactories with all modern improvements, among which may be mentioned one of the largest soap-factories in America, several large wholesale establishments, banking-houses, etc.

There are many romances regarding buried treasures in Durango. There is no doubt that there has been deposited all through the state in caves and other secret places a vast amount

THE PRINCIPAL STREET, DURANGO.

of treasure, the proceeds of robberies committed by bands of brigands and outlaws during the numerous revolutions.

To Governor Don Juan Manuel Flores the state owes the greater part of the progress it has made for some years past, and to him was given the duty of driving the last spike on the International Railroad, which owed its construction largely to his indefatigable zeal. When that road was formally opened and the hitherto remote capital of Durango made accessible to travellers for the first time, it was a veritable revelation to the world. No one had imagined that up among those mountainous solitudes would be found a city so beautiful, so advanced, or so fully equipped to compete with modern national capitals; and the whole country did honor to the untiring genius and progressive spirit of Durango's able governor, General Flores.

CHAPTER XXVI

SAN LUIS POTOSÍ

EAST of Zacatecas and Aguas Calientes is San Luis Potosi, one of the most important states in the republic. It has an area of twenty-eight thousand eight hundred and eighty-nine square miles, and a population at the last census of about five hundred and forty thousand.

This state, lying in the most central position in the country and crossed from north to south and from east to west by important railways, is mostly free from mountains, lying principally in the temperate district. Coahuila and Nuevo León join it on the north; Tamaulipas and Vera Cruz on the east; Querétaro, Guanajuato, and Jalisco are its southern neighbors; and Zacatecas bounds it on the west. It is within touch by railway of all the trade-centres: Tampico and Vera Cruz give it ports through which to reach all Atlantic points, while the railways from Laredo, El Paso, and Eagle Pass make the United States a very near neighbor. Salado, Parida, Matehuala, Catorce, San Venado, Moctezuma, El Maiz, Salinas, Valles, and Rio Verde are among its jewels.

If there is any one country which is beautiful in its picturesque vegetation and useful for the products of that kingdom, it is the Huasteca of San Luis Potosi. There the highest trees give support to a multitude of creeping vines and to a swarm of vegetable parasites, which create an agreeable confusion and form obscure thickets where the foot of man has never yet penetrated. The multitudes of shades of color of the green leaves and the divers hues of the flowers, with the half-light produced in many places by the shade of the trees, allowing an occasional vista of purest blue sky; the silence of the bosks at certain hours of the day; the harmonious songs of the birds at the rising and the setting of the sun, are all poetical, and invite to meditation and the adoration of the Author and Source of so many marvels. The entire state is a gem of varied beauty, worth travelling thousands of miles to see.

In the towns to the southeast and east of the capital there are lands well adapted for agriculture. The enterprise which is directed to this class of work will find there every kind of products which temperate and torrid climates know, not only in cereals and fibre-bearing plants, but also in fruits and hard woods. In all portions of the state Indian corn is cultivated, as well as wheat and beans, all most useful as food for the inhabitants; but the branches of agriculture which have been most developed are the cultivation of coffee and that of tobacco. The coffee-plants number about four million, with a mean yield of forty thousand quintals. Sugar-cane is another of the products which are most abundant. In fine, having, as this state has, lands in all three climates,—cold, temperate, and torrid,—it can produce all the fruits of every zone.

In the rural districts, to the north and northwest, there is an abundance of cattle and sheep, yielding hides and wool. *Palmito*, the central tender part of a palm-tree grown in the

Huasteca, when cooked in any one of several manners, is an agreeable and nourishing food. The *hualpoy* is a species of bean having the flavor of peas. The *pimienta* of Tabasco is a stout and aromatic tree, the odor of which may be noted in various parts of San Luis. Its spherical fruit is like that of the ordinary pimienta; its leaves make an agreeable beverage like tea. The *mora*, which is exported in great quantities, is a stout tree, the wood of which yields a yellow die; the *mohuite*, a dark velvet; the *ixquitl*, a blue. Among textile plants, besides the varieties of magueys and pitas, there is *jonote*.

In the different rivers fish are found in great abundance and large variety. They are not only handsome in appearance, but are declared by epicures to be of a very fine flavor, being fed by the many natural undergrowths.

Nature has been most prodigal in trees suitable for construction, as well as for cabinet-making. Some of these are peculiar to this district. Among them may be found the *chicol*, with dark brown wood, which when dry is like iron, and which petrifies when buried in a moist place.

In some of the mountainous parts there is no necessity for oxen or ploughing, a hoe being sufficient to enable the planter to raise a good crop,—corn, for instance. In the level country ploughs are used with oxen.

In the coffee district they use plants which have come up of themselves. The plant at the age of two years is in the best condition for replanting.

SEÑOR GENERAL DON CARLOS DIEZ GUTIERREZ, GOVERNOR OF SAN LUIS POTOSÍ.

In the moist months of winter it is transplanted where it will be shaded in the summer while growing. After it has a fair start, the overshadowing trees are pulled up in order to give the more important plants light and air. This and fencing with wood are the only labors necessary. A coffee plantation lasts many years when once started. I have seen plants thirty years old and still bearing.

Rice is cultivated in some parts with the plough; no more care is required than to cut the plant. In Xilitla, Huehuetlan, Coscatlan, and Aquisman there is an abundance of this crop, which brings good prices. When it is ripe it is cut as wheat is, dried, threshed, and winnowed in the wind, a picturesque process that has died out in our country. Sugar-cane grows in abundance. It is crushed with rude wooden rollers, and the sugar and molasses are made in a primitive manner. Tobacco is exported from the state, but not in nearly as large quantities as it should be. Vanilla is very easily grown, and yields a large profit.

The mineral deposits throughout the state are already known, and there is considerable national and foreign capital invested in working the mines, and each year more American capital becomes interested. There are in the state seventy-two mines, of which forty-three are in Catorce, twenty-five in Guadalcazar, and four in the capital. Of these, forty-eight produce silver, eleven lead, two copper, one sulphur, and ten mercury. The mines of San Pedro in this state were discovered in the middle of the sixteenth century, and it is they that have made the reputation of the state. There are here no regular veins, but metalliferous masses produce lead, oxide of iron, native silver, and sulphur, and almost all contain a trace of gold. The mining industry is notably progressive, and the "plants" for carrying it on are of the most modern type. The installations of the Concepcion and Santa Nuna are most complete and costly. There is an immense metallurgical establishment at Morales, with five buildings and eleven furnaces. The state of San Luis produces over three million dollars of silver per year. Silver comes in considerable quantities from San Antonio de Guascama.

In the northern part of the state is Catorce, "The Silver City." Catorce means in Spanish fourteen, and these mines were discovered by a group of fourteen banditti. These are of the

PALACE OF THE GOVERNOR, SAN LUIS POTOSÍ.

most celebrated mines in Mexico. The great mining city is eight miles from the station of the same name, and since the discovery of queen silver, about 1780, the town has grown into a population of about twenty thousand. The plaza occupies the only level spot in the place. The mines are particularly interesting, with miles and miles of shafting and tunnelling. Enormous quantities of ore have been taken out, and still there is an annual output of several million dollars.

When we visited these mines we went on horseback, attended by one of the officials and a boy. The path is rugged and steep, but not dangerous, and gives a magnificent view of the town, stream, and cañon hundreds of feet below. Conducted by the proprietor of the mine (which, by the way, in its first year produced one million six hundred thousand dollars), we inspected it thoroughly, and found it very interesting. We were conducted through a large iron gate across the patio into the warehouse, where we were struck by the extreme neatness of the place. With lights and guides we passed through the tunnel, which was at first like a cold-air passage, but afterward grew uncomfortably warm. As we proceeded we had to dodge the little cars that flew by with the rapidity of lightning, to dispose of their rich burdens. Once in the mines, every man was at his place, watching his part of the machinery with the utmost care.

Then we went down the shaft. It was like going down an elevator through the darkness of the Inferno into the very bowels of the earth. Once at the bottom and standing again on *terra firma*, we found another scene of strange and busy activity. But, alas, the activity grew less as the miners discovered our presence. Probably they had never seen two women down there before, and they feared terrible consequences, as there is a common superstition among the miners that a serious accident will surely follow a woman's visit to the mines. Indeed, while we were in Mexico City a band of thirty Indian miners walked all the way from the sulphur-mines of Popocatepetl, where they were working, because a woman had set foot in the place.

We could see no trace of silver on the sides of the gloomy black walls until small, greenish-mouldy spots were pointed out to us as indicating veins of silver. When we finally landed at the mouth of the shaft we felt that we had had an experience not to be missed for worlds, but not to be repeated if possible to avoid it.

Other important mines besides San Pedro (discovered about the middle of the sixteenth century) are Guadalcazar, Matehuala, Durazno, Cedral, and Salinas. The Concepcion is worked by a powerful company, of which Governor Gutierrez is president. This is perhaps the most important and wealthiest in the state, seeming to be inexhaustible, although worked on an enormous scale, with a subterranean railway of its own. The mines of Charcas contain many minerals, and the salt-works of Peñon Blanco have made the fortune of their owners.

There is a large metal foundry, the most extensive on this continent, near the border of the state, which is proving valuable as an inducement to enlarge the workings in all these mines.

There are many manufactories in this state, especially in the capital, where are made soap, candles, varnishes, sombreros, tobacco, pottery, and wine. In the eastern towns are many small aguardiente stills and a few sugar-houses. The principal manufactures are cotton goods in Venado, wool in Santa Maria del Rio, linen in San Luis, and gilt and silvered articles.

The Mexican National Railway traverses the state from south to north, from the capital of the republic to Laredo, Texas, a distance of thirteen hundred and fifty kilometres. The trip from San Luis Potosi to Tampico affords one of the most delightful and interesting trips on the American continent. The views afforded passengers on this line are justly styled the "Swiss scenes of Mexico."

From San Luis Potosi, at an altitude of six thousand one hundred and eighteen feet above sea-level, the plain gradually slopes downward, by a series of terraces, cut through here and there by cañons giving passage for the watercourses descending from the table-land to the sea. Through one of these openings the train descends into and through the wild San Isidro valley, the mountain-sides of which are densely wooded. Soon after leaving Cardenas the road descends abruptly into the pleasant valley of Canoas, and thence enters the great cañon of Tamasopo. Winding along the shelf hewn in the sides of the almost perpendicular cliffs, around curves, and through a succession of tunnels, the train finally reaches the mouth of the cañon, where a magnificent view suddenly presents itself. Before and beneath spreads out a beautiful valley encircled by mountains. Twelve hundred feet below is seen the dense, luxuriant tropical forest, interspersed with fields of growing cane and tropical fruits. Running along the almost perpendicular mountain side, with grand cliffs towering above, there can be seen beneath, at three different places, the line of track over which the train is to pass before reaching the valley below. Here a new surprise awaits the traveller. He is passing through a coffee plantation. Under the giant trees, literally covered with an infinite variety of orchids, grows the coffee, with its glossy evergreen leaves and bright red berries. Shortly after leaving Rascón the cañon called "Abra de Caballeros" is entered, at the mouth of which the river tumbles down a series of cascades over three hundred feet. These falls are called "El Salto del Abra." The water in the pools is of a lovely green color, which as it rushes over the falls appears turned into a snowy foam, presenting an effect long to be remembered. Just beyond the "Boca del Abra" the train passes, on an iron bridge, directly over an opening in the top of "Choy Cave," from which rushes, more than two hundred feet below, a beautiful stream of water, which winds its way through the valley toward the Gulf.

CHURCH AND FOUNTAIN AT GUADALUPE.

The Mexican Central system has another line from San Luis to the port of Tampico, four hundred and forty-six kilometres, said to be the finest piece of engineering in the republic. Both systems of railways have their stations respectively in the east and in the north of the Alameda, a few metres from the principal plaza, these being elegant edifices, especially that of the National Mexican, without doubt the best in the country.

The railway from Vanegas to Rio Verde, a local enterprise, is in operation between Vanegas and Matehuala. Of similar origin is a line from Cedral to Potrero, the lines together amounting to seventy-two kilometres. This railway runs with great regularity, contributing principally to mercantile progress, and above all to the local improvement of mines.

Primary instruction is given in about nine hundred schools, of which seven hundred and eleven are public, ninety-one private, and nine sustained by religious associations. There is in the capital a college for secondary instruction, called "Scientific and Literary Institute," in which are followed the studies preparatory to the professions and the regular courses in medicine and law, and in topographical, geographical, hydrographical, mining, and mechanical engineering. In this institute there are thirty-one resident students and two hundred from outside. A normal school for male and one for female teachers have in the first thirty-nine students, all resident, and in the second sixty-eight, all non-resident.

An industrial military school, designed for the poorer class, has two or three hundred pupils, all receiving in the establishment primary instruction and devoting themselves to various trades, which they are there taught. The printing and lithographic establishments of this school are the best in the city. The presses are steam-driven, and the director in each shop is most capable.

These pupils, as well as those in the normal schools, receive instruction in military tactics, in which they have shown great aptitude and proficiency. The students in each school receive board, clothing, and books free. In the industrial school there is a military band for young men and boys, conducted by a competent leader, who says that it is one of the best in the country.

In the school of arts and trades for girls are taught English and French and occupations adapted to the gentler sex, as millinery, flower-making, printing, lithography, and telegraphy. In this school there is a loom which is turning out satisfactory products, and some of the students have formed an orchestra, which is heard with great pleasure. All these establishments are supported by the government.

There are one civil, one military, and one children's hospital, the first supported by the state, the second by the general government, and the third by private means.

The capital of the state is San Luis Potosí. Other important towns are Valles, Matehuala, Venado, Guadalcazar, Rio Verde, Tamazunchale, Tancanhuitz, Santa Maria del Rio, Cerritos, Salinas, and Alaquinas, capitals of *partidos* or counties.

CASCADE DEL SALTO, SAN LUIS POTOSÍ.

San Luis Potosí has a population of seventy-five thousand people, and is one of the most important business centres in the republic of Mexico. It is situated in a fertile valley surrounded by mountains rich in mineral wealth, and is the principal distributing point for a large section of Northern Mexico. The successful opening of the port of Tampico gives San Luis Potosí commercial advantages equal, if not superior, to those of any other city in the republic of Mexico. There is located at this point the smelting plant of the Compañia Metalúrgica Mexicana, the most extensive silver-lead reduction works on the North American continent.

This city may justly lay claim to a first rank among the cities of the Mexican republic. This is true whether she be considered from an historical, a political, or a commercial point of view. Founded in the days of the Spanish conquest, the geographical position of San Luis (almost in the centre of the great Northern Mexican plateau, some six thousand feet above the level of the sea) secured for her pre-eminence from the earliest times. She stands prominent in the country's history, colonial, imperial, and republican. The military commander, the political leader, the railroad or mining engineer, the commercial agent and capitalist, each in turn has made her the centre of his operations. The history of the city may to a great extent be read in its outward appearance. Grand old Spanish churches, such as that of San Francisco, dating from the sixteenth century, the Carmen, with its two-hundred-year-old carvings, and the Guadalupe, with its sacred associations, are almost within view of the handsome but essentially modern railway depots of the Central and National companies. The imposing French-built government palace and the Mexican cathedral, flanking the old Spanish plaza, with its American tram-lines and electric lights, the old fortified mint, telling of revolutionary times, the college hospital, the library, and the splendid new theatre, seating three thousand, with other new and elegant buildings, speak for the prosperity and advancement of the present day.

It has always been a very busy and flourishing place, holding the same relation to Eastern Mexico that Guadalajara holds to Western Mexico. The surrounding country is a very fertile district, and San Luis furnishes a ready market for its produce. The rapid growth and the display of enterprise in San Luis have given it the right to be called the "Chicago of Mexico."

There are many fine buildings in San Luis Potosi. The government palace is attractive in appearance; the cathedral shows some fine stone-work on its towers. There are characteristic paintings of high quality in the church of El Carmen. Much may be seen in a given time in San Luis by taking a street-car or carriage to the church of Guadalupe, as the visitor thus enjoys the Paseo, the fountains, and the market on the way, and reaches something worth going to see at the end of his ride. The old church has a clock which was given by the King of Spain in return for the largest piece of silver ore ever taken from a mine. On the entrance to this beautiful sanctuary are these comforting and inspiring words:

> Aqui el que pide recibe,
> El que busca halla,
> Al que toca se le abre.

("Here he who asks receives, he who seeks finds, to him who knocks it is opened.")

The two tall towers of this church form the most striking feature of the city to the traveller approaching from the south.

A new theatre in San Luis Potosi, one of the handsomest in Mexico, is a monument to the progressive spirit of Governor Gutierrez. The building is of stone, massive and large. Immense columns of stone and iron adorn the front. The entrance is very much like that of the Grand Opera in Paris. It is elegant yet massive in design, and would be a credit to any republic. There is a grand and beautiful lobby, which is approached by wide marble steps and covered by a dome of heavy stained glass. Seen from below, this last has a magnificent appearance, with a huge balcony winding around in the interior, with heavy iron railing. This is entered above by beautiful glass doors, opening from an immense hall, large enough for a ball-room, with marble-tiled floors. The theatre is on a magnificent scale, and beautifully upholstered boxes with brass railings and handsome effects add greatly to the grandeur of the parquet below. The stage has all the latest improvements, and the whole theatre is a noble example of what taste can do when backed up by immense wealth. It is one of the finest in the republic, and was built under the supervision of General Gutierrez. The governor's private box, facing the stage, is magnificently fitted up, with the coat of arms of the state in silver and bronze, while the brass railings around the boxes above and below add to the beauty of this massive theatre.

San Luis Potosi is a capital place to visit, as there are fine hotels there, with a great deal to interest a sight-seer. Not only are the streets wonderfully clean, but the law requires that the houses shall be kept freshly painted, so that the city is fresh and bright in every quarter. The markets are particularly interesting, with picturesque water-carriers, many fountains, and many novel types. A fine statue of Hidalgo formerly occupied the Plaza de Armas, but has been removed to a more important place and a costly and elegant kiosk erected in its place. When the evenings are warm and serene, as most nights are in San Luis Potosi, this plaza presents a most attractive appearance, with whole families promenading to the gay music under the silvery light of the moon or the more brilliant radiance of the electric light.

There are several other handsome buildings, including the governor's palace in the Plaza Hidalgo, built in 1767, and the ex-municipal palace of two stories and with magnificent arcades.

An account of this historic city may well end with the record of the fact that here was made

THE GRAND THEATRE "LA PAZ," SAN LUIS POTOSI.

the first discovery of silver in Mexico, a discovery which went so far to found the country's future greatness. The pretty tradition is that early in the sixteenth century an Indian goatherd was climbing the San Luis hills, his foot slipped, and to save himself he clutched at a neighboring bush, which, giving way beneath his weight, was uprooted and exposed to view the native silver beneath.

In the capital there are two prisons, one for men and the other for women. The first, connected with the penitentiary system, is in a beautiful building of modern construction, as may be easily seen from its ornamentation. It can accommodate about four hundred and fifty criminals, all of whom are fed there, and in the same building there is an efficient hospital department. The institution has already cost three hundred and fifty thousand dollars, and fifty thousand more will be spent on its gardens. The women's prison is a building of ancient construction, with a chapel for Roman Catholic worship, and is large enough for its usual number of offenders, about sixty. It was given by a former resident of the city in the early years of this century, on condition that it should be used only for the purpose designated. Each principal town in the state has a prison for men and one for women.

North of San Luis is the very pretty village of Bocas, a typical town of Mexican beauty. Fine haciendas with walled gardens, blossoming flowers and fruits, towered chapel and ancient court-yards, may be seen, with plenty of green foliage to soften the landscape on every side. In the northern portion of the state, at La Maroma, the line separating the Temperate from the Torrid Zone is marked by a pyramid erected by the Mexican National Railroad.

Up to the present time we have described only the inanimate features of this wonderful state. But there are other treasures, more precious than mines of silver and of gold: her men of action and of soul: her patriots and warriors; her defenders in time of war, her leading citizens in days of peace.

Of these, the "noblest Roman of them all" is he who has long stood at the helm of government in the state of San Luis Potosi, and whose career is at once the record of the progress of this state and one of the principal features of its advance. General Carlos Diez Gutierrez was born in the city of Maiz, in this state, in 1845. As governor and military commander of San Luis he has given a vigorous impulse to all public duties, reformed the postal service and the gendarmerie, and completely reorganized the government and its departments. As governor of his state he has brought to the front rank the penitentiaries, industrial schools, asylums, hospitals, telegraphy, railways, and other public institutions and improvements.

CHAPTER XXVII

ZACATECAS

ZACATECAS is another inland state, south of Durango, and surrounded by Coahuila, San Luis Potosi, Aguas Calientes, and Jalisco. It has an area of twenty-six thousand five hundred and eighty-eight square miles, and is a flourishing state in many ways. It is one of the most mountainous, being traversed by the Sierra Madre with numerous spurs and branches. The hilly country of the middle and west is interspersed with fertile and wide valleys and deep gorges and ravines, furnishing a variety of wild and beautiful scenery. The state is rather poorly watered, there being no large streams. The climate is very generally salubrious, warm in the valleys, and rather cold in the elevated portions. Silver is very abundant in this state, which long ranked first in importance among the great mining regions of Mexico. Guanajuato, however, has taken precedence of it in this respect. Mining is the chief industry, although agriculture is extensively and profitably carried on.

Zacatecas is divided into twelve *partidos* or districts,—Zacatecas, Fresnillo, Sombrerete, Nieves, Mazapil, Ciudad Garcia, Pinos, Villanueva, Sanchez Roman, Juchipila, Nochistlan, and Ojo Caliente.

The capital is Zacatecas, a city of about eighty-five thousand population, lying in a deep gorge of the mountains about three hundred miles northwest of Mexico City, on the Mexican Central Railway. It has many churches, a hospital, a mint, good schools, and a literary institute founded in 1868. The city is justly celebrated for its enormous output of silver. Its first mine was discovered in September, 1546, and on July 1, 1818, it was estimated that the total output of the mines since their discovery aggregated the sum of six hundred and sixty-seven million three hundred and forty-three thousand two hundred and nineteen dollars. These

SEÑOR GENERAL JESUS ARECHIGA,
GOVERNOR OF ZACATECAS.

silver-mines are steadily producing immense quantities of ore, and recent new discoveries have been made which indicate that Zacatecas may become famous as a gold-ore producing point also.

The city is reached by a steep slope from the railway station, and the narrow streets are wonderfully clean, well paved, and have raised pavements at one side. Everywhere the little court yards are seen through open door-ways and are glowing with flowers and sunshine. There are many market-places, and the central one has a great circular stone fountain, around which at almost every hour of the day may be seen women and children with great red earthen jars and little gourd-shaped cups, which they use to fill the jars; these latter are then swung easily to the left shoulder, and the women walk off with all the grace and self-possession of ball-room belles.

To see Zacatecas you must go down a steep side street to the beautiful old church, with its great façade of carved freestone and three unique spires, and the arcade covered with its double row of arches. Everything glows with color,—the sky, the frescoes, the flowers, the trees, the gayly dressed people, and the broad stone seats. The inner court of the government patio is finished with a dado and frieze of blue and yellow; the slender pillars in double columns between the arches of the first and second floors are brilliant with stencilled wreaths of flowers; the broad stone steps curving away to the upper galleries are ornamented with pots of tropical plants. From a corner of one of these galleries one sees a beautiful picture. The red sandstone towers of the cathedral, with their beautiful carving, are barbaric in splendor and still harmonious. Against the sapphire sky their outlines are wonderful, and there is no end of novelty. One market-place is devoted entirely to coarse potteries, jars for water, and cooking articles and kitchen utensils.

THE CATHEDRAL, ZACATECAS.

Many travellers say the low-topped houses and domed churches remind them of Palestine. Indeed, Zacatecas is called "The Jerusalem of Mexico." Far up on the mountain called "La Bufa" is the shrine which the Mexican devotees visit to obtain remission of their sins, many of them scaling the steep sides of the mountain upon their hands and knees, as an exceptional self-imposed penance. The people wear their peculiarly picturesque garb, and should it be Sunday and the band playing in the plaza, the moving throngs will form a veritable kaleidoscopic scene, wonderfully pleasing to the eye.

Water is a comparatively scarce article in Zacatecas. The fountains in the plaza are always thronged with people with their water-jars, and as early as four A.M. men and women of the poorer classes are at the fountain filling jars with water, which they sell to later arrivals at a centavo for four gallons, the quantity a jar holds. The schools and the markets, the latter with their many varieties of fruit unknown in our country, are very interesting. Many of the venders, spreading a shawl on the pavement, divide their articles into sundry little piles, each of which is sold for one cent. These sometimes consist of cooked articles, and many a passer-by gets a meal for that sum.

Passing along the streets, through the open door the mother of the family or a young girl can often be seen preparing the family meal. Corn, having been first soaked in a weak lye, is placed on a flat stone, over which a stone two inches in diameter and perhaps ten inches long is rapidly rolled by the hands of the woman, who kneels on the floor. The softened corn is soon reduced to a coarse paste, and is then flattened by hand into very thin wafers, which are immediately baked. These are the tortillas which, together with the frijoles, constitute the staple diet of the masses. Some of the tortillas are laid out for dishes and plates on which to place the beans; another tortilla is twisted into a spoon; and when the beans have been eaten,

A GENERAL VIEW OF ZACATECAS.

then the spoons, dishes, and plates are eaten, and, the hands being wiped on a tortilla that is left, that is eaten also. Thus the meal is over and the table cleared, with no dishes or table-cloth to wash. This, of course, obtains only among the poor classes; nowhere can be found more charming manners and true refinement than among *la alta sociedad*.

Of course the principal interest of the people of Zacatecas is mining. Among the principal buildings is the Aduana, built of red sandstone, with handsome carving around the entrance and the yard. Then there is the handsome market, which is exceedingly tidy and clean, and of which the upper floor is used as a hall or occasional theatre. There is another fine theatre, with a seating capacity of eight hundred, handsome decorations, and all the modern improvements. Close to the market is the cathedral, built of red stone, with a wonderful frontage on three sides, magnificently carved. The interior is equally rich, and cost many thousands of dollars. Toward the back of the theatre is the old church and convent of Santo Domingo. This formerly was very large, and the centre of the Inquisition, as were all the convents of the Dominican order almost everywhere. The portion forming the city convent is now the city prison ; the old church and the chapter assembly-room still belong to the order of Santo Domingo.

This church was the first one built in the state of Zacatecas, and was erected between 1560 and 1570. All that remains to show that it belonged to the Inquisition under the Dominican order is the assembly-room, or "Sala de Actas." The decoration of the church is very fine. The next place of interest is the church and convent of San Francisco. The church is small and very poor ; the frontage is of carved stone, and the interior decoration appears to have been very rich in former years. The convent now is almost in ruins, a small part being used as a *meson*, another as a dwelling-place for the poorer class, a small piece as a brick-yard, but by far the greater portion has become dilapidated with age and neglect. The old convent of San Augustin has been almost entirely turned into dwelling-houses, but the church, a very fine building, has been left entire, and belongs to the Presbyterian missions.

THE THEATRE CALDERON, ZACATECAS.

From the balcony of the Hotel Zacateno there is a magnificent panorama, the whole city seeming like one great fortress of stone. Huge stone walls and mountain-sides are everywhere, with patches of green here and there, making up a picturesque combination.

There are several silver-mines in the vicinity of Zacatecas, some of them exceedingly valuable. The principal mining districts in the state besides Zacatecas are Fresnillo, Sombrerete, Chalchihuites, Nieves, Pinos, Mazapil, Ojo Caliente, and Mezquital del Oro. These furnish, in addition to large quantities of gold and silver, copper, tin, lead, iron, cobalt, antimony, cinnabar, arsenic, sulphur, and alum. The patio process is in common use, although calcination and the *tonel* method are also employed. The product of these Zacatecas mines averages yearly from five to six million dollars, the mint coining five hundred thousand dollars per month. The climate is perfect ; no case of consumption was ever known.

In February, 1896, Zacatecas enjoyed the novelty of a snow-storm, during which the people gave themselves a holiday and battles with snow-balls became the rage. Students built snow forts and erected snow statues of General Escobedo and Minerva. Over three feet fell, and the sight was something almost unheard of, the climate usually being delightful all winter.

Having exhausted the sights of Zacatecas, Guadalupe, a suburb of about nine thousand people, some six miles distant, may be reached by tramway. The cars, operated by the "gravitation system," start slowly, but are soon whirling down the steep hills, passing by the queer adobe houses, the track now crossing over a bridge beneath which are seen droves of burros carrying the ores from the mines, again through a gulch around some huge boulders, or past the yawning mouth of some mine ; the magnificent views and the varied objects creating a thousand vivid impressions. Indeed, the experience of this tramway ride is one not soon to be forgotten by the tourist.

In Guadalupe the market-place, as in all other Mexican cities, is a point of interest, where every variety of vegetable is offered for sale, and the venders themselves are not the least attractive features of the scene.

The cathedral of Guadalupe, with its tiled dome and its beautiful surroundings, presents a delightful appearance as one approaches through the plaza, planted thickly with roses and

THE LITTLE PLAZA OF VILLAREAL, ZACATECAS.

countless varieties of flowers. As we enter the cathedral, we pause in astonishment. Upon the altar are life-size figures representing the crucifixion, and in the background is a painting of the hill of Calvary, with the attending Roman soldiers and Jews grouped around. Attached to the cathedral is an art gallery containing many magnificent paintings, the subjects drawn from the Holy Scriptures, and in their treatment showing the work of some master-hand. The new chapel, on the north of the cathedral, the gift of a lady of great wealth, is considered one of the finest in the world. The steps leading to the altar are of onyx, only the rarest kinds being used ; the rail of the altar is of solid silver, and the altar itself in parts is constructed of solid silver and gold. The magnificent dome is beautifully frescoed, and one's eyes never tire of feasting on the many lovely figures so skilfully portrayed.

The remainder of the convent is now occupied as a school. In this school there are over two hundred boys from the poorer classes of Guadalupe and Zacatecas, who are being taught the trades of wool-working and weaving, printing, bookbinding, carpentry, carriage- and car-building, blacksmithing, and shoemaking, as well as other trades. The blankets and wraps made in this school are equal in manufacture to any that may be bought either in the States or in Europe, and compare very favorably in price with them. This school was awarded medals in the Paris Exposition of 1887 and the Exposition at Chicago in 1893 for woollen and silk goods made on the premises. There is a band of well-trained musicians connected with the school. The establishment is self-supporting, and certainly is well worth visiting. This is the pet institution of the governor, who manifests the deepest interest in the progress of the pupils.

THE CHURCH OF GUADALUPE, ZACATECAS.

Near Guadalupe is the establishment of Señor Don Serapio Galvan, Fábrica de Providencia. This factory is in the shape of the letter L, and occupies thirty thousand square yards. The street front is a handsome façade, with square tower and large entrance; inside is a handsome court, with offices for the various departments. The owner's private house is also here, and has a large court with covered galleries from which opens a suite of handsome rooms gorgeously furnished. Carriages and all sorts of vehicles are manufactured in this factory, to compete with the best American or European products.

The governor of Zacatecas is General Jesus Arechiga, under whose wise administration many improvements have been made in public and private enterprises. Among the achievements of his terms are the new theatre, costing nearly two hundred and fifty thousand dollars; a magnificent hospital, of rose-colored stone, fitted with all the requirements of modern science; an elaborate system of lighting; a beautiful school for girls with ample grounds and all the latest appliances known to educators, a scientific institute, a normal school for boys, and other public buildings and improvements of importance to the capital city. His efforts have not been confined to the seat of local government, however, as many useful public improvements have been made throughout the state, including new schools, city halls, public gardens, and markets. A word should be added in praise of the fine system of public schools in Zacatecas. The state spends nearly three million dollars in primary and higher public instruction. There are about twenty-five thousand students in these schools, with two thousand more in private schools maintained by the clergy and other individuals. With her vast resources, her educational system, and her public spirit, the state of Zacatecas has already become a power in the republic of Mexico.

CHAPTER XXVIII

AGUAS CALIENTES

ONE of the smallest states in Mexico is Aguas Calientes, having an area of only two thousand two hundred and sixteen square miles. It is almost entirely enclosed within the state of Zacatecas. According to the last census, the state of Aguas Calientes has four cities, four villages, forty-nine haciendas, three hundred and fifty-five ranches, eighteen thousand five hundred and two houses, besides three hundred and eighty-one that are being constructed, sixty-eight Catholic churches, and two Protestant. The eastern districts consist of elevated table-lands, some five thousand to six thousand feet above the level of the sea. The western portion includes the sierras of Laurel and Pinal, spurs of the Sierra Madre or Cordillera. The table-lands produce abundant crops of cereals and a variety of fruits, including olives, figs, grapes, and pears. It is divided into four districts,— Aguas Calientes, Rincon de Romos, Asientos, and Calvillo.

The capital is Aguas Calientes, which means hot waters. It is a very attractive city of about forty thousand inhabitants, noted for its hot springs, well-appointed bath-houses, and healthy climate. At this point there is now being erected what will be one of the largest silver-copper smelting plants in the world. One of the most celebrated and largely attended fairs of the republic (the Feast of San Marcos) is held at Aguas Calientes in the month of April in each year, when thousands of people from all parts of the country throng the streets and plazas of this old and beautiful city. Aguas Calientes has especial attractions for lady tourists because of the beautiful needle-work (drawn-work) which is brought to all trains by the venders, for sale at very low prices.

SEÑOR DON RAFAEL ARELLANO,
GOVERNOR OF AGUAS CALIENTES.

The city takes its name from the warm mineral springs in its neighborhood. The old roads

STREET SCENE IN AGUAS CALIENTES.

from Mexico to Sonora and Durango and that from San Luis Potosi to Guadalajara meet here. The baths are reached by a long avenue of superb cottonwood-trees, and are well built of a soft red stone. The baths are very cheap and much frequented. On one side, through a canal, flows the surplus water from the springs, which is used gratis for bathing by those unable to pay the small charge of the bath establishment and by the washer-women. There is a handsome alameda (or park) and a paseo, as the grand avenue of these towns is called. The country around is very fertile and highly cultivated. The climate is delightful, the air being warm and the changes in temperature between November and April varying less than twenty degrees.

From Aguas Calientes a branch of the Mexican Central Railway extends to Tampico, on the Gulf of Mexico, passing *en route* through Salinas, noted for its extensive salt deposits, probably the greatest on the American continent, and San Luis Potosi, the capital of the state of the same name.

In the tropical altitudes of Mexico, and in the hot springs sections, as at Aguas Calientes, without regard to altitude, there is a sort of Egyptian disregard of the conventionalities in attire and a disposition to take a daily fashion hint from the Garden of Eden instead of from Paris, the children discarding even the fig-leaf. The water-carrier of Cairo is much like his brother of Guanajuato, where a long earthen jar is used. The groups about the fountains all over the republic, with jars of pottery borne on the women's heads on protecting turban-like rings, or balanced on the men's shoulders, are also Oriental.

Aguas Calientes, although small, is one of the important states in Mexico. It is half-way between the city of Mexico and the northern border, with a

KIOSK IN THE PARK OF SAN MARCOS, AGUAS CALIENTES.

TEMPLE OF SAN MARCOS, AGUAS CALIENTES.

branch line to San Luis Potosi. It is noted for its warm, healthy climate and its constant sunshine. Many invalids from the southern portions go there, and it is destined to become an important health resort. No tour of Mexico is complete without a visit to this beautiful state. The drawn-work manufactured by the Indians excels in beauty the celebrated Fayal work, which is so much better known.

The governor of Aguas Calientes is Señor Don Rafael Arellano, and to his wise administration the state owes its present peaceful condition and its marked progress in all the arts and sciences.

CHURCH OF THE ASCENSION, AGUAS CALIENTES.

CHAPTER XXIX

QUERÉTARO

SOUTH of San Luis Potosí and just west of Hidalgo is the old state of Querétaro, with an area of three thousand four hundred and twenty-nine square miles. It occupies a part of the Cordilleran plateau, and, while it contains much fertile land, is traversed by numerous mountain spurs. In these, however, many minerals lie waiting for the enterprising capitalist. Gold, silver, copper, lead, antimony, quicksilver, and tin are found. Cotton is grown in some parts, grain, tobacco, and sugar are extensively cultivated, and a good many cattle are raised. Fine forests of timber and precious woods abound also. The state is divided into six *partidos*,—Querétaro, San Juan del Rio, Amealco, Jalpan, Toliman, and Cadereyta.

The chief towns, besides the capital Querétaro, are San Juan del Rio and Toliman. Querétaro will arrest the attention of the traveller because of its beauty, and also because the career of Maximilian was there brought to a tragic close upon the "Hill of the Bells." It is an old city, dating back to the Otomites, in 1400. Its churches are numerous, imposing, and beautiful. A small stream flows through the town, furnishing irrigation,—all that is needed in this whole land to make it prolific in crops and fruit.

Querétaro has a population of fifty thousand, and is situated one hundred and ten miles northwest of Mexico, on a plateau six thousand feet above sea-level. It occupies the sides and summits of several hills, and is separated from picturesque little suburbs by a small stream. The streets are well laid out, the houses are regular, and the city is one of the finest in the republic. Palms and bananas grow in the open squares, with an occasional tree of scarlet hibiscus. The houses are more pretentious architecturally than most Mexican cities can boast, and give an air of comfort and wealth. The parish churches are magnificently decorated. The town has about fifty churches

SEÑOR CORONEL DON FRANCISCO COSIO,
GOVERNOR OF QUERÉTARO.

in all, a college, an art school, and an academy of design. Water is supplied by an aqueduct five miles long, which crosses a plain upon arches some of which are ninety feet high. This aqueduct is connected with a tunnel, through which the water is brought six miles, and is a marvel of skilful and substantial work. The expense was borne mainly by one generous person, to whom the city has gratefully reared a beautiful monument on one of its plazas. The water-carriers, in their quaint dress, gather about the public fountains to fill their jars for domestic purposes.

There are manufactures of woollen and cotton goods, leather, soap, cigars, and pulque. It is interesting to visit the large cotton-factory known as the "Hercules Mills." A colossal statue of Hercules, which cost fourteen thousand dollars before it left Italy, stands near a fountain in the midst of ornamental trees. Some fifteen hundred women and girls are employed in this mill, the best operatives receiving about forty cents per day.

Querétaro is noted for its opals, which have been worked for centuries and are still unexhausted.

This city has a melancholy interest because here Maximilian was shot. It will be remembered that Napoleon "the Little" undertook, while the Civil War was in progress, and because the United States government was occupied in suppressing a rebellion, to establish an empire in Mexico. He took upon himself the task of exporting an emperor to Mexico,—Maximilian of Austria, a dreamer imbued with the idea of the divine right of kings. He listened to the seductive assurances of an emperor who himself had secured the right to rule by rapine and blood. Carlotta, the beautiful wife of Maximilian, was ambitious, an ardent Catholic, and the Pope gave the new rulers consecration and his blessing. The history is interesting, though both emperor and empress exhibited a spirit of vanity and frivolity and a disregard of the rights of the people that was lamentably weak and heartless. When the Civil War was closed, the United States government put sixty thousand troops into Texas on the Mexican border, and then the Little Napoleon was told in unmistakable language that the French troops who sustained Maximilian must be withdrawn. Maximilian was advised to abdicate, and would have done so but for the proud and ambitious Carlotta. She volunteered to go to France to intercede

FAÇADE OF THE RUINS OF SAN AUGUSTIN, QUERÉTARO.

MONUMENT TO DOÑA JOSEFA ORTIZ DE DOMINGUEZ, QUERÉTARO.

with Napoleon. He was deaf to her entreaties, and she then fled to the Pope for relief, but with no better success. Repulsed, her finely strung nature succumbed, and she became a maniac,—perhaps the best surcease, except death, from the humiliation, the defeat, and the greater grief that were to follow.

Maximilian, with a few thousand troops, was shut into this city. On the night of May 19, 1867, the city was captured, and he was tried and condemned to be shot, together with his two

COURT-YARD OF THE FEDERAL PALACE, QUERÉTARO.

trusted generals, Mejia and Miramon. The execution took place two miles out from the city one month later. Maximilian said, as the fatal pilgrimage was begun, "I am ready; it is a beautiful day to die." Holding the crucifix over his breast, as an indication to the soldiers where to fire, and with his faithful generals at his side to share the same fate, he received the death-dealing bullet. The place is marked by three rude stones within an iron-railed enclosure, each stone bearing the name of one of the victims. Thus ended the last attempt to plant a monarchy upon this continent.

Querétaro possesses two of the masterpieces of Tresguerras, the churches of Santa Clara and Santa Rosa. Tresguerras was an architect, a sculptor, an engraver, a painter, and a poet, and he trained a great many workmen to carry out his ideas. He was born at Celaya in 1765, and died there in 1833. The church of Carmen at Celaya, with its wonderful dome, was one of his great works, and the interiors of Santa Rosa and Santa Clara, both of them old convent churches at Querétaro, are two others. Both have been mutilated by the removal of the grand altars and of the decoration of the chancels, and by the substitution of tawdry modern constructions. Otherwise they are both superb examples of art, Santa Rosa being much the

AQUEDUCT AT QUERÉTARO.

finer. There is nothing in Europe more beautiful than this interior decoration. They are possessions of which Querétaro should be proud and which she should guard with jealous care as incomparable monuments of Mexican art. Words are inadequate to describe the splendor of the wonderfully rich wood-carving, heavily gilded, the elaborate and graceful metal-work, including balconies and grilles of wrought iron, and the painting and sculpture, all from the hand or design of this great artist. As the work of a great Mexican they should be cherished by the entire nation, and it is to be hoped that no further act of vandalism will be tolerated.

In the government palace of Querétaro Governor Cosio has established a museum known as "The Historical Chamber," which is full of famous relics that have a bearing on great events of Mexican history. On the walls hang the portraits of former governors, including that of the present one. Among other curious objects are the mortuary casket in which the remains of

Doña Josefa Ortiz were brought from their former resting-place in the city of Mexico. Above it, in a glass case, is the identical old lock through the keyhole of which Josefa Ortiz (who was the wife of the corregidor) gave warning that the plot for Mexican freedom had been discovered. On the wall above the casket hangs her portrait, with that of Hidalgo and other heroes of the independence. On the wall are the portraits of the generals who fought against the French, and facing them are those of the imperial leaders. In this room is also preserved the rude coffin in which Maximilian's remains were brought back to the town to be embalmed before being sent to Austria, the blood-stains still showing on the bottom. On the side is the full print of the back of his hand where in jolting it struck against the side of the coffin. His remains now rest in the lovely castle of Miramar, by the sounding Adriatic. The bodies of

GENERAL VIEW OF THE HERCULES FACTORY, QUERÉTARO.

Miramon and Mejia were carried to Mexico and buried beneath stately monuments in the mausoleum of illustrious dead, in the pantheon close by the church of San Fernando, and near them, under a still handsomer monument, lie the remains of President Juarez, who refused to pardon them. The remains of Miramon have been lately claimed by his native city, Puebla, and they have been reinterred there with honors.

Querétaro was founded by the Otomite Indians in 1400, captured by a lieutenant of Cortez in 1531, and besieged in the Mexican revolution of 1810, when it stood for the cause of freedom and suffered for it. "Many a tempest's breath and battle's rage" has passed over Querétaro.

In the public square is a monument to Columbus. On one side of this are the names of the distinguished men the city has produced, on another the names of those who deserve remembrance for their benefactions to the city, on the third side are inscribed the memorable events in the city's history, with their dates, and on the fourth the elevation of the city above sea-level, its latitude and longitude, its mean temperature, with its highest and lowest range, its rainfall, and similar information.

The church of Santa Rosa was built as a thank-offering for the suppression of bandits and contrabandistas about 1752, and toward the end of the century was thoroughly reconstructed by Tresguerras. Mr. F. W. Church, the artist, has made a very close study of Persian architecture, and he thinks it remarkable that an artist who had never been outside of Mexico should have reproduced some of the most delicate characteristics of that architecture.

The country about Querétaro dimples and curves into a nest of sunny valleys, rounded into great beauty and widely different from the arid plains of some of the plateau regions.

San Juan del Rio is a pleasing little town of about eighteen thousand inhabitants. From here the train climbing the sides of the mountains gives the passenger a fine view of the beautiful valley below, and at Marquez station reaches the highest point on the line, eight thousand one hundred and thirty-three feet above sea-level. From this point there is a gradual descent of fourteen hundred and seventy-six feet in twenty-six miles.

WATER-CARRIERS AT THE PUBLIC FOUNTAIN, QUERÉTARO.

The condition of public instruction throughout the state is most gratifying. Besides the numerous primary and grammar schools there are a normal school, a civil college, and the academy of San Fernando, so that the beneficent influence of good schools is felt even in the smallest villages.

Governor Cosio, of Querétaro, is in hearty sympathy with the importance of preserving such noble works as the churches of Santa Rosa and Santa Clara, the monuments of a great Mexican architect. Governor Cosio is a fine type of the Mexican gentleman and statesman. He is a man of sterling character, universally esteemed, patriotic, public-spirited, and progressive. He speaks excellent English, and would be an honor to any country. A distinguished gentleman of honorable ancestry, his tact and integrity of purpose make him a credit to the high post which he has so long occupied and in which he has become firmly intrenched in the hearts of a loving people.

CHAPTER XXX

GUANAJUATO

JUST west of Querétaro is the larger state of Guanajuato, which is one of the most important states of Mexico on account of its mining interests, by far the richest in America. It has an area of eleven thousand one hundred and thirty square miles, with about a million population. This state is divided into five *partidos*,— Guanajuato, León, Celaya, Allende, and Sierra Gorda. Almost the whole of the surface lies within the plateau of Anahuac, at an average height of six thousand feet above sea-level, although it is extremely irregular, being traversed by two mountain-chains, and containing three peaks upward of nine thousand feet,— Los Llamios, El Gigante, and El Cubilete.

There are many picturesque and fertile valleys in the southern half. Lake Juriria, near the capital, is twelve miles long and four and one-half miles wide, and abounds in fine fish. Most of the mountains are porphyritic, although the Cerro del Cubilete is chiefly basaltic. The soil is exceedingly fertile, even for Mexico, and large crops of all kinds of grain can be depended on. The climate is generally salubrious, and there are numerous hot springs frequented by invalids. Chile, from which *Capsicum annuum* is obtained, is one of the staple products; maguey is plentiful; the sugar-cane does well in the warmer valleys; the olive and most of the European fruits flourish; and fine timber is found in the mountains.

Mining is, however, the chief industry, although the native Indians devote much care to agriculture. Guanajuato is one of the oldest mining regions of the New World. Only one-fourth of the area of the state has been scientifically explored, and yet there are already over three hundred mines perfectly studied and capable of giving good profits. The first mine worked was at a place called Veta de la Cruz, in the year 1548. Later, in the year 1554, work was undertaken

SEÑOR JOAQUIN OBREGON GONZALEZ,
GOVERNOR OF GUANAJUATO.

in the Veta Madre. The great value of these mines can be guessed at from the magnificent buildings in that region that are still standing in a state of admirable preservation. The first mining settlement was called Santa Ana; afterward Guanajuato was built, the first church occupying the situation of the present Municipal Pantheon. In 1558 the mines Rayas and Mellado were opened within the emplacement of the Veta Madre. The principal mines are La Luz, Valenciana, Rayas, Mellado Peregrina, La Loca and Adjuntas (annexes). The total product of all, according to the data that have been gathered, amounts to eight hundred and fifty million dollars.

La Luz in about ten years yielded some eighty million dollars. Rayas and Mellado during forty-four years rendered nearly one hundred and eighty million dollars. Rayas has made

THEATRE JUAREZ, GUANAJUATO.

fabulous yields of gold. It has been related that in some instances the quintal has been sold at one hundred and thirty-two dollars. On other occasions the product of one hundred and twenty-six arrobas (an arroba is about twenty-five pounds) has yielded twelve hundred marks.

The celebrated mines of Valenciana, discovered in 1770, and abandoned during the war of independence, in 1810, had up to that time produced two hundred and seventy-one million dollars. Since the workings have been taken up by several more or less powerful companies, the results have always been proportional to the amount of capital engaged. It has been figured that the Valenciana has been worked only one-eighth of its extent, and that it is susceptible of producing five million dollars per year for the next three centuries. The Valenciana mine is situated on the great Guanajuato vein, one of the most considerable that exists,—the Mother Vein (*Veta Madre*), which is in some places sixty metres wide. The ores of this vein are silver sulphuret, black prismatic silver, native silver, seleniuret of silver and gold, gray copper- and silver-bearing blendes. The working of the mines of Guanajuato is carried out with a great deal of intelligence. In several of them are shafts and tunnels of colossal dimensions, that of Cayetano especially being more than two thousand metres long. The wealth of the Valenciana is proverbial throughout the world; Baron de Humboldt, on his visit to Guanajuato, found a shaft eighteen hundred feet deep. He made a special study of that mine, an account of which is to be found in his printed works. Suffice it to say that the working company has spent the enormous amount of one million two hundred thousand dollars in the construction of shafts for the extraction of the metal, the deepest of all, called Guadalupe, being three hundred and forty-five metres in a vertical direction. These mines produce at present more than two thousand loads of mineral weekly, with which the mills of the company are fed.

A PRETTY LITTLE HOME ON THE ROAD TO THE PRESA DE LA OLLA.

Santa Rosa is one of the oldest and most promising mines for its wealth of gold and silver, and also for the economy with which it is worked. The yield of gold is marvellous, and no other mine of the Veta Madre region has ever rendered equal products. The Purisima de los Hernandez, for instance, has yielded ore valued at thirty-one thousand two hundred and forty-six dollars and eighty-one cents for a load of fourteen arrobas, or three hundred and fifty Mexican pounds. Public attention is now concentrated on Santa Rosa, as some of its mines are in full bonanza. Some of them, for instance, San Guillermo and Trinidad, yield weekly from five thousand up to twenty thousand dollars each. Labor is extremely cheap, the highest price being twelve dollars the metre of depth. Richly endowed by nature, the country contains throughout its immense extent rich metalliferous deposits exceeding "the wealth of Ormuz or of Ind." The innumerable enterprises for developing the country have produced, with more or less profit, colossal sums. If the work had been directed from the beginning with intelligent economy, the importance and profits of the exploitations would have been much greater. As for the riches already extracted from the hills in the principal mining regions, they are insignificant compared with those still shut up in the bowels of the earth.

The name Guanajuato is derived from an Indian word meaning "the hill of the singing frog." The earliest settlers were the Tarrascan Indians, who, upon arriving here, found a large stone in the shape of a frog, of which they made an idol, and they named the site of the future city Guanajuato, or the Hill of the Frogs. It was founded in 1554, and made a city in 1741. The site of the city was a gift from Mendoza to Don Roderigo Vasques, one of the conquistadores, as a reward for his military services. Guanajuato is one of the three greatest mining centres of the republic. It is the capital of the state. The peculiar situation of the city, with its crooked and irregular streets and its fortress-like houses, makes it look very ancient and feudal, and, oddly, amid all this antiquity stretch the wires of the telegraph and telephone, linking the old civilization with the new in a way that is strangely paradoxical. The heart of the city is the Plaza de Mejia Mora, where there is a tablet which states that here Benito León Acosta, Mexico's distinguished engineer and man of science, was born.

The climate of Guanajuato is temperate: no extremes of heat or cold mar its comfort. It is a land of blue skies and fresh breezes; the atmosphere is clear and invigorating. Mellow sunlight pours its flood of gold on fruitful fields. The forests are rich in timber of great value: oak, laurel, magnolia, mahogany, gum, rosewood, ebony, cedar, and many other woods abound.

MUMMIES AT THE PANTHEON, GUANAJUATO.

All the oil-bearing and medicinal trees and plants are found within her borders. Fruits and vegetables grow luxuriantly and in endless variety. Every possible taste can be satisfied with honeyed or acid fruits, rich, delicious nuts, and nourishing, palatable vegetables. The streams swarm with fish fit for the table of an epicure. Although as yet the farm appliances are somewhat primitive, improvements are being introduced rapidly, and the land is surprisingly productive of all the known grains and other valuable agricultural growths. It is a land where the sky is as deeply blue as sapphire, where the sun is rarely hidden, where tropical flowers of unspeakable magnificence deck every hedge and swing from every limb, and where the birds are like bits of flying flame or winged jewels.

Guanajuato is one of the quaintest and most delightful places in the world,—a walled city among the mountains, set upon the sides of heights so steep that the houses seem to cling to the rock, and that a misstep might precipitate one into the midst of a plaza three or four hundred feet below.

This lovely, bewildering spot is full of lanes and archways and winding market-places, where the picturesque people seem to be selling every oddity imaginable. The upper balconies of the beautiful homes are gay with awnings and flowers; the old church of the Jesuits is magnificent in fine arches of soft pink stone and carvings like lace-work; the overhanging hills show brilliantly against the blue sky wherever one turns; through a hundred different arches some vision of slender-pillared inner courts bright with blossoms and fresh greenery continually flashes out.

THE CASTLE OF GRANIDITAS, GUANAJUATO.

In fact, such is the unevenness of the streets that in many cases the houses seem to have been built in an amphitheatre, and often the doors of one dwelling are almost on a level with the roofs of the next. Many of the streets are too narrow for a wheeled vehicle, and all the older ones are extremely irregular. A mountain torrent passes through some of the eastern ones, which sometimes rises to a flood.

The streets are for the most part irregular, precipitous, rock-paved paths, upon which a wheeled vehicle is seldom seen, and down whose steep inclines half-naked men, women, and children of the peón class contest the right of way with gorgeously accoutred horsemen and droves of patient pack-laden burros.

The fame of Guanajuato, however, rests on her great mining industry, and a visit to one of her haciendas for the reduction of ore and to a mine is essential to even a cursory understanding of her resources. Many of the mines of Guanajuato are of comparatively easy access, some being entered by tunnel direct into the mountain, along which rails are laid for convenience in removing ore by horse-car, and others by steps cut in the rock. Should the would-be visitor be a woman, however, she will probably meet with obstacles, on account of the strange superstition in regard to the presence of a woman in a mine. But Friday is pay-day, and on Saturday the men frequently prefer to drink rather than to work; consequently, on the latter day she can visit the mine to her heart's content.

A visit to a hacienda or reduction works where the whole process of milling ore is executed by mule-power is one of the curiosities of Mexico, and nowhere is this process to be seen to better advantage than in the Hacienda de la Purísima.

In addition to its other points of interest, Guanajuato can boast of a theatre building just completed after the expenditure of twenty years of labor and a million of dollars. It is surpassed in elegance by no other structure of its class on the North American continent, with the possible exception of the Auditorium of Chicago. The interior of the Juarez Theatre is magnificently decorated, and is a dream of color. The proscenium arch is of the horseshoe form, in red, gold, and blue stucco relief. The noble parterre gives ample space to the large and comfortable seats, and these, with the three tiers of boxes, draped in old-gold plush, give a seating capacity of thirteen hundred people. The walls of the boxes and of the whole interior are stencilled in the Catalan style with dull reds and golds, which set off superbly the costumes of the señoritas and their lovely faces, for the ladies of Guanajuato are uncommonly beautiful and gracious.

A visitor who inclines rather to the curious than to the picturesque or practical will perhaps give the cemetery of Guanajuato, or "pantheon," precedence among the "sights" of the place. This burial-place is on the top of a steep hill which overlooks the city, and consists of an area

DAM MANUEL GONZALEZ, GUANAJUATO.

enclosed by what appears from the outside to be a high wall, but which proves from within to be a receptacle for bodies placed in tiers, much as the narrow confines of their native valley compelled them to live. The pantheon is enclosed by high walls, entered through ponderous gates. The dead are buried for the little time that the peculiar dryness of the soil and air takes to mummify them. Then they are filed away in pigeon-holes in the walls. Each pigeon-hole may contain the remains of a citizen, but it is not so occupied unless a specific rental is paid promptly. It is customary to pay this rental for a couple of years, but if the relatives of the deceased are particularly wealthy and have an unusually high social standing, they sometimes continue to pay the dues for five years, while if the relatives are correspondingly below the average the assessment may be paid for only a few weeks or months. When the rentals are no longer forthcoming, the partially mummified remains are taken out of the pigeon-holes and corded up in subterranean chambers tunnelled out of the solid rock. Here the skeleton-guarded walls are musty, the light is pale and gruesome, and the air is laden with the odor of the decaying dead. On all sides are the spectral forms. They are arranged upright around the walls, and there they keep their silent vigil until disintegration proceeds so far that the bones are no longer articulated. Once they fall asunder, they are heaped up from stony floor to rocky roofs, and there are many tunnels full of these human bones.

They are often no more than skeletons, these corpses that fringe the walls of the vaulted passages. Eyeless sockets stare at one, and gaping mouths look as if death had come with pain, while a piece of dried flesh with hair, with now a boot and then a fleck of trousers, remain attached to all that is left of what may once have been a prominent citizen.

Indeed, in many ways this old town of sixty thousand inhabitants is a very strange admixture of a new world and the centuries-old Orient. The walled streets, the white clothing, the public fountains, the stone balconies, the sandalled feet, the deep sky, all make one realize that yesterday is joining hands with to-day in bringing Guanajuato to the front as one of the most enterprising towns of the republic.

The dam "Manuel Gonzalez" cannot fail to interest the reader. The works of the reservoir were commenced on the 5th of March, 1887, and completed in 1893. The amount of expenses, including prizes, was over two hundred thousand dollars. The material employed is a metamorphic rock, known in the locality as green rock, and exceedingly handsome. In the ornaments are used sandstone of different colors, called loseros, and the red stone from the Bufa quarry. The effect of these combinations is beautiful beyond description; and all these varied materials are the products of the immediate locality. A wall, containing over forty thousand cubic metres, has been built, measuring one hundred and sixty-six metres in thickness at the base or foundation and twenty-four at the upper part. The maximum height in the interior is thirty-three metres and eighty-eight centimetres. This dam contains one million six hundred thousand cubic metres of water. On account of the short distance from the capital—only five kilometres—and the difference in the height of the ground, the city of Guanajuato is supplied with water enough for all its needs, and it will be possible to establish hydraulic motors of incalculable usefulness.

Public instruction has been pushed to the front, the systems of teaching being in conformity with the progress of modern times. The result has been the increase of the school population. There are now in the state no less than five hundred schools, with an attendance of thirty thousand pupils of both sexes. The cost of maintaining the schools of public instruction and of employing teachers of high ability is over two hundred thousand dollars. There are five institutions, with all the requirements of modern times, devoted to the highest branches of teaching. The government of the state, attentive to the welfare of its people, issued a decree making public instruction obligatory, and assuming control of it.

While we were in the state of Guanajuato we were shown through the great woollen-mills of Soria, which are a short distance from Celaya. These are very handsome factories, belonging to the Gonzalez family. There is a very complete little village around them, and the mills turn out beautiful fine woollen goods, equal to the best produced by the manufactories of Europe.

Among other interesting towns of Guanajuato is Salamanca, a busy little city, celebrated for the straw and leather goods manufactured there.

San Miguel de Allende was named for, and was the birthplace of, the patriot Allende. The city is on the east side of the railroad and about a mile and a half from it. It is spread out on the sloping sides of a great hill,—one of the most picturesque towns in Mexico, and

THE PRESA, GUANAJUATO.

famous for its baths, where the water gushes from the rocks on the hill-side, and is conveyed fresh to the baths at a most comfortable temperature. These ever-running springs, furnishing an abundance of water, run down in sparkling streams and miniature cascades through the most lovely gardens of fruits and flowers. The plaza is a beautiful one, densely shaded by luxuriant trees, under which the natives, in brightly colored costumes, group themselves on market-days, when the band plays in the evening, making pretty pictures fit for a canvas. The hotels face the plaza, the windows overlooking the novel scene. On one side is the Casa de

Loreto. The modern spires of the chapel, designed by an untutored native, contrast strangely with the square and Moorish style of the older buildings beside it.

San Juan de las Vegas is a typical Mexican town, primitive in style, where no foreigner has his home, where there are groves of oranges and lemons and bananas, where fruits may be had for the picking, and where the native "lazies" the time away in indolent do-nothingness behind the rows of cactus that hedge the streets.

Celaya was founded by the Spaniards in 1570. But, for that matter, the Spaniards penetrated a thousand miles farther north than this and founded Santa Fé, in New Mexico, and then over five hundred miles farther than that and founded Monterey, in California, before the English had established their first feeble colony at Jamestown, in Virginia.

Celaya is a city of great beauty in the midst of a fertile country. Here the tourist meets the vender of opals, strawberries (at all seasons), and dulces, a native confection, or rather the vender meets the traveller on all trains, night or day. At Celaya are many fine old churches, especially Our Lady of Carmen, which contains some frescos of note and several paintings well worth seeing. It is built on a level plain in the valley of Laja.

Salvatierra is noticeable in the distance from the glittering of its many church domes, which, being covered by glazed tiling, present a pleasing contrast to the dark green of the many shade-trees with which the streets are lined. Salvatierra has a population of ten thousand, and is something of a trading-centre. There is a large woollen-mill, which gives it some manufacturing importance.

Acambaro is the most satisfying town in Mexico. It is delightfully primitive, and the fact that it is an important railway junction-point has not deprived it of its antique quaintness. The town lies westward of the station, and, although scarcely half a mile away, is so completely hidden by the trees that only the church-towers can be seen peering above them and showing their white outlines against the blue background of the high hills beyond the town. The lover of the quaint and antique will find much to charm in this old town. Acambaro is the junction of the western division of the Mexican National Railroad, leading to Morelia and Patzcuaro and the beautiful lake region of Mexico.

The very pretty town of Maravatio has the usual complement of queer-looking old churches and attractive plazas. Its red-tiled houses give it a picturesque appearance. At Maravatio connection is made with the Michoacán and Pacific Railroad, under construction, to the west coast of Mexico.

Skirting the valley of Solis is a beetling cliff, called by the natives "El Salto de Juan Medina," the tradition being that a famous bandit, one Juan Medina, being hotly pursued by the authorities, leaped his horse from the precipice and was dashed in pieces on the rocks below.

Near Rio Hondo is a great meteoric stone as big as a car, called by the natives the "moonstone," as they believe it fell from that planet. There are some strange hieroglyphics on the stone, and, from its engraving, it is believed to have a more ancient origin than the famous Calendar stone.

León is situated in a valley noted for the fertility of its soil, and has a population of about one hundred thousand people. It is a great manufacturing city, and one of its principal productions is the beautiful soft leather clothing, delicately embroidered in gold and silver bullion, worn by the wealthier classes on their estates, although largely discarded in the cities.

Away back in 1680 a Spanish garrison was established around the infant city of León. León in the early history of New Spain became celebrated for its shoes, rebozos, saddles, spurs, small ironware, leather, etc., a reputation which it still retains. It is pre-eminently a city of small factories. In thousands of houses hand-looms are running, producing blankets and rebozos, and small shoe-factories are scattered all over the city, where the head of the family can be seen in the front room working, assisted at times by the wife and younger members of the family. They are a prominent and ever-present feature of this quaint city. The general cleanliness of the streets is noticeable. There is no poor quarter. The houses of the well-to-do and of the working classes are to be found together on every block. There are miles of streets of one-story houses, with whitewashed fronts and little gardens or patios in the rear, where the workmen live. It is common for two or three trades to be represented in one family. Zapateros (shoemakers), rebozeros (weavers), and factory girls all belong to the same family.

One of the interesting sights of the city is on Sunday mornings to see the artisans carrying their wares about the streets for sale or delivery to their employers. Men loaded with shoes, saddles, leather, clothing, rebozos, spurs, small ironware, etc., crowd the sidewalks, anxious to realize on their week's work before noon.

León is known as the "Queen of the Bajío," and is the largest city in that section of the republic. It has a population of about seventy thousand. The city is regularly laid out, with a central plaza and twelve minor plazas, and among its more notable buildings are the Casa Municipal (city hall), Alhondiga (commercial exchange), barracks, and jail. The main plaza has a fountain in its centre and is planted with trees. Special mention must be made of the calzada and the park. The former is a magnificent promenade about a quarter of a mile in length by two hundred feet in width, the centre tiled and paved for pedestrians, with seats extending its entire length, and carriage-drives on both sides, also shaded with magnificent rows of trees. This is a favorite resort of the public in the afternoon, and on Sunday many equipages may be seen there that would do credit to the metropolis.

TRIUMPHAL ARCH IN THE PASEO AT LEÓN.

León has an opportunity to possess at a small cost a boulevard of exceeding beauty by connecting the Rio Calle and the park; the cultivation of the trees should then be pushed, and the city would have a paseo of two miles more reaching from park to calzada; add electric light to this, and a fairy-land would be the result.

On one side of the plaza is the Casa Municipal; on the other three sides are portales lined with shops. Just outside of the city, on the road leading to Silao, is a picturesque causeway shaded by trees, that is the paseo of the town. This pretty place is reached by a tramway from the plaza.

The curacy of León was founded before the year 1586, for in that year the first curate, Alonzo Espinoso, was slain by the Chichimec Indians. During the ensuing two hundred years the curacy was administered by the Franciscans, by whom the existing parish church, dedicated to San Sebastian, was erected early in the last century. It was remodelled in 1834. Adjoining this is the small church of the Tercer Orden, also a Franciscan foundation. The church of Nuestra Señora de los Angeles, also a Jesuit foundation, and the oldest church in the city, contains some noteworthy carvings by the artist Sixto Muñoz, a native of León. La Soledad is believed to be contemporaneous with the foundation of the town.

The climate of Silao is equable and delightful. Many who find the capital too high for comfort come to Silao, which is two thousand five hundred feet lower, and therefore affords relief and a radical change from the hurly-burly of the city, at an elevation of more than seven thousand feet.

Irapuato is a thriving business town of some fourteen thousand inhabitants, and is widely known as the "strawberry station," from the fact that fresh ripe strawberries can be purchased here at the train-side every day in the year for twenty-five cents, Mexican money, per basket.

The present governor of Guanajuato is Señor Joaquin Obregon Gonzalez.

CHAPTER XXXI

JALISCO

JALISCO is one of the richest, most important, and most populous of the Mexican states. It has an area of one hundred and one thousand four hundred and thirty square kilometres (forty-eight thousand nine hundred and sixty-seven square miles), with a population of one million three hundred thousand. Its principal river is the Grande, or Santiago, which forms near the village of Juanacatlan a beautiful cascade, which tourists have aptly named the "Niagara of Mexico," and which is reached by an electric road from El Castillo station. It may be mentioned that these falls furnish the electric lighting for the city of Guadalajara, fifteen miles away. The river is here five hundred and sixty feet wide, and it pours the waters from Lake Chapala and an area of forty thousand square miles over the shelf of rock sixty-five feet high at a single leap. There are smaller rapids above and below.

Besides this, the same river has many other picturesque falls on its way to the Pacific Ocean. Among the lakes which stud with beauty this prosperous state is Lake Chapala, larger than Lake Geneva, and the largest and most beautiful in the republic. This lake, by reason of its area of eight hundred and ten square miles, is sometimes known by the name of the Chapalan Sea. Lake Chapala is a summer resort of the highest grade, and is frequented by the most prominent residents of Guadalajara and other large towns. There has recently been discovered a large deposit of petroleum discharging from the bottom of the lake.

SEÑOR GENERAL DON LUIS C. CURIEL,
GOVERNOR OF JALISCO.

In this state there are fifteen silver-mines, besides three of gold, five of copper, three of lead, two of mercury, and eight of iron. The richest mining district is that of Comanja.

The soil of Jalisco, by reason of its varied climate, produces all kinds of fruits. Its mountains are covered with trees, some of which are valuable and in great demand. In the group of mountains forming the Sierra Mascota lies a rich mineral district, that of Tepic, nearly all silver-mines; beside which there are other districts which could be worked to advantage.

Jalisco borders on the Pacific Ocean, as well as on the states of Sinaloa, Durango, Zacatecas, Guanajuato, Michoacan, and Colima. In colonial times it was known as the kingdom of Nueva Galicia. It is divided into eight cantons, Guadalajara, Lagos, La Barca, Sayula, Etzatlan, Autlan, Tuscacuesca, and Colotlan. The Sierra Madre crosses the eastern portion of the state, and the principal mountains are Tapalpa and Tigre in Sayula, and in the south the Nevado and the Volcan de Colima, the latter twelve thousand feet above the sea and in eruption most of the time. There are many beautiful valleys and rivers, the largest of the latter, the Santiago, being six hundred miles long, rising in Lake Lerma in the state of Mexico and flowing through Lake Chapala, which is in itself ninety miles long and from ten to thirty-five wide. Lakes Sayula and Magdalena are smaller, but noted for their delicious fish.

A STREET IN GUADALAJARA.

The climate of Jalisco varies from generally cold in the higher and northern altitudes to delightfully mild in Guadalajara and hot on the west coast.

The capital of Jalisco is Guadalajara, the population of which is estimated at one hundred and twenty-five thousand. Beautifully located as it is and having a delightful climate and fertile soil, the city is constructed with elegant blocks of houses fronting on clean, wide, and well-paved streets, and inhabited by a population noted for hospitality, culture and refinement, cheerfulness, politeness, and frankness of character. It easily holds the position of the queen city of the republic. Its cathedral, while smaller than that of the metropolis, is much handsomer and of greater architectural merit. One of the theatres, the Degollado, is the largest and most beautiful in the country. A superb granite penitentiary, built and managed in accordance with the latest developments and improvements in that line, is greatly admired by visitors. An entire square is covered by the government palace, which, while somewhat resembling the national palace in the city of Mexico, is even more harmonious and elegant in its architecture. The young ladies of the city rival the dark-eyed heroines of Shakespeare; and, in fact, during the local history love and dark eyes have had a most important influence. It was a romantic love-episode and its disastrous termination that caused the short duration of the government of New Galicia, a neighboring city, which was intended to be the capital of the province.

The history of the founding of the city is worthy of notice. In the year 1530, in the expedition made by Nuño de Beltran Guzman for the conquest of the northwest, the Spaniards penetrated into Jalisco and gave to this region the name of Nueva Galicia. Here, in the year

THE PALACE.

above named, the Captain Juan de Oñate founded the Villa del Espiritu Santo de Guadalajara, which name was given to the town in compliment to the oidor, whose birthplace was the Spanish city Guadalajara in New Castile. But the site then chosen proved undesirable, and a year or two later the town was removed to the valley of Tlocatlan,—not by the free choice of the townsfolk, but by order of the oidor,—where, by a royal cédula of the Emperor Charles V., dated November 8, 1536, it was granted a coat of arms as a city. But this second site became the more distasteful the longer they remained in it, and especially because they were exposed to the frequent and cruel assaults of the wild Indians. Yet they dreaded to move, for fear of the wrath of the oidor, although that functionary had been recalled to Spain to stand trial for his many crimes. While the men of the town, in council together, debated what they should

SANTUARIO ZAPOPAN, JALISCO.

do, a certain brave woman named Doña Beatriz Hernandez broke in upon them, crying. "Look at these fellows who are going on with questions and answers and never coming to the point! The king is my master! What has Don Nuño to do with us,—he who has been the cause of all our troubles? Let us go where it is good for us to go, without asking leave of Mr Guzman or Mr. Anybody Else, only our master the king!" And then, with one voice, they all shouted, "Well spoken! Let us do as Doña Beatriz has declared!" So commissioners were appointed to choose a site, and decided upon a fair valley called Atamazac; and eight days later all the townsfolk went out together in good order, and in that fair valley made they thenceforward their home. In which spirited fashion was the present city of Guadalajara founded, in the year of our Lord 1541.

In this city is the celebrated "Assumption" of Murillo, which belongs to the cathedral and hangs in the sacristy. Its authenticity is not a matter of doubt. When Maximilian ruled the land with the assistance of a French army under Bazaine, the marshal, who knew a thing or two about art, made an offer to the cabildo of forty thousand dollars, which was rejected.

Murillo in this picture represents the Virgin borne through the blackness of space by the archangel Michael in a cloud of exquisite light, with which mingle floods of glory from the heavens which Infinite Love has opened for Perfect Purity and Maternal Love. The joyous cherubs lie at her feet below the crescent moon. In the left-hand corner are cherubs winging their way to glory through the blackness of infinite space. On the extreme left of the group of thrice-blessed cherubs at the feet of the Virgin, and in full splendor of her cloud, is a beautiful little creature who is waving his hand at the star that had guided him, and seems to be saying, "Good-by, dear star!" But all these exquisite details, so full of tenderness and adoring love, are subject to and dominated by the chiaroscuro, whose graduation has never been equalled.

The foundation of this cathedral was laid in 1548. The present building was commenced in 1561, and the corner-stone was laid in 1571, by Bishop Ayola. The building was completed in 1618. Its towers were thrown down by the earthquake of 1818, and the clock between the towers was badly injured. The interior is rich in decorations and paintings. The two towers of this cathedral are wholly unlike any others in Mexico. In one of them is the "campanilla del correo," the little bell of the courier, which rang only in announcement of some important event. Another bell, called San Clemente, was in former times rung during a thunder-storm to ward off lightning. An important adjunct to the cathedral is the Sagrario, a comparatively new structure, commenced in 1808 and completed in 1843. The other churches are the San Francisco, San Augustin, San Felipe, La Campania, Guadalupe, Mexicalcingo, Jesus Maria, Capuchinas, Santa Teresa, Santa Maria, San José de Añalco, San Sebastian de Añalco, La Parroquia de Jesus, San Juan de Dios, Aranzazu, La Soledad, San Diego, Belen, La Concepción, La Trinidad, and La Parroquia del Pilar, with others in course of construction.

A MONUMENT TO PIUS IX., JALISCO.

One of the most famous of the institutions of Guadalajara is the Hospicio. It is one of the most noted in the world. The building is an imposing one of white stone, handsome and attractive, covering an entire square, and containing twenty-five patios or courts, with fountains, flowers, shrubs, palms, and trees, from which echo the melodious reverberating songs of children and birds, which seem to touch the hearts of all who visit it, and to embody almost a life in itself. It is, in fact, not a hospital, as is popularly supposed, but a home for the poor of all ages, from the baby in the cradle to the aged nearing the grave. The institution is admirably managed, under authority of the state of Jalisco. Children are taught all that may be learned in schools of the highest order, and as they grow older they learn some useful occupation in the higher arts and sciences. The product of their labor is offered for sale in support of the Hospicio, and includes some of the most exquisite embroideries and laces, made by the girls. Music, painting, drawing, and calisthenics constitute a part of the tuition, while the more practical matters of life receive serious attention.

The public squares and *jardines* in Guadalajara are pretty and well kept. Twice a week and on Sundays an excellent band discourses sweet music in the plaza, attracting a large crowd of people. There the best society and the prettiest young ladies are seen. By common consent the sexes and classes separate on the promenade. The inner or wider promenade is

THE CATHEDRAL, GUADALAJARA.

reserved for the better class. On both sides are benches and chairs. The gentlemen keep in line on one side and in one direction, while the ladies do the same, but in an opposite direction, the two streams passing each other constantly. It would be considered *mauvais ton* to go against these rules. Thus, no matter how great the throng, perfect harmony exists among the promenaders. The lower class, clean and well-behaved, walk on the outside, never mixing with their social superiors.

There is no doubt that Guadalajara deserves her name as the queen city of the west, and any one who knows her cannot but appreciate her picturesque Mexican name, La Perla del Occidente.

No other city approaches it, unless it be Puebla; but the real beauty of Puebla is outside, while Guadalajara has many charms within her gates. The centre of its charms is its plaza, a beautiful garden surrounded by magnificent buildings. On one side is the government palace, on another the cathedral, and on the other two sides are long rows of portales, with their graceful arches. One can never forget the first evening on the plaza in Guadalajara. Guadalajara is one of the brightest of Mexican cities. Its cathedral is approached only by that of the capital. The government building has a modern air that is pleasing; its stucco is colored a light gray, and its white trimmings are decidedly agreeable to the eye.

One is reminded here of the Royal Exchange in London by seeing on a government building an inscription of a Bible passage. Here the passage is "Nisi Dominus custodierit civitatem, frustra vigilat qui custodit eam" ("Except the Lord keep the city, the watchman waketh but in vain"). In one of the principal squares is the monument commemorative of General Ramón Corona, a brave soldier, whose memory is loved by all true Mexicans, and who was assassinated by a lunatic in 1880.

In its loyalty to the Church Guadalajara is second to no other city in Mexico, and makes good its claim by works of charity and mercy.

Days may be spent pleasantly in this beautiful city, and other days in exploring the grand surroundings. A visit to the famous barranca should not be omitted.

AVENUE LEADING TO THE HOSPICIO, GUADALAJARA.

The Santiago River has here cut its way from the plateau to the lower level, and has made an enormous cañon, the perpendicular sides of which are two thousand feet high. At the top of the chasm you are in a temperate climate, at the bottom you get a taste of torrid temperature. Nowhere else in Mexico, and probably nowhere else in the world, can so satisfactory an excursion be made so easily; two hours' ride from the city brings one to the barranca, but the visitor should devote the whole day to the excursion to this region of the banana and the palm.

The scenery is grandly magnificent and wholly indescribable, so wildly picturesque. Here you are in the midst of castellated rocks, frowning precipices, and unfathomable abysses. Passing first the scraggy mountain-oaks, till, in the lower road, the path is through a forest of thumb-bananas, and shaded by their broad leaves, one finds at the bottom of the barranca the Rio de Santiago, while on either side the towering mountains lift up in perpendicular cliffs the grandest picture of sublime magnificence.

The big barranca of the Rio Grande de Santiago, from its point of departure from Lake Chapala at Ocotlan, is the narrowest valley in the world. It is probably exactly like a Norwegian fiord, from the cosmographical point of view, but while it is full of Indian villages, fruit-trees, and slopes terraced for maize, and laughter and merry voices bubble up along its course, the fiords are solemn and silent and awe-inspiring.

A trip to San Pedro is delightful. The ride is along the ancient calzada, under great trees kissed by the sun for a hundred years, and more paved streets, handsome residences, fine stores, beautiful gardens, and happy faces will greet you at San Pedro. This is the favorite suburb of Guadalajara. Here the wealthy people have out-of-town homes. Here also the famous Guadalajara pottery-ware is made.

The celebrated Guadalajara ware is known the world over. It is sold at greatly reduced prices from those asked in the curiosity stores in the city, where there is no certainty of genuineness. A warm welcome is extended to the visitor at the low adobe by Juan Panduro, the Indian sculptor, who shows and sells samples of his exquisite handiwork, made by himself and son. If one desires a bust or statuette of himself, or a life-like likeness, it may be modelled while he waits and afterward baked and sent to his hotel, or the artist will call at the hotel and do the modelling at one's room. This young Mexican made himself famous at the Atlanta Exposition by his wonderful work. In the much frequented "Mexican village" he was the centre of attraction, and specimens of his remarkable craft were carried by admiring visitors to every part of the United States. The work of these artists is all the more interesting and remarkable because they not only never received any art education themselves, but have never even seen the work of other artists except as it may be found in Guadalajara. Their material is the native clay, made and fashioned with their fingers and a small pointed stick; and so perfect is their work that not only are the features carefully reproduced, but every line and wrinkle and even the smallest buttons or bit of lace-work are finished with the minutest detail.

The city of Atemajac is situated to the north of the city of Guadalajara, and is reached by street-cars, which leave the cathedral every forty minutes. On the road to this village you pass the hamlet of Mezquitan, where the Tastoanes meet annually to commemorate the anniversary of the assassination of Saint James. This spectacle is ludicrous in the extreme, as the Indians dress themselves in primitive and barbaric costumes and go through the mock tragedy as they suppose it was enacted. On the way you pass also the famous baths, which have the rare property of being cool in summer and hot in winter. The trip is a very enjoyable one, as the cars pass through a lovely tract of country.

Up toward the northeast, on the Mexican Central's main line, is the town of Lagos, which has a population of forty thousand, and an elevation of six thousand one hundred and thirty-four feet. This is a fine manufacturing city, at the edge of one of the most fertile agricultural districts of the republic. There are numerous stories about the people of Lagos, which, if true, show them to be somewhat like Falstaff, not only witty in themselves, "but the cause that wit is in other men." They say that the council of twelve was to hold a meeting in the hall where was a bench on which all should sit. Six came, and each put his hat beside him on the bench. When the other six came there was no room for them. It was decided to stretch the bench. Each man put his hat on his head, and the twelve men pulled on the bench, six at each end. Then they all sat down, for the bench was now long enough for them all. Here is another: The parish priest lay ill in his bed of a grievous sickness; desiring to know the time of day, he sent his servant up to the *azotea* (roof) to find out the hour from the sun-dial which was there. The domestic, after studying the matter carefully, came to the conclusion that he knew nothing about this contrivance, so he placed the dial on his shoulders and brought it to the priest, saying, "Here is the watch, that your worship may see the hour, because I don't understand it."

From Irapuato, in Guanajuato, a branch of the Mexican Central Railway extends to Guadalajara, one hundred and sixty-one miles west, running through a rich agricultural and fruit-growing country producing large crops of wheat, corn, and sugar, and the finest oranges grown in the republic. Passing through Penjamo, a quaint old place of some eight thousand people, and La Piedad, with about the same population, the next station of importance is La Barca, a city of twelve thousand people, situated on the Lerma, or Santiago, River, near where it empties into Lake Chapala. Fifty miles west of La Barca and fifteen miles east of Guadalajara, at the station of El Castillo, a tramway conveys passengers to the famous falls of Juanacatlan, justly termed the "Niagara of Mexico." The river at this point plunges over a precipice sixty-five feet in height to the rocks below, making a picture of grandeur and interest well worth seeing.

Sixteen miles beyond La Barca lies Ocotlan. This pretty place is on the river Sula, a short distance above its junction with the Lerma. The station is connected with the town by street-cars, which run to the bridge just above the steamboat landing. Ocotlan is situated on

SCHOOL OF JURISPRUDENCE, GUADALAJARA.

a plain, which slopes southward a few miles into the shore of the lake. With its pretty plaza, its beautiful church spire, its portales, and its two bridges, Ocotlan is very picturesque.

At Poncitlan, eleven miles from Ocotlan, are a beautiful bridge and some charming scenery. This is the best wheat country of Jalisco.

Atequiza, thirteen miles farther west, is a good station for any one to stop at who wishes to visit a great hacienda comfortably and without a ride through the country. The station, as is common along the whole line, takes its name from the great hacienda nearest. Atequiza is in sight, half a mile away on the left. This hacienda has miles of wheat-fields, hundreds of oxen and other animals, and thousands of men at work on its farms or ranches. Here are the head-quarters of the vast estate,—storehouses, corrals, workmen's homes, mills, hospitals, school-houses, and a church, besides the princely residence of the owner. As for the interior of these haciendas, they are much alike,—a great stone building, which is neither farm- nor country-house, but has a character peculiar to itself, solid enough to stand a siege, with floors of painted brick, large deal tables, wooden benches, painted chairs, and whitewashed walls; one or two painted or iron bedsteads, put up only when wanted; kitchen and outhouses; the court-yard, a great square, around which stand the house for boiling sugar, whose furnaces blaze day and night, the house with machinery for extracting the juice from the cane, the refining-rooms, the places where it is dried, etc., all on a large scale. If the hacienda is a coffee plantation also, then there is the great mill for separating the beans from the chaff; and sometimes there are buildings where they make brandy. There are four or five hundred men employed, exclusive

FALLS OF JUANACATLAN.

of boys, and a hundred horses and mules. The property is very extensive, containing fields of sugar-cane, plains for cattle, and the pretty plantations of coffee, so green and spring-like, the latter containing, say, fifty thousand young plants, all fresh and vigorous. Besides there is a great deal of uncultivated ground, abandoned to the deer and hares and quail, of which there is great abundance. This hacienda or plantation is thought to be the place called "Miraflores" in Christian Reid's beautiful story "A Cast for Fortune."

The completion of the Mexican Central's branch from Guadalajara to Ameca has opened up a rich agricultural and mineral region to the outside world. Between La Venta and Orendain the road runs through a succession of hills, where some heavy work was done. At Metaconejo the Rio Salado is crossed on an iron bridge; on the right may be seen some fine sugar-cane. The next stop is Orendain, distant eight leagues from Tequila, a town of about six thousand inhabitants, and the centre of the great Tequila industry. The famous hacienda of El Refugio belongs to Orendain Hermanos, of Guadalajara. The village of Tala, with its three thousand inhabitants, is about two miles south of this station. La Vega is the last station before reaching Ameca, and, no doubt, will be the most important one on the line.

From La Vega to Ameca the line runs through a beautiful valley lying between two ranges of mountains. Ameca, the terminus of the road, is an interesting place of some eight thousand people. The Ameca River, a wide and deep stream of water, flows through the town. A solidly constructed bridge of stone unites the two banks of the river. The principal industries of the districts are agriculture and mining.

That the arrival of the railroad has aroused Ameca from a Rip Van Winkle sleep there is no doubt. All the large and fertile valleys in every direction produce enormous quantities of corn, that can now be transported to market rapidly and cheaply. Coffee-growing has never been attempted to any extent, but with the coming of the iron horse attracting new capital, energy, and brains, it is only a question of time when the region is developed, thus adding to the wealth of the great state of Jalisco.

Etzatlan is a charming little town upon the shores of the Laguna de Magdalena, which lies in the hollows at the foot of the high mountain called the Cerro de Tequila. It is quite large, and is navigable. It is, in fact, navigated, for a small steamboat plies from Etzatlan on the south of the lake to Magdalena on the north. There are several fine beaches, and General Curiel, the governor, intends to make this a summer resort for the people of Guadalajara during the heated term, March, April, and May. The air is cooled by the evaporation of so great a body of deep water, and Etzatlan will be a sort of tourist's paradise, for it is within easy reach of the best meat and poultry in the republic, and the boats will bring tropical fruits from Magdalena, which is only six miles from Tequila, with an excellent wagon-road.

The Cerro de Tequila is bold and rugged, and a most picturesque feature of the landscape, and there is another huge mountain to the south. The ground is open toward the west in the direction of San Marcos, but otherwise Etzatlan is surrounded by high mountains. It is bowered amid semi-tropical vegetation, and is constantly cool, affording a most pleasing contrast to the city of Guadalajara during the hot months.

The Guadalajara branch of the Mexican Central has not only brought railway communication to one of the great cities of the republic, but has also made easily accessible an extensive and productive agricultural region. It is in this part of the country that the oranges are produced which have lately begun to be shipped to the United States. At present, however, it is not the cultivation of the orange, but that of coffee, that is attracting special attention. The possibilities of the western slope with reference to this product are but imperfectly determined, while on the eastern slope much progress has already been made.

Capitalists who seek a sure and productive investment for their money should take into account not only the richness of the soil, the mildness of the climate, and the thousand attractions offered by life in that zone, but also and principally the assured importance of Guadalajara as a railway centre of the first rank, with facilities for transportation at least equal, if not superior, to those of the city of Mexico, being able to send its varied products rapidly at low rates of freight not only to the principal markets of the republic, but also to those abroad, for which it will have seven or eight points of outlet.

One of those products which will seek speedy exportation will be the mineral wealth of Jalisco, which exists in great quantities, and which possesses a richness of which we assuredly have had but a hint as yet.

The mining districts at the present time are Mascota, Talpa, Hostotipaquillo, Tapalpa, Comanja, and Bolanos, with a total of more than two hundred and fifty mines, the greater number being of silver with some traces of gold, three or four of gold, some of copper, and others of quicksilver, iron, lead, and other metals.

The city of Guadalajara has had for many years a mint in constant activity, coining silver and gold from the mines of Jalisco, among which those that have sent the greatest amount have been the mines in the districts of Talpa and Mascota.

In spite of this, it may be asserted that mining in Jalisco is in its infancy, and awaits only the energetic and decisive action of companies with sufficient capital to astonish the continent with the fabulous riches of its veins, many of them as yet untouched.

And so it will be seen that, with all the modern progress and enterprise of Guadalajara, the resources of the great and important state of Jalisco are yet to be developed, and that neither

THEATRE DEGOLLADO, GUADALAJARA.

the world at large nor the inhabitants of Jalisco themselves dream of the wealth that lies locked in her natural resources.

It is impossible to over-praise the climate of Jalisco. With its constant sunshine, its skies even bluer than those of far-famed Italy, and its mellow, genial warmth, Guadalajara is one of the most beautiful garden-spots of the world.

The intellectual condition of Jalisco is up to the standard of modern times, and lifts the people into a state of intelligence rather above the ordinary. The schools are of the best, the state and the cities spending large sums of money on them, so that the primaries are being extended even to the distant ranches, while the secondary and professional schools rank among the best in Mexico. Jalisco's lawyers have attained the highest reputation, her doctors command the respect of all, her engineers have attained national fame, and her "Seminario de los Obispos" (Seminary of the Bishops) is known everywhere as having graduated some of the most notable of the Mexican clergy.

The governor of Jalisco is General Luis C. Curiel, a young and energetic statesman, of whose abilities his people are justified in expecting much. Governor Curiel, after serving his country in the cause of Mexican freedom, had the advantage of several years in Paris in an official capacity, where he became familiar with the most progressive ideas of good government, the benefit of which is being felt by the people of Jalisco to-day. This noble statesman is one of the "coming men" of Mexico, and undoubtedly will be heard from in the future as prominent in the making of Mexican history.

CHAPTER XXXII

COLIMA

COLIMA, just south of Jalisco, is one of the smallest states in Mexico, only Morelos having a smaller area. Colima contains two thousand three hundred and ninety-three square miles, and has a coast-line of one hundred miles. The surface is generally level, although there are a few mountains rising to a height of one thousand feet. The volcano of Colima, as has been stated, is over the line in Jalisco. It was inactive from 1830 till 1869, and was supposed to be extinct; but on July 12 of the latter year it began to smoke, and a few weeks later it poured forth intensely hot pumice-stone enough to cover hundreds of acres at its base, keeping up the eruption for several years.

The climate of Colima is very hot, and the soil is exceedingly fertile, producing large yields of coffee, tobacco, vanilla, indigo, cacao, and various fruits.

Colima was founded in 1522 by Gonzalo de Sandoval. It was incorporated, under the name of Santiago de los Caballeros, by Philip II., and was finally made a city in 1824. It is the capital city, and has a population of some twenty-five thousand. It is situated in a fertile plain. Although the inhabitants of the state are largely Indians, those of Colima are intelligent whites, and the streets are handsomely laid out, with many fine residences. There are a government house, a college, and several good schools, besides a number of churches.

The city of Colima is a very gay and lively place, with plenty of blossoming flowers and luxuriant foliage and many beautiful plazas, the principal of which is the Plaza de Armas, with an elegant iron kiosk in the centre. The government palace is large and beautifully decorated with a magnificent public clock with a luminous dial in the front façade. There are many other beautiful buildings of a public character in Colima, as well as many imposing private residences of good architectural features.

SEÑOR CORONEL DON FRANCISCO SANTACRUZ,
GOVERNOR OF COLIMA.

HACIENDA OF SAN ANTONIO, NEAR THE CITY OF COLIMA.

LAKE JABALI, HACIENDA OF SAN ANTONIO.

INDIANS FROM THE VILLAGE OF SUCHIBLAN, IN WORKING CLOTHES.

The city of Colima and its surrounding district are connected by railway with the magnificent port of Manzanillo, one of the most important ports on the Pacific coast. This gives Colima commercial advantages with the United States and with Europe, although its citizens are shut off by the Sierra Madre from direct communication with the interior of their own republic. The Mexican National Company has a concession for carrying this line on from Colima to Guadalajara, and, although there are many difficulties to be overcome, this will probably be done some time in the future, thus not only opening up a wonderful mountain country, but connecting the fertile little state of Colima with the centre of Mexico's modern progress. At the present writing, however, the difficulties look to an ordinary observer almost insurmountable. Never shall I forget the fatiguing journey of two or three hundred miles on horseback, zigzagging between tremendous barrancas of unfathomable depth, ascending and descending hills almost perpendicular, which we took under the hot summer sun across the Sierra Madre from Guadalajara to Colima in June. It was one of many wonderful experiences in a wonderful country never to be forgotten, a journey we could never have either undertaken or accomplished but for the generous assistance and kind courtesy of President Diaz, who furnished us letters to the governors of all the states through which we passed. The journey was accomplished on horseback in less than a week, during which we were accompanied by two trusted Indian guides and our body-servant. The magnificent scenery of the mountain district in Jalisco and Colima is not to be easily described. It is wild with all the fragrance and luxuriance of a tropical country, and picturesque with the beauty of peaks and cañons of a noble mountain-range.

INDIAN WOMEN FROM THE PUEBLAS NEAR COLIMA.

It was in Colima that we saw the process of making tuva, a most delicious and refreshing drink. It is made from the sap of the cocoanut palm, which is drawn from the very top of the tree. Señor Francisco Santacruz, the governor's son, kindly escorted us through the gardens adjacent to the palace and showed us the process. An Indian servant came to the bottom of the tree and devoutly crossed himself; then he ran up the tree with the agility of a monkey, seating himself at the topmost part, where the leaves branched out after the manner of the cocoanut palm. With a sharp knife he made a deep incision in the top of the tree, and then fastened a bowl made of the native gourd so as to catch the sap. Afterward this sap was brought down and fermented, making a delicious light wine of peculiarly delicate flavor.

THE GOVERNOR'S HOUSE IN COLIMA.

Some of the barrancas of the country are terribly precipitous, and almost as picturesque as the barrancas of Jalisco. In colonial times the Spaniards hewed the mountainroads out of solid rock, and the feet of men and mules passing over them for so many years have made them as smooth as glass,—which will give some idea of the great risk in travel.

The lake of Cuyutlan, along the border of the state, is the next to the largest lake in the country, and is navigable for its entire length.

The schools of Colima are models of their kind, the state expending annually many thousands of dollars for their support. The people of Colima, in consequence, are an intelligent, educated, and thriving class.

There are but three political districts in Colima,—Central, Alvarez, and Medellin. There

STREET SCENE, COLIMA.

are seven municipalities.—Colima, Villa Alvarez, Comala, Coquimatlan, Tecoman, Iztlahuacan, and Manzanillo.

Both the hot lands and the temperate regions are wonderfully fertile and rich in products of every species. Colima coffee is famous everywhere for its excellence, and is raised here in

PLAZA DE LA LIBERTAD, IN FRONT OF THE GOVERNOR'S PALACE IN COLIMA.

great abundance. Owing to the climate, tropical fruits grow in astonishing luxuriance, and, as there are no mines in Colima, the people devote themselves to the pursuit of agriculture with remarkable results.

Manufacturing is not neglected in Colima. There are three important cotton-factories in the state, known as San Cayetano, La Armonia, and La Atrevida. There are two larger mills, also, for making sugar and brandy from cane, besides numerous manual industries on a smaller scale.

The governor of Colima is Coronel Francisco Santacruz, who is a progressive, well-educated man, and under whose fostering care the state is making a fine record for itself. He is particularly interested in the cause of public education, realizing that no true progress can be accomplished in any country except upon a foundation of thoroughly good common schools. I made a thorough personal inspection of the public schools of Colima, and found them conducted according to the most approved modern methods now in use in European and American cities. Thus it will be seen that while Colima is a small state it is neither poor nor unimportant.

CHAPTER XXXIII

TEPIC

THE territory of Tepic was to us a surprise and a wonder. We were the guests of Mr. Ernest Lonergan, who met us with carriages and took us through the capital and entertained us handsomely at his lovely home. We were shown over the sugar-refineries at Puga and the immense plantation of the Barron's, and took horses from Tepic to San Blas, from which place we went on one of the Pacific Mail Steamship liners to Mazatlan. At Tepic we had the pleasure of meeting General Romano, the governor of the territory. We had heard so much about this energetic man, who had crushed out brigands in that part of the country, that we expected to meet quite a piratical personage, but were most agreeably surprised when we met a charming gentleman with delicate manners and exceedingly courteous.

The territory of Tepic originally belonged to the state of Jalisco, but President Lerdo de Tejada, on account of the power which the famous one-eyed Indian chief Lozada had acquired, declared it a free territory. When Lozada attacked Guadalajara with his hordes of Indians he was met by General Corona with only twelve hundred men and repulsed. General Corona was assassinated on the 10th of November, 1880. This general, an intimate friend of Benito Juarez, had rendered great service to his country during the war of intervention of the French.

The territory of Tepic contains about one hundred and eighty thousand inhabitants, the principal towns being Tepic, with ten thousand; Santiago, six thousand; Ixtlan, five thousand; San Blas, two thousand; Ahuacatlan, two thousand; and Acaponeta, three thousand. Immediately around Tepic, however, there are factories containing as many inhabitants as some of these towns. Among these are the Hacienda de Puga sugar-factory and the Escondida. Near Tepic there are large cotton-factories, "Fábrica de Jauja." The proprietors of these factories, Messrs. Barron and Forbes, own large estates near the town of

GENERAL LEOPOLDO ROMANO,
Governor of Tepic.

Santiago, where they raise nearly all the cotton worked up in their factories, supplying any shortness in their crops from Acapulco, in the state of Guerrero. Both these factories run about six thousand spindles and one hundred and eighty looms, turning out excellent cotton goods, which are sold in the Tepic territory and in Jalisco, Sinaloa, and Sonora. Messrs. Barron & Forbes Company's "Fábrica de Jauja" has extensive bleaching-works on the most improved plan, turning out white cotton cloths which compete favorably with the products of Manchester manufactories. These cloths are sold all over the republic of Mexico.

Besides his sugar estate of Puga, Mr. Francis Barron owns the hacienda of Mora, where sugar-cane is also cultivated, the product being worked up by an open jamaica-train into brown sugar, called *panocha*, which is largely consumed by the natives. The Hacienda de la Laguera, at the door of Tepic, also deserves mention. At one time this was a lake surrounded by mountains, and evidently formed an enormous crater of a volcano, but in 1866 a tunnel was driven through the hill at one end and a deep ditch cut in the pasture-land that, although only four thousand five hundred acres in extent, has at least three thousand head of cattle feeding on it the year round.

CATHEDRAL, TEPIC.

The country round about Tepic is remarkable for its excellent pasture-land and fertile soil.

Both Puga and Escondida have large distilleries attached to their sugar-factories, where the refuse is worked up into a species of rum (aguardiente). Mr. Barron's estate embraces about one hundred thousand acres, and extends from the city of Tepic to the other side of Santiago.

Tetitlan, another large estate on the same road, deserves mention on account of its fertile lands and abundant water, at the foot of the extinct volcano called Sevoruco.

Below Tetitlan are the lands of General Leopoldo Romano, governor of the territory; these extend to San Blas and Santiago. Here is found a splendid breed of cattle, the general having spared no trouble or expense in raising them on his pastures. An extensive coffee-plantation has been laid down also by the general. Large quantities of salt are produced from his lands adjoining San Blas.

Santiago is a town situated on the river which bears its name, the largest river in the republic. A tract of land was ceded for the building of the town, and cotton, corn, beans, and tobacco are extensively cultivated. India-rubber trees grow readily here. Corn yields three times as well as on the higher land.

To the south of San Blas an extensive and fertile estate is being opened up by a German firm. These lands have been planted with coffee, teas, tobacco, etc., and are yielding most satisfactory returns.

With the exception of sugar-cane cultivation, agriculture in Tepic is carried on by a species of partnership between the owner of the soil and the laborer. The owner opens an account current with the laborer, giving him land, oxen, plough, and seed, the laborer putting in his labor. Any advance in cash, justified by the size and condition of the crop, that may be required by the laborer is allowed by the owner, who receives back the equivalent from the share of the laborer. Generally a stipulated price is named at which the owner purchases the laborer's share, which usually yields a large profit to the owner. This system has one advantage, that the crop is carefully tended by the laborer, which is rather difficult where such extensive crops are grown.

PLAZA AT TEPIC.

The Tepic territory is noticeable for the quantity of waterfalls it contains, of which as yet only a few are utilized. This abundance of water is of great importance to a country where pasturage is so expensive an item.

The town of Tepic is situated about two thousand nine hundred and eighty feet above the level of the sea, and enjoys a most delicious climate from the month of November till the end of April, possibly the most delicious climate anywhere. The nights are cool, with slight frosts in December, January, and February. The days are warm and bright. Rain seldom falls except in June, July, August, and September, the rainfall averaging sixty-six inches in the year. During the hot months frequent heavy storms fall, mostly at night and scarcely ever before the afternoon, the mornings being delightful. The drives around Tepic are most picturesque. The town boasts a very pretty plaza, where fruit and flowers are sold. This square presents an animated aspect on Sundays, when the country-people bring in their produce from miles around. The alameda, or park, as well as other smaller squares, is beautifully laid out.

The government buildings are handsome, and in the Plaza Principal a fine stone municipal college is in course of erection. The merchants and shopkeepers are enterprising and thriving, but feel sadly the want of railway communication with the interior, which would open up the fertile district capable of being the granary of the interior of Mexico.

Even now, with their limited means of transport, Tepic cultivators of the soil and manufacturers hold their own and compete with more favored districts in the Jalisco and Sinaloa markets; but they can send only produce which will bear the heavy freight charges, such as cotton goods, sugar, tobacco, coffee, and rice.

A very important product is cocoa oil, which is raised in large quantities on the coast lands and sold in Jalisco, Sinaloa, and other neighboring states.

COTTON-FACTORY "JAUJA," TEPIC.

Ixtlan is a flourishing little town, with several small sugar-factories in its immediate neighborhood; its principal source of revenue is mining.

The territory of Tepic owes its prosperity in great part to its able and courteous governor, General Leopoldo Romano, who received his charge in a state of semi-revolution and completely overrun with brigands.

Jauja is situated on the outskirts of the city of Tepic, and is noted for its extensive and beautiful gardens. Bella Vista is situated about three miles from Jauja. Between these two places the Tepic River forms a splendid cascade, about five thousand cubic feet per minute falling one hundred and ten feet.

The factory of La Escondida is situated a mile below Bella Vista, and uses the Tepic River for irrigating its cornfields. This factory, if not the largest refinery in the republic, is equal

La Escondida Sugar-Factory, Tepic.

in size to any other, and has unquestionably the best refining machinery plant in this country. The lands of Escondida are excessively broken, and great ingenuity has been shown in perfecting them for corn cultivation.

The Hacienda de Puga has a splendid water-power and moves therewith all its machinery, such as sugar-mills, centrifugal, etc., steam being used merely for boiling. This hacienda, as well as the Escondida, turns out perfectly white cube sugar, which is sold in the immediate vicinity and in the neighboring states of Sinaloa and Jalisco.

Large quantities of muscovado sugar are shipped annually to San Francisco from these refineries, being forwarded to San Blas in carts and mule-trains and thence by sailing-vessels to their destination. This sugar compares most favorably with that of the West Indies.

Three stage-coaches leave Tepic daily for Ahuacatlan, Ixtlan, Guadalajara, Santiago, Acaponita, Rosario, Mazatlan, and San Blas.

The Central Railway is extending its line from Guadalajara in the direction of Tepic, its line already having reached Ameca. It will open a world of riches in the interior, and also will connect the Pacific Ocean by way of San Blas or Mazatlan with the Gulf of Mexico.

Unquestionably no state enjoys to-day more perfect security from brigandage than the territory of Tepic. In effecting this the governor has been ably seconded by the prefect of the territory, Señor Don Nicholas Perez.

General Romano is a highly cultivated gentleman, besides being a well-known military man of Mexico. He took a prominent part in the war against the French, having been taken prisoner and sent to France, where he refused to give his parole and escaped, returning to his beloved country after suffering hardships the recital of which

The Village of Puga, Tepic.

CASCADE OF EL INGENIO, TEPIC.

would fill a volume. Besides being a valiant military man, he has proved himself an accomplished diplomat in the way in which he has pacified the territory of Tepic, which under the

PUGA DWELLING, VIEW FROM FACTORY.

dictatorship of Lozada had been virtually severed from the Federal government. For the result I point to the flourishing state of the territory and the well-deserved affection and esteem the general enjoys.

CHAPTER XXXIV

SINALOA

NORTH of Tepic, stretched along the Pacific coast and broken up by the Sierra Madre, lies Sinaloa. The formation of the country would naturally, therefore, consist of mountains in the eastern part, and sloping, extensive plains toward the west coast. It has an area of twenty-five thousand nine hundred and twenty-seven square miles, and a population of something over two hundred thousand. Sinaloa is not perhaps so well developed as the eastern and central states of Mexico, but it, too, has enormous possibilities of wealth. The coast is indented by several bays which make good harbors, such as Mazatlan, Angeles, Altata, Tamazulla, etc. The chief rivers are the Canas and the Fuerte, which form the southern and northern boundaries, and the Sinaloa and the Culiacan. Some of the rivers overflow their banks at stated periods, thus enriching the surrounding country. There are several gold- and silver-mines, and the mountains contain in addition promising deposits of copper, iron, platinum, lead, and sulphur.

The soil is fertile, and offers great opportunities to the rice- and coffee-planter, as well as to the sugar industry. Guavas, bananas, and other tropical fruits can also be raised to great advantage.

Agriculture and mining are the principal industries of Sinaloa, although there are extensive manufactures of castor oil and mezcal, and a great deal of pearl- and tortoise-fishing on the west coast.

The capital of Sinaloa is Culiacan, and the chief port is Mazatlan. The town of Sinaloa is on the right bank of the river of the same name, with a population of some ten thousand, was the old capital of Sinaloa. The town has good houses, schools, and churches.

GENERAL FRANCISCO CAÑEDA,
GOVERNOR OF SINALOA.

It is in the midst of a gold-mining district, and

Culiacan is on the Culiacan River, with a population of not far from twelve thousand. It is

CITY OF MAZATLAN.

in the midst of a well-watered and productive country, with rich gold- and silver-mines in the vicinity, which are being worked with considerable success. The city has a fine public square with a handsome colonnade, and the streets are well laid out and regular. Among the principal buildings are a large cathedral decorated with valuable paintings, a mint which cost three hundred and fifty thousand dollars, and a very fine club-house. It occupies the site of the Aztec city of Colhuacan, famous in Mexican history.

In Culiacan there are a large cotton-factory, a sugar-refinery, and several manufactories of lesser importance, and between Culiacan and Altata there is a large wine-establishment, connected with another sugar-refinery.

Altata is the seaport of the city of Culiacan, and the outlet for a large agricultural and mining country. The entrance to the bay is over a bar, but, once inside, the harbor is safe and commodious. The interior produces large quantities of gold and silver and lead ore. The Novelata sugar-plantation is within twenty-five miles of this harbor. The export of ores and sugar, together with that of brazil-wood, forms the trade of this port. It is a port of entry of the sixth order. The climate is healthy, and similar to that of Mazatlan.

The river Culiacan is about two hundred miles long, and empties into the Gulf of California at Altata.

Mazatlan, however, is by far the most important town of Sinaloa. It lies beautifully situated at the head of a bay at the entrance to the Gulf of California. Its population ranges from ten thousand to twenty thousand, but it is impossible to give it accurately, because much of it is a floating

MAZATLAN, SHOWING THE HARBOR.

THEATRE IN CULIACAN.

CALLE DE ROSALES, CULIACAN.

population. In summer merchant-traders resort here from Chihuahua, Sonora, Jalisco, Colima, Durango, and other states, to look after heavy business interests. The upper town stands in front of rocky hills, and is somewhat uneven, but the section facing the bay has handsome streets, with fine residences, mostly in the Castilian style of architecture, with some of the more modern types intermingling. There are several public squares, but the chief public buildings stand surrounded by orange-trees in the Plaza de Armas. The custom-house, the residences of the commandant and the captain of the port, and the public stores are all tasteful buildings in another square nearer the beach. The vegetation is tropical and abundant, the annual temperature varying from seventy to ninety degrees.

Silver-mines are worked all around Mazatlan, the largest being owned by Americans and valued at several millions. The chief exports are gold and silver, dye-woods, and fine pearls, amounting to two or three million dollars in some years. There are several good public and

PLAZA, MAZATLAN.

more private schools, and in many ways Mazatlan offers splendid opportunities for the capitalist or the colonist, provided the tropical heat of the country be taken into account. Its natural advantages will always make it an important shipping port and the gateway to the Gulf of California.

Mazatlan impressed us with its beautiful approach from the ocean, the flanking mountains and the blue Pacific waters made such a remarkable and beautiful contrast with the shore, all abloom with tropical palms and ferns. The scenery is very fine. We found good hotels and schools. There was some talk, when we were there, of the removal of the capital of the state of Sinaloa from Culiacan to Mazatlan, but it will probably remain where it is. The steamer took us to Altata, and thence we went to Culiacan by railroad. At Culiacan we visited several other schools and factories, and had occasion to note once more the growing attention paid by the state governments throughout Mexico to the system of public schools. It is a system scarcely excelled anywhere in general excellence.

Throughout the state there are pretty villages with comfortable-looking houses and patios that are models of neatness and beauty. In Eastern Sinaloa are some beautiful pine districts that approach in beauty and value those among the mountains of Pennsylvania, united to the semi-tropical vegetation of Florida. It is a section of country not yet much developed, but contains a wealth of lumber which will make several fortunes in the course of time. There are some splendid specimens of pines in the region, which can be readily marketed in that part of Mexico. On the border between Sinaloa and Tepic there is a section of forest yielding some of the best yellow pine in the country. The district is supplied with an abundance of mountain streams, and has already been bought up by a syndicate of Eastern and Southern men, who are developing the entire region.

The governor of Sinaloa is General Francisco Cañedo, a brave soldier and a man whose one thought is his country and whose one aim is to conduct his state to an elevated plane of prosperity and intelligent progress. Under his guidance Sinaloa is fast coming to be one of the most important as it is one of the largest states in the republic. The unusual productiveness of the mines now in operation and the vast extent of mining-lands yet unexplored offer great inducements to prospectors.

CHAPTER XXXV

SONORA

NORTH of Sinaloa lies the state of Sonora, between the state of Chihuahua and the Gulf of California. Sonora has an area of eighty-one thousand and twenty-two square miles. All the eastern portion is extremely mountainous, and, as in Sinaloa, there are extensive western plains.

Sonora is noted for the longevity of its people. At the time of the discovery of America it was inhabited by the most vigorous and robust of all the Indians. The old Spanish explorers commented on the healthfulness of its climate, and in modern times there are few countries in the world where the death-rate is lower and the average age of the people is greater. These conditions extend even to the vegetable kingdom; diseases that trouble the fruit-growers so much in California and the north seem to lose their virulence under the bright sun and balmy sky of Sonora; and various orange scales, to which the Agricultural Department of the United States has devoted so much time and money in the vain effort to eradicate them, are unknown. There seems to be something in that dry but soft climate that conduces to universal health. The cattle industry is one of the most important in Sonora, and offers great opportunities to the farmer or other individuals who will go into stock-raising.

The Yaqui River is the largest stream in Northern Mexico, being four hundred and fifty miles long. It rises away up in the summits of the Sierra Madre, and its head-waters extend even into Arizona. The other principal rivers are the Mayo and the San José. All three empty into the Gulf of California, as, in fact, do all the waters of Sonora.

The water of the Yaqui has most wonderful fertilizing qualities. It is of about the color and consistency of chocolate. The material in suspension is so fine that it takes a long time to settle, and let the water stand as long as you will it never gets entirely clear. This silt or coloring matter thus carried in suspension is the richest kind of fertilizer. It is this that makes the valley of the Nile of an inexhaustible fertility; it is this that has enabled the Pima Indians to raise wheat in the valley of the Gila, in Arizona, for more than three hundred years on the same land without exhausting the soil and without supplying to it any other plant food than the water used for irrigation; and it is this that has made the Yaqui valley so rich and fertile.

There is no better land in the world. For fruits no lands can be better. Sonora already, notwithstanding the deficiency of its rainfall and the backwardness of its development, sends to Kansas City and Chicago the best oranges that are found in their markets, and all its fruits are celebrated wherever they are known. The banana, the cocoanut, the pineapple, and nearly all other tropical fruits reach a perfection here that they never have attained upon the Mediterranean, and the figs of Sonora are superior to those of Smyrna.

Sonora is, generally speaking, a mountainous state, but it is not by any means all mountain. The Yaqui and Mayo valleys bear a larger proportion to the whole state than does the Hudson

River valley to the Adirondack region of New York. All through, the percentage of mountains in Sonora is about double, and that of level land about half, what it is in New York State.

There is a difference, however, between our mountains and those of Sonora. Ours are for the most part barren of mineral wealth, but Sonora is the California of Mexico. Three hundred years ago the Jesuit Fathers, coming into this country to save the souls of the Indians, found its mountains full of silver and gold. Although concerned principally with the affairs of the world to come, they never entirely neglected the things of this world: so the priests became prospectors and their Indian neophytes were turned into miners. Laymen had to render an account and pay tribute to the crown on all their mines produced, but these pious explorers claimed exemption from all such burdens, and the world will never know how much gold and silver was shipped in those early days by the Jesuit Fathers to the Church of Rome.

BAY OF GUAYMAS.

There are traditions floating now all through the sierras and the Rockies of lost mines of fabulous wealth, and the credulous of both countries—and the Yankee can be quite as credulous as the Mexican—have been exploring these terrible cañons and hunting through these mountain fastnesses, chasing sunbeams everywhere, in the vain effort to find something that probably never existed.

But we can safely cast aside all these fancies. There is enough of actual riches easily to be found in these mountains to satisfy the wildest dreams of avarice, and Sonora has already shown that she is a state of great mineral resources.

There are numerous gold- and silver-mines in Sonora. All the products of the temperate zone flourish here, besides coffee and much fruit.

In a mining way Sonora offers a vast and virgin field to American capital. The great gold lode at Minas Prietas is but in the infancy of its development, and it has already produced many millions. Those who know assert that there are a number of such lodes in Sonora, which need only to be developed by the requisite capital to make them rivals of the Prietas lode, and nowhere in the world can mining operations be conducted more cheaply.

Gold-mines are found all over the state, especially in the Altar district, where so many well-known old gold-mines have been known to exist. With the certainty of saving nearly all the gold by using the by-products, as in South Africa and other parts of the world, many new efforts have been made. Las Prietas and La Dura are the most productive in Sonora now. Las Prietas group has a population of five thousand people, and La Dura and surrounding may have two-thirds as many. Lampasas, in Northeast Sonora, is a silver camp that promises to grow, with additional machinery contemplated by its owners.

Batuc, in Ures district, has two paying mines, newly discovered, which, with the employment of capital, will become very productive. These are of silver, with some gold.

Lead is being found in larger amounts than ever known before.

Copper is also a new product, notably the Nacozari discoveries.

Sonora, generally speaking, is well timbered and watered, and a very little coke added to the hard woods will furnish cheap fuel for lead smelting. In the great enterprises of irrigation, development, and cultivation of the natural resources in agriculture and horticulture there is a vast and virgin field to be occupied.

On the Yaqui River the Sonora and Sinaloa Irrigation Company, with Mr. Walter S. Logan, of New York, as president, has completed its canal, which will reclaim nearly four hundred

PRINCIPAL STREET IN THE CITY OF GUAYMAS.

thousand acres of land. But the great work of colonizing and bringing into productiveness all that vast tract of fertile soil remains to be done. Numerous similar projects of great magnitude and importance are capable of development in Sonora, none of which should be neglected or overlooked by American capital.

This early completion of the Yaqui Canal will produce a better state of things in that section, and safety to life and property. Most likely an extension of the railroad to that fertile section will follow.

The principal railway in the state runs from Guaymas northerly to Benson, Arizona, connecting with the Southern Pacific. This opens up one of the most fertile valleys of Sonora, together with some very picturesque scenery.

European banking-houses have long had their eyes fixed on the state of Sonora, which is indeed, as a distinguished statesman has termed it, "the treasure-house of Mexico." President Diaz is lending his powerful influence to the construction of the railway which is projected from the main line of the Mexican Central at Chihuahua, and has undoubtedly had in view the realization of the predictions of eminent geological and mineral experts, who have pronounced Northwestern Mexico far richer in minerals than the older and better-known sections of the republic.

Sonora is divided into eight cantons,—Ures, Hermosillo, Guaymas, Alamos, Montezuma, Zaguarita, Altar, and Magdalena. Nogales is the northern railroad terminus, and lies next to the United States.

Guaymas is surrounded by hills, and is a hot place. Before the railway reached it from Nogales the streets were dirty and narrow and the place was unhealthy, but it has much

GOVERNMENT PALACE, HERMOSILLO.

improved of late. The port is commodious, with excellent anchorage, and furnishes safe harbor for many vessels. It is the port of entry for Sonora and Chihuahua, and its foreign trade is very large. The Indians carry on a large fishery business, and the chief exports are wheat, flour, and hides.

Guaymas is one of the most important ports of Mexico. While there we had ample opportunity to see the beautiful girls for which the city is justly famous. They dress stylishly. Strange to say, light hair and blue eyes predominate, and there is many a fair head covered with Cleopatra-auburn hair. The water in the bay is beautiful, with more phosphorescence than I have ever seen elsewhere. Altogether, this was one of the loveliest ports we found in Mexico.

The most beautiful sight in all my travels was the view of the bay at night around Guaymas.

This vicinity is remarkable for the immense quantities of phosphorescence in the water, so dense that it coats everything with which it comes in contact. Hundreds of fish, coated with phosphorus and all aglow with silvery light, can be seen darting in every direction; even the bottoms of boats and the paddles of the boatmen shine with the strange evanescence as they come in contact with the water. The sight from the bow of the steamer Orizaba was simply wonderful as we left the port for Lower California: hundreds of these phosphorescent fishes were following us in eager pursuit of the refuse from the ship, and a streak of silver light extended backward, caused by her passage through the water, as far as we could see.

The capital of Sonora is Hermosillo, in the midst of a region famous for producing delicious oranges and figs; as much as thirty-five thousand dollars has been cleared here in one year from

VIEW OF THE CITY AND BAY OF GUAYMAS.

one orange plantation alone. Hermosillo is an extremely Mexican city, and is very picturesque, resting in the shadow of rugged mountains. It has a population of from fifteen to twenty thousand people, including many Yaquis. It lies in a valley near the junction of the Horcasitas and Sonora Rivers.

The climate is hot, but healthy. A great deal of wheat is raised in the adjacent country, and there are several flourishing flour-mills in the town. Large quantities of brandy are manufactured from grapes, which abound in the valley. Hermosillo was, up to 1800, a military station, and was formerly the seat of the presidio of Pitic. After the discovery and opening of gold-mines in Sonora the population of Hermosillo grew rapidly, and the town is still the chief *entrepôt* of Sonora.

In the mountainous regions of Sonora are numerous predatory bands of Indians, who have long retarded the development of the state. The Tauri Mauri Indians number many thousand. They occupy fertile valleys far up among the mountain-trails and severest roadways. The largest city or pueblo among them is that of Norogochi, containing about eleven thousand people. The altitude of the town is seven thousand two hundred feet, and all the mountainous valleys occupied by the Tauri Mauri have an average altitude of six thousand four hundred and fifty feet. These Indians have a contempt for Mexican rule, which they show by their refusal, even after several centuries of authority, to speak Spanish or to allow it to be taught to their children.

In physique and facial appearance the Tauri Mauris resemble the Apache Indians of the United States. They wear their hair like the Apaches, and their clothing—a waist-cloth and

VIEW OF THE CITY OF GUAYMAS.

sandals—is almost similar. They travel entirely on foot, and their arms are arrows and a bow. Thousands of them who work in the fields do not seem to know the use of a burro or a horse. They carry their burdens on their head and shoulders, and it is common to see an old man trotting along with a cigarette in his mouth and a load of merchandise weighing over one hundred and fifty pounds fastened to his shoulders. As a race the Tauri Mauris are intensely proud. They have never had war with the Mexican government, but they have threatened it several times when the republic has proposed to settle the land question among them on a plan similar to that of the United States with its Indian wards. Strangers are permitted to pass unmolested through the Tauri Mauri country, but are not allowed to get a living there. There are very rich gold and silver ledges in the mountains all about the Tauri Mauri valleys, but so many venturesome prospectors have gone there and never come back, that no American, at least, has dared to make a trial of prospecting in that region for several decades. The Tauris live in houses of poles roofed with hewn planks. Their farms are fenced, and their stock is well cared for.

There are about three hundred wild and rebellious Yaqui Indians hidden in the fastnesses of the Bacatete Mountains, and some thirty thousand peaceful Yaquis working all over Sonora, among the best workers, the most successful farmers, and the quietest citizens in the whole state.

There are few things in the history of the native races of North America of more absorbing interest than the career of the Yaqui Indians. The Spanish conquistadores found them living in this country three hundred and fifty years ago. They were a strong and stalwart race. Put a Yaqui by the side of an Iroquois, and you can hardly tell them apart. Put a Yaqui and an Iroquois by the side of any other Indian in North America, and their physical superiority is seen at once. Compare them physically with all the other races of the earth, and you will find that they have few if any superiors.

The Yaquis were not, however, like their prototypes the Iroquois, dependent upon the chase for their food. From the beginning they were not woodsmen, but farmers. Cabeza de Vaca, after his long, romantic, and perilous journey across the continent, found great fields of Indian corn waving on the Yaqui River as far back as 1536. When the early Spanish missions were established in the Californias they obtained their supplies from the agricultural Indians in the Yaqui valley, and many a Spanish army was saved from starvation in times past by the Yaqui cornfields.

At Quergache are the "Gambucinos," or miners who live by creeping into the old mines and working out enough of the rich silver ores to support them for a few days. They are an ignorant, shiftless, and thievish set, who will not cultivate the ground any more than they can possibly help. Here, too, is a cathedral erected three hundred years ago, when the Spaniards worked the mines around this place. The church, built in honor of Señora Pillaro, has suffered from fire and has been only partly restored. It is a lofty, roomy affair, of cut stone carved by artists from old Spain, and patched with adobes by lazy mestizos.

In such a church and in such a city one feels as if the spirit had gone back into the ages of the past. This is not a part of the busy, bustling nineteenth century; it is a day-dream in the world of three hundred years ago.

The state of Sonora is fortunate in having for its governor Don Ramon Corral, to whose integrity of purpose and wise supervision it owes its recent prosperity.

CHAPTER XXXVI

BAJA CALIFORNIA

THE peninsula of Lower California forms one of the territories composing the republic of Mexico. This peninsula was discovered by Cortez in 1536. The Jesuits began to form establishments there about 1690, and instructed the native Indians in the arts of agriculture and civilization. They were taught the arts of irrigation, and exported agricultural productions to the mainland of Mexico. The Jesuit fathers remained there until 1767, when they were expelled, and the missions which they had established were placed under the charge of the Dominican fathers at Mexico City, under whom they greatly declined, so that in 1833 they were all secularized. The region settled by these Jesuit and Dominican fathers in the eighteenth century is extremely beautiful, and the ruins of the old mission are to-day exceedingly picturesque.

While everybody knows of the beauties of Southern California, there is dense ignorance among most readers of the fact that the peninsula of Lower California is equally beautiful. It is, in fact, a continuation of the same general features.

The imaginary line that separates Southern California from Baja California marks no difference in soil or climate. The valleys and *mesas* on the Mexican side are as good as those upon the American. All they need are irrigation works and roads. When these are supplied, and it becomes known that fruits, cereals, and wines can be profitably produced there, Mexico will be an open market, and the peninsula will gradually fill up with an industrious population.

COLONEL RAFAEL GARCIA MARTINEZ,
JEFE POLITICO, LA PAZ.

Taking the steamer Orizaba at Guaymas, we went to La Paz and San José del Cabo. At La Paz we visited the pearl-fisheries, and were duly initiated into the mysteries of the hideous-looking diving apparatus. The Mexican government leases these fisheries to the companies that operate them, and some fine pearls have been brought up from the depths of the ocean off the rocky coast of Lower California. We were told of a black pearl worth ten thousand dollars in gold that was sold to Madame Carnot, the wife of the former president of France; and recently another exquisite pearl was sold in the American market for thirty-five thousand dollars. The pearl industry, conducted as it is under perilous surroundings, has its incidental curious phases. The divers are all the time attempting to steal these gems, and a common practice it is. While working, if they find a pearl, their faces never change expression; but if detected, the diver, who also opens the shells, will simply swallow the pearl. In such cases it is restored to its rightful owner by a prompt dose of tartar emetic.

These deposits have yielded the finest pearls discovered in modern times. They are still yielding, and to-day more pearls are found there than anywhere else along the coasts of the two Americas.

More than a thousand divers are employed during the season, which lasts from the month of May to November of each year. They are furnished with boats, money, and diving paraphernalia by local merchants, with whom they contract for all the pearls they can find. The total annual product is estimated at five hundred thousand dollars.

Baja California contains some fifty-seven thousand five hundred square miles. The population is composed largely of Indians and mixed races, and is principally in the southern part.

PORT OF LA PAZ, SHOWING THE GREAT PEARL-FISHERIES OF BAJA CALIFORNIA.

It is divided into eight districts, each having an *alcalde* as judicial head. The coasts are low and sandy, and broken up by many islands and bays along the entire length. La Magdalena, the bay, has been regularly visited for fifty years past by American whalers, sealers, and fur-hunters. The bay of La Paz is the most important in the gulf, penetrating inland some twenty-five miles. The cove opposite the town of La Paz may be reached by vessels not drawing over twenty feet of water. Loreto, Los Angeles, and San Felipe Jesus are the other ports of any importance.

The entire peninsula is traversed by a volcanic range of mountains. This is divided into three sections, the Sierra de San Lázaro, with an average height of six thousand feet, forming the principal backbone of the lower peninsula. The Sierra de la Gigantea has an average elevation of three thousand or four thousand feet, with occasional peaks six to eight thousand feet high, and lies north of the San Lázaro range; and still farther north is the Coast range, having an average breadth of one hundred and thirty-five miles. These are barren and desolate near the summits, with cactuses of enormous size at their base, and some very fertile valleys. Toward the interior there are many springs which send out streams that afterward lose themselves in the sand. Along the coast lagoons there is much good soil, and in the plains and most of the dry river beds water is found a few feet below the surface, offering easy and inexpensive means of irrigation. Wherever irrigation in any form has been practised the crops are exceedingly abundant.

The summer temperature along the Pacific coast varies from fifty-eight to seventy-one degrees, but that on the gulf coast is higher. The scenery is in many places picturesque. The sky is remarkable for its transparency and deep azure color, save at sunset, when it is often variegated by the most beautiful shades of purple, violet, and green. In winter there are heavy rains and terrific tornadoes. In summer and autumn, especially on the gulf coast, rain often falls from a cloudless sky.

The vegetable productions of Baja California are corn, wheat, beans, peas, manioc, grapes, oranges, lemons, citrons, prunes, dates, plantains, pineapples, olives, and figs. The sugar-cane has also been cultivated, and some cotton was raised by the Jesuits. Several varieties of the agave family are abundant, and many kinds of acacia-trees, such as mesquites, algarrobas, and locusts, are common. Two varieties of native palms bearing edible fruit are frequently found. The pine, cedar, oak, wild plum, cottonwood, sycamore, willow, and elder are also met with. The principal animals are wild sheep, goats, horses, horned cattle, mules, and swine. The adjacent seas abound with excellent fish. The pearl-oyster is found at intervals along the coast. It is most abundant in the bay of La Paz, near Loreto,

GOVERNMENT HOUSE, LA PAZ.

and in the bays of Muleje and Los Angeles. Fossil remains are found in various parts. Argentiferous galenas are very common above Muleje Bay, and pure sulphur occurs in the same region. Copper ores are found in several places between the northern boundary and the old mission of Rosario, on the Pacific coast, and also on the northern gulf coast; the deposits on Ceralbo, San José, and Espiritu Santo Island are very rich. Quicksilver is also said to have been found near Santa Catalina Mission, at the head of the gulf. The salt-beds of the Pacific coast, from San Quintin to Magdalena Bay, are numerous, and the salt is readily obtained. The salt-mines on Carmen Island are very rich, and large quantities of salt have been exported to San Francisco. The Mexican government has derived considerable revenue from these mines.

There is a great deal of activity in the mining districts adjacent to Ensenada. The history of the Pueblo mine is well known to miners. The fabulous deposits of gold found in pockets near the surface and the number of coyote-holes that can be seen give evidence of the methods employed in days gone by. This and the Castillo were the first gold-mines worked in that section. The latter was started forty years ago, and gave birth to the town of Real del Castillo.

Besides these, there are the San Nicolas, San Francisco, San Luis, Suiza, Accidente, Tepeyac, and San Rafael in the Real district; and the China, Piedad, Mina, California, Cristo, San Luis, and other valuable properties in the Jacalitos district.

Politically the peninsula is a territory, not a state, of the Mexican republic. It has two capitals,—La Paz in the south and Ensenada in the north,—and two governors appointed by the federal authority, as governors of territories are appointed with us. The great length of the peninsula and the difficulty of passing through this length have made necessary its division into these two districts. There is no territorial legislature. The few government employees are paid out of the federal treasury, and, with the exception of customs duties, there are no taxes, except for local improvements. There are therefore no "politics" in this quiet land.

CORONEL AGUSTIN SAGIÑES,
JEFE POLÍTICO, ENSENADA.

The government requires the inhabitants to obey the laws and keep the peace, and ample powers are given to the governors to maintain order and punish violence. At La Paz there is a small force of troops; at Ensenada the governor had until recently under his control a police force of fifteen mounted men, well armed and active, who were sufficient for all purposes.

Ensenada is a real American town, and is exceedingly attractive in appearance. It is beautifully situated in a healthful location, and is the natural outlet of considerable inland business and mineral wealth. Here lives the governor, Agustin Sagiñes, of the upper portion of the territory, and the several public buildings do credit to the place and to him.

Magdalena Bay is one of the most beautiful places along the Pacific coast, and is surrounded by a beautiful country. The climate all along here is uncommonly salubrious, and Magdalena Bay offers a very desirable site for a sanatarium. The bay is of large dimensions and is accessible in all weather. Orchilla is a parasitic moss which hangs from the trees throughout this region, adding a touch of picturesqueness to the natural beauties of the place. Large quantities of it are gathered on the sea-shore and in the vicinity, pressed, and shipped to Europe, where it is used for the purpose of dyeing sealskins, etc. A large fortune has already been made by an enterprising company in handling this innocent-looking gray moss which has such valuable properties.

The region all through this district is particularly productive and offers great inducements for investment. The missionaries, after 1730, introduced the Arabian date-palm, which succeeds admirably and yields abundantly, and also oranges, lemons, and all the species of the citrine family, pineapples, bananas, and plantains. They planted the vine, olive, fig, pomegranate, almond, peach, quince; and even plums, apples, pears, melons, watermelons, and such like, in more elevated and cooler districts. The vine, fig, olive, currant grape, almond, quince, and peach are more luscious and grow much more quickly, and with less labor and expense, than in Alta California, and in many localities are unsurpassed in the world for luxuriance, sweetness, and flavor. The fig and grape are much sweeter, and the grape ripens more quickly and better, from hotter and drier suns, and makes much richer wine, brandy, raisins, and currants.

There is much good land near the missions of Rosario, San Vicente, Santo Domingo, and Santo Tomas. Several permanent streams and a number of coast lagoons furnish abundance of excellent water for animals and irrigation.

THE BAY AT ENSENADA.

The region around Cape San Lucas is beautiful in the extreme, and not far from there lies the picturesque little village of San José del Cabo, which is a shipping port with a coast custom-house section. The Orizaba and the Coos Bay, steamers of the Pacific Coast Company, stop at all principal ports, and furnish the best possible means of communication between San Francisco and Guaymas, Sonora.

PIER AT ENSENADA.

La Paz has a population of three thousand. This is the residence of the governor, Coronel Rafael G. Martinez, and his official assistants for the southern district, and is an exceedingly picturesque town, especially as approached by the sea. Although not a large town, many of the houses are tasteful and convenient, and indicate that the place has long been the abode of luxury. The port is well sheltered, the climate hot, and the surrounding country productive. The shipping is growing, and the pearl-fisheries still form an important source of revenue.

There are great resources in Baja California, although its position is unique. While it is isolated from all the other states of Mexico, it has more seaports than any state, and many

CITY OF ENSENADA.

other advantages for future growth and prosperity with the development of the rest of the republic of Mexico.

From Ensenada, which is the last Mexican town in Baja California, we went by way of San Francisco, taking the Southern Pacific Railroad, and going back to the republic of Mexico at El Paso, Texas.

CHAPTER XXXVII

MICHOACÁN

THE state of Michoacán has been given a name which, according to some authors, means "fisherman's country." Its territory is extremely mountainous and its scenery strikingly picturesque. It is characterized by enchanting gorges, beautiful valleys, and vast plains of fertile lands along the banks of glistening streams, whose course, sometimes impeded by huge rocks, occasionally acquires great rapidity, as can be observed especially at the falls of Onendo. At times, after meandering over the ground, a stream will sally forth in the midst of exuberant vegetation and drop again from festooned falls in myriads of crystalline threads, which sparkle in the sunbeams, reflecting all the prismatic colors. This wonderful spectacle is particularly noticeable on the banks of the Cupachito.

Cortez took an excursion through Michoacán after the fall of Mexico, and was delighted with what he saw. It was at that time a powerful and independent state, inhabited by one of the kindred Nahuatlac races. The Spaniards advanced across the state and erected a cross on the Pacific coast in the name of their Catholic majesties. On their return they took back samples of gold and California pearls, and the report of the great southern ocean beyond. Cortez wrote, "Most of all do I exult in these tidings of the great ocean. For in it, as cosmographers and those learned men who know most about the Indies inform us, are scattered rich isles, teeming with gold and spices and precious stones." For even then had Spaniards begun to look on Mexico as a great treasure-house to be drawn upon to support their own extravagant country.

SEÑOR ARISTEO MERCADO,
GOVERNOR OF MICHOACÁN.

Michoacán lies on the western slope of the great cordillera of Anahuac; it is bounded on the north by Jalisco, Guanajuato, and Querétaro, on the east by México, on the south by Guerrero and the Pacific, and on the west by the sea, Colima, and Jalisco. Its area is twenty-one thousand six hundred and nine square miles. Its most noted mountain peak is the volcano of Jorullo. The highest point is the Cerro de Santa Rosa, in the district of Tlapujahua, about seventeen thousand feet. Between the ridges stretch elevated and fertile valleys, watered by several rivers, the principal being the Lerma and the Mescala, or Balsas, besides many mountain torrents.

Of the eleven lakes, the most noted are Lake Chapala, partly in Jalisco, Lake Patzcuaro, and Lake Cuitzeo.

Along the one hundred miles of coast the ports are San Telmo, Buceria, and Maratua. The first was once open to foreign traders, but, owing to a lack of shelter, none of these harbors are of importance.

Michoacán has a variety of climates, corresponding to its altitude, but it is generally very healthy. The mean annual temperature at Morelia is seventy-one degrees. The mines are

GOVERNOR'S PALACE, MORELIA.

principally silver, though gold, copper, cinnabar, iron, coal, sulphur, copperas, emery, lead, marble, and lithographic stone are also found.

The soil is extremely fertile, and the state is like one great garden. Corn usually yields four-hundred-fold. Cattle, horses, mules, and hogs are extensively raised, and there is excellent opportunity in this beautiful state for the enterprising agriculturist.

Among the manufactures are rebozos, serapes, blankets, and fine silver-ware. There are numerous flour-mills, one or two glass-factories, and steam weaving-factories in Morelia. There are excellent roads in this state, and for twenty-five years past the principal telegraph lines have been in communication with Morelia and other points. There is a state college, as well as a large number of schools, both public and private.

MICHOACÁN

There are seventeen districts in Michoacán, and the chief towns are Morelia (the capital), Puruándiro, Zamora, Ario, Tacámbaro, and Taretón.

Morelia stands upon a rocky hill six thousand four hundred and thirty-eight feet above the sea. The streets are wide and regularly laid out. On one side of the Plaza de los Martires, the principal square, stands the noble cathedral, and extensive arcades are along the others, as this is the principal business centre. The houses are very substantially built, and the government building is very handsome. The San Nicolas College, which was built in the sixteenth century and remodelled in 1868, is one of the finest edifices in the republic of Mexico. It is in the renaissance style, with many departments, including law, medicine, pharmacy, and agriculture. There were at one time a great many convents and nunneries, but these were suppressed in 1859. Here is one of the finest bull-rings in Mexico. There are also several asylums, hospitals, and a fine prison. Morelia is always admired by strangers for its broad and airy streets, fine houses, and general beauty. There is a crowded market-place that is always interesting, and the climate is ever delightful. The alameda is broad, paved with flat stones, shaded by fine old trees, and bounded by a low stone wall with stone benches alongside. This, as usual, is the social resort of the town. It is crossed by a fine aqueduct of solid masonry, constructed in 1788, with vast and lofty arches and very imposing in effect.

MONUMENT TO OCAMPO, MORELIA.

Morelia was founded in 1541 by the Spaniards, and received the name of Valla-dolid. The patriot José Maria Morelos, however, was born here and served as curate of Nucupétaro, and after his death the name of the town was changed in his honor.

Morelia is one of the prettiest cities in all Mexico, and its women enjoy the same reputation for beauty. The beautiful plaza, the magnifi-cent cathedral, the Paseo de San Pedro, the Calzado de Guadalupe, and the aqueduct, are objects of attraction; but the hospitality of the people, the beauty of the women, the music, and the flowers all combine to make a most in-teresting visit to the traveller. If there was nothing else at the end of it, it is worth the journey to Morelia to view the cathedral and the great towers thereof, that may be seen from afar off overtopping the high hills, giving the first glimpse of the city as the train comes up the valley from the east.

There is not a finer edifice anywhere in Mexico, outside the capital, than the cathedral of the see of Michoacán, and even the cathedral of Mexico is not superior except in size. The towers, the great organ, the silver altar-rails, vestments and vessels, images and candelabra of fine silver, have not an equal anywhere, though these are only a remnant of what used to be, nearly half a million dollars' worth having been confiscated by the government some twenty years ago, though one can hardly miss what has been taken away or tell where they put it when it was here. The silver font from which Iturbide and Morelos were baptized is still in use. The cathedral is beautifully situated, with the main front facing the Plaza de los Martires, and the eastern looking over the Plaza de la Paz. In the Plaza de los Martires, which means the plaza of the martyrs, are the most beautiful trees and flowers, and in the midst of them a pavilion where the band plays in the evening,—that famous, magnificent band that was at the

New Orleans Exposition, the favorite band of Mexico. And to this plaza come also the "four hundred" of Morelia. In the afternoon there is music in the beautiful Parque de San Pedro, and the walk thither, not a long one, is through the Calzado de Guadalupe, a paved way shaded by immense elms, the walk-way being in the centre and the drives on each side in front of the residences. The trip can be made on the horse-cars, but there is everything to recommend the delightful walk.

The state is called in full Michoacán de Ocampo, in honor of one of the great heroes of Mexican independence. We were shown through the handsome library, in which is preserved the heart of Ocampo, and it was my privilege to hold in my hand the gold and white enamel casket which contains that relic, which is almost worshipped by the patriotic Michoacanos.

The story of Ocampo adds another to the many romantic episodes of Mexico's revolutionary days. He was one of the greatest heroes who sacrificed life for the sake of the country he was so determined to free from foreign tyranny. When he was captured by the enemy and condemned to be shot, his last request was that his heart should be taken from his dead body and carried back to his native state. This was done, and the state was rechristened in loving memory of one of its greatest heroes, Michoacán de Ocampo.

By moonlight Morelia looks like a panorama of Mexico, with its fine square, beautiful streets, and good houses. Near by is the hill of Las Bateas, where by the order of Morelos two hundred Spaniards were murdered in cold blood to revenge the death of the curate Matamoros, who had been taken prisoner and shot by Iturbide. It is singular that the great leaders of the independence should have been ecclesiastics,—the curate Hidalgo, its prime mover, and the curates Morelos and Matamoros. Hidalgo, it is said, had no plan, published no manifesto, declared no opinions, but rushed from city to city at the head of his men, displaying on his colors an image of the Virgin of Guadalupe, and inciting his troops to massacre the Spaniards. Morelos was an Indian, uneducated but brave and enterprising, and considered the mildest and most merciful of these soldier-priests. Matamoros, equally brave, was better informed. All were good generals. When Morelos became generalissimo of the revolutionary forces he formed a congress, which met at Chilpancingo, and was composed of lawyers and clergymen. Disputes and divisions arose among them, and in 1814 they published a useless document in the village of Apatzingan to which they gave the name of the "Mexican Constitution." The following year Morelos was defeated in an engagement which took place in the environs of Tesmelaca, taken prisoner, led to Mexico, and after a short trial degraded from his ecclesiastical functions and shot in the village of San Cristobal Ecatepec, seven leagues from the capital. The revolutionary party considered him as a martyr in the cause of liberty, and he died like a true hero. The appellation of Morelia given to the city of Valladolid keeps his name in remembrance.

As Agustin de Iturbide was a native of Morelia, and his career forms a part of Mexican history, a condensed account of him may not be out of place here.

He was born of Spanish parents, who came to Mexico a few months before his birth. When he was only fifteen years old he became heir to and assumed the care of his father's estate, and was also made lieutenant of one of the militia infantry regiments of Valladolid, as it was then called. In 1805 he joined the army at Jalapa. On his return in 1809 he aided in repressing a revolutionary movement, which was followed on September 16, 1810, by the revolution planned by Hidalgo. Iturbide took the field "in the service of the Mexicans, the King of Spain, and the Spaniards," vying with the latter in rigor toward the insurgents. He gained distinction in the battle of Cruces, and was made a captain in the southern army, but ill health compelled him to go to the city of Mexico, and he was sent to Michoacán as second in command under Garcia Conde. Here he again aided in quenching the revolutionary fire, rekindled by Albino Garcia, whom he captured; and he was soon afterward made colonel. From that time till the end of 1815 he took part in all the engagements of the royal troops, directed for the most part against José Maria Morelos, who after the execution of Hidalgo succeeded him as leader of the insurgent forces. The year 1816 found him in command of the provinces of Guanajuato and Michoacán and of the northern army by which they were then occupied; but he had incurred the displeasure of some leading citizens, and grave accusations were preferred against him, which led to his dismissal. On returning to private life Iturbide set about maturing his long-cherished project of independence. The news of the Spanish consti-

LAKE PATZCUARO, MICHOACÁN.

tution, proclaimed in the peninsula in 1820, filled Mexican soldiers with the desire of freeing their country. The movement soon became general, and Iturbide, seeing that the time for action had come, secured command of the southern army, about to march against Guerrero, who was then at Acapulco at the head of the remaining rebel forces. On November 16, 1820, he set out from the capital, and to lull the suspicions of the government simulated some encounters with Guerrero, to whom he in reality communicated his project; and, having concerted with him relative to future operations, he informed the viceroy that the rebellion was entirely at an end.

This intelligence restored confidence among merchants, and a convoy was despatched to Acapulco, with five hundred and twenty-five thousand dollars, which money Iturbide seized, promising to refund it to its owners. With these resources at his disposal and secret agents in all parts of the country, he promulgated, on February 24, 1821, his plan of independence, known in history as the "Plan of Iguala," from the name of the town where it was put forth. The principal bases of the plan were "religion, union of Spaniards and Mexicans, and independence; Ferdinand VII., or, in case of his refusal, such other member of a reigning family as the congress soon to be organized might choose, to be called to the new empire." His next step was to inform the viceroy of what had taken place, and the latter immediately organized an army to crush the revolution in its infancy. But this measure came too late. Meantime the newly appointed viceroy, Don Juan de O'Donoju, arrived from Spain, and, finding the suppression of the new order of things to be impossible, he concluded with Iturbide, at Córdova, August 24, 1821, a treaty in accordance with the plan of Iguala, except in the clause relating to the election of emperor, who, in case of the refusal of Ferdinand VII. and of some other princes enumerated, should be "any one designated by the Córtes." On September 27 Iturbide made his entry into the capital amid the acclamations of the people. The junta gubernativa prescribed in the plan of Iguala was at once organized, and Iturbide, who at Iguala had prudently refused the title of lieutenant-general and accepted that of first chief of the army, was formally installed in office. Peace was soon established; the few Spanish troops in garrison at important stations became discouraged; the only stronghold left the Spaniards was the fortress of San Juan de Ulua, off Vera Cruz; and the peninsula of Yucatán, with the province of Chiapas and several towns in Guatemala, declared their independence, and were ultimately united to the Mexican empire. Such of the Spanish residents as desired to leave the country were permitted to do so without restraint, which liberal measure, with numerous others emanating from the new government, served to increase its short-lived popularity. But Iturbide, who had been successful in organizing and carrying out a bloodless revolution, was unable to establish a government upon a solid basis. A regency composed of three members, according to the plan, was appointed. Iturbide was proclaimed generalissimo of the land and marine forces and president of the regency, with an annual salary of one hundred and twenty thousand dollars, an immediate donation of one million dollars, twenty square leagues of land in Texas, and the title of serene highness. Before long signs of discord between Iturbide and the junta became visible. The treasury was depleted and nearly all sources of revenue were cut off, while the national expenses were greatly enhanced; the army was without discipline; and public opinion was divided between republicanism and the new form of government. Iturbide hastened the convocation of the first congress, in the hope of immediate relief; but that body obstinately refused to grant him money for the troops, and even

PORTAL DE MATAMOROS, MORELIA.

declared the command of the army to be incompatible with the executive power. But the generalissimo had sixteen thousand men at his disposal in the capital, and through the agency of his partisans he was proclaimed emperor on the night of May 18, 1822. On the 21st the proclamation was confirmed by congress, which declared the crown hereditary in his family, fixed the civil list at one million five hundred thousand dollars annually, created an order of knighthood and other accessories of a monarchy, established the imperial household with the customary pomp, and ordered money to be coined with his effigy. He was crowned on July 21. The symptoms of anarchy had not disappeared, however, and a conspiracy organized in Valladolid led to the arrest of several persons, among them fifteen deputies. This, with the arbitrary seizure by the government of one million three hundred thousand dollars deposited at Perote and Jalapa, exasperated the people; and Iturbide, harassed by the continued opposition of the congress, dissolved that body on October 31. But Santa Anna proclaimed the republic at Vera Cruz on December 2; the junta instituyente, which had succeeded the congress, was unable to establish order; defection became general among the army officers, and the republican troops were fast advancing towards the capital. Iturbide, in despair, hastily reassembled the congress and tendered his abdication; but that body, not recognizing the abdication, annulled the election of the emperor, and decreed that he should at once leave the country and "fix his residence in Italy," granting him a yearly pension of twenty-five thousand dollars, and declaring null the plan of Iguala and the treaty of Córdova. On May 11, 1823, Iturbide set sail for Leghorn, where he arrived on August 2. Impelled by an insane desire for the recovery of his crown, he proceeded to England, and on May 11, 1824, embarked for Mexico. During the year a new government had been formed, with a republican constitution, and Iturbide had no influential friends left in the country. The government, apprised of his movements, declared him "a traitor and an outlaw in case he should at any time and under any title whatsoever set his foot upon Mexican territory, and that by that act alone he should be regarded as a public enemy of the state." Iturbide arrived at Soto la Marina on July 14, and landed in disguise; but he was apprehended by the military commandant, who detained him a prisoner at Padilla, awaiting the decision of the congress of Tamaulipas. That body sentenced him to immediate execution. He was shot on the morning of July 19, 1824. The congress of Mexico decreed that his family should reside in Colombia, and settled upon them a yearly pension of eight thousand dollars; but, as there was no ship for a Colombian port, his wife was permitted to go to the United States. She lived for many years in Philadelphia, and then went to Bayonne, in France. Angel de Iturbide, the eldest son of the emperor, died in the city of Mexico in 1872, leaving a son, who had been adopted by Maximilian as heir to the throne; and the Emperor Iturbide's younger son died in Paris in May, 1873, where he had earned a precarious subsistence as keeper of a public-house. The claims of the Iturbide family in recent times are too recent and too well known to need any comment here.

About five or six leagues from Morelia are the natural hot springs of Cuincho. These baths are resorted to by many invalids, and will doubtless come to be quite a health-resort. All the streams that come pouring down from these rocky hill-sides are hot, evidently coming from volcanic sources, as they are heavily charged with muriatic acid. Humboldt ventures the supposition that in this part of Mexico at a great interior depth is a fissure running east and west for about four hundred miles, through which, bursting the external crust of porphyritic rock, the volcanic fire opens now and then a passage at different points from the Mexican gulf to the Pacific. The famous volcano of Jorullo is on this vein, and boiling fountains are common in various portions of it. The baths at Cuincho are delightfully agreeable, and the temperature of the water deliciously refreshing. For many decades these baths have been enclosed in great stone walls, the light coming from a high window near the roof.

Jorullo, some twenty leagues to the south, has been ascended many times. As far back as 1803 M. de Humboldt and M. Bonpland ascended to the crater of this burning mountain, which was formed in September, 1759. Its birth was announced by earthquakes, which put to flight all the inhabitants of the neighboring villages; and three months afterwards a terrible eruption burst forth, which filled all the inhabitants with astonishment and terror, and which Humboldt considers one of the most extraordinary physical revolutions that ever took place on the surface of the globe. Flames issued from the earth for the space of more than a square league. Masses of burning rock were thrown to an immense height, and through a thick cloud of ashes

PASEO DE SAN PEDRO, MORELIA.

illuminated by the volcanic fire the whitened crust of the earth was seen gradually swelling up. The ashes even covered the roofs of the houses at Querétaro, forty-eight leagues distant, and the rivers of San Andres and Cuitumba sank into the burning masses. The flames were seen from Patzcuaro; and from the hills of Agua-Zarca was beheld the birth of this volcanic mountain, the burning offspring of an earthquake, which, bursting from the bosom of the earth, changed the whole face of the country for a considerable distance around. In a letter written at the time of this event to the Bishop of Michoacán by the curate of the neighboring village, he says that the eruption finished by destroying the hacienda of Jorullo and killing the trees, which were thrown down and buried in the sand and ashes vomited by the mountain. The fields and roads were, he says, covered with sand, the crops destroyed, and the flocks perishing for want of food, unable to drink the pestilential water of the mountains. The rivulet that ran past his village was swelled to a mighty river that threatened to inundate it; and he adds that "the houses, churches, and hospitals are ready to fall down from the weight of the sand and the ashes," and that "the very people are so covered with the sand that they seem to have come out of some sepulchre." The great eruptions of the volcano continued till the following year, but have since become rare.

The scenery around Lake Patzcuaro is extremely picturesque. At the foot of the hills which slope back from the northern end lies the village of Tzintzuntzán, which possesses the finest picture in Mexico, an excellent specimen of the great master Titian. Although only a small village, Tzintzuntzán was formerly the capital of the independent kingdom of Michoacán, an important city, and called in the time of Cortez Huitzitzila. It was formerly the residence of the monarch Calsonsi, who was an ally of Cortez, and with his Indian subjects assisted him in his Mexican war. It is now an Indian village, though it is said that some remains of the monarch's palace still exist apropos of which there may be seen all through the state large stones lying in fields or employed in fences, with strange hieroglyphic characters engraved on them, some of which may be very curious and interesting. The view as we approach Patzcuaro, with its beautiful lake studded with little islands, is very fine. An old church nestles like a bird-house among the trees, and stands at the outskirts of the city. Here, it is said, his majesty of Michoacán came out to meet his Spanish ally when he entered this territory.

Patzcuaro is a pretty little city, with sloping roofs, situated on the shores of the lake and in front of the little Indian village of Janicho, built on a beautiful small island in the midst of the lake. There are churches bearing the date of 1580. The first

COLLEGE OF SANTA MARIA DE GUADALUPE, MORELIA.

bishop of Michoacán, Vasco de Quiroga, who died in Uruapan, was buried in Patzcuaro, and the Indians of this state still venerate his memory. He was the father and benefactor of the Tarascan Indians, and went far to rescue them from their degraded state. He not only preached morality, but encouraged industry among them by assigning to each village its particular branch of commerce. Thus, one was celebrated for its manufacture of saddles, another for its shoes, a third for its bateas (painted trays), and so on. Every useful institution of which some traces still remain among them is due to this excellent prelate; an example of what one good and zealous and well-judging man can effect. The old church of Patzcuaro is handsome and rich in gilding. At the door is printed, in large letters, "For the love of God, all good Christians are requested not to spit in this holy place." The better classes in Patzcuaro seem fairer and have more color than is general in Mexico. In this old town, too, one may see specimens of that mosaic-work which all ancient writers upon Mexico have celebrated, and which was nowhere brought to such perfection as in Patzcuaro. It was made with the most beautiful and delicate feathers, chiefly of the picaflores, the humming-birds, which they called huitzitzilin. But it is now many years since the last artist in this branch lived in Patzcuaro, and, though it is imitated by the nuns, the art is no longer in the state of perfection to which it had been brought in the days of Cortez. Then several persons were employed in each painting, and the work required extraordinary patience and nicety in the blending of colors and the arrangement of the feathers. The sketch of the figure was first made, and, the proportions being measured, each artist took charge of one particular part of the figure or the drapery. When each had finished his share, all the different parts were reunited to form the picture. The feathers were first taken up with some soft substance with the utmost care and fastened upon a piece of stuff; then the different parts, being reunited, were placed on a plate of copper and gently polished till the surface became quite smooth, when they appeared like the most beautiful paintings; or, according to old writers, more beautiful, from the splendor and liveliness of the colors, the bright golden and blue and crimson tints, than the paintings which they imitated. Many were sent to Spain and to different museums both in Europe and in Mexico; but the art does not belong to the present utilitarian age. The lake from this point is as clear as one vast mirror, and covered with thousands of wild ducks, white cranes, and herons, all seeming to whiten their plumage by constant dipping in pools and marshes and lakes.

Patzcuaro is well entitled to its name, which being interpreted means "a place of delights," and it certainly means this to anybody who goes there. The station is on the lake-shore; a diligence runs to the town, two miles up the hill, and the drive is a most charming one, as the beautiful view grows wider and wider as the hill is ascended, and when at the top the lake with its islands, and the valley with its fields of green and its four dozen towns and villages, are included in the scope of vision. The quaint plaza, shaded by great trees, surrounded on four sides with heavy columned portales, the market-place, the narrow, crooked streets, with shrines and crosses in every nook and corner, and the grand view from Los Balcones, at the crest of the Cerro de Calvario, are all subjects of the greatest interest. There is a little steamer on the lake, which runs from the dock to the northern shores, making several landings at away-back towns where there are no railways and perhaps never will be. The object of the voyage on the lake, and, in fact, the trip to Patzcuaro, is the famous painting in the old church at the village of Tzintzuntzán, on the east shore of the lake,—The Entombment, by Titian, presented to the bishop of Michoacán by Philip II. of Spain. Many noted writers and artists have made the pilgrimage and returned with the feeling that the trip was amply paid for in the seeing of so celebrated a picture.

Among other curiosities there is a Virgin entirely covered with Indian embroidery. The organist's place is hereditary in an Indian family, descending from father to son.

Tzintzuntzán was once the capital of the powerful empire of Tarasco, which successfully resisted to the last the incursions of the Montezumas. After the Spanish conquest this was the seat of the bishopric of Tarasco, and was held in such high esteem by Philip II. of Spain that its cathedral was presented by that puissant monarch with this fine creation of the brush of Titian. Its authenticity is unquestionable. The old church is fast crumbling to decay, and its pristine glory has departed from it; yet such is the veneration of the Indians for this beautiful painting that the bishop has refused to allow it to be removed. Enormous sums have been offered by enthusiastic art-lovers, but the church authorities have declined to entertain them, and the picture still hangs where it was first placed by the loving hands of its original owners more than three hundred years ago. The old city is now only a little hamlet with a grand old church and a great picture. The steamer runs irregularly, but need not be depended upon for the trip to Tzintzuntzán. It may be made by canoe, the wide-bottomed boats of the Tarascans, or on horseback or burros, in three or four hours. Patzcuaro and the beautiful lake have all the attributes of a fine health- and pleasure-resort. In the very near future the American will begin to find out why the Indians call it a place of delights.

At different points on the other side of the lake are other Indian villages, where the life that is lived to-day is essentially the same as that of five hundred years ago, and the features of the scene at this moment are surely of the ancient world. From all points of the lake more than a hundred canoes, or "dug-outs," may be seen moving in converging lines to a point on this shore. The modern art of making boats has not influenced the builders of these primitive vessels,

CATHEDRAL, MORELIA.

which are in the shape of a Chinaman's shoe, with the width less in proportion to the length. The bottom is flat, and the sides slope inward toward the top. They are propelled by rude paddles, which consist of a straight stick with a circular disk, about ten inches in diameter, at the end. They are manned by men and women, or by men or women, as it may happen. Three times a week they make this trip across the lake, bringing their wares to a common market-place, and return late in the afternoon with the produce of their exchanges. The wares which they offer are such as their ancestors might have brought to market centuries before the conquest. In fact, this part of Mexico remains yet to be conquered, if by that term is meant subjected to the forces and laws of progressive civilization. And yet it will be but a little while before Lake Patzcuaro and its surrounding villages will all be modernized by that greatest civilizer of the world—the railroad.

Uruapán, farther west, is perhaps the gem of Indian villages. It has a few good houses and fine streets; but its boast is in the Indian cottages, all so clean and snug and tasteful, surrounded by fruit-trees. To reach it one rides through shady lanes of trees bending under their weight of oranges, chirimoyas, plantanos, granaditas, and every other sort of delicious fruit. We visited the place under care of a military escort provided by Governor Mercado. The Indians here, as all through Michoacán, are Tarascos,—the Otomites and Chichimees,—and their language is most harmonious. The dress of the Indian women of Uruapán is pretty, and they are altogether a clean and good-looking race. They wear *naguas*, a petticoat of black cotton with a narrow white and blue stripe, made very full and rather long, and over this a sort of short chemise made of coarse white cotton and embroidered in different-colored silks. It is called the *sutunacua*. Over all is a black rebozo striped with white and blue, with a handsome silk fringe of the same colors. When they are married they add a white embroidered veil and a remarkably pretty colored mantle, the *huepilli*, which they pronounce guipil. The hair is divided and falls down behind in two long plaits, fastened at the top by a bow of ribbon and a flower. In this dress there is no alteration from what they wore in former days, save that the women of a higher class wore a dress of finer cotton with more embroidery and a loose garment over all, resembling a priest's surplice, when the weather was cold. Among the men, the introduction of trousers is Spanish; but they still wear the *majtlatl*, a broad belt with the ends tied before and behind, and the *tilmatli*, or *tilma* as they now call it, a sort of square short cloak, the ends of which are tied across the breast or over one shoulder. It was on a coarse tilma of this description that the image of the Virgin of Guadalupe was found painted. In this region the finest coffee in the world is raised, the "Uruapán" being everywhere recognized as the finest of brands.

In the environs of this town is the river Marques, amidst a most extraordinary union of tropical and European vegetation,—the hills covered with firs and the plains with sugar-cane. The river pursues its course through an enchanting landscape, now falling in cascades, now winding placidly at the foot of the silent hills and among the dark woods, and in one part forming a most beautiful natural bath by pouring its waters into an enclosure of large smooth flat stones overshadowed by noble trees.

A number of old Indian customs are still kept up here, modified by the introduction of Christian doctrines, in the marriages, feasts, burials, and superstitious practices. The citizens also preserve the same simplicity in their dress, united with the same vanity and love of show in their ornaments, that always distinguished them. The poorest Indian women still wear necklaces of red coral or a dozen rows of red beads, and their dishes are still the *jicalli*,—or, as they were called by the Spaniards, *jicaras*,—made of a species of gourd, or, rather, a fruit resembling it, and growing on a low tree, which fruit they cut in two, each furnishing two dishes. The inside is scooped out, and a durable varnish given it, by means of a mineral earth, of different bright colors, generally red. On the outside are painted flowers, and some are also gilded. They are extremely pretty, very durable, and ingenious. The beautiful colors which are employed in painting these jicaras are composed not only of various mineral productions, but of the wood, leaves, and flowers of certain plants, of whose properties these people have no despicable knowledge. Their own dresses, manufactured by themselves of cotton, are extremely pretty, and many of them fine.

About six miles from Uruapán are the celebrated Falls of the Sararaqui. At the foot of the oak-covered mountain is a great enclosure of lofty rocks, prodigious natural bulwarks, through a great cavern in which the river comes thundering and boiling into the valley, forming the great cascade of the Sararaqui, which in the Tarascan language means sieve. It is a very fatiguing descent, but it is worth while to make the whole journey from Mexico to see a sight so wildly grand. The falls are from fifty to sixty feet high and of great volume. The rocks are covered with shrubs and flowers, with small jets of water issuing from every crevice.

The Indian cottages are all clean, the walls hung with fresh mats, and the floors covered with the same; their kitchen utensils of baked earth are neatly hung on the wall, from the largest size in use to little dishes and jarritos in miniature placed there for ornament. The operation of making and painting jicaras is very curious. The flowers are not painted, but inlaid, and their like cannot be procured anywhere else.

There are other Indian villages almost equally interesting, but the more central and important parts of Michoacán are fast becoming civilized. Querendaro, on Lake Cuitzeo, is one of these places which are passing from the old to the new phase. The scenery around this lake is extremely lovely. Trees and flowering shrubs are plentiful and varied, and one may ride for hours with scarcely any fatigue. Bluebirds are particularly plenty here, and are called by the people guarda-bosques, "wood-guardians."

Around Querendaro are some fine haciendas, and among those may be found the most cordial hospitality in the world. I think the Mexican character is never seen to such advantage as in the country among these great landed proprietors of old family, who live on their own estates, engaged in agricultural pursuits, and entirely removed from all the party feeling and petty interests of a city life. It is true that the life of a country gentleman here is that of a hermit, in the total absence of all society, in the nearly unbroken solitude that surrounds him. For leagues and leagues there may be no habitation but his own; the nearest village may be distant half a day's journey, over an almost impassable road. But he is "monarch of all he surveys," a king among his farm-servants and Indian workmen. Nothing

An Entrance to the Paseo, Morelia.

can exceed the independence of his position. To enjoy this wild country-life he must be a first-rate horseman and addicted to all kinds of country sports; and if he can spend the day in riding over his estates in directing his workmen, watching over his improvements, and redressing disputes and grievances, and can sit down in the evening in his large and lonely halls and philosophically bury himself in the pages of some favorite author, his time will probably not hang heavy on his hands.

At Querendaro a canoe may be hired from the Indians for a voyage across to the Island of the Burros, one of the many islands of the lake, and the only one inhabited. The people are a hardy, sturdy race; the men are hunters and fishers, the women have nothing to do but to eat and sleep and grow fat, which they have made a complete success of; there are some fine specimens of almost Amazonian proportions, the finest Indians in Mexico. The lake abounds in myriads of water-fowl of every description.

Near the landing-place of Querendaro there are some hot springs, and the water is hot enough in the streams that flow from them to cook an egg. In scores of places columns of steam are rising from the fissures in the ground, and to walk over or near them is to feel the ground sink beneath. In a thicket near the railroad is a most primitive bath. A pit dug in the ground near one of the spring-streams is filled with water by damming the little brook, and when full is turned back to its own channel again. It must be a spring of wonderful curing waters. On the

LA TZARASACUA, URUAPAN.

trees and bushes, in the ground, everywhere near, there are hundreds and hundreds of crosses, the thank-offerings of those who have bathed and been cured.

While mining is not the most important interest in Michoacán, still there are many claims which have paid well for some time. The Trinidad and Tajo have been worked for more than one hundred and fifty years. The Los Llanitos pays well, and the Zinda group, about thirty-five miles from Morelia, gives excellent prospects. The best known mining-camps are the Curucupaceo in the district of Morelia, those in the district of Tlalpujahua, and those of Inquirán in the district of Tacámbaro. Perhaps the mines most familiar to residents of the city of Mexico are El Oro, which is now in bonanza, La Borda y Anexas (from which eight millions have been taken), Seis Señores, Santa Rosa, and La Concepción.

More important, however, in the mineral wealth of Michoacán is the copper that is found in large nuggets, some of which are exhibited weighing at least thirty pounds. At Santa Clara del Cobre, ten miles from Patzcuaro, one may see cooking utensils in common use whose shape indicates that the copper in that region was worked by the Tarascans. With a copper smelter in the city of Morelia the copper interest of the state would be on a splendid footing. There can be no question that the prospect is a magnificent one, and would be still more so if there were railroad communication with Patzcuaro, or if there were steamboats on the Balsas River. It is certain that there are large deposits of high-grade copper ore in the southwestern parts of the state, and Oropeo and Churumuco are specially named. There are both copper and cinnabar in Pungarabato, which is in the extreme southeast and lies upon that part of the Balsas which is called the Mexicala.

Finally, there are ores of galena in the districts of Zinepecuaro and Huetamo.

The schools of Michoacán are excellent, those of Morelia being of very high standing. The Industrial and Military School, named for Porfirio Diaz, President of Mexico, is a very fine institution, as is also the Normal Training-School for Girls. The San Nicolas College is a very old institution, which is the pride of the city and one of the centres of higher education in the Mexican republic.

This state is most fortunate in having as its governor Señor Don Aristeo Mercado, who is a man too great for petty rivalry and too clear-headed not to appreciate the value of what has already been done in Michoacán. He is a man of original ideas, with the courage and ability to carry them out; the result is seen in the admirable condition of the state, the high standing of the public schools, and the progressive spirit of the people.

CHAPTER XXXVIII

GUERRERO

THE state of Guerrero has enormous possibilities of wealth, and is destined to play an important part in Mexico's future financial resources and developments. It lies on the southern coast, bordering on the Pacific coast, between Michoacán and Oaxaca, with Mexico and Puebla to the north. Guerrero was not a state until 1849, when three districts taken from Mexico, two from Puebla, and one from Michoacán were put together to form it. It has an area of twenty-four thousand two hundred and twenty-six square miles, and a very large Indian population, although, as in most parts of Mexico, the whites are increasing very rapidly.

The state was named in honor of Vicente Guerrero, who was born at Tixtla about 1770, and executed at Cailapa, February 14, 1831. Guerrero was a mulatto and originally a slave. In the struggle for the independence of Mexico he exhibited great courage, and after the death of Mina became one of the leaders of the insurgents. In 1820 he entered the service of Iturbide, upon whose overthrow in 1823 he gave in his adherence to the provisional government and to the republic. In 1827 he was a candidate for the presidency, but was defeated by Pedraza by a majority of two votes in the electoral college. The partisans of Guerrero alleged that the election was carried by fraud, and rose in insurrection. Pedraza resigned in 1829, and Guerrero took possession of the presidency. On September 15 of that year he issued a proclamation abolishing slavery. The next year a Spanish force invaded Mexico, whereupon dictatorial power was conferred upon Guerrero, and his troops under Santa Anna defeated the Spaniards; but soon afterwards Bustamente and Santa Anna, on pretence that he ought not to have prolonged his dictatorship after the defeat of the Spaniards, revolted against Guerrero, who was deserted by his troops and compelled to take refuge in his hacienda

SEÑOR CORONEL ANTONIO MERCENARIO,
GOVERNOR OF GUERRERO.

at Tixtla. He was popular, and the people rallied to his support. He renewed the contest, but it was brought to a sudden close through the agency of a Genoese ship-captain, who invited him to a dinner on board his vessel at Acapulco and betrayed him to his enemies. He was tried by a military commission and shot. And thus perished another native hero of Mexico.

The state of Guerrero is traversed by the Sierra Madre with its many spurs, and is consequently very mountainous, its climate varying with the elevation, from very hot in the low countries to cold in the higher portions. The chief river is the Rio de las Balsas, which rises in Tlaxcala and, flowing southwest, finally forms the dividing line with Michoacán. There are great mining possibilities in Guerrero, some of which are already being developed. Both silver and gold abound, the mines of San José and Piedras Blancas being among the most important. Cinnabar is abundant elsewhere, as are likewise lead, sulphur, saltpetre, and copperas; and anthracite is found in Chilpancingo. The soil is very fertile; vegetation, particularly arboreal, is rich and varied, and there are extensive virgin forests, containing excellent timber and many species of precious woods.

IN TIXTLA, GUERRERO.

Maize and beans are the chief agricultural productions, the former yielding three large crops annually. Cotton, sugar-cane, coffee, cacao, yucca, and tobacco are also cultivated, and cochineal and indigo are extensively produced. Agriculture is, however, little attended to, save in the central portions of the state. The chief articles of export are cochineal, indigo, cacao, wool, and hides; the imports consist of cotton and silk fabrics, spices, and hardware. The foreign trade, once very important, is carried on through the port of Acapulco. Manufactures are limited to coarse cotton and woollen stuffs, rude agricultural implements, and household utensils. Many of the inhabitants are miners, and on the coasts numbers are engaged in pearl-fishing.

The first capital of Guerrero was Tixtla, which on its selection in 1849 was immediately raised to the rank of a city. It is picturesquely situated in a narrow gorge of the Sierra Madre, but has not yet become of great importance in any respect. It is five thousand feet above sea-level, and its chief occupations are coarse manufactures and agriculture.

The present capital is Chilpancingo, a few miles southwest of Tixtla, and situated on a pleasant table-land on the western side of the mountain-range.

Acapulco is, perhaps, the most important town in Guerrero, as it has one of the best harbors on the entire west coast. During the Spanish dominion Acapulco was the focus of the China and East Indian trade, and was a place of considerable importance. The California trade later gave it a period of transitory commercial life, as it was a coaling station for steamers between Panama and San Francisco; but with the new railroad now in process of construction, Acapulco is destined to see greater days than ever. The region around Acapulco produces the best lemons in the world, the fruit being large and juicy and far more desirable than either the Californian or the Sicilian product. As soon as the railway is completed from Cuernavaca, the way will be opened for marketing this product in New York and other ports, when the lemon industry is likely to blossom out into the greatest agricultural one of Guerrero.

CHILPANCINGO, THE CAPITAL OF GUERRERO.

This new railroad, "The Mexico, Cuernavaca and Pacific," is a line that is to give Mexico standard gauge connection with the old and historic port of Acapulco, whither came once the richly freighted galleons of Spanish commerce from China and Japan. In this connection it is worthy of note that the first fair and equitable treaty with Japan in modern times was made by Mexico. This new line pushing on to the Pacific, C. P. Huntington's in Northern Mexico and Colonel Joe Hampson's in Central Mexico, will enable Mexican manufacturers, working on a silver basis, to reach out for the west coast trade of South America. It is believed that the Mexico, Cuernavaca and Pacific road will open up extensive coal-fields and gold-mines in the state of Guerrero, cheapening fuel over a large region, and that eventually steamships from the Orient will touch at the piers of the Mexico, Cuernavaca and Pacific Railway at Acapulco. This port of Mexico presents an enormous field for investment. The day is not far distant when millions of American dollars will find their way there to be utilized. Guerrero is at present practically an unknown land, but for the man with a little capital at his disposal it presents a great future.

M. Le Royal, a French engineer staying in Mexico, reports that he has discovered a cave in the district of Guerrero which is much larger than the famous cavern of Cacahuamilpa, situated some distance south of Cuernavaca, a description of which is given in the next few pages, and which has hitherto been supposed to be the largest natural cave in existence in Mexico. The French engineer, after a few visits to the entrance, decided to make a thorough investigation. Accordingly he took five companions, candles, food for twenty-four hours, magnesium light, barometer, compass, etc., and set forth. It was not so easy a task as he had imagined, however, to find the end of the cave. At first the bottom of the cave was a gradual slope downward, then it changed upward, and afterward alternated for the most part between descents and ascents. Here and there a level bottom of great width was found. The height of the cave varied very much, as might naturally be expected. In some places it was several hundred feet high. For some distance from the entrance no trace of human beings was found, but occasionally magnificent stalactites and stalagmites—the finest M. Royal had ever seen—were met with. After proceeding for ten miles he came upon what had evidently been a cemetery, as there were at least four hundred petrified bodies there, together with ancient idols, stone tools, etc. Curiously enough, there was also a fountain of beautiful, clear, sparkling water. The aneroid barometer showed that this spot was six hundred feet lower than the mouth of the cave. M. Royal and his men went inward some twenty miles and then did not find the end; on the contrary, he concluded that the end of the cave was yet some distance from him. Finally, after being twenty-six hours under ground, the company found themselves under the blue sky. What possibilities of conjecture this cave calls up! Was there once a people there, who buried their dead in this immense cavern? Was it a prison-house? The ancient Toltecs and Chichimecs must have made use of it for something, but what? And now, late in the nineteenth century, this old cave with its hundreds of petrified bodies was lighted up for the first time in ages.

PALACE, CHILPANCINGO.

A discovery of great archæological value and importance has also been made in Guerrero by Mr. William Niven, a well-known mineralogist of New York City.

Mr. Niven is a life-member of the American Society of National History, and owner of the Rose Garnet quarries near Cautla, Morelos. While on a prospecting tour in 1894 he discovered a great and unknown prehistoric city in the mountains northwest of Chilpancingo.

The ruins are even more numerous than he had at first supposed, and cover an area of ten leagues square, or nine hundred square miles; he found in every foot-hill and mountain-ridge the remains of houses and great buildings. In most instances these prehistoric structures were little more than foundations, but many of the walls are standing from three to eight feet high and all substantially built of stone and lime. Mr. Niven has visited the ruins of twenty-two temples, occupying a space averaging six hundred square feet each, with altars in the centre from five to twenty feet high and from ten to fifteen feet square.

At Quechomictlipan (Aztec for "what a quantity of bones on top") he found that the building-stone in some of the edifices had been carefully cut of equal dimensions; and while excavating in one of these rooms great quantities of bones of animals were secured. This room proved to be a circular chamber, or tower, about twelve feet in diameter, which was filled with dust and broken plaster. On the floor, which was also of plaster, there were large quantities of stone beads and many very curious and interesting objects, with great abundance of broken pottery, metals, etc. Excavations at Jabalin revealed plastered walls and a great quantity of broken pottery. The walls of the temple at Yerba Buena are in some places eight feet high, and the altar is twelve feet high, with parts of the stairs still remaining. Here were also found many objects of terra-cotta. Photographs were made of a stone in hieroglyphics a short distance from Xoquiapán, and on the top of a hill were the ruins of a temple, with the usual altar in the centre. At Organos the ruins were almost entirely under ground. An excavation was made into one, and at ten feet the foundation of the walls was not reached. Three chambers were partly cleared out, and they were found to be filled with clay, ashes, and broken pottery. Another temple was found near there, at a place called Tejas, with more subterranean dwellings. One large cut stone at Xochocolzin, seven feet long by two feet wide, had a figure of an idol carved on one side, with head-dress complete. About eight hundred yards west of the summit of the hill were two large idols, one weighing about five hundred pounds. At Yexcal the buildings were all under ground, and near the roof of one were twelve prepared stones of the shape and size of a sugar-loaf built into the walls, placed side by side, with their broad ends projecting. On the summit of the Cerro Porterrio, as well as at Chalchintepetl, there are what appear to be great pyramids over sixty feet high.

TEMPLE AT QUECHOMICTLIPAN, OMITLAN.

Perhaps the most remarkable find was made at a place called Guaybo. Here were the ruins of a temple six hundred feet by two hundred feet. At the depth of nine feet from the surface, under the altar, an olla of terra-cotta was discovered filled with dirt, secreted in which were seventy-two beautiful objects of mother-of-pearl. Four were carved heads with a peculiarly shaped head-dress, and the others were carved representations of fish, etc. To reach the ruined city one must go over the route of the new railroad to Acapulco.

The governor of Guerrero, Señor Coronel Antonio Mercenario, is doing everything in his power to further the interests of his state and so to develop its resources as to bring it to the front rank in the Mexican republic. The people of Guerrero are wide awake and earnestly

GIRLS' COLLEGE, CHILPANCINGO.

desirous of keeping abreast with modern progress, and in this laudable purpose they are led by their valiant Governor Mercenario.

CHAPTER XXXIX

MORELOS

MUCH larger in the old days was the state of Morelos, which yielded up a part of its borders to Guerrero; but, in turn, the state was once a part of the state of Mexico. It is now a very small state, with an area of only eighteen hundred and eighty-seven square miles, but it has a large and rapidly increasing population and is a perfect garden of beauty. It is very mountainous, and is a part of the central table-land, with an elevation of four thousand five hundred feet above the sea. Popocatepetl, that most beautiful of volcanoes, is on the northeastern boundary, and there are other high peaks; but between them are most beautiful valleys of remarkable fertility, and these are being cultivated by enterprising Americans as well as Mexicans, and offer the best possible field for Northern men.

Numerous streams water the plains, the most important of which are the Cuernavaca and the Cuautla, tributaries of the Amacusaque. This is the greatest sugar-cane-producing state in proportion to its area, and immense gardens are laid out everywhere for the cultivation of exquisite fruits. Enormous quantities of sugar and molasses are made.

Of the thousands of tourists who yearly visit the city of Mexico, few now fail to make a trip up to the summit of the Mexico and Cuernavaca road as it crosses the lofty sierra. From the train, as it winds up the mountains, one gets a wonderful panorama of the valley of Mexico, seven thousand square miles in extent, guarded by its snow-capped sentinel volcanoes, a panorama of unsurpassed beauty and grandeur. Once upon the plains of Ajusco, over nine thousand feet above sea-level, you are in a region of pine-trees and potato-fields. But go on a few miles, and, looking from the cars, your gaze is fixed on another vast valley, that of the state of Morelos, the

SEÑOR CORONEL MANUEL ALARCON,
GOVERNOR OF THE STATE OF MORELOS.

richest sugar-growing region in Mexico. You look down from the pine-clad uplands, says one writer, "into a region of palms and tropical vegetation, and the ancient city of Cuernavaca seems to be riding out on an ocean of green sugar-cane. And yet the half has never been told."

AZTEC MONOLITH, CUERNAVACA

Poets have sung of nature's enchanting loveliness and beauty bordering the right of way of this great scenic line; orators have painted word-pictures of the beauties of its travel which charm the senses with unspeakable variety; writers have crowded glowing words into most befitting rhetorical effects; and yet, with all this combination of effort and intelligent description, to know, to understand, to appreciate, and fully to realize and enjoy the picturesque views, one must see them. Born with an indomitable will and intelligence, Colonel J. H. Hampson has written the realization of another of his great railway projects and public benefactions in letters of railway-steel along mountain-sides and rugged ways, and the Mexico, Cuernavaca and Pacific Railway is, and will ever be, a lasting monument to his energy and genius.

There are many mines in operation in Morelos, silver, gold, cinnabar, lead, chalk, and kaolin all being found in abundance on her mountains.

Morelos is divided into five districts, and the chief towns are Cuernavaca, the capital, Cuautla de Morelos, Yautepec, Jonacatepec, and Tete-Cola.

Cuernavaca has an ideal climate, dry and uniform, and the air is delicious. Among its chief attractions are the ancient palace of Cortez and the famous garden of La Borda, on which over a million dollars were lavished. Maximilian, when emperor, had his winter home in Cuernavaca, as had Cortez long before. The former lived for a time on the La Borda estate, and Carlotta and the emperor breakfasted under its trees and spent long days in the great walled garden. The empress used to go about the street like a young girl, attended by a

A BRIDGE BUILT BY CORTEZ IN MORELOS.

single maid of honor, her head covered with a silk rebozo. Maximilian also took a small country house outside the town, which still stands, and dwelt there some months.

Cuernavaca is situated at the foot of the southern slope of Ajusco, where the cold storms which sweep the gulf coast in winter can hardly gain access; hence it enjoys the perfection of a winter climate. Fields of tender vegetables planted in November for fruiting in winter attest the absence of frost. Its summer climate is also agreeable, for its elevation of five thousand feet above sea-level precludes oppressive heat. Moreover, the rain is said to fall here mostly by night. From this point one has a nearer view than from the city of Mexico of the great snowy summits rising above forested slopes, and here the interest of the view is greatly enhanced by the striking contrast afforded by an intermediate range of bare red rock, disordered masses, serrated, castellated, and pinnacled beyond description. Above and about the town the mountain-side is furrowed by many ravines so deep as to receive the name of

PALACE OF CORTEZ, CUERNAVACA.

barrancas. Below the town these open out into a wide valley which is green throughout the year with plantations of cane. Streams of pure water course down through every street, and fountains are frequent. To this quaint and quiet town, verdant and shady under bright, warm skies, was attracted the ill-fated Maximilian, and hither he was wont to ride by night to hide from assassins in the thick wood of his high-walled garden. The several barrancas of this neighborhood, with their brooks and waterfalls, their thickets of shrubs, their cliffs and bluffs, shaded or exposed, dry or wet, and the swampy meadows at their bottoms, offer a prospect for the tourist seldom excelled. The mountain woods more distant are hardly less inviting. The character of its plants indicates that this region belongs to the same floral zone as Oaxaca and Guadalajara. As a health-resort, a place to restore weak lungs and to rest weary nerves, Cuernavaca has no superior.

Cuernavaca (cow's horn), the ancient Quauhnahuac, was one of the thirty cities which Charles the Fifth gave to Cortez, and afterward formed part of the estate of the Duke of Monteleon, representative of the family of Cortez, as Marquis of the Valley of Oaxaca. It was celebrated by the ancient writers for its beauty, its delightful climate, and the strength of its situation; defended on one side by steep mountains, and on the other by a precipitous ravine through which ran a stream which the Spaniards crossed by means of two great trees that had thrown their branches across the barranca and formed a natural bridge. It was the capital of the Tlahuica nation, and after the conquest Cortez built a splendid palace, a church, and a convent of Franciscans, believing that he was laying the foundation of a great city. And, in fact, its delicious climate, the abundance of the water, the minerals said to exist in the neighborhood, its fine trees, its luscious fruits, and its vicinity to the capital combined to strengthen this belief. The conqueror's palace is now a half-ruined barrack, though a most picturesque object, standing on a hill, behind which starts up the great white volcano. There are some good houses and the remains of the church which Cortez built, celebrated for its fine arch.

CASCADE OF SAN ANTONIO.

It would be difficult to imagine anything more picturesque than the coffee plantations and orange walks. In this region the orange-trees are covered with their golden fruit and fragrant blossoms; the lemon-trees bend over, forming a natural arch which the sun cannot pierce; the air is soft and balmy and actually heavy with the fragrance of the orange-blossom and the starry jasmine. All round the orchard are streams of the most delicious clear water, and now and then a little cardinal, like a bright red ruby, perches on the trees. One may pick orange-blossoms, jasmine, lilies, double red roses, and lemon-leaves at the very moment when Winter is wrapping the world in his white winding-sheet in the United States.

The cave of Cacahuamilpa, whose wonders equal the descriptions of the palaces of the genii, was until the present century known to the Indians alone, or if the Spaniards formerly knew anything about it, its existence had been forgotten among them. But although in former days it may have been used as a place of worship, a superstitious fear prevented the more modern Indians from exploring its recesses, for they firmly believed the evil spirit had his dwelling there, and in the form of a goat, with long beard and horns, guarded the entrance of the cavern. The few who ventured and beheld this apparition brought back strange tales to their credulous companions, and even the neighborhood of the enchanted cave was avoided, especially at night-

FIELD OF RICE IN MORELOS.

fall. The chain of mountains into whose bosom it leads is bleak and bare, but the ravine below is refreshed by a rapid stream that forms small waterfalls as it tumbles over the rocks, and is bordered by green and flowering trees. Among these is one with a smooth, satin-like bark of a pale golden color, whose roots have something uncanny and witch-like in their appearance, intertwining with each other, grappling as it were with the hard rock, and stretching out to the most extraordinary distance. The entrance to the cave is a superb portal, upward of seventy feet high and one hundred and fifty feet wide, according to the computation of a learned traveller; the rocks which support the great arch are so symmetrically disposed as to resemble a work of art. Down a declivity, it may be one hundred and fifty feet, surrounded by blocks of stone and rock, is a gloomy subterranean palace, surrounded by the most extraordinary, gigantic, and mysterious forms, which it is scarcely possible to believe are the fantastic produc-

Borda Garden, Cuernavaca.

tions of the water which constantly trickles from the roof. The vast labyrinth is indescribable. It is said that the first sala is about two hundred feet long, one hundred and seventy wide, and one hundred and fifty in height. The walls are shaded with different tints of green and orange; great sheets of stalactites hang from the roof, and white phantoms, palm-trees, lofty pillars, pyramids, porches, and a thousand other illusions, are on all sides. One figure, concerning which all agree, is a long-haired goat, the evil one in that form. But some one has broken the head, perhaps to show the powerlessness of the enchanted guardian of the cave. In the second sala the architecture is decidedly Egyptian, and the strange forms of the animals resemble those of the uncouth Egyptian idols. These, with the pyramids and obelisks, indicate that perhaps the ancient people took the idea of their architecture from some natural cave of this description, just as nature suggested the idea of the beautiful Corinthian pillar. Again, it seems to be a tract of petrified country. Fountains of congealed water, trees hung with frozen moss, pillars covered with gigantic acanthus leaves, pyramids ninety feet high, look like works of the pre-Adamites, yet no being but He who inhabits eternity could have created them. The second hall may be nearly four hundred feet in length. But why go on? It is said that this cavern has been explored for four leagues, and yet that no exit has been discovered. The skeleton of a man was once discovered by some travellers, lying on his side, the head nearly covered with crystallization. He had probably entered these labyrinths alone, either from rash curiosity or to escape from pursuit, lost his way, and perished from hunger. Indeed, to find the way back to the entrance of the cave is nearly impossible without some clue to guide the steps among these winding galleries, halls and issues, and entries, and divided corridors.

Among the celebrated Humboldt pictographs are some very interesting ones which are supposed to be relics of this region. These documents may have been a record of the methods of the early Franciscan missionaries, and were presented early in the nineteenth century to the Royal Library at Berlin by Baron Humboldt.

The pictographs consist of fourteen pieces, of different sizes and widely varying contents. One entire document and the fragment of another belong to a period prior to the conquest.

PLAZA, CUERNAVACA.

The former is a schedule of tributes paid to a certain temple. There is nothing to show what or where the temple was, but it probably belonged to a tribe inhabiting the state of Morelos. The tributes consisted of blankets, gold in plates and in dust, etc. The blankets may have been for the personal use of the priests of the temple, but not necessarily so, for blankets, like other articles in general use, were eagerly sought after as a species of money, or, in other words, as instruments of barter or exchange.

Cuautla de Morelos has been the theatre of important historical events. Here it was that the curate Morelos shut himself up with his troops until the Spaniards under Calleja besieged it and the priest and his party were compelled to abandon their position.

The state of Morelos has already thousands of bright, clever, pushing Americans and Englishmen engaged in active endeavor. All through the hot country one finds them growing cane, maturing their coffee-trees or gathering their fruit, raising maize and bananas, and leading the independent lives of small planters and cultivators, their manual labor being done for them

FIELD OF SUGAR-CANE IN MORELOS.

by the native Indian. One could easily enumerate scores of men who took only a few thousand dollars to start with, some less, who are now on the way to wealth, and not a few who are very substantial people indeed.

Cuernavaca is the home of Mr. J. Hamer, at whose factories in the city of Mexico a practical test is being made of successfully spinning the native flax and manufacturing linen cloths of all kinds. We visited this flax-factory and the residence of Mr. Hamer; and in this connection might say that we made the entire trip through Mexico in beautiful linen travelling costumes which were woven at this factory. While there we had the opportunity of meeting Governor Alárcon and his newly wedded bride, finding them both among the most charming people in Mexico.

Although Morelos is the smallest state in Mexico, it certainly equals in importance even the greatest. In Governor Manuel Alárcon it has an executive head fitted to carry its industrial and its native wealth to a fitting climax, and make the region named after that noble patriot Morelos one of the most progressive spots, as it is one of the most beautiful, in the world.

CHAPTER XL

CHIAPAS

CHIAPAS is the most southern state in the Mexican republic, and presents an almost virgin field of unsurpassed natural resources. It is bounded on the north by the state of Tabasco, which separates it from the Gulf of Mexico, on the east by the republic of Guatemala, on the south by the Pacific Ocean, and on the west by the states of Vera Cruz and Oaxaca. The Sierra Madre mountains run almost parallel with the Pacific Ocean in their course through the state, there being between the two a stretch of level land which is uncommonly fertile, including the districts of Soconusco and Tonalá. North of these mountains, and exactly in the central section of the state, there are also fertile plains in the districts of La Libertad, Chiapa, and Tuxtla, and in Comitán along the Guatemalan frontier; and, finally, along the boundary of Tabasco are situated the humid forest-plains of the districts of Pichucalco and Palenque. From the southern limits of these two districts and toward the centre of the state the mountain-slopes begin to rise, finding their extreme height in the district of Las Casas, whose county-seat is more than seven thousand feet above sea-level; but the coast range in its descent to the sea slopes more abruptly. In the districts of Mezcalapa, Pichucalco, Simojovel, Chilón, Comitán, and Palenque the landscape presents a picturesque undulating country, with ridges of mountains of moderate altitude, and traversed by numerous navigable streams, such as the Grijalva, Mezcalapa, Tapijulapa, El Salto, and Usumacinta. The number of rivers of lesser importance is very considerable, and Chiapas may be counted among the best watered states of Mexico. As there are no really low or swampy districts, the climate is healthy, and it is generally tempered by prevailing breezes from the gulf and the Pacific Ocean, which supply the atmospheric moisture favorable to plant life and give abundant rainfall.

SEÑOR CORONEL FRANCISCO LEON,
GOVERNOR OF CHIAPAS.

The general aspect of the country is very unlike that of Northern Mexico. Chiapas has no barren country except in the very highest parts of its mountains, the medium and lower regions generally being covered by forests of valuable woods, while its cultivated parts show fields of all kinds and abundance of crops.

Lake Tepancuapán, in the southern part, is eighteen miles long and three miles wide, and abounds in crabs. There are several smaller lakes in the state.

It is a mistake to assume that all of Chiapas is mountainous, and hence inaccessible. Through the ports of Tonalá and San Benito on the Pacific the rich districts of Tonalá and Soconusco can be reached, and from the former port the towns of Tuxtla, Chiapa, and San Cristóbal are accessible by means of a good wagon-road. Six water-ways give access through

PALACE, CHIAPAS.

the gulf to the districts of Mezcalapa, Pichucalco, Simojovel, and Palenque. Ascending the Grijalva River, in Tabasco, and following the Mezcalapa, the districts of Mezcalapa and Tuxtla are reached; the district of Pichucalco is reached by the river Blanquillo, Simojovel by the Tapijulapa, and Palenque by the rivers Tulija and Chacamas. Palenque is also accessible from Lake Términos by ascending the rivers Palizada and Usumacinta into Lake Catazaja to the town of Catazaja. The Mezcalapa is navigable for low-draught boats up to within twenty-four Mexican leagues from Tuxtla-Gutierrez, the capital of the state. The department of Comitán is not easily reached by either the gulf or the Pacific Ocean, but its proximity to Guatemala offers great advantages for the exportation of its products to that country, which will always contribute to the enrichment of the inhabitants. The road to Guatemala is hilly, but is in fit condition for travelling. The Tehuantepec National Railway has opened new and advantageous means of egress to the state. By taking the train at Coatzacoalcos, the railroad's terminus on the Mexican Gulf, or at Salina Cruz, its terminus on the Pacific Ocean, San Gerónimo station is reached, from which place a good wagon-road leads to the capital city.

Chiapas has over three hundred thousand inhabitants; the majority of them are Indians. They are of a peaceful disposition, and there are among them tribes which are intelligent and highly civilized, as may be seen in Tuxtla, Ocosocuautla, Copainala, and other places. The inhabitants of Chiapas are remarkable for their hospitality. Foreigners are well received, and no distinction is made on account of nationality. The necessaries of life are generally cheap and excellent. There are schools distributed throughout the state according to the size of the towns. In the cities of San Cristóbal, Comitán, and Tuxtla there are high schools for girls, supported by the city and state governments, and under the guardianship of the latter government. In Tuxtla and San Cristóbal there are preparatory schools where students receive preliminary instruction for any professional college of the federal government.

BETWEEN ORTEGA AND LA PUERTA.

Commerce is the most developed of the resources of Chiapas. Tonalá and Soconusco supply themselves through their ports; Pichucalco and Palenque are supplied from San Juan Bautista; the remaining departments do their trading for foreign products with Tuxtla, which is the commercial metropolis of the state, and here capital and wealth have concentrated themselves. Trade in Chiapas is susceptible of great possibilities.

Agriculture is in its infancy, but will be the means of adding materially to the wealth of the state. Coffee, which has been cultivated for some years, is greatly enriching some of the departments. Soconusco has two million coffee-trees, Tuxtla about one million, Mezcalapa five hundred thousand, the other departments one million, making a total of four million five hundred thousand, one million of which are in production, and the remainder will be bearing inside of two years. There are several sugar-cane plantations, and in Simojovel some interest is taken in tobacco culture.

Coffee is considered the best paying product of Chiapas. In a hectare (2.4711 acres) of land nine hundred trees are planted. It is not advisable to increase the number, as is done in the other states, on account of the extraordinary growth of the tree in Chiapas. The minimum product of a tree in full bearing is two pounds of dry coffee; many plantations produce on an average three, four, and five pounds to the tree. Trees are found in Simojovel and Chilón that bear twenty pounds, and there is one particular tree in Tuxtla, on the Mezcalapa River, forty years old, that yields forty pounds; but of course these are isolated cases.

The cacao- or chocolate-tree can be planted also, nine hundred to the hectare. Each tree produces half a pound of seed a year, and begins to yield after five years' cultivation. The advantage that cacao has over coffee is that its crops can be gathered four times a year. In the city of Mexico and other interior towns cacao is worth from fifty cents to one dollar a pound.

Tobacco can be harvested six months after planting. The best tobacco-lands are situated in Simojovel, Mezcalapa, and Matastepec, in Tonalá.

In the lands best adapted for the cultivation of sugar-cane the cost of production does not exceed twenty-five cents per arroba of twenty-five pounds, and this could be much reduced by using modern appliances, as yet unknown in Chiapas. The fine sugar-lands of Chilón, Palenque, Pichucalco, and Mezcalapa require no irrigation, and the plantations last twenty years without replanting.

The cultivation of the rubber-tree is known to be very lucrative. It is found wild in Mezcalapa, Tuxtla, and Soconusco; only in the latter district has it been cultivated.

Vanilla is found wild in Tuxtla and Mezcalapa, where good-sized plantations could be established in connection with rubber-growing. In a few years such experiments would yield profitable results.

In all the departments where the climate is warm the tropical fruits, such as pineapples, bananas of various kinds and of excellent quality, lemons, oranges, mangos, and zapotes, are raised. The traffic in semi-tropical fruits obtainable in Las Casas is in itself the way to a fortune, for these fruits sell well in the state, in Tabasco, and along the Isthmus of Tehuantepec.

The production of cereals is abundant, and in some sections corn yields four hundred for one. The ears of corn raised in Juncana (Comitán) very often exceed twenty Mexican inches in length. Wheat, which can be raised on a large scale in Las Casas, is sold for a good price throughout the state.

Cattle-raising is one of the best enterprises in Chiapas, on account of the splendid pasture-lands.

Mining is a new industry in the state. The gold-mine of Santa Fé in Pichucalco is worked with good financial success; other mines have been discovered and gradually developed. Those in Motozintla (Comitán) and several others in Tuxtla and Chiapa demonstrate the fact that the state is wealthy in minerals.

Other exportable articles are the skins of crocodiles caught in the rivers and lakes of Palenque and Tonalá. In the same district herons are numerous, the feathers of which have been sold as high as forty-eight dollars gold per ounce. Notwithstanding the extensive exportation of cedar and mahogany, there are yet many unexplored forests of this fine timber.

Good land can be had in any of the districts, the prices varying according to the kind of land, accessibility, and location. Waste lands belonging to the federation are obtained by denouncement before the resident agent of the Department of Encouragement (Fomento).

Of all the states in the Mexican federation, Chiapas has the least burdensome system of taxation. Improved farms pay six dollars taxes for every thousand dollars of assessed valuation. The law exempts from taxation all kinds of buildings, machinery, unproductive plantations, and breeding animals imported from foreign countries to improve the stock. City property pays no taxes to the state, but the municipalities or cities collect six-tenths per cent. on very low assessments. Twenty thousand dollars tax is imposed on all the merchants doing business in the state, the pro rata being adjusted by the assessment boards. Freighters in making use of the highways pay a road tax. On the amounts collected for state and city taxes the federal government imposes an extra tax of thirty per cent.

The district of Palenque is located in the descent which the Sierra Madre mountains make on their extension toward the northern part of the state, and covers a great portion of the plains that stretch out to Tabasco and Campeche. The country consists of high and low lands: the former are the extension of the rich coffee-belt of Simojovel, but more fertile in this section; the lowlands do not inundate, are higher, of better quality, and their climate less hot, than those of Tabasco. El Salto, head-quarters for the department officials, is situated at the head of navigation of the Tulija river. Catazaja, on Lake Catazaja, is probably the most important city. Whilst crocodiles have been almost annihilated in Tabasco by killing them to export the hides, they abound in the lakes and rivers of Palenque. In like manner herons are plentiful, and their fine feathers have reached a very high price.

Near the town of Palenque are the famous ruins of that name. They were discovered by the Spaniards in 1750, but no one knows what they were originally intended for or by whom they were built. They consist of artificial terraces, or terraced truncated pyramids, of cut stone. They are surrounded by edifices of elaborate plan, covered with hieroglyphics and bearing evidences of having once been painted in bright colors. The principal structure, called the palace, is built upon a truncated pyramid three hundred and ten feet long. The palace itself is two hundred and twenty-eight feet long and twenty-five feet high. It is built of cut stones cemented with lime and sand, and was once painted. The hieroglyphics which ornamented the piers and bas-reliefs show a much better knowledge of human anatomy than is shown in other American aboriginal work of like nature.

TYPES OF INDIAN WOMEN IN CHIAPAS.

In one of the courts are a number of stucco tablets and one of stone which shows a cross-legged seated figure like that of Buddha in some of the Hindoo pictures. It is on a seat carved with figures of jaguars, and before it is another richly dressed figure presenting some highly ornamented object. There are hieroglyphics on the tablet that doubtless tell the whole story, could we but read them. Near by is another building seventy-five feet long, and with solid walls except on the north, where there are five door-ways and six piers. Four of the latter are ornamented with well-executed female figures, and the whole is ornamented with stucco-work and plenty of hieroglyphics, outside the house and in. In another structure is a group of human figures apparently in the act of making a solemn sacrifice. Many of the buildings seem to have been lived in, and others were probably devoted to religious purposes. Two stones in the shape of a tongue, about a yard long and two-thirds of a yard wide, inscribed with hieroglyphics, are objects of awe and adoration to the Indians. Throughout the state are scattered evidences of ancient occupancy, and it is remarkable for the numerous ruins of ancient cities and monuments. The tombs at Palenque are objects of deep interest to archæologists. One who has not visited the forests of Palenque cannot imagine the inextricable confusion of great roots, overturned tree-trunks, climbing vines, and decaying vegetation that buries everything under a seething, gloomy, deceptive covering. One step forward may land one on a fallen column, and the next bury one waist-deep in the rotten trunk of a fallen forest giant among scorpions and biting ants.

The district of Chilón shares the extension of the salubrious mountain-lands of Palenque in the north and the fertile plains of Comitán in the south. The land is well timbered, has an abundance of water and pasture-fields, and offers splendid inducements for agricultural enterprises. Capitalists from Comitán and San Cristóbal have established fine estates that bring them a good income.

ON THE ROAD TO BONITO.

Tuxtla-Gutierrez, the capital and residence of the state officials, is situated in the extreme east of the district and a few miles from the Chiapa River. It is the best trading town, being in communication with all sections of the state, the supply-store of the other towns, and the warehouse for a good many of them. Suchiapa, Ocosocuautla, Zintalapa, and San Fernando are towns whose inhabitants exceed one thousand. A wagon-road connects Tuxtla with the port of Tonalá, and a branch near the coast touches the Tehuantepec Railway. Good wagon-roads connect the capital with the towns of Suchiapa and Chiapa, and the plains that follow the left side of the Chiapa River render the country accessible clear up to Guatemala. There are mule-roads to San Cristóbal, Comitán, and Copainala, and another is being constructed to Pichucalco. Twenty leagues below Tuxtla-Gutierrez the Mezcalapa River is navigable to Tabasco and the gulf.

Tonalá, the county-seat and the residence of the Jefe Politico and Judge of First Instance, lies six leagues from Arista; it has five thousand inhabitants. It is quite a commercial point. Arista is the only port of the district. The federal government has established here a maritime custom-house and an office of Captain of Ports. The principal wagon-road of the state is the one that starts from Arista through Tonalá and then ascends the Sierra Madre into the department of Tuxtla. A branch of this road connects the department with the Tehuantepec Railroad. The Mexican Pacific Railroad is built from Arista to La Aurora, and will continue to the capital, Tuxtla-Gutierrez.

Soconusco is the best known of all the districts of Chiapas, owing to the rapid development of its natural wealth. From a poor, unknown section it has grown up within a few years to be the most famous and prosperous coffee district. Here foreign capitalists have invested ungrudgingly and made fortunes. Soconusco is situated at the southeast corner of the state, adjoining Guatemala, and occupies the widest section of the strip lying between the Sierra Madre and the Pacific Ocean. The country is mostly level along the coast, but rises gradually toward the Sierra, where splendid coffee-lands are found, rivalled by none in the republic, unless by the other rich coffee districts in Chiapas. Soconusco cacao has been known ever since the conquest of Mexico by the Spaniards, and always has had the reputation of being the best in the world. Soconusco is the most southern point in North America.

Throughout Chiapas large amounts of foreign capital are coming into the country for investment. The successful results already accomplished are encouraging, and there are more new ventures being planned than ever before. Indeed, quite recently contracts have been made for bringing over several hundred Japanese colonists, nearly all of whom will locate in Chiapas and become factors in the coffee cultivation. The climatic conditions in the lower coast sections of the country, the soil, and the river transportation facilities in most of the coffee districts all offer peculiarly good inducements for the investment of capital in coffee-lands.

The governor of Chiapas is Señor Coronel Francisco Leon, who conducts the affairs of his state with a commendable spirit of economy.

CHAPTER XLI

CAMPECHE

JUST beyond Tabasco, and between that state and Yucatán, is Campeche. It has an area of twenty-six thousand and ninety square miles, and, like its neighboring states, the population is largely Indian. It was formerly a part of Yucatán, but was separated in 1858. The principal river is the San Francisco. The Champotón also is important, and there are numerous smaller streams. There are, besides, some small lakes; so that, taken as a whole, Campeche is a well-watered state. The soil is for the most part sandy, except near the capital and in the forests. There are

PALACE OF JUSTICE, CAMPECHE.

good pasture-lands, and cattle-raising is an important industry. Salt, rice, and sugar are prominent among the products, and henequin is raised in prodigious quantities. There is a great future for this part of Mexico as soon as capitalists shall discover what opportunities are open there for the manufacturer who will work up the textile material that can be raised in Campeche.

The capital of the state is the city of Campeche, which is also an important seaport for all the surrounding states. It is situated on the Bay of Campeche, at the mouth of the San Francisco River. It has a population of about twenty-five thousand, and is fast growing. The streets are irregular, and the houses remarkable for their uniform height of one story, their square form, and for all being built of the limestone which abounds near the city.

We were charmed with Campeche; it is very picturesque, with its great wall surrounding the city, built in defence against Indian raiders and French and English buccaneers. Governor Montalvo and others entertained us. We were struck with the affectionate regard

CALLE DE ZARAGOZA, SHOWING THE WALL WHICH SURROUNDS THE CITY.

shown for the family of Honorable Joaquin Baranda, minister of justice. The Barandas have been intimately associated with the history of the state, and I believe the records show that Minister Baranda's father was admiral of the tiny Mexican fleet that operated against the Spaniards in the colonial struggle for independence. The state is now called Campeche de Baranda, in his honor.

Campeche was founded in the middle of the sixteenth century, and has figured in history more or less ever since. It was sacked by the British in 1659, and again by pirates in 1678, and by filibusters in 1685. Its site has been twice changed, the present one being honey-combed with subterranean chambers which were dug out ages ago by the Mayas Indians, ruins of whose structures may be seen in the vicinity of Campeche even now. The city of to-day has several churches and convents, a museum containing interesting aboriginal relics, a theatre, and several schools and colleges. It has a beautiful alameda, embellished with alleys of orange-trees and seats of the native marble. There is a lack of good water at Campeche, and living is consequently higher than in some other Mexican towns. The port is defended by three fortresses. The roads are extremely shallow, and few of the numerous vessels can approach the mole. Vessels drawing ten feet of water have to anchor a mile off shore, and those drawing fifteen feet from six to seven miles away.

The commerce of Campeche was, under the Spanish colonial system, in a most flourishing state, as it had the monopoly of the imports to Yucatán; but it is now confined mostly to salt, sugar, hides, henequin and articles manufactured from it. Logwood and other dyestuffs are still exported in quantities, but the cigar industry is greater. The Campeche cigars are made

PLAZA DE LA INDEPENDENCIA, CAMPECHE.

from Tabasco tobacco (which is superior to that of Yucatán), and are often sold in foreign markets for the Havana.

In many respects, nature has been kind to Campeche. It needs only good judgment and industry to develop its riches. There are plenty of rivers for irrigation, each worth a gold-mine, if properly used, but now comparatively valueless because unemployed. There is but one railway in the country, that to Minatitlán, three hundred and eighty-five miles long, a branch of the celebrated Tehuantepec route.

Everybody has heard of the "Mysterious City," which tradition places somewhere in this region. Deep in the wilderness, on some far-off unnamed tributary of the Rio Usumasinta, is supposed to be hidden a splendid city, whose white walls shine like silver in the sun, and inhabited by unconquered aboriginal Indians who yet worship the hideous idols of their ancestors. At least it is true that several adventurous explorers of our own time, who have made this region the study of years, believe in the mysterious city. Stephens, Morelet, Squier, and Le Plongeon tried hard to find it; and Ober, being on the border of the wilderness, was strongly tempted to venture alone in search of it, but was dissuaded from the undertaking.

It is said that only one person in the world claims to have actually sojourned within the aboriginal city and lived to tell the tale. This is Señor Don Pedro Velasquez, a Guatemalan. He says that he accompanied two young gentlemen from Baltimore, Maryland, who, with several Campeche Indians, were prospecting the wilderness in search of mines and india-rubber, and who, after many hardships and hairbreadth escapes, reached the shining city. According to

RUINS OF HOCH-OB, CAMPECHE.

his account, the wonder is that they were allowed to enter at all. But once inside the city, they were safe enough so long as they showed no desire to depart. At the first attempt to leave it they were bound hand and foot and thrust into a pen adjoining the temple. That same evening one of the Baltimoreans was sacrificed on the blood-stained altar of the sun, having the heart torn from his living body and placed reeking before the idol just as the sun sank below the horizon. The others expected the same fate, but during the night they managed to effect an almost miraculous escape. Only Don Pedro, however, and one of his Indians returned to civilization, the rest having perished in the wilderness.

Carmen, while it has the best harbor on the Mexican coast, is one of its least known ports. As no regular line of ocean-steamers stops there, it seldom falls to the lot of tourists or travellers to visit the place; yet there are from a dozen to two dozen foreign vessels anchored there a great part of the time. At the lower extremity of Yucatán a fringe of islands hems in a portion of the gulf, forming a large lake. The early navigators, believing this lake to be a strait separating Yucatán from the mainland, and here terminating their voyages for the time being, gave it the name of Términos, which name still remains. But the lake is really the estuary of the great Usumasinta River, which drains an area of country extending from the Cockscomb Mountains of British Honduras on the east to the rugged mountain-peaks of Chiapas on the west and the cordilleras of Guatemala on the south. Since its birth the wealth of Carmen has consisted in the logwood cut in the vicinity and on the banks of the Usumasinta, with large quantities of mahogany felled in the interior and floated down the streams to the port. For the shipment of these valuable woods many vessels are required.

Travelling in the jungles of Campeche is not particularly inviting as yet. Wild beasts and

PALACIO CENTRAL, RUINS OF HOCH-OB, CAMPECHE.

hostile Indians are not the greatest perils in that tropic forest. Terrible tales are told of enormous serpents which hurl themselves from the trees with the force of a catapult, by one twist of their sinuous coils crushing the life out of a man on horseback, and swallowing small animals in the twinkling of an eye. Even worse than the giant boa is the small *víbora de sangre*, whose bite causes the blood of man or beast to ooze through the pores of the skin until the veins are empty and the victim dies from exhaustion. There are also tiny vipers, the exact color of the leaves under which they lurk, whose sting is certain death.

And yet, life in many parts of the state is almost ideal; and invariably the stranger in Southern Mexico is astonished at the magnificence in which the wealthy planters live. Each is like a king in his own extensive domain, absolute monarch of all he surveys, as well as lord of the lives and destinies of his peons.

The hacienda garden is a wonder in its way. In it are cocoanut-, mango-, and red-pear-trees, clumps of oranges and limes, thickets of figs and pomegranates, while the flower-beds, raised a foot from the ground and bordered with beautiful shells bedded in mortar, are filled with roses, narcissus, pansies, and tuberoses, almost unrecognizable as the familiar favorites because grown to such perfection. On the average hacienda, too, the proprietor's residence is a model of elegance and comfort, suited to the climate and typical of the rural homes of wealthy Mexicans.

The governor of Campeche is Señor Don Juan Montalvo, whose administration is distinguished by prudent foresight and wise economy.

CHAPTER XLII

TABASCO

TABASCO lies north of Chiapas and stretches along the coast of the Gulf of Mexico, covering an area of twelve thousand seven hundred and sixteen square miles. It lies also between Campeche on the east and Vera Cruz on the west. The population is largely Indian, of a peaceful disposition, although Tabasco, like all the other Mexican states, is fast being developed by white men from various northern points. There are many lagoons and inlets along the coast, with the islands of Laguna Carmen and Puerto Real. The surface is flat and marshy, except in the southern portion, where it rises toward the mountains of Chiapas and becomes more healthy.

GENERAL ABRAHAM BANDALA,
GOVERNOR OF TABASCO.

The Usumasinta and Tabasco Rivers are the most important streams: these are navigable, carrying a large amount of freight, and being the principal thoroughfares of the state. Oak, cedar, ironwood, and mahogany abound. Coffee, cacao, sugar-cane, pepper, palmetto, tobacco, and rice are extensively cultivated, offering magnificent opportunities for further development. Corn yields three and often four crops a year in this land without a winter. Wild bees furnish large amounts of wax and honey, and indigo grows spontaneously.

The capital and largest city is San Juan Bautista. Cortez and the Spanish army discovered Tabasco and made a landing there before they went on to Mexico. Bernal Diaz speaks of the town of Tabasco, with its wooden walls. It was then a very populous place, with the better houses built of stone and lime, and the others of mud or adobe. The inhabitants, the Tabascan Indians, gave proof of superior refinement as well as unusual valor. Their stout resistance, however, did not prevent Cortez and his soldiers from finally gaining possession and capturing it "in the name of the Crown." This he did with three sword-cuts on a large ceiba-tree, proclaiming aloud that he took possession of Tabasco in behalf of his Catholic sovereigns, and would defend and maintain it with sword and buckler. He did not find this so easy as he had hoped, for soon the whole adjacent country was ready for battle, and on the 25th of March (Lady Day), 1519, a fierce contest was waged on the plains of Ceutla, a few miles from Tabasco. Even then this country was well irrigated with numerous ditches crossing off the land like a checker-board. Maize and cacao were growing in great abundance, and great plantations of them were fed by numerous canals and reservoirs of water, with only a narrow roadway between. Cortez's troops triumphed, however, after a fierce battle lasting some hours, and in the interchange of slaves following

FARM-HOUSE, TABASCO.

the great Spanish conqueror came into possession of the beautiful slave Doña Marina, who had so much influence in Mexican matters afterward.

Her father was a rich and powerful cacique, but died young, and her mother married again. In order to secure the estates for the son of this second marriage her mother sold Doña Marina into slavery; and after one or two changes she fell into the hands of Cortez, who first made her his interpreter, then his secretary, and finally his mistress. Afterward she had it in her power to have her mother properly punished, but refused to do so. Her son, Don Martin Cortez, was Comendador of the Military Order of St. James. She always felt sympathy for the conquered race, and her name of Malinche (the Aztec word for Marina) was always remembered with kindness in Mexico. Many an Indian ballad commemorates her good qualities, and it is said that her gentle spirit even now watches over Mexico, and that oftentimes the spirit of an Indian princess is seen at evening flitting among the grottos and groves around Chapultepec.

PORT OF SAN JUAN BAUTISTA.

Many of the Spanish conquerors settled in Tabasco, others in the cordillera toward the rich slopes and valleys of Oaxaca. When Cortez endeavored to discover a strait in Central

America which should connect the great oceans, he again marched through Tabasco. He halted in Coatzacoalcos and hunted up a map of Tabasco. From there on to Honduras the Spanish army had a most discouraging time in the marshes and overflowed watercourses. They were obliged to build fifty bridges within a hundred miles, and one of them was more than nine hundred paces across. They found Iztapán, which was then a considerable village. They passed near the famous ruins of Palenque, and the village of Las Tres Cruzes still has a trace of their visit in the three crosses which they left there. And yet, with all this, no description of the ancient capital is found in Bernal Diaz's or Cortez's accounts. Was it even then a heap of

STREET IN SAN JUAN BAUTISTA.

ruins mouldering in a mass of vegetation and hidden from the knowledge of the surrounding country?

Farther on,-in the province of Aculán, was for many years the famous "Bridge of Cortez," which contained one thousand pieces of timber sixty feet long and the thickness of a man's body, and yet was built in four days. Until the present century this bridge stood as a monument of Cortez's commanding bravery and energy. It was in Aculán, too, that Cortez was informed that Guatemozin, the last of the Aztec chiefs, who had accompanied him from Mexico, had formed a conspiracy against the Spaniards. And in spite of his protestations, Cortez ordered his execution. He, with the chief of Tacuba and one or more inferior princes, was executed by being hung from a ceiba-tree beside the road. They had been "converted to Christianity," but died by the hands of those who converted them, and thus perished the last Aztec emperor.

A good deal of the country is sloping and very much broken, but at least four-fifths could be well cultivated. Coffee always requires a slope. The present population, which is sparse, consists principally of Indians. These people work faithfully and cheerfully at light work, such as coffee-gathering.

There is no finer country in the world awaiting development than this general slope. The rainfall is abundant. The climate is very healthy. Any observant man who will look at the Caucasian type of Mexicans among the scattered ranches of people born and raised there will find that they will compare favorably for bone, muscle, color, and physical strength with the best Mexican type. The water is plentiful, pure, and nearly always soft.

There is a good quantity of water-power available all through this state; the supply of it toward the wilder end of the slope is practically unlimited.

There is plenty of building-stone in the country. Part of the slope has an unlimited

SAN JUAN BAUTISTA.

quantity of marble of all colors. The state is especially attractive on account of the harmless, gentle, industrious nature of the few Indians that occupy it.

The trade of the state is controlled by Spaniards, who also own nearly all the steamers sailing under the Mexican flag in the Gulf of Mexico. They are all hard workers, and most of them fine fellows. They send home to Spain about a million dollars annually. A good many marry in the country, and their children are among the best types in the state.

This country unites all the conditions necessary for happy, reasonable living. The climate is temperate, the water excellent and abundant; there is plenty of timber and plenty of building-stone; it is a fine coffee, corn, cane, and cotton country.

The capital, San Juan Bautista, is on an island of volcanic origin thrown up in the midst of the alluvial plain of the Grijalva, about sixty-five miles from the sea. It has a population of twelve thousand, and is provided with two street railroads and a first-class electric-light plant, comprising one hundred arc lamps and one thousand incandescents. The latter are extensively used in private houses. More than a million dollars have been put into new buildings since 1887, about half of that amount having been invested by foreigners, who would not be likely to place their money in turbulent communities. There has been only one burglary in San Juan Bautista for the last eight years, and that was committed by people from the interior.

GOVERNMENT PALACE, SAN JUAN BAUTISTA.

San Juan Bautista is almost a Yankee town in point of progress. All through that country we were impressed with what we have noted elsewhere, and that is the devotion of Mexicans to their dead heroes. The Mexicans have fine feelings, and perhaps nowhere is this better illustrated than in the regard thus shown for those whose gallant endeavor formed the cornerstone of their country's unparalleled prosperity.

The governor of Tabasco, General Abraham Bandala, is a hard-working and able functionary, to whose heart the interests of the people under his care are ever the first consideration.

CHAPTER XLIII

YUCATÁN

DOWN in the little strip of country between North and South America once flourished a rich and powerful empire. It marked a prehistoric millennium, for at the height of its development the empire had grown beyond warfare and capital punishment. There was no shedding of blood. The relics of its inhabitants, sculpture, and architecture challenge comparison with those of Greece. The laws seem to have been far better than those of to-day. Its people had a literature from which other ancient nations seem to have borrowed copiously, if not always accurately. They were a physically perfect race, and theirs was the day of Methuselahs. Their religion forms the basis of the more modern religions. They worshipped one God, the creator of all things, and believed in the immortality of the soul. Their women were equal with the men, fighting with them side by side in battle, as well as sharing in all social, civil, and religious honors. It will thus be seen that the new woman is not so very new after all; she is something over ten thousand years old. The seat of this ancient empire, which included all the land of Tehuantepec to the Isthmus of Darien, was known as Mayax. Uxmal was the seat of government, while the centre of learning, the metropolis of the empire, was Chichen-Itza. To it came pilgrims from the adjacent country to see its glories and taste of its wonderful knowledge or to sacrifice in its grand temples.

LIC. CÁRLOS PRÓN,
GOVERNOR OF YUCATÁN.

Knowledge, as in all the old civilizations, was a matter of caste. The masses were taught in figurative language. The Mayan scholars had an excellent knowledge of geography, with primitive maps. It is not likely that the maps would be of much practical value to modern geographers, as the different countries were represented under the forms of certain animals or

Governor's Palace, Mérida.

objects. The ancient rulers of Mayax received their title of Can (serpent) from the shape of the country. Any one who looks at a map of Central America can see how it resembles a serpent. This title was a general one; every ruler was a king. After his death the ruler was deified, and thus may be accounted for the origin of serpent worship. The serpent is held sacred, as is the tree, in the mythology of every country. Both have been closely related, and no better explanation has been found for this relation.

Mayax of old also figured as a tree planted in the continent of South America, with Yucatán as its principal branch. The sacred tree, its representative, the ceiba-tree, is an evergreen-tree, with wide-spreading branches, and is to-day planted in front of the churches in that part of the country. It was supposed to be the Tree of Knowledge or Life. It was truly "placed in the middle of the garden," the empire of Maya being between the two continents, North and South America. Yucatán, consequently, is supposed to be the seat of the oldest civilization in America. But, although it was "discovered" by Europeans in 1506, this ancient civilization had then died out and only the ruins of it remained. Archæologists and scholars have speculated without end, and almost without results, on this ancient civilization. Some think that here was the lost Atlantis; some believe it to have been the seat of the Garden of Eden, and imagine that here Adam and Eve founded the human race; some believe it to be mysteriously connected with ancient Egypt; but probably the theory above stated with regard to the Mayas is most correct.

With some writers it is the fashion to say that Columbus was the discoverer of this peninsula, because when at Pine Island in the summer of 1502 he sighted a canoe, evidently from the adjacent mainland. Had Columbus followed that canoe he would doubtless have added to his own glory; and, at any rate, his mention brought hither three years later Vincent Yañez Pinzon and Diaz Solis, who are generally known as the real discoverers of Yucatán. Córdova reported great cities with splendid palaces and many high pyramids, and, landing at Campeche, found stately temples, with their walls covered with serpents carved in basso-rilievo, similar to those of the great teocalli in the city of Mexico. From the little that can be learned it seems that previous to the Spanish conquest there existed in Yucatán a powerful and populous nation, of an origin so remote as to be altogether unknown, and ruled by caciques according to fixed principles of law and order. The first European to explore its shores was Fernando Cortez, in 1517. He gave it the name of Yucatán. One account says that on landing and asking the name of the country the natives answered, "Tectetan," meaning, "I do not understand you," and that Cortez took the phrase for Yucatán.

Bernal Diaz says it came from the Indian word "Ouyouckatan,"—"Listen to what they say." Cortez's nephew, Juan de Grijalva, explored the region, and, being impressed with the evidences of civilization, the extraordinary character and number of the ruins, and the numerous shrines and crosses, which reminded him of his own country, named the entire peninsula New Spain; a name afterward taken to cover all Mexico, but which, happily, has not stood.

The conquest of Yucatán was finally completed under Grijalva's son in 1541, and Yucatán belonged to Spain till 1821. After three years of independence, it was united to Mexico in 1824. It was again independent from 1840 to 1843, and from 1846 to 1852. It has since belonged to Mexico, first as a single state, until 1858, when Campeche was separated from it.

The area of Yucatán is thirty-two thousand six hundred and fifty-eight square miles. It is divided into fifteen districts,—Mérida, Motul, Izamal, Valladolid, Espita, Tizimin, Ticul, Sotuta, Tekax, Peto, Maxcan, Temax, Tixkokob, Hannama, and Acanceh. The population is still largely Maya Indian. The coast of Yucatán is generally higher and bolder along the Caribbean

Sea than elsewhere, and has several excellent harbors. The northern portion has sandy shores, with the two sandy ports or roadsteads of Progreso and Sisal. On the west coast is the Laguna de Términos, the principal inlet. The chief islands are Carmen, or Perla del Golfo, across the mouth of Laguna de Términos, the Alacranes group, and Cozumel, where Cortez first landed and held his communications with the Mayas. Except for the chain of hills across the interior, the country is mostly low and rather flat. The Usumasinta, which rises in Guatemala, is the chief river, and empties into the Laguna de Términos. A most remarkable feature of Yucatán is the number and magnitude of its subterranean rivers. The climate, though generally very hot, is on the whole salubrious, except on the gulf coast, which is periodically visited by yellow fever. The seasons are two,—the dry, from October to May, and the wet, embracing the remaining months. Most of the interior is covered with dense forests, rich in many varieties of precious woods, including mahogany and rosewood. The soil in the south and east is of great fertility, yielding abundant crops of maize, pulse, rice, indigo, tobacco, coffee, vanilla, sugar-cane, and, above all, the precious henequin, or pita plant, which furnishes sisal-hemp. Copal and other resins and gums are plentiful. The chief occupations are agriculture and cattle raising, the manufacture of coarse cotton fabrics and of various articles of henequin, and fishing. The evidences of a higher civilization possessed by the race that originally inhabited Yucatán are abundant and interesting.

The ruins of Uxmal, Chichén, Izamal, Mayapán, etc., have been explored by Stephens and other archaeologists. Those of Uxmal, the most remarkable, are situated about fifty miles south-south-west of Mérida. They comprise numerous massive lime-stone structures, built on broad terraced platforms, and all highly ornamented. The largest single building, called "the governor's house," has a front of three hundred and twenty-two feet, and contains twenty-four rooms. The most beautiful structure is the "house of the nuns," composed of four ranges enclosing a large court-yard, with eighty-eight apartments. The "house of the dwarf," on a very steep mound eighty-eight feet high, was a teocalli for human sacrifices. But little, if

TYPE OF YUCATACOS.

anything, definite is known of the uses of the temples and other vast edifices, which, from their size and profuse ornamentation in carved and colored figures and bassi-rilievi, are, even in their ruined state, among the most wonderful architectural relics in the Western world. Nor does any certainty exist relative to the building of the edifices and cities, though Morelet, Orozco y Berra, and others contend that they could have been constructed only by the Toltecs.

Equally interesting are the ruins at Chichén. Notwithstanding the appearance of great antiquity of these ruins, which are perhaps the most remarkable in Yucatán, they are in a better state of preservation than any other; but they have the distinguishing feature common to all of them,—namely, the impossibility of ascertaining the purposes or uses of the extraordinary structures which still stand in testimony of the high degree of civilization of a people long since forgotten. According to Stephens, the most curious and at the same time the most incomprehensible ruins he met with were a series of columns at Chichén, the highest of which do not exceed six feet, so disposed as to form a vast parallelogram, the rows being respectively three, four, and five feet deep from the outside to the enclosed space within. In the immediate vicinity of the area comprised within these pillars is the castillo, or castle, rising from the same plane and occupying the top of a lofty pyramidal mound which measures at its base on the north and south sides one hundred and ninety-six feet, and on the east and west sides two hundred and two feet, and is seventy-five feet in height. The four sides of the building itself measure forty-three and forty-nine feet respectively, in the same direction as the mound.

The capital of Yucatán is Mérida, situated about twenty miles from the port of Progreso, on the Gulf of Mexico. Mérida was founded in 1542 by Francisco de Montejo the younger. It occupies the site of the ancient Maya town of T'hoo. It was made a bishopric in 1561, and became an important town early in the Spanish dominion of Mexico. The decisive battle which conquered the country, in 1541, was fought on the spot where Mérida now stands, between two hundred Spaniards and forty thousand Indians—according to Spanish accounts. Probably the figures are not exact, though doubtless the defeated army was greatly superior in point of numbers.

Mérida was built almost entirely from the material of the Indian city, and upon the ruins of another ages older. T'hoo, the Maya city which the Spaniards found and razed to the ground in the year 1542, was the site of many temples, palaces, and pyramids, and so ancient that enormous trees were growing on the "hills made by hand," as the historian describes the artificial mounds. Each pyramid was crowned by a temple, and on the tallest, which stood in the place now occupied by Mérida's main plaza, was the principal sanctuary, H-chun-Caan, where human sacrifices to unknown gods were offered amid imposing ceremonies by a long retinue of priests. Beyond these facts even tradition is silent concerning T'hoo and the people thereof.

The Mérida of to-day is laid out in the chess-board fashion of New Spain, with streets running at right angles and square blocks of buildings. The exact centre is occupied by an extensive plaza, and in it are gardens of flowers and trees and a handsome fountain, which seems to have been constructed without any expectation of its containing water. The streets are broad, and the sidewalks are four feet wide, but paved with rough stones. The oddest thing about the streets is their nomenclature by object-lessons, so plainly portrayed that they may be read without the aid of letters. Of course the subjugated Indians could not read print, and for convenience the Spaniards called the streets after the names of familiar objects, with representations at the street-corners as perpetual reminders. Thus, one street is named Calle del Flamingo, and has a huge red flamingo painted on the corner house. Another is the Street of the Elephant, and the representation is a well-moulded figure of an elephant with exaggerated trunk and tusks. There is the Street of the Old Woman (Calle del Mujer Viejo), and on its corner is the caricature of an aged female with huge spectacles astride her Hebrew nose. The Street of Two Faces has a double-faced human head; and there are others equally striking.

In every street of Mérida a few blocks distant from the centre stands an ancient gateway, arched high above the pavement, and just beyond are the barrios, or suburbs. Over each gateway is now a dismantled niche, which once held its Christ or saint or Virgin, before which the people were forever kneeling and crossing themselves. There are no fewer than fifteen public squares in the city, each facing a church. Around the great central plaza are arranged the principal edifices of church and state. One whole side is occupied by the cathedral and the bishop's palace. The cathedral, erected early in the sixteenth century, is one hundred and seventy-nine feet wide by nearly three hundred feet long. On its otherwise severely plain façade is a central pavilion, in which is the main entrance, ornamented by a Corinthian portico; one hundred feet above this is a grand vaulted arch supporting a gallery, and on each side are two steeples, with a number of galleries narrowing in upward succession, each ornamented with light balustrades of stone. The interior of the church is equally imposing. It consists of three naves, with round arches supported by twelve immense columns of solid stone, while twenty other pillars of like dimensions are embedded in the walls. Small chapels with splendidly decorated shrines are placed along the sides; over the door-way are carved the arms of Mexico, flanked by saints in bas-relief.

Among Mérida's many churches are several almost as fine as the cathedral, and hardly less remarkable for the power and influence of their particular saints in the public estimation. There is St. Anne's Church, which ladies frequent to pray for good husbands. It is said that in many instances the supplications of spinsters have brought about most gratifying results. In another

TEKAX.

sanctuary, which enshrines an image of St. Barbe, is a vast collection of figures in wax and ivory, representing parts of the human frame which had been healed through the efficacy of prayer, with hundreds of discarded crutches, models of vessels miraculously preserved at sea, and pictures representing deliverance from many perils.

On the south side of the plaza, in strange contrast to the governor's palace and the great Casa Municipal, is the oldest house in the city, one of the most remarkable buildings in Mexico. It is the house of Montejo the younger, built in the year 1549. Tall pillars on either side of the main entrance bear aloft two Spanish soldiers, and on the first floor, by the window, are two wonderful knights, armed with visors, breastplates, and helmets, standing upon the bodies of prostrate Indians, a graphic portrayal of the subjugation of the Mayas. Most of the houses of Mérida are low, having but the ground floor, all of stone and stucco, and the building materials include massive blocks from the pyramids, beautifully carved and polished in past ages. All have flat roofs, with balconied windows stoutly grated by half-inch iron bars, projecting a foot or two beyond the walls. The unpromising exterior is but the outside, however, of spacious apartments opening into the patio, encompassed by Moorish arches. The patios are planted with flowers, shrubs, and palm-trees, and the whole effect savors of Granada, Morocco, and the Byzantine empire. Glass window-panes are almost unknown. The walls are so thick and the window-openings so large that people place chairs in the embrasures and pass many hours looking at the street scenes. In the bedrooms one sees wooden knobs on the walls, which are to fasten hammocks to, for all Mérida sleeps in a hammock,—that is, every individual sleeps in his or her hammock. Those moving in the highest circles of society, as well as the most lowly,

MÉRIDA, YUCATÁN.

are born, live, and die in hammocks,—not the kind of hammocks exported to other countries, but fine white ones, made from sisal-hemp. The natives excel in their manufacture. Only the coarser kinds are sent away, for at home the best ones, costing from ten to fifteen or even thirty dollars apiece, find a ready market. These are of remarkable length, width, and fineness,—indeed, sometimes almost resembling lace,—but always they are very strong.

All the rooms of the houses are large, and the ceilings lofty. Some of the floors are of tile, and others of a dark red polished substance resembling stone. The drawing-room is usually about sixty feet long and thirty feet wide. The walls are delicately frescoed, although the basis is only coarse cotton cloth stretched and covered with a heavy coat of sizing, upon which the beautiful and delicate paintings are laid. The patio, however, is the most attractive part of the establishment, and in it, sheltered during the heat of the day by the cool shade of palms, the inmates lie in hammocks hung in the corridor or porch and pass the time in blissful comfort.

The architecture of the Mexican house, with its barred windows and well-guarded doors, which prevent intrusion, along with the climate and customs, tends to incline the people to lead exclusive and perhaps lazy lives; and yet, once within the massive doors, the beauty and care and love of the home life are seen in many ways. In such homes the lives of the Meridans are directed in gentle and lovely ways, and we recognize the charm of it all, and are ready to accord these Mexican sisters all their accredited beauty and gentleness of heart.

The Mérida market is in a court between high buildings. Here small tables and bits of straw matting are placed on all sides, and upon these the men and women display their wares. Vegetables, fruits, and goods of all descriptions are arranged in heaps; here one can find the products of every zone and clime, and all very cheap. The people are sheltered from the intense rays of the sun by awnings of cloth or matting. They are all polite, and, with their bright smiles, easily gain customers. Under nearly every awning, mixed up with the vegetables or flowers, are fat round babies with black eyes and always sweet and charming. The flower-market is the place of enchantment, for the love of flowers is a strong trait of character in these people. Here are men and women arranging great bunches of exquisite blossoms with a delicacy of taste which both delights and surprises the visitor.

There are institutes of law, of medicine, and of pharmacy; there are a literary institute, private colleges, academies, and fine public schools. Manufacturing is in a flourishing state.

A few words about the ancient marriage customs of Yucatán may prove interesting. From time immemorial the Maya women have worn a simple form of dress which they never vary. It consists of two pieces, a very full skirt falling to the ankles, and a loose upper garment called *nipil*. Joined under the arms only, being made very ample, it hangs in graceful folds, after the manner of the Greek peplum. Cotton or linen is the material, always plain white, though trimmed with colored embroidery. As for jewelry, each woman loads her neck, fingers, and ears with it. Decked out in this finery, the bride was formerly conducted to the home of her betrothed. All the relatives of both families had been invited, and sat in a line around the room. The father of the bridegroom began the ceremony by scattering cacao-beans over the floor. These were picked up and kept by the guests, being symbolical of the hospitality that the young couple must always bestow on their fellow-men. The beans having been gathered, the young couple knelt side by side on a mat to receive the blessing of the young man's parents, his mother's first, then his father's. This benediction consisted in sprinkling them with a twig of rue dipped in pure water. This was followed by a second scattering of cacao beans, after which the bride and the groom had to partake of a mixture of pinole and honey. The parents of the bride took no active part in this ceremony. To-day none of the natives confine themselves to this simple form of marriage. The priest assures them that without the sanction of the Church they are not properly married, so they go to the altar. The Mexican law alone can make their union legal, therefore they are usually married twice over.

The scenery of Yucatán impresses travellers as strangely unique. Just back of the coast dunes stretches a broad lagoon many miles in extent, and varying in depth with the season. Here millions of northern birds spend their winters, and when the passing train startles them to wing, the sky is literally blackened by ducks, teal, ibis, egrets, and herons, blue and white. Beyond the lagoon the bed of coral which composes the entire peninsula of Yucatán rises slightly above the sea-level, presenting the appearance of a dry swamp. Wheel-roads follow the railways, and upon them patient oxen plod painfully along, their heads bowed under heavy wooden yokes, hauling great loads of henequin in rude carts with wheels of wood. Finally the region of henequin plantations is reached, with miles and miles of the so-called "sisal" on either side. The immense fields are neatly walled, and the picturesque homes of the planters are mostly built of stone, shaded by rows of cocoa-palms, and approached by long avenues through arches and stuccoed gateways.

The great industry of Yucatán is the cultivation of henequin, or *yashqui*, that species of the cacti family known as "sisal." Few people not directly concerned in the business have any idea of its magnitude and its enormous importance. Henequin grows wild in great profusion all over Yucatán, and, as it requires almost no water, it seems to thrive best on barren rocks and desert sands, or in very thin soil, where nothing else could find foothold. A henequin plant attains its full perfection in seven years. A stem shoots out from the centre of it, and the leaves gradually detach themselves in the form of an immense spear or "Spanish bayonet," with sharp thorns along the edges, terminating in a strong needle-like point. A bale of henequin fibre (four hundred pounds) represents the product of about seven thousand leaves. In most places the old process of making the fibre by hand is discarded as unprofitable, and the stripping of the leaves is done with great machines driven by powerful steam-engines. The scraper consists of a large wheel with strong blunt knives all around its rim. The henequin leaves are pressed against this rim, and, by means of a lever, worked by the hand and foot of an Indian, the knives remove in an instant the pulp which covers the fibre. The pulp having been removed, the fibre is taken from the leaves in long strips, like very fine silk thread, of a beautiful green tint. It is made into small bundles and placed in the sun to dry, care being taken to turn it over frequently, that all the moisture and vegetable matter may be expelled, as otherwise it would ferment after baling, and fermentation means a considerable reduction in its commercial value. In the packing-house the dried hanks are put up into four-hundred-pound bales by a cotton-press. It is then ready for market, where its average value is seventy dollars a bale; but of course, like other commodities, it has its ups and downs in price.

SECTION OF THE NUNNERY, CHICHEN-ITZA.

Henequin-raising is a good business for an enterprising young man. Wild land may be had almost for the asking, either from the government or from private owners,—generally the descendants of some old-time hidalgo,—who have more land than they know what to do with. Any wild henequin plants will do to stock the hacienda, using young shoots cut from the base of older growths. When set out in holes about eight feet apart they invariably take kindly to their new quarters and flourish, and once fairly under way the plantation requires very little attention. Three years after the shoots are set out the plants are large enough for the first crop to be cut; the cutting goes on for ten or twelve years; and in the mean time new shoots are set out every year, so that the plantation is constantly being renewed.

The grain crop and its products consume an astonishing amount of fibre. Binders' twine, cordage, hemp sacks, and ropes are necessary for handling all products, and all these are made of the fibre.

Next in value to henequin comes the *Bromelia pita*, locally known as "ixtle," the ancient Aztec name. From this the Maya's clothes were made, and it formed the foundation of the beautiful feather cloaks of Montezuma's time. Though the best ixtle grows near Tehuantepec, there are a dozen varieties of the plant in other parts of Mexico. Some of the fibres grow to the length of fifteen or twenty feet, silky as floss, yet strong as wire, and capable of being subdivided into threads from which may be woven the coarsest bagging or the finest cloth, ship cables or spool thread. To this day the ixtle furnishes the poorer natives with their garments and the hammock-beds in which they are born and die, and with their baskets and household utensils; paper is manufactured from the fibre; from the roots of the plant a favorite intoxicant is brewed; the juice of its bruised leaves is the best known remedy for wounds; its thorns are the Indians' pins and needles; in short, there is no telling all the uses to which it is put. A few years ago some ixtle fibre was sent to England to be experimented with in the great cloth manufactories, and from it some handkerchiefs were woven which have since figured in several world's fairs to the astonishment of all beholders.

It is probably true that there is no natural product of Mexico and Central America which so well repays intelligent industry as fibre plants, of which there is an inexhaustible supply, while the demand throughout the world is unfailing. However wars, panics, and monetary depressions may affect other industries, the nations of the earth must be clothed and fed, and the great land products must be transported. By the use of fibre-made sacking, twine, and cordage these are prepared for transportation, and test and experiment prove these articles very useful. During the last decade the amount of henequin and ixtle exported from Mexico has increased tenfold. Already they assume the second place on the export list, precious metals coming first.

In addition to these fibre products, it has been demonstrated that India jute can be grown to better advantage here than in the Orient. It is made into portières, curtains, furniture linings, etc. And now that the brilliant colors and beautiful finish of silk are imparted to it, some hemp fabrics vie with the choicest products of Persian looms.

In the state there are four railways, one broad-gauge and the others narrow-gauge. The first named has a total of seventy-five miles in operation; the others average each about sixty miles completed, and are in active course of construction. They are owned and operated exclusively by natives. Tariffs for passengers and freights are about one-half the rates charged for local business by the railways of the United States.

CASTLE, CHICHEN-TIJA.

Except wheat, rye, and small grain, almost any plant thrives here when the seasons are favorable, but the principal products are corn, beans, sugar, and hemp. The latter is phenomenally hardy, and flourishes almost as well without as with rain; but corn, beans, and sugar require irrigation.

The passenger for Yucatán usually comes from the north by water and lands in the Broadway of Yucatán's principal port, Progreso. Groups of dark-faced men lounge idly in shaded doorways, and women in garments of spotless white are squatted along the curbstone with bowls of cooked meat for sale or tamales red-hot with grease and garlic. There are a tiny market-place full of fruits and fish, and a big railway station walled with lattice-work. There is a hotel, a stone structure with thatched roof, whose ground floor is used for a stable, the whole space above being one long, unpartitioned sleeping apartment, in which transient guests may hang their hammocks upon waiting hooks. Progreso's custom-house is a handsome building, as modern architecture goes in Yucatán, and your luggage is not usually subjected to very rigorous inspection, there being manifestly little temptation to the smuggler in this outlying territory of Mexico. The population is a little less than two thousand. The place is a shipping-point, and nobody lives there unless compelled to. Just back of it are fever-breeding swamps full of decaying vegetation. Yet swarms of pleasure-seekers from Mérida and other interior towns come to Progreso for sea-bathing during a certain portion of every year. The main harbor of Yucatán was formerly Sisal, on the northeast coast, which gave its name to the hemp for which the country is famous; but the requirements of increasing commerce long since transferred the harbor to Progreso. And unprepossessing as it is, the little town of Progreso is of much importance, for it is the shipping-point of vast quantities—in fact, all—of the sisal-fibre of Yucatán.

The railroad to Mérida, while scarcely comparable to other systems in Mexico, is far from poor. On leaving Progreso it crosses a large lagoon which extends for many miles just inside the coast-line. This is at certain times of the year a great resort for the wild fowl of the north, and is a sportsman's paradise. The railway then passes through great sisal plantations, with here and there a palm-surrounded house relieving the monotony. The fields are all walled with stone, solidly built, showing industry and thrift. Frequently groups of Indians, men, women, and children, always dressed in white, gaze curiously at the passing train and start nervously when the whistle blows. Evidently the iron horse has not ceased to excite their wonder and fear.

Sailing due east from Progreso, one passes from the open sea into the Yucatán Channel, which connects the Mexican Gulf with the Caribbean Sea. The harbors are few along these unoccupied coasts, and for many miles there is little to be seen. Blue-green white-capped billows stretch away to the horizon, with a monotonous line of sandy beach on one side, broken by occasional dark patches of forest, with here and there a rugged mound or a pyramid overgrown with verdure indicating the site of some prehistoric city. M. Charney states that he "found the country covered with ruins from end to end." Stephens says that he visited forty-four ruined cities, most of which were entirely unknown to white men before his coming, even to the people of Yucatán, and that in all the cities he found relics of wealth and architecture and advanced civilization. Baldwin in his "Ancient America" says that near all the principal ruins are traces of beautifully constructed artificial lakes, the bottoms of which were made of flat stones laid in cement several layers deep. There are also numerous remains of a very ancient paved road, raised above the graded level of the ground and very smooth. It ran north and south, and doubtless led to other cities in the unknown interior, perhaps greater ones than any yet discovered. It is now many years since Stephens's visit to Yucatan, and only twenty-six more ruins have been added to his list, while the whole interior is still a literal *terra incognita*.

Yalahau is an insignificant port, but is celebrated in Mexican annals as a resort of old-time buccaneers. Its harbor commands a wide view both up and down the gulf, so that all vessels passing from Cuba and the Spanish main could be critically studied at a safe distance by the pirates, most of whom were "leading citizens" of Yalahau and owned sugar-plantations in the neighborhood. The village consists of a single street of cane-stalk cottages elevated a few feet above tide-water, both the town and the swamp behind it being completely hidden under groves of palm and cocoanut. Cut off from communication with the outer world and connected with the interior only by dangerous and toilsome roads, the little hamlet is about as independent as a separate republic. Time was when golden doubloons were more plentiful in Yalahau than pennies are now. There is a disused fortress here which the federal government built and garrisoned for the suppression of piracy, but the soldiers soon joined hands with the free-hearted brigands whom they had been sent to capture and shared their pleasures and plunder. The only stone house in the village is the residence of the present alcalde, and used to be the head-quarters of the buccaneers. Here unlucky captives were sometimes held as

LAS MONJAS, UXMAL.

hostages, and if ransom were slow in coming, a finger, a toe, or an ear was sent to hurry up the relatives, followed by larger portions of the victim if the first instalment did not bring speedy returns. The old house stands so close to the sea that restless waves have washed away part of the foundation.

The island of Cozumel is one of the most interesting spots in the vicinity. It was discovered by Juan de Grijalva in 1518, and Cortez set sail for it in the following year. Eight years afterward Montejo came with four hundred soldiers and took possession of the island, which is about thirty miles long, is now almost uninhabited, and is covered with a dense growth of trees and tangled creepers. Its name signifies in the Indian tongue "the place of swallows." The Spaniards declared that on this island they found a populous city "composed of stone houses, white and lofty." Many vestiges of ancient inhabitants are still visible. Not more than two hundred feet from the sea, visible above the tree-tops from the decks of passing vessels, is a magnificent relic, a structure sixteen feet square standing on a terrace, with exterior of plain stone stuccoed. It has stone steps on each side leading up to four doorways that face the cardinal points and open into narrow corridors encompassing a small room. Near it is a similar structure, upon which the remains of paintings are visible under a queer triangular arch.

A little north of Cozumel, about five miles from the coast of Yucatán, is Isla de Mujeres (Women's Island), a tiny speck in the Caribbean Sea, only six miles long by half as wide. It is not a resort of the omnipresent "new woman" of to-day (who is not, by the way, objectionably present in Mexico), but I venture to assert that more astonishing things are crowded upon it—suggestions of strange doings in far-away centuries—than can be found in any other place of equal size. Cortez's soldiers named it Women's Island because in the four great temples which they found here all the idols represented colossal female figures. The island is singularly beautiful, encompassed by the green-blue sea. Mangrove- and cocoanut-trees crowd to the water's edge, except where broken by tiny clearings around the palm-leaf hut of some fisherman. Turtle-catching is quite a business here. Three kinds abound: the cahuamo, whose eggs serve for food, its carcass being useful only for oil; the tortuga, of which both the meat and the eggs are eaten, and whose shell is worth twenty-five cents a pound; and the jare, whose shell sells for eight dollars a pound.

MOUNT SEBATSCHE.

Another interesting spot, about thirty miles from Mérida, is the village of Tixkokob. It has a fine old church, and the quaintest cemetery ever seen. All around its outer walls rows of skulls are arranged; skulls grin along the arms of the crosses with which the interior space is thickly set, and several huge vases are piled high with the same ghastly relics. In the middle is a promiscuous heap of human bones several feet deep. Inside the walls, dangling from cords fastened to the top, are baskets and boxes and bundles, each containing a skeleton, appropriately labelled. Everywhere there are fragments of shrouds, shoes that have dropped from fleshless feet, arms, legs, trunks to which dried flesh still adheres, and scores of skulls with hair still clinging to them, in some cases the long beautiful tresses of women. Inside the church the floor is a series of trap-doors, each covering a vault filled to the brim with former citizens of Tixkokob. In the choir of this church and on all the window-ledges are more skulls, each labelled on the forehead, and some of them bearing startling inscriptions. On All Souls' Day (November 2) all these skulls are placed upon a black-draped dais surrounded by lighted candles, and mass is said and incense burned and holy water sprinkled amid the prayers of the people.

Valladolid is a very old town, and was once the most flourishing centre of trade on the peninsula. It lies on the line of the railway, about one hundred miles southeast from Mérida. Half a century ago the first cotton-mill of the country was erected here, and several manufactories flourished. Here the bishop made his residence, as well as some of the proudest Castilian families of New Spain, whose coats of arms may still be seen upon the fronts of tenantless casas. The last great uprising of the natives occurred almost fifty years ago, and inflicted injuries from which Valladolid will never recover, for, besides actual murder, rapine, and conflagration, the Indians left such terror behind, threatening to come again, that the remaining citizens

FAÇADE OF LAS MONJAS, UXMAL.

fled to safer quarters. The population is now less than ten thousand, after half a century of comparative peace, and lands close by, the best in Yucatán, may be bought for twenty cents an acre.

Founded soon after the Spanish conquest, Valladolid was built in a style commensurate with the wild dreams of the conquistadores, and bears marks of ancient grandeur. But desolation now broods over it. The central plaza, where hidalgos and ladies of high degree were wont to promenade to the accompaniment of moonlight and music, is now ankle-deep in sand, its benches of crumbling stone overrun with scorpions, centipedes, and lizards, and its ancient palms and elms too ragged to cast a shade. At one side of it is an enormous parochial church, with convent and cloisters, fast falling into decay. There are other large churches,—Sisal, San Serircio, San Juan de Dios, Santa Lucia, Santa Anna, and Candelaria,—all dilapidated. Most of the private houses show the same signs. In the principal street—the Calle de Sisal—are extensive crevices in walls with the coats of arms of forgotten families emblazoned on them.

According to tradition, Valladolid has been the theatre of remarkable events. It is asserted that the place was long haunted by a demon of the worst character, which even now is spoken of with bated breath as El Demonio Parlero (The Talking Devil), because he held nightly discourse with any who chose to question him, answering in the voice of a parrot. In fact, he carried his pleasantries to such an extent, and made himself so troublesome, that the bishop was obliged to invoke divine assistance, and with the combined powers of earth and heaven succeeded in ousting the devil and driving him to the woods. The records go on to state that this demon, after having been thus banished from Gulciba and several other villages, returned to Valladolid

MUNICIPAL PALACE, MÉRIDA.

with new schemes, but was finally barred out altogether by the device of surrounding the town with consecrated crosses set close together on the hill-tops. These the devil could not pass, and to this day there are hundreds of wooden crosses standing guard around Valladolid.

Before the days of Valladolid's decline most of the largest land proprietors and "substantial citizens" generally were opposed to separation from Mexico, while the bulk of the population —those who owned no property and had nothing to lose—raised a cry for "libertad," which to them meant license. After independence was achieved another agitation arose, as to whether Yucatán should again become part of Mexico or form a separate republic, and local feeling ran high. Both factions invoked aid from the natives, placed arms in their hands, and filled their ears with promises. When quiet was restored, these offers of reward were forgotten, and the Indians were dismissed empty-handed. But they retained their arms and the knowledge they had gained of warfare, all of which they turned to account against the whites at the first opportunity. In 1847, when an imbroglio arose between Mérida and Campeche, the revengeful Indians saw their chance. With fire and sword they swept the eastern part of the peninsula, obliterating every town and village in their course, and nearly destroying Valladolid, which had then a population of twenty thousand or more. Remembering the centuries of wrong endured by their fathers, they entered upon a war of extermination. They possessed themselves of more and more territory in the northern, eastern, and southern portions of the peninsula, ravaging the country, pillaging, burning, murdering. The terrified Creoles, huddled together at Mérida, appealed to the United States, to Spain, and at last to the republic of which they had declined to become a part, Mexico. Just having concluded her war with the United States, the latter sent troops to Yucatán, and gradually the Indians were driven into the interior. By calling on Mexico for aid, Yucatán lost her place as an independent republic, and soon after she became one of the states of the Mexican federation.

According to the popular legend, Quetzalcoatl (the serpent, or twin, with peacock or trogon feathers), a mythical personage, went out from Yucatán to the region about Panuco and appeared to the Huastecas in a long white robe and holding a staff. He introduced the honors belonging to the cross, taught the people many arts, and instituted a form of worship, finally returning to Yucatán. In the mythology of Yucatán, however, he was called Cuculcan, and they make him return to Mexico. At any rate, although the accounts of him vary, he was ultimately honored as a god, and his religious ideas extended throughout the old Mexican empire. Probably he was the Aztec prototype of the Messiah.

Still unconquered, these Indians hold all Southeastern Yucatán, and for upward of forty years they have been in armed rebellion against the government. Numerically they are probably less than a thousand, but what they lack in number they make up in ferocity. They are not of the same race as the timid Indians about Mérida,—patient hewers of wood and drawers of water, whose ancestors perhaps built the magnificent temples which are scattered all over the country. The yet unconquered tribe is probably descended from the Caribs,— cannibal savages who once possessed the Mosquito coast, the Spanish main, and the southern islands of the West Indies. The wildest stories are told of their atrocious cruelties. The chief tribe, Chan Santa Cruz, has a city or stronghold of the same name somewhere in Southeastern Yucatán, supposed to lie between thirty and forty miles west of Ascension Bay and fifty miles below Lake Bacalar. No white person has seen the city of Chan Santa Cruz, or, if he has, he has never returned to tell the tale. It is supposed that its citizens practise the aboriginal arts and retain the aboriginal customs, with some borrowed from their civilized neighbors. They have strict laws, and any shortcoming is severely punished, the murderer of a Chan Santa

Cruzan being executed in exactly the same manner as he inflicted death upon his victim. As a rule they are monogamists, and their besetting sin is drunkenness. They have always much corn in store, and in times of drought, when Yucatán has been threatened with famine, they have sold some to the whites at exorbitant prices.

For many years Yucatán has been the Siberia of Mexico, to which are sent offenders whom the government does not know what else to do with, since the amended constitution practically does away with capital punishment. Consequently Chan Santa Cruz includes among its heterogeneous population many people not of Indian blood,—negro slaves, escaped convicts, Chinese, and castaways and outlaws of various colors and nationalities.

It seems almost incredible that next door to the United States, within less than a week's journey from New York or Chicago, is a section of country almost unknown to Europeans, whose unconquered people still live as their progenitors did before the Christian era; and even more incredible is it that the powerful Mexican nation, which claims that bit of territory, knows as little about it. The greater portion of the peninsula is a *terra incognita*, of which white men know absolutely nothing beyond what may be seen along the coast and gathered from Indian tradition. The Rio Hondo forms the boundary between it and Belize, a few nameless streams flow into the Caribbean Sea, and beyond the dense forests that girdle the coast is a great central desert, crossed by a ridge of unknown hills. Between the forest belt and the coast are undulating tracts where corn, tobacco, rice, and sugar-cane are grown and cattle are raised in such numbers as to furnish exports of hides and salted meats next in value to the export of the fibre industry.

To the uninitiated, perhaps, there seems little in Yucatán to attract the average tourist, yet many world-famous savants have spent years there in enthusiastic and well-rewarded research. Scattered all over the country are remains of stupendous and richly carved edifices and wonderful monuments of vanished people, and the very air seems filled with the mystery of the melancholy of *los antiguos*. And yet how many people realize that some of the most wonderful relics of antiquity on the face of the earth lie within a week's journey of New York? Why do archæologists pursue their quest everywhere else on the globe, when here are remains more curious than those of Pompeii and Herculaneum, older than those of the Aztecs in Mexico and the Incas in Peru?

Yucatán is a part of Mexico that is positively distinct and rare, cut off as it is at the eastern point of the crescent gulf. We could not help noticing a similarity in features between the Japanese and the Mexicans as found in Yucatán, although E. H. Thompson, formerly United States consul of Mérida, an archæologist of reputation, inclines to the opinion that there is no such relationship and that the first settlers came from the other side of the Atlantic.

The governor of Yucatán is Señor Lic. Carlos Peón, under whose administration the state is making rapid strides toward modern advancement. Señor Peón, being a very wealthy man himself, does not have to limit enterprises of importance by the condition of the treasury in the state he governs so wisely and so well.

CHAPTER XLIV

CITIES AND INHABITANTS; PECULIARITIES OF THE INDIANS; SOME NOBLE FAMILIES; LITERATURE OF MEXICO; FOLK-LORE.

THERE are now twenty-eight states and two territories, and it is estimated that there are more than eleven million inhabitants, about three-eighths of whom belong to the pure Indian race, while the rest is made up of mixtures of Spanish and Indian, with a few hundreds of thousands of pure Spanish origin and still fewer of other foreign elements.

There are in the country three cities of more than one hundred thousand inhabitants: Mexico, in the federal district, with three hundred and fifty thousand; Guadalajara, in Jalisco, with one hundred and five thousand; and Puebla, in the state of the same name, which has slightly over the limit figure. Guanajuato has over fifty thousand people. Of cities having more than twenty thousand inhabitants there are sixteen,—from León, with fifty thousand, to Celaya, in the same state, with twenty-one thousand.

There are supposed to be seven castes in Mexico, which are kept distinct. First, the Gachupino, or Spaniards born in Europe; second, the Creoles,—that is, whites of European family born in America; third, the Mestizos; fourth, the Mulattoes, descendants of whites and negroes, of whom there are a few; fifth, the Zambos, descendants of negroes and Indians, the ugliest race in Mexico; sixth, the Indians; and seventh, the remains of the African negroes.

Of pure Indians, Humboldt in his day calculated that there existed two millions and a half in New Spain (without counting Mestizos), and they are probably very little altered from the inferior Indians as Cortez found them. The principal families perished at the time of the conquest. The priests, sole depositaries of knowledge, were put to death, the manuscripts and hieroglyphical paintings were burnt, and the remaining Indians fell into a state of ignorance and degradation from which they have never emerged. The rich Indian women preferred marrying their Spanish conquerors to allying themselves with the degraded remnant of their countrymen, —poor artisans, workmen, porters, etc.,—of whom Cortez speaks as filling the streets of the great cities and as being considered little better than beasts of burden; nearly naked in the tierra caliente, dressed pretty much as they are now in the temperate parts of the country, and everywhere with nearly the same manners and habits and customs as they now have, but especially in the more distant villages, where they have little intercourse with the other classes. Even in their religion, Christianity, as I observed before, seems to be formed of the ruins of their mythology; and all the festivities of the Church, their fireworks and images and gay dresses, harmonize completely with their childish love of show, and are, in fact, their greatest source of delight. To buy these they save up all their money, and when you give a penny to an Indian child it trots off to buy crackers as a white one would to buy candy. Attempts have been made by their curates to persuade them to omit the celebration of certain days, and to expend less in the ceremonies of others, but the indignation and discontent which such proposals have caused have induced the Church to desist.

Under an appearance of stupid apathy they veil a great depth of cunning. They are grave and gentle and rather sad in their appearance when not under the influence of pulque; but when they return to their villages in the evening, and have taken a drop of comfort, their white teeth light up their bronze countenances like lamps, and the girls especially make the air ring with their laughter, which is very musical. Their smile is extremely gentle, and the expression of their eyes very severe. As they have no beard, if it were not for a little moustache which they frequently wear there would be scarcely any difference between the faces of men and women.

The Indians in and near the capital are, according to Humboldt, either the descendants of the former laborers or remains of noble Indian families who, disdaining to intermarry with their Spanish conquerors, preferred to till the ground which their vassals formerly cultivated for them. It is said that these Indians of noble race, though to the vulgar eye indistinguishable from their fellows, are held in great respect by their inferior countrymen. In Cholula, particularly, there are still caciques with long Indian names, also in Tlaxcala, and, though barefooted and ragged, they are said to possess great hidden wealth. But it is neither in nor near the capital that we can see the Indians to perfection in their original state. It is only by travelling through the provinces. The Metis reside by preference in the great centres of population, where they work at all sorts of trades. They are also scattered throughout the country, engaged in its development as employees in the agricultural, mining, and manufacturing lines. Nearly all the working class is from this group. Spanish, mixed with provincialisms and words of Indian origin, forms their language.

THE MAIN CANAL AT TLAHUALILO, DURANGO.

The working class shows its intelligence and activity in printing, bookbinding, carpentry, cabinet-making, blacksmithing, turning, wood- and stone-carving, hat- and shoe-making, and the spinning and weaving of cotton, silk, and wool. Its members have a somewhat advanced social organization.

While the Indians have preserved their customs, diametrically opposite to those of the other two races, there is a very notable change for the worse in those of them who live near the great centres; but most of them who live in the mountainous districts have preserved in all their purity the ancient customs and the primitive language. Their general bearing and their brilliant clothing, and above all their cleanliness, greatly distinguish them from the degenerate Indians of the central plateau.

In some districts, as in the fertile regions of the Sierra, they preserve their imitative dances of the Cegador, Tehuacanzi, and Zempoa Ixochitl. During certain religious ceremonies they execute their dances in the churches before the most venerated images, as, for example, that of the Virgin of Guadalupe.

The Indian in general likes fermented drinks; but he is brave and sober, and shows these good qualities whether as a hunter in the ravines of the sierras or as an intrepid soldier going into battle after a severe march of sixty miles. His robust countenance explains why, despite a frugal and often insufficient diet, and in defiance of hygiene, piled pell-mell in cramped and damp huts, so many reach a very advanced age.

The numbers of these natives who, thanks to education, have become notable in office and in the Church, prove beyond all question that they can reach, like members of the white race, a high degree of civilization.

The degeneracy of some of the Indian tribes proceeds from several causes, among which may be mentioned too early marriages. Pestilence has decimated them, and wars and a mixture with the white and Metis races have aided in wiping them out.

Their minds are affected by the same variety of passions as are the people of other nations, but not in an equal degree. Mexicans seldom exhibit those transports of anger or frenzies of love which are so common in other countries; they are slow in their motions, and show a wonderful tenacity and steadiness in those works which require time and long-continued attention.

They are patient of injury and hardship, and where they suspect no evil intention are most grateful for any kindness.

They are by nature taciturn, serious, and austere, and show more anxiety to punish crimes than to reward virtues. Generosity and perfect disinterestedness are the principal features of their character. Gold with the Mexicans has not the value which it seems to possess elsewhere. They give without reluctance what has cost them the utmost labor to acquire. The respect paid by children to parents and by the young to the old seems to be a feeling born with them. Parents are very fond of their children also.

Courage and cowardice alternate in their minds, so that it is often difficult to determine which predominates. They meet dangers with intrepidity. Their singular attachment to the external ceremonies of religion is very apt to degenerate into superstition, as happens among the ignorant of all nations of the world, but that they are prone to idolatry is nothing more than a chimera formed in the brains of ignorant persons. The customs of a few mountaineers are not sufficient to justify an aspersion upon a whole people. To conclude, the character of the Mexican Indian is a mixture of good and bad.

Many Mexican families of noble lineage can point to a family history dating back to the eight hundred years' war against the Moors, when their ancestors were ennobled for gallantry or services to the kings. There are living many families of noble descent who cherish their titles in secret and hold aloof from the mass of the people. Some of these ancient families are wealthy, being still possessed of great estates. The newer families are the descendants of successful soldiers, who stood somewhat in the same relation to the old aristocracy as did the marshals and generals of Napoleon I. to the old French nobility. Consequently, when we talk of an American aristocracy we should look to Mexico for the best and most genuine specimens.

Descendants of Hernando Cortez exist, some bearing his name; one gentleman of this race and name, a man of cultivation and refinement, is living to-day in Tacubaya. Descendants of Santa Anna also live in Tacubaya.

Descendants of presidents constitute another sort of aristocracy. In fact, service to the state in high place seems always to give one's family and descendants a claim on popular consideration and respect.

Every little while interesting information regarding the descendants of the Aztec monarchs is made public, and, as the people who sprang from the earliest known monarchy on the soil of North America, they may rightfully claim precedence socially. The young son of Don Luis G. Sierra y Horcasitas and his wife Señora Maria Dolores Abadiano, Roberto Luis Cuauhtemoc, is the fourteenth in descent from the Emperor Cuitlahuac, although it is disputed that he is descended from the last Aztec monarch, the ill-fated and heroic Emperor Cuauhtemoc, whose statue adorns the Paseo de la Reforma.

Cuitlahuac, from whom the boy referred to descends, and Montezuma II. were brothers of Matlazinca, the cacique of Coyoacan. Among the descendants of Cuitlahuac are Don Pedro Patino Itzolinque, who lives in Holland, and another Don Pedro Patino Itzolinque, who is a soldier in the state of San Luis Potosí.

HACIENDA OF ZARAGOZA, TLAHUALILO, DURANGO.

As is known, Cuauhtemoc was the son of the Emperor Ahuizotl, son of Axayacatl, and consequently a nephew of Montezuma II. He married the princess Tecuichpocli, a daughter of Montezuma.

It is sufficient to know that there are many well-proved descendants of the Aztec monarchs living and borne on the pension-roll of the Mexican government. Some of them reside in Spain and other European countries, among them being the Duke of Abrantes, the Marquis del Aguilar Fuerte, and the Count of Miravalles.

In this connection it is of interest to note that the direct descendants of Montezuma are living to-day, and boast a family tree which reaches back to the fourteenth century. They reside at Salamanca, in Spain. They have not a large fortune, but possess sufficient means to enable them to appear at court. The present head of the family is Señor Don Agustin Maldonado y Carbajal Cano Montezuma, Marquis of Castellanos and of Monroy. There are three children, —two sons and a daughter. The latter is the widow of the Count de Monterrón, who was one of the principal noblemen in the Basque provinces. The Countess of Monterrón, notwithstanding her large fortune and high position, has followed a scientific career, and is prominent in Spanish educational work. Of the two sons, Don Fernando is a lawyer and a deputy and Don José is an eminent musician. The Maldonado family is connected by marriage with the

English house of Lancaster, and also with the houses of Abrantes and Medinaceli, which are of the first nobility in Spain. The Marchioness de Castellanos has furnished a genealogical tree of the family showing the lineage from the Emperor Montezuma to the Maldonados of the present day. It is as follows:

Montezuma I. (king in 1469) =

Princess Atotozli = Prince Tezozomoctli.

Axayacatl = Princess Azcalochitl.

Cuitlahuac. Princess Teotlalico = Montezuma II. (king in 1502).

Princess Tecuichpoctli, afterward baptized Isabel de Montezuma, = (1st) Alonso de Grado. No issue.

= (2d) Pedro Gallego.

Juan Gallego de Montezuma.

= (3d) Juan Cano de Saavedra.

Pedro Cano de Montezuma. Gonzalo Cano de Montezuma. Isabel Cano de Montezuma. Catalina Cano de Montezuma.

Juan Cano de Montezuma = Doña Elvira de Toledo.

Juan Cano Montezuma Toledo = Mariana de Carbajal.

Juan Cano Montezuma Carbajal = Isabel Maria Antonia Pizarro.

Mariana Cano Montezuma Pizarro = Alvaro de Vivero.

Maria Vivero Cano Montezuma = Juan Carbajal y Londa.

Bernardino Carbajal Cano Montezuma = Maria Josefa Lancaster.

Juan Carbajal Carbajal Lancaster Cano Montezuma = Francisca Zuñiga Enriquez Fernandez de Córdova.

Manuel Bernardino Carbajal Zuñiga Cano Montezuma = Maria Micaela de Gonzaga.

Angel Carbajal Gonzaga Cano Montezuma = Maria Vicenta Fernandez de Córdoba.

Angel Carbajal Maria Fernandez de Cordoba Cano Montezuma = Manuela Isidra Tellez Giron.

Manuela Carbajal Tellez Giron Cano Montezuma = José Maldonado y Acebes.

Agustin Maldonado y Carbajal Cano Montezuma, the present Marquis de Castellanos.

Among other descendants of Montezuma is Eugenie de Guzman y Porto-Carrero, the ex-Empress of the French,—a fact not known generally. It is therefore apparent that the wife of Napoleon III. was of older imperial stock than her husband, and brought to the alliance more dignity than she acquired by it.

In the city of Mexico there is a gentleman by the name of Mercado who is a descendant of Montezuma, a very intelligent person, who has preserved many relics of his illustrious ancestors, and is extremely well versed in the family history of the Montezuma race.

Among the older famous men of Mexico were Hidalgo, Morelos, and Matamoros, accounts of whom have been given elsewhere in this volume. The earliest of Mexico's famous men, whose fame has come down through several hundred years, were the Montezumas. Montezuma was the name (Monctecumatin, the sad or severe man) of two emperors of ancient Mexico.

Montezuma I. was born about 1390, and died in 1464. After his accession in 1436 or 1438 he made war upon the kingdom of Chalco in defence of his allies the Tezcucans. The Chalcos were routed in a great battle, and their chief city was entirely destroyed. A war followed with the king of Tlatelolco, who was defeated and killed. Montezuma next conquered the province of Cuihixcas, and subsequently that of Tzompahuacan. In a war with Atonaltzin, a chief of the Mixtecas, he suffered reverses which led to a confederacy between Atonaltzin and the Huexotzincas and Tlaxcalans against the Mexicans; but Montezuma in his first encounter with them gained a signal victory, which greatly enlarged his empire. In 1457 he conquered Cuetlachtan, a province on the Mexican gulf, and carried six thousand two hundred of the people to Mexico, where they were sacrificed to the god of war.

Montezuma II., the last of the Aztec emperors, was born about 1480, succeeded his uncle Ahuitzotl in 1502, and was killed June 30, 1520. He was both a soldier and a priest, and had taken an active part in the wars of his predecessor. When his election to the imperial dignity was announced to him he was sweeping the stairs of the great temple of Mexico. At the commencement of his reign he led a successful expedition against a rebellious province and brought back a multitude of captives to be sacrificed at his coronation. For several years he was constantly at war, and his campaigns, which extended as far as Honduras and Nicaragua, were generally successful. He made important changes in the internal administration of the empire, especially in the courts of justice, and became noted for strictness and severity in the execution of the laws, as well as for munificence to those who served him and in his expenditures for public works. He became equally noted also for arrogance, pomp, and luxury, and his heavy taxes led to many revolts. At the time of the arrival of Cortez in Mexico, in 1519, Montezuma was alarmed not only by the internal troubles of his empire, but also by the appearance of comets and other strange lights in the sky and of mysterious fires in the great temple, which the seers interpreted as omens of the approaching downfall of the empire. Thus disheartened, he did not meet the invasion of the Spaniards with his usual energy. He at first forbade the white men to approach his capital, and then sent an embassy to welcome them. When Cortez entered Mexico (November 8) he was received by Montezuma with courtesy and apparent good will, and at first he treated the emperor with the greatest deference, but a collision between the Mexicans and a Spanish garrison at Vera Cruz soon afforded a pretext for a change of measures. At the end of a week after his arrival he waited upon Montezuma with a few of his officers under pretence of a friendly visit, and, after upbraiding him with the transaction at Vera Cruz, took him captive and carried him to the Spanish head-quarters. The emperor, fearing instant death if he made any opposition, assured his subjects, who were about to attempt a rescue as he passed through the streets, that he accompanied the Spaniards of his own free will. Montezuma was for a while put in irons, and was so completely humbled that when Cortez offered to liberate him he declined to return to his palace, apparently ashamed to be seen by his nobles. He was subsequently induced to swear allegiance to the King of Spain, and was kept a prisoner for seven months, till, in June, 1520, the people of the capital rose in insurrection and besieged the Spaniards in their quarters. He was induced by Cortez to address his subjects from the battlements of his prison in hopes of appeasing the tumult, but, though at first listened to with respect, his appeals in behalf of the white men at length exasperated the Mexicans, a shower of missiles was discharged at him, a stone struck him on the temple, and he fell senseless. He refused all remedies and nourishment, tore off the bandages, and died in a few days. Some of the children of Montezuma became Christians and were carried to Spain. From them descended the counts of Montezuma, one of whom was Viceroy of Mexico from 1697 to 1701.

Do not imagine that because Mexico is a land of almost tropical languor, hitherto little comprehended by her northern neighbors, she has no taste for literature. No: when you make up a mental picture of Mexico and its tropical capital, do not leave out of it the men of books, the writers of prose and poetry, the ardent students of history, all the dwellers in that calm empire of the intellect where peace reigns alway.

Poets, writers, and great orators are held in high esteem, as witness the honors paid to the remains of Altamirano, the Aztec orator and littérateur, deceased in Europe. The popular respect shown to the poet Guillermo Prieto, one of the signers of the constitution of 1857, a venerable man but full of intellectual vigor, is another proof of this. The ability to write well and to talk well is highly considered in Latin-American countries.

Mexico is a land of book-readers. Among the upper classes a genuine love of literature is universal. Mexico is a good market for the best books of the modern literatures of France

RAVINE OF INFIERNILLO, INTEROCEANIC RAILROAD.

and Spain. The lawyers and physicians and the old families of the landholding caste are great readers and buyers of costly editions. Nor must it be supposed that during the last generation the people of Mexico have confined their attention and energies entirely to putting their fair country on a peaceful footing and insuring her material prosperity. On the contrary, in no country in the world has the race for wealth been more subordinated to the proper provision of facilities for intellectual development and enjoyment. Spain still feeds the intellectual appetite of Mexico, as in ancient days: shops which could not exist except for the presses of Madrid and Barcelona live and prosper.

At the same time Mexico is producing, as she has for centuries produced, a literature of her own. As far back as 1680 the Abbé Clavigero referred to previous Mexican historians to whom he was indebted, and King Nexahualcoyotl of Tezcuco, before the Spanish conquest, had written that wonderful poem on the "Mutability of Life."

Among Mexican novelists one finds remarkably good descriptive power. Just as the country of the Mexicans glows with color and intense life, so does their fiction and their poetry glow with fervid passion and feeling; yet there is a tendency to epigrammatic terseness in sentence and paragraph. There is invariably a deep admiration for and a love of nature, expressed in the most beautiful of word-painting, and always there is intense patriotism with luminous force in the expression of it.

Señor Irenio Paz, who is an editor as well as a novelist, may be taken as a fair sample of the modern Mexican writer. He has written a score or more of popular novels, in a simple, direct style that always appeals to his readers. Especially valuable are they for the pictures they contain of home-life among the Mexican people.

Vicente Riva Palacio holds a first place, also, for the elegance and purity of his language. His prose is imbued with the spirit of poetry, and is full of delicate imagery and rhythmic force. This writer's tender and loving sympathy often overflows in descriptive passages of great beauty, and his scope of expression ranges from a spirit of gentle revery and limpid thought up to the richest exuberance of melodramatic intensity. His "Calvario y Tabor," for instance, is an historical novel covering the period of struggle which culminated in the overthrow of foreign power and the downfall of Maximilian, and treats of almost every possible range of emotions. It is a tale of the death-agony of the old empire and the transfiguration of the new republic, intermingled with the loves and romances of the people, their habits and hospitalities and supreme charity. The historical portions of the novel are superb, and here and there are remarkable thoughts forcibly expressed; as, for instance, "Nations, like Christ, have their Tabor and their Calvary; only, when the Son of God passed first to transfiguration and thence to the cross, it is the contrary with them, for nations are composed of mortals. The Spirit of God can alone support the sorrow of Calvary after the glory of Tabor."

Ignacio Manuel Altamirano has been equally well known as orator and as author. His "Paisajes y Leyendas" of the customs and traditions of Mexico is as marked for its temperate and even style as is Palacio's work for vehemence and contrast. Confining himself principally to the religious festivals of the country, he gives us charming pictures of a primitive race carrying into their observance of Christian rites many suggestions of the more innocent forms of their old worship. He is evidently as widely read in the modern classics as El Periquillo Sarniento was in the ancient. French, English, German,—all literatures laid their flowers at his feet, and his versatile fancy culled from each in turn.

Juan Mateos is famous not only at home but abroad. He has reached a point at which a man becomes a prophet in his own country. His brother authors quote him as they would Goethe or Lord Byron. His novels are mainly historical. In "El Cerro de las Campanas" he gives intense and dramatic expression to the story of the "Usurpation." With only a thread of narrative to sustain interest, he places before us a careful *résumé* of the episode of Maximilian. Being a dramatist as well as an artist, his actors naturally group themselves upon the stage of history or fiction, and each succession of scenes culminates in a tableau. The rush and power of his expression sweep eloquently toward the author's conclusion.

Señor Ignacio Mariscal, the distinguished secretary of foreign affairs, is also a writer of great ability. He has translated into Spanish some of the choicest poems of our best American writers, and has written several noted works on the occult sciences. He is also a fine linguist, speaking fluently nearly half a dozen languages.

Señor Matias Romero is likewise a writer of great distinction.

The list of Mexican authors stretches almost indefinitely. Besides those already mentioned as novelists, Manuel Payno, Pedro Castera, Peon Contreras, Garcia Cubos, Vicente Morales, and José Maria Esteva are well known as brilliant and forcible writers. Upon more serious topics, whether of political or social importance, are writers like Zarco, Mariscal, Prieto, Baranda, Siliceo, Arriaga, Ocampo, Alcaraz, Lerdo, Montes, Zamacono, Yanes, and many others, who have contributed largely to the education of the people.

As poets, a still greater number of popular and celebrated men and women find honorable place in the ranks. Guillermo Prieto is probably best known in national songs of originality and patriotism. José Maria Esteva follows closely in giving expression to the natural traits and habits of the country. Acuña, Luis G. Ortiz, Silva, Gutierrez-Najera, Dias-Miron, Covarrubias, Juan Valle, Eduardo Zárate, Francisco Colina, Firso de Córdova, Apapite Silva, Manuel Romero, Laureana Wright de Kleinhans, Esther Fapia, Rosa Carreto, Refugio Argumeda de Ortiz, and Miguel Ulloa are poets not without honor in their own country. Justo Sierra, one of the most virile and forceful of singers, and Manuel Flores, by his tenderness and sweetness, have taken high rank among Spanish poets even outside their own country. In fact, almost every popular Mexican romancist is also a popular poet.

Among famous religious writers are Sister Juana de la Cruz, Señor Carpio-Pesado, Arango, Bishop Montesdeoca, and others. As dramatists, Gorostiza and Alarcon rank well among Spanish classics; while Calderon, Rodriguez-Galvan, Chavero, Mateos, Contreras, Acuña, and others have produced much skilful and remarkable work. Señors Juan de Dios, Pesa and De las Rosas hold an enviable place as poets of home and domestic life.

As linguists, Señors Mariscal, Altamirano, Iscalbalceta, and Pimentel are best known, the latter having made important studies upon the Indian dialects of the country; while Orozco y Berra in his "History of Ancient Mexico" has excelled all previous writers upon the same subject. The best author upon constitutional subjects, or those relating to political economy, is probably Señor Vallarta; but each of these lists of authors could be reënforced by numberless names.

However, enough have been given to prove that Mexico is not behind other lands in the number of her literary workers.

And this is largely due to the fact that the Mexican people are great readers. The city of Mexico contains many large private libraries, and has been from the time of the conquest a city of book-lovers. Books were printed there before they were known in what is now the United States. You smell the clean, pungent odor of printers' ink away back in the annals of the city of Mexico. There are hundreds of cultivated men in Mexico who live in the enchanted ground of literature, contented in retirement from politics and business, asking only an occupation that may give them a few hours' leisure every day to devote to their reading.

Again, Mexico besides being the commercial and political centre of the country is the university town. Students one meets at every turn. Professors are numerous. And it requires more than twenty daily journals to satisfy the demand for the news. Whatever may have been true of the past, in these modern times a bookish impress has been given to the people by the existence of the great government schools, where thousands of youth from all over the republic are being educated. Public instruction, which is of the utmost importance, and is so considered by all in authority, is favored by the happy influence of peace, thanks to which schools have multiplied, the number of pupils increased, and civilization triumphed, and the nation is enjoying therein the fruits of an educated people.

What a difference is presented to-day in the picture of public instruction, sheltered under the mantle of peace, compared with that which was offered during the times of political agitation and revolution! This interesting feature, and the principal and most solid foundation of the future prosperity of this country receives each day further development, thanks to the vigorous impulse impressed upon it from all sides. While public authorities in all branches, moved by generous emulation, have made living and enduring souvenirs of their occupancy of office, this is particularly the case with the department of public instruction. Outside of the great cities the academy diffuses the light of civilization, and even in the smallest hamlets public and private schools extend the knowledge of the people in every useful department. Primary instruction is given almost everywhere. In all the largest municipalities the governments either directly support or subsidize a great number of these establishments. Many schools the creation of which is due to private initiative are endowed by individuals or are under the direction and surveillance of beneficiary societies, such as the Lancasterian and the Catholic.

The reforms of public instruction became, as it were, general in the principal states, such as Puebla, Vera Cruz, Nuevo León, Colima, Guanajuato, etc., the governors of which could not but cherish the idea of such reforms and of instituting normal schools, which are already yielding their fruit in the republic. Among the governors who have distinguished themselves in matters relating to education are ex-president of the republic General Don Juan N. Mendez, the late General Juan Enriquez, Gildardo Gomez, General Manuel Gonzalez, and others.

Among the important labors in behalf of public instruction of Minister Baranda, who all through General Diaz's administration has worked incessantly

COTTON-GROWING AT TLAHUALILO, DURANGO.

to effect radical reforms in the Mexican modern educational system, enabling the common people especially to look better to their future, there must be mentioned the institution, in 1889-90, of a pedagogical congress, composed of representatives from the several states of the republic, at which compulsory education, together with other matters relating to public instruction, was fully discussed, and in 1892 this was put in force.

According to this law, education is obligatory for all children from six to twelve years old, and the course of study is to extend through four years, embodying morals, civil instruction, the national language (including reading and writing), arithmetic, rudiments of physical and natural sciences in the form of object-lessons, practical notions of geometry, rudiments of geography and natural history, drawing outlines of common and simple objects, singing, gymnastics, and military drill ; and for girls, besides the branches mentioned, manual labor and work for ladies.

Nearly all the states of the Mexican confederacy have adopted the principle of compulsory and free primary instruction. In order not to make too light of the principle of obligation, certain penalties are incurred by parents or guardians who do not comply with the law, and prizes are given to the pupils who attend the regular course of instruction.

Señor Serrano, professor in the normal schools of Mexico, has been for many years actively interested and engaged in the work of higher education. He went through all the public schools of Europe, particularly of France, and adopted all the improved methods and appliances there to be found for the schools of Mexico.

There are in the capital of the republic and in the capitals of the states, as well as in some of the principal cities, important public libraries, among which may be mentioned the National Library, of one hundred and fifty thousand volumes, and nine others, in the city of Mexico, one of twenty-five thousand volumes in Guadalajara, and another of the same size in Puebla, besides many others of from seven thousand to fifteen thousand volumes. The college libraries usually treat principally of the special subjects which form part of the curriculum. There are also special libraries, some of which contain notable editions and very rare works and rich collections of manuscripts bearing on the history and archæology of Mexico. In the national archives there are preserved documents and manuscripts of great historic value, which occupy fourteen large halls and hold for Mexico an importance equal to those of Spain.

The museums of Mexico play no small part in her educational system, as well as being of great interest to visitors. The principal ones are The National Museum of Antiquities and Natural History; the Academy of San Cárlos, comprising collections of paintings, sculpture, engraving, metals, and coins; the museums of the preparatory school and of the schools of medicine and agriculture, and special collections in zoology, botany, mineralogy, and palæontology.

One of the signs of the development which has taken place in Mexico during the last fifteen years is the flourishing condition of the press of the country. Throughout the republic hundreds of periodicals and newspapers are published, treating on every topic from politics to science and industry. But it is in the city of Mexico that we find the greatest progress in this regard. It may seem strange to our readers to learn that there are in the city of Mexico more daily papers in proportion to the population than there are in New York City, besides numberless weeklies, semi-monthlies, and monthlies.

The *Mexican Herald* is the leading paper published in English. The editor is Mr. Frederic R. Guernsey, a brilliant young journalist who made a fine record for himself in Boston and New York newspaperdom before coming to Mexico. As correspondent for Northern papers he first visited Mexico City and saw the opportunity for a live, up-to-date American daily, conducted on the lines of newspapers in the United States, an opportunity which he has improved to good advantage.

Of course, however, the majority of the inhabitants of Mexico read papers printed in their own language. Of these the most universally read are probably *El Universal*, *El Imparcial*, and *El Mundo*, which are published in the capital of the republic. Then there is *El Siglo XIX*, the oldest paper in Mexico, having been published first in 1841. It has numbered many of the ablest men of Mexico among its contributors, although it has of late years been of most value as a financial journal. The next oldest paper was *El Monitor Republicano*, which suspended publication January 1, 1897. *El Partido Liberal* is supposed to be a favorite paper with Presi-

dent Diaz, and is therefore one of the most widely read journals in the country. These are by
no means all the daily papers published in Mexico; in fact, I have not sufficient space even to
enumerate them all.

Thus it will be seen that the people of Mexico are quite "up to date" in literary and educational matters, and that as education spreads among the masses day by day the growth of her press will keep up with that of the country.

The customs of the common people of Mexico, like those of all rapidly developing countries, are fast changing, and in a few years there will be no habits and fashions to distinguish Mexico from any other land. In olden times, however, the Aztecs modified their customs in the

PICTURESQUE SCENE ON THE MEXICAN CENTRAL NEAR TAMPICO.

same way, and after the conquest the whole country adopted many distinctly Moorish features, several of which are easily traced to-day.

For instance, the churches of Mexico follow the model of those in Spain, and the little half-orange domes of the Moors are to be seen in some of the beautiful mission churches. While the *artesonado*, or bread-tray roof, is not unknown, the beautiful convoluted double horseshoe arch, or *ajimez*, never was adopted. The canopy used in religious processions is still called *baldaquin*.

The Mexican manner of eating, in which all those at the table dip their hands into the common dish, is still to be noted off the lines of railroads. This custom every one will remember as being common in Old Testament times, and was followed by our Saviour: "And he answered and said unto them, It is one of the twelve that dippeth with me in the dish."

Pulque and mescal are Aztec, of course, but the other Mexican drinks are direct inheritances from the Moslem.

On entering a Mexican church the stranger is immediately struck by the number of women who, closely wrapped in black rebozos or tápalos, kneel on the floor of earth during the service. This uniform method of covering the head and shoulders is Moorish: "No maiden went to a mosque where there was not a place set apart for the virgins, and every woman was carefully wrapped up and covered with her veil."

At the doors of Mexican churches are still to be found venders of wax tapers and small candles, which are purchased by the pious and burned in front of the altars, sometimes held by the devout suppliant, sometimes placed upon the altar itself. The men very frequently, when impelled by an excess of devotion, will pray stretched at full length, or bent low to the floor, or with arms extended in the form of a cross. A Mexican may give in a number of different ways. There is the usual *limosnita*, or alms to beggars; the *regalo*, or ordinary present; the *recuerdo*, or souvenir; the *dones* to the affianced wife; *estrena*, Christmas gift; *albricias*, present made to the bringer of glad tidings; *aguinaldo*, or New Year's gift; and *propina*, much like the American's philopœna. Mention should be made, too, of the *penitentes*, or contrite sinners, who many years ago publicly whipped and otherwise mortified themselves in the streets of every village throughout the republic. They were of the same class as the *flagelantes* of Spain, and are the outcome of the same morbid spirituality that once surrounded the Moorish santones with the halo of godliness. The power of the Church has been exercised remorselessly, and in most of the villages effectually, to stamp out this survival of savagery and barbarism. But from time to time they are still heard of and described.

Carmen Day has been a great religious feast-day for six hundred years in the Catholic calendar. Hundreds of houses are annually made happy with visits and gifts to the "Carmens," who are remembered by their friends, and there is even something in the opera of "Carmen" that goes direct to the Mexican heart. Since Señora Diaz has been the "first lady in the land," however, "Carmen Day" has been more popular than ever, as celebrating, in a way, her saint's day.

Scarcely a town in the republic is so poor that it has not its alameda or its public garden, with its winding paths, in which twice a week one can listen to fairly good music and witness the promenade of sedate men who march leisurely, arm in arm, two by two, in one direction, while señoras and señoritas, equally sedate, march with equal leisure in the opposite, a custom referred to elsewhere in this volume.

A very curious custom is that of pelón, by which, after a certain amount of purchase at a shop, the buyer receives a rebate or gratuity, either in money or in goods. The word *pelón* means a stone or weight of some kind used to balance the crude scales in the country parts of Spain. The custom of pelón as it exists in Mexico is analogous to that of *l'agniappe* in Louisiana, and is copied under various names by many great Northern emporiums to-day. The Arabian fashion of selling bread from trays carried through the streets of Jerusalem and other cities is paralleled in many Mexican villages, and there is a striking resemblance between the street-cries and those of the land of the Moslem. "Algo de fruta! algo de dulce!" is the common cry of the itinerant candy- and fruit-peddlers of Monclova, Celaya, Morelia, Querétaro, Laredo, and elsewhere. There seems to be a great liking for sweet things, the *dulceros*, and in Morelia there are thirty kinds of candy on sale.

The piñon and pecan are indigenous to Mexico, and the candy made of them is called *dulce de cacahuate*. The frijole, the native bean, is a Mexican specialty,—*el plato na-*

cional,—and is cooked in a variety of ways and served at every meal. The mescal constituted the primary food of the nomadic tribes of Northern Mexico, the word *chichimec* meaning mescal-eaters. Chie is a peculiar seed which when boiled with water makes the water emulsive. It is used as a preventive against sudden chills and stomach troubles. Nothing can be more Mexican than chile, called *aji* and *quauhchilli* by the Aztecs. No Mexican dish of meat or vegetables is deemed complete without it, and its supremacy as a table adjunct is conceded by both garlic and tomato. If, however, chile is pungent, the *chilchipin* is vegetable fire. On a small bush grows the *cocotillo*, and a dangerous thing it is, too; for swallow the small seeds and paralysis of the lower limbs ensues.

The beautiful filigree silver-work of Mexico, or *filigrana*, is too well known to need description. Its derivation is undoubtedly Moorish, and the talent for it a direct inheritance from Spain. Not only the filigree jewelry, but the dainty, filmy *deshilada*, or drawn-work, may claim an Arabic origin.

Mexican courtesy is not put on as a garment to be worn at balls and on occasions of ceremony, but is ever present, and has become as it were a second nature. Mexicans in meeting embrace one another, as the Moors and Arabs do. The proudest gentleman in the land will take off his hat to return the salutation of the beggar who begs a light for his cigarrito, or will beg his pardon in the name of God when declining his supplication for charity.

The Mexican comadre appears to the best advantage when a new baby is to be admitted into the church. The

INTEROCEANIC RAILROAD LEAVING THE CITY OF MEXICO.

party having returned from the christening at the sanctuary, the house is thrown open. There are music, conversation, and dancing, with refreshments to which all are made welcome, even the beggars on the streets.

The fondest term of endearment that can be given to a Mexican is *tocayo*,—namesake. And name-days, not birthdays, are celebrated in Mexico. Invitations are extended for celebrations on the day of the saint whose name is borne by the host, and consequently there is much feasting on the minor saint-days.

The older funeral customs of Mexico are very interesting. These mortuary ceremonies of the Mexicans, with slight allowance for time and distance, are found among the Moors to-day. When little children died among the Mexicans, the body was dressed in white, with a helmet of gilt paper or a garland of artificial flowers. It was then laid upon a temporary bier and borne to the church, and thence to the grave, by surviving comrades, preceded by musicians playing soft, sad music. Grown people were buried in much the same way. The male mourners, wearing above their elbows bows of black crêpe, marched two and two, each bearing a candle, which was lit as the procession entered the church. Ladies did not attend funerals; the evening after the funeral they would meet in some convenient house, light candles, and talk about the dead and his virtues until the candles burned away.

Customs connected with courtship and marriage are changing, as in other countries, but even now the relations between the sexes are under strict surveillance among the Mexicans, and young men and young women have not the same opportunities for becoming acquainted as in many other countries. A jóven who feels the first impulses of the tender passion has few opportunities for meeting the object of his affections alone, or for conversing with her save in the presence of parent or grim dueña. He may dance with her at parties, speak to her at christenings, or kneel near her at mass or vespers, but his chief pleasure is to be found in *jugando el oso*, or *oseando*, as the term goes. He takes his station close to the lattice of the young señorita, and there remains until she approaches and looks down and (of course) by accident drops a flower or a handkerchief; then, animated by hope, he may venture to send some female relative to sound the girl's parents and find out what are his prospects. Among the rural Mexicans, who adhere most strictly to old usages, a betrothal is still an affair of considerable formality. The aspirant accompanies his declaration by the tender of the *dones*, generally jewelry, the acceptance of which gives him the right to walk with the young lady and her family to church and places of entertainment. As the wedding-day approaches, he buys the trousseau for the bride. This custom is now dying out in all but the remote Mexican districts.

CHAPTER XLV

NATURAL ADVANTAGES

NOWHERE in the world do we see a country which has come forward more rapidly than has Mexico in the last half-century. Few Americans realize that Mexico was "discovered" and settled by Cortez a hundred years before any settlement was made in the United States. And in natural advantages no other portion of this marvellous western hemisphere can claim a place above her.

Mexico is the geographical centre of the earth, an imperial place in the great highways of the world. The country extends between 14° 30' and 32° 42' north latitude, and between 88° 54' and 119° 25' of longitude west of Greenwich.

It is bounded on the north by the United States, on the east by the Gulf of Mexico, on the southeast by Guatemala, and on the south and west by the Pacific Ocean.

The frontier line which separates Mexico from the United States starts near the mouth of the Rio Grande from a point in the sea three leagues from the coast, follows the line of the river to its intersection with the parallel of latitude 31° 37' 47" N. (at Ciudad Juarez), runs in a straight line westward one hundred miles, then bends to the south to 31° 20', then follows the parallel westward to 111° of longitude west from Greenwich, and continues in a straight line to a point on the Rio Colorado twenty miles from its confluence with the river Gila, then it turns toward the north of this confluence and bends toward the west, following the line between Lower and Upper California. From Ciudad Juarez westward the boundary lines are marked with two hundred and fifty-eight massive iron and stone monuments. It has a northern frontier of fourteen hundred and a southern of three hundred and forty-five miles. It has a seaboard of sixteen hundred and seventy-seven miles on the Gulf of Mexico and the Caribbean Sea, two thousand and forty on the Gulf of California, and four thousand four hundred and eight on the Pacific Ocean, making six thousand and eighty-six in all.

The area of this immense republic is nearly two million square kilometres, say seven hundred and fifty-two thousand square miles, that of the United States being about three million six hundred thousand square miles, so that Mexico has an area of about one-fifth that of our great territory, a fact which few realize. The greatest length of the country is two thousand eight hundred kilometres (seventeen hundred and fifty miles), and the greatest width twelve hundred kilometres (seven hundred and fifty miles), while the least is two hundred and eighty-five metres (one hundred and seventy-five miles) at the Isthmus of Tehuantepec.

So few outsiders have anything more than a general idea of Mexico that I may be pardoned for going into still further details.

Mexico comprises an elevated table-land one thousand kilometres (six hundred and twenty-five miles) in width in the north, and from one hundred and eighty to two hundred kilometres (one hundred and twelve to one hundred and twenty-five miles) at the south, in the

Isthmus of Tehuantepec. The central table-land, a continuation of the Rocky Mountains of North America and of the Andes of South America, is formed by the chain of mountains called the Sierra Madre, which divides in the state of Oaxaca into three branches, the southern, the eastern, and the western. The face of the country is extremely diversified. The littoral regions are in general low and sandy, especially on the Atlantic side, where they were probably submerged at no remote period as far as the foot of the mountains. In no part of the republic within thirty miles of the sea does the land rise higher than one thousand feet, except, perhaps, in Chiapas, where the chain of the Mexican Andes presents a mural barrier facing the ocean, toward which the descent is exceedingly rapid. But the traveller journeying inland from either side, north of the Tehuantepec isthmus, climbs by a succession of gigantic terraced mountains to a table-land with a mean elevation of eight thousand feet, extending far beyond the northern limits of the republic. On the railway from Vera Cruz to the capital every variety of climate is experienced within the space of a few hours, and the natural productions peculiar to each are successively passed in review, from the sugar-cane, indigo plant, and plantain of the tropics, to the pines, firs, and lichens of the north.

The valley of Mexico is an elliptical plain with an area of about nine hundred and forty square miles, fringed on the east, south, and west by lofty peaks, some of which are active volcanoes; indeed, the plain may be regarded as one vast volcanic hearth, roughened at intervals by isolated hills rising abruptly from the surrounding level. The most elevated summits are at the southeast, where Popocatepetl and Ixtaccihuatl tower majestically over all the rest. So regular is the great plateau (formed exclusively by the broad, undulating, flattened crest of the Mexican Andes, and not the swelling of a valley between two mountain-ridges, such as the alpine valley of Bolivia or that of Thibet), and so gentle are the slopes where depressions occur, that the journey from Mexico to Santa Fé, New Mexico (about twelve hundred miles), might be performed in a four-wheeled vehicle. From Mexico south to Oaxaca, in the centre of the plain of that name, with an elevation varying from three thousand to six thousand feet, the route is almost as level as from the capital northward.

There are seventeen mountains—ten of which are volcanoes—which are over ten thousand feet in height. Popocatepetl ranks first, at seventeen thousand five hundred and forty feet, and Orizaba next, at seventeen thousand one hundred and seventy-six feet.

The central table-land has toward the north a height of from twelve hundred to eighteen hundred metres (say from three thousand nine hundred and fifty to five thousand eight hundred feet) between $32°$ and $22°$ north latitude, where it is called the table-land of Chihuahua, and from eighteen hundred to two thousand seven hundred metres (say from five thousand eight hundred to twelve thousand two hundred feet) in the table-land of Mexico, which extends from $22°$ to $17°$ north latitude. The table-land of Chihuahua is level, arid, and covered with a nitrous soil.

Near the nineteenth parallel the table-land of Mexico is broken by a line of volcanoes.

The volcanic zone is about nine hundred kilometres (five hundred and sixty miles) long from east to west, and ninety kilometres (fifty-six miles) wide. Its central line starts at the volcano of Colima, near the Pacific, and ends in the volcano of San Andres Tuxtla, near the north of Mexico.

As has already been said, from the coast toward the interior of the country the land rises by gradations, forming grand plateaus and picturesque and deeply bordered valleys, with sudden changes of level. The waterfalls precipitate themselves in imposing cascades, adding greatly to the beauty of the country.

The crest of these vast cordilleras, seen from the savannas of the coast, is defined from afar sometimes against a blue and transparent sky, sometimes against a misty background. Granitic rocks or snowy peaks accentuate a country which is more broken up, and which rises in vast echelons to the central plateau. Bounded on the east and on the west by a succession of heights, which merge into the axis of the two grand mountain-chains into which the cordillera divides, it is different in many points from those which traverse South America, and of which they are the continuation.

In going inland from the state of Vera Cruz one encounters savannas, or grand prairies, broken by woods and forests, then numberless spurs, which jut out from the foot of the cordillera. On the flanks of these are echeloned valleys, and at the summit the plain of Puebla, to which one rises by the gorges of the sierra, that of Boca del Monte being two thousand three hundred metres above the sea-level.

The mountains in the extreme southeast are mainly composed of porphyry, with some limestone and clay slate, in which lie embedded unnumbered veins of silver, copper, and lead, awaiting the enterprising hand which shall seize them and turn them into wealth untold.

The Oaxaca system is chiefly of granite, especially the loftiest peaks. Granite also forms the foundation to the central table-lands, where there are richly in evidence also the porphyries and precious metals. The Cerro del Mercado, in the state of Durango, is said to be almost a solid mass of iron.

The rocks of Mexico throughout belong to the granitic, porphyritic, basaltic, and limestone formations. The porphyries form the summits of colossal masses of bizarre and capricious form. Sometimes they are found in thick strata, when they are traversed by metal-bearing veins, and form, in the Sierra de Hidalgo (Pachuca), large deposits of great richness.

The limestone cavern of Cacahuamilpa, described in the chapter on Morelos, affords, with its vast and enormous galleries, its infinitely diversified and beautiful concretions, and its fantastic aspect under the electric light, one of the wonders of the world.

The mineral deposits of Mexico, so far as hitherto known, are richer than those of any other country, not excepting Peru; and it is supposed that still richer mines of silver and gold are likely to be discovered. The quantity of silver annually extracted is estimated at five hundred tons, and that of gold at a ton and a half.

The mines during the colonial period were crown property, and those who worked them paid one-fifth of the product to the king. When Mexico became independent they were declared public property, and miners were required to pay into the national treasury only a small percentage of the yield. Even this tax was afterwards abolished, and any one can, by right of discovery, denounce or record a mine and obtain authority to work a certain number of varas free of tribute. A slight tax is, however, imposed on melting and coining the metal.

No country in the world is more favored than Mexico. Situated below the tropics, the climate of Mexico is not less uniform than diversified. The temperature of each locality is almost always the same, yet the different localities present a thousand distinct temperatures.

There is comparatively little difference between summer and winter, except that one is the wet season and the other the dry. The climate can, as a whole, be classified as temperate, yet the country may be considered as divided into three zones,—the hot, the temperate, and the cold. The first is comprised between the sea-level and one thousand metres of height, the second between one thousand and two thousand metres, and the third extends from two thousand metres up. Longitude and latitude do not influence the climate so much as does height, and one often finds these three distinct climates within a few miles of one another, according to the height above the sea.

A marked instance of sudden changes in climate may be instanced in the trip from Esperanza, where the descent from the temperate to the torrid zone is made in about two hours, the drop in altitude being over four thousand feet.

Within the torrid zone the only distinction in the seasons is the wet and the dry,—the first between June and October, the second from November until May.

The torrid region of this country comprises the peninsula of Yucatán, the state of Tabasco, and the greater part of the states of Vera Cruz and Tamaulipas near the coast. The torrid district on the Pacific Ocean extends to the territory of Lower California.

The lands in the torrid district near the coast are of wonderful fertility, thanks to the abundant moisture of the soil kept up by a permanent dew and by the copious rains, and are generally healthful.

Perpetual spring reigns on the slopes of the cordillera between one thousand and sixteen hundred metres above the sea-level; the thermometric variations do not exceed four or five degrees C. (eight or nine degrees F.), and the main temperature varies between twenty-three and twenty-five degrees C. (seventy-three to seventy-seven degrees F.), cold and excessive heat being unknown.

Europeans and North Americans may settle here without danger; they soon get acclimated. This district offers the agricultural laborer and the intelligent artisan many opportunities for fortune.

The cold district and the central plateau occupy the plains on the north of the states of Michoacán and Mexico, the federal district, the northern and eastern parts of the state of Puebla, the

LA SEDEÑA BRIDGE, INTEROCEANIC RAILROAD.

states of Tlaxcala, Hidalgo, Querétaro, and Guanajuato, part of Jalisco, the state of San Luis Potosí, except its western part, the states of Aguas Calientes and Zacatecas, and the plains of Durango.

The healthiest climates are, of course, the driest ones, whether hot or cold. Mineral springs abound on the table-lands and on the slopes of the cordilleras.

The mean temperature of the city of Mexico is about fifty-eight degrees of Fahrenheit the year through. In no other country does the temperature become so much cooler after sunset, and one may walk a mile even at noon under the tropical sun without fatigue.

The rainy season begins at the end of May and lasts into October. During this time the sun comes out brightly in the morning, about noon pleasant showers without wind or violence come up, and by sunset all is bright again. The same is the case in the table-lands; but on the

Pacific coast between the twenty-fifth and thirty-fifth parallels the case is reversed, and the rainy season falls in the winter months. The difference between winter and summer, therefore, is hardly felt; indeed, in the rainy season the climate during the daytime is slightly cooler, but altogether delicious. There is probably no other country on which God has bestowed so delightful a climate.

The nature of the surface and the character of the seasons prevent there being many large bodies of water and the formation of navigable watercourses; but what is lost in this direction is gained by the numberless water-powers which abound on every hand.

There are, however, five groups of lakes: those which are without outlet and which have no streams as feeders, being fed directly by the rains; those formed by the enlargement of watercourses, as of rivers which flow through them; those which receive no watercourse, but which give rise to one or more rivers as outlets; those which receive watercourses which are lost therein; and lagoons which communicate with the sea, some of which might be considered as estuaries.

The soil throughout Mexico is, for the most part, extremely fertile. Artificial irrigation is in many places resorted to, and is effected by dams or aguages and canals. The landed property is estimated at over one billion, and the vegetation everywhere is magnificent.

Every variety of edible fruit known in Europe or America is found there, usually growing spontaneously. Owing to the peculiar structure of the country, too, all fruits, with every kind of garden vegetable, may be obtained in the Mexican markets the year round.

The flowers of Mexico are among the richest, most beautiful, and most varied in the world. On Sunday mornings the streets of the capital are literally enamelled with blossoms of the most fragrant odors and most brilliant colors.

The fields in the hot district are adorned with the beautiful green of the tobacco, the sugar-cane, and the pampas grass of the coast region; and the plantations of mangrove-trees and the bamboo, with its branching foliage, give shade to the river banks. In the virgin forests gigantic fig-trees are found, with immense cedars, mahogany-trees, and many others, beautiful in foliage as well as useful for their fruits and woods. The most luxuriant vines trail from the highest branches of the trees, with choicest flowers hanging in festoons, making the forest almost impenetrable. In Mexico, where the language of flowers is understood by all, the orchidaceæ seem to compose nearly the whole alphabet. Not an infant is baptized, not a marriage is celebrated, no obsequies are performed, at which the aid of these flowers is not called in by the sentimental natives.

In the temperate regions the character of the vegetation changes, but its beauty does not lessen. Magnificent forests of liquidambar, various kinds of oak, laurel, magnolia, and myrtle, cover the base of the mountains; mosses, ferns, and lichens carpet the smooth surface of the rocks, as also the rough bark of the trees. Every dale or glen is an orchard where one can gather the most palatable of fruits while enjoying the most delightful breezes, and where the sighing of the winds, the singing of the birds, and the murmur of the waterfalls make sweetest music.

In the colder regions one finds a rich variety of the coniferous plants and trees crowning the heights and waving in the extensive fields of golden grain and among the green corn, whose cultivation is so general in the central table-land, while adorning the valleys and meadows are the leafy ash, the immense ahuehuete, and the beautiful willow with its hanging branches.

In travelling through Mexico one sees all varieties of vegetation; therefore, on the bleak and hilly parts are to be found scanty growths, although invariably, even here, there are surprises wherever there is a little rivulet bathing trees and flowers in dew; or the loveliest blossoming trees, bananas, oranges, and lemons mingled with bright flowers and combining into an orchard and a garden.

Lilac-trees, scarlet wax-flowers, the trailing white jasmine, tall white lilies, vie with one another in the valley, varied higher up the slopes of the mountains by stunted nopals and blue-green magueys,—a beautiful, bountiful, blossoming land.

In a country so teeming with luxurious foliage and brilliant flowers the soil is naturally fertile and productive. Agriculture is, perhaps, the easiest and most natural occupation, from the formation and richness of the country.

In the cultivated regions we find the maguey, or agave, from which is extracted the national drink pulque. The maguey grows on the great plains of the plateaus, at a height of over seven thousand feet above the sea. On the plains of Apam, about one hundred miles from the city of Mexico, as far as the eye can reach it encounters straight rows of maguey plants, about nine feet apart.

The maguey is the most useful plant in the country, taking the place in Mexico that the cocoa palm does in the South Sea Islands. With great justice Father Acosta called the maguey *la planta de las maravillas,*—"the marvel plant." There are maguey plantations which produce a revenue of from ten thousand to twelve thousand dollars a year.

The city of Mexico consumes over two hundred and fifty thousand pints of pulque a day, and there are in the city eight hundred or nine hundred shops which sell nothing else. The Mexican Railway has one train which daily leaves the plains of Apam carrying nothing but pulque, the freight on which amounts to one thousand dollars a day.

The maguey, or *Agave americana,* grows not only in fields, which are planted thickly, but in ditches set along the fences, and in many odd corners which seem to be good for nothing else. It grows in good land to an enormous size, the central stem often attaining a height of twenty-five or thirty feet and a diameter of twelve or fifteen inches; the branches in some instances are a foot and a half wide and four or five inches thick. One maguey plant frequently yields a hundred and fifty gallons of pulque. A single plant will often yield four hundred and fifty-two cubic inches in twenty-four hours, and keep it up for four or five months, which would amount to nearly three times the quantity I have given.

One can scarcely imagine the appearance of these immense maguey plantations. In the country between Mexico and Vera Cruz, for instance; here for hundreds of miles the plains and hill-sides are covered with long, close lines of agave in every stage, from the strong, large, generous beauty of the full-grown plant to the young, tender green of the newly transplanted shoots. If one can conceive the symmetry of these regular forms, with the spiked, fleshy leaves, eight or ten feet long, falling in a whorl around the central blossom-stalk with the regularity of sculpture, and conceive also the effect of seeing them spread over such vast tracts of country, he will have before him one of the most novel pictures in this land of novelty. The plant combines within itself a dozen different materials for comfort and use. Growing on an absolutely dry soil, with no help from irrigation, it has the property of condensing moisture and coolness about its roots, which makes it yield at full growth an incredible amount of liquid.

What attraction to taste, sight, or smell this thin, sticky, sour, pale beverage can have is one of the mysteries a stranger can never hope to elucidate. Still, as nearly every luxury in every land is an acquired taste, from the decayed fish and edible bird's-nest of the Chinese to the Roquefort cheese and the olive of Western civilization, we ought not to quarrel with this manifestation.

With this common drink, which is to the Mexican what beer is to the German or light wine to the Frenchman, the maguey furnishes two others, not unlike our brandy and whiskey, very intoxicating, but very little used.

It supplies the native, besides, with a primitive needle and thread, which he obtains by tearing off one of the sharp spikes and a long thread of fibre; it gives a species of hempen cloth from the coarser tissue and of paper from the fine inner pulp; it provides a good thatch for houses; and the débris, dried, makes fuel in regions where wood is scarce.

The maguey and its produce, pulque, were known to the Indians in the most ancient times, and the primitive Aztecs may have become as intoxicated on their favorite *octli*, as they called it, as the modern Mexicans do on their beloved pulque.

It is not often that we see the superb flower with its colossal stem, for the plant that is in blossom is a useless beauty. The moment the experienced Indian becomes aware that his maguey is about to flower, he cuts out the heart, covers it over with side leaves of the plant, and all the juice which should have gone to the great stem of the flower runs into the empty basin thus formed, into which the Indian thrice a day, and during several months in succession, inserts his *acojote*, or gourd,—a kind of siphon,—and, applying his mouth to the other end, draws off the liquor by suction,—a curious process. At first this is called honey-water, and is sweet and scentless and tastes like sweet champagne, but soon ferments when transferred to the skins or earthen vases in which it is kept. To assist in its fermentation, however, a little old pulque—*madre* pulque, as it is called—which has fermented for many days is added to it, and in twenty-four hours after it leaves the plant you may imbibe it in all its perfection. It is said to be the most wholesome drink in the world, and remarkably agreeable when one has overcome the first shock occasioned by its rancid odor. At all events, the maguey is a source of unfailing profit, the consumption of pulque being enormous, so that many of the richest families in the capital owe their fortune entirely to the produce of their magueys.

The strong and pointed thorns which terminate the gigantic leaves were used by the ancient Mexicans as nails and pins. With these the ancient sanguinary priests were in the habit of piercing their breasts and tearing their arms, in acts of expiation.

Together with the maguey grows another wonderful production of nature, the *órganos*, which resembles the barrels or pipes of an organ. The plants, growing close together and about six feet high, and being covered with prickles, make the strongest natural fence imaginable, besides being covered with beautiful flowers.

So much for the maguey plant, always of deep interest to strangers.

The sugar-cane was unknown to the ancient Mexicans, who made syrup of honey and also from the maguey, and sugar from the stalk of maize. The sugar-cane was brought by the Spaniards from the Canary Islands to Santo Domingo, whence it passed to Cuba and Mexico. The first sugar-canes were planted in 1520, by Don Pedro de Atienza. The first cylinders were constructed by Gonzalo de Velosa, and the first sugar-mills built by the Spaniards at that time were worked by hydraulic wheels, and not by horses. M. de Humboldt, who examined the will of Cortez, informs us that the conqueror had left sugar-plantations near Coyoacan.

In a general way it may be said that all the coasts of the hot districts of Mexico are favorable to the cultivation of the sugar-cane. It varies in quality according to the latitude, but there is one zone specially adapted to the culture, the cane there being notable not only for its exuberant production but also for its fine quality.

There is probably no enterprise in or out of Mexico at the present time which can be compared to coffee-culture as a money-making business. Mexico is admirably adapted to coffee-growing, and her coffee ranks among the finest in the world. Coffee of the finest quality is produced in Colima, Oaxaca, Michoacán, Morelos, and Vera Cruz, and there is no other country in the world which produces such good coffee with so little cultivation as Mexico does. In India, for instance, where the cultivation of the coffee-plant is carried to a very high pitch indeed, it is reckoned that it is necessary to employ one person (man, woman, or boy) to every acre of the coffee plantation. In Mexico it is doubtful whether more than one person is employed for every twenty acres.

Go where you will over the republic of Mexico, you will find current opinion to be peculiarly favorable to the extension of coffee-raising. There is probably no country in the world,

RAVINE OF METLAC, MEXICAN RAILROAD.

not even Ceylon, so admirably adapted in all its conditions to the successful production of coffee as Mexico. This coffee production in Mexico is one of the few lines of business which can be successfully pursued by the poor man as well as by the man of moderate means and the millionaire. Within the last few years very much has been written and said about coffee-raising. There is, perhaps, no other investment that will give such enormous results and is at the same time non-speculative in its nature. A right understanding of coffee-raising, and the application of proper business methods, are the chief requisites to success, and it involves little or no risk to the investor.

The soil and climatic conditions necessary to the successful production of the coffee-berry are so peculiar that, though it grows in all countries between the tropics, the acreage exactly adapted to it is comparatively small. Entire absence of extremes of heat and cold, a moist atmosphere, fertile soil, and freedom from drought, are indispensable to the production of remunerative crops. On fertile lands and under the climatic conditions above referred to the energetic man of moderate capital can be assured of returns to be found in no other industry.

There has been but little of what is termed "high cultivation" of the plant here. Notwithstanding this, however, estimates given by coffee-growers in various parts of the republic show beyond doubt that the profits of the business have for some time been from one hundred to two hundred and fifty per cent. per year on the whole cost of the plantation, including the land.

Mexico, which hardly counts as an exporter of coffee, could alone easily furnish as much of it as all other coffee-producing countries together, Brazil excepted. It grows in Mexico everywhere, both in the temperate and tropical zones,—a circumstance worthy of remark,—and Mexican coffee is of superior quality. The celebrated Uruapán coffee is considered equal to Mocha; that from Colima is also greatly praised. Orizaba and Córdova sell their crop every year to the United States.

Reports from Jalapa and neighborhood are to the effect that land is being rapidly bought there for coffee-growing purposes, and that new coffee plantations are to be met with in all directions. Owing to the convenient situation and transport facilities, the coffee-growing districts of Vera Cruz are likely to become more and more resorted to by coffee-planters.

Tea-growing is an industry to which the climate and situation of Mexico and the cheap labor there to be obtained lend themselves most admirably. Tea thrives best at an altitude of from three to five thousand feet above the level of the sea. It requires a good soil, the best being black well mixed with leaf-mould or vegetable deposits. It also requires plenty of sunshine and a good rainfall. Hill-sides with a southern or southwestern exposure are admirably adapted to tea-growing. There are several localities in Mexico which are well fitted for this venture.

Cacao, or, as we ordinarily know it, cocoa, which yields chocolate, grows to best advantage in the republic of Mexico. That of Soconusco (in Chiapas) has the reputation of being the best in the world. There is also very good cocoa produced in the state of Tabasco.

There is but little information to be given on this head. This much, however, is certain, and every one knows it in Mexico, that Soconusco can produce as much as Nicaragua, and that the small quantity gathered there can be sold at any price demanded. It is certain that railways will develop this productive industry.

Among the few districts in the world where the vanilla bean grows are the states of Jalisco and Hidalgo, and above all Vera Cruz, Chiapas, and Oaxaca. One of the places where it grows best is Misantla, a canton of the state of Vera Cruz.

The exportation of this product, which of late years had decreased, has taken a new start. The reputation of Mexican vanilla leaves nothing to desire, its qualities being well and favorably known abroad.

By the Mexican plan of cultivation land will yield three crops every two years, one of wheat and two of corn, the wheat averaging twenty bushels per acre, and the corn fifty on irrigated land and thirty on dry. There are fifty-two thousand square miles of land suitable for growing these two crops.

Tobacco is cultivated in several places in the state of Vera Cruz, also in the states of Tabasco, Campeche, and Yucatán. An excellent grade is raised in Oaxaca and Chiapas, and in Tepic and Compostela in the state of Jalisco. The increase in the exportation of Mexican tobacco during the last thirteen years has been remarkable.

About 1868 (during the Cuban war) several Cuban refugees commenced to make cigars in Mexico. There had always been planting and manufacturing in the country, but never before exportation. Shortly after, the first Mexican cigars were received in London. They had a homely appearance, but burned well and had a very agreeable fragrance. At that time the London journal *Tobacco* expressed itself as being pleasantly surprised by Mexican progress in cigar-making, by the exceptional quality of the tobacco from that source, and also by the increase in the demand and the prices received. Thus the Cuban war opened out for Mexico what might be called the era of tobacco.

To the processes of manufacture which the Cuban emigrants brought into Mexico is due the progress made in this branch of the national industry. Now the future of Mexican tobacco is assured. Mexican growers have been called on to fill up the gap caused by the diminution of the production in Cuba; they are called on to furnish tobacco equal in quality to that of Havana, and yet at a lower price. The markets of Antwerp and Hamburg are already theirs.

Here, then, is a line of important industry to recommend, to which there is nothing lacking thus far but capital to make it prosper.

Mexico, above all other regions on the earth, is suitable to the development of textile plants. They are found everywhere in a wild state, but little and poorly exploited, furnishing, however, work for an important percentage of the Indian class. In no place have these plants been the object of any serious attempts at cultivation, although they have been a source of brilliant profits.

When we consider all the land which possesses favorable conditions for cotton-culture, we see that Mexico might easily rival the United States and the Indies. From time immemorial cotton has been the object of important cultivation and manufacture, which, however, was much more considerable under the Aztec monarchy than in our day. The use of cotton clothes was, in fact, general with the ancient Mexicans; and from the beginning of this century cotton was worth at Vera Cruz three or four times less than anywhere else. But Mexico from the agricultural point of view has remained stationary, or even has gone back in such a way that not only is she not counted to-day among the countries which export cotton, but is obliged to buy it each year from the United States. The superiority of Mexican cotton, notably that of Vera Cruz, over the American product is, however, sufficiently proved by the fact that from one hundred and thirty to one hundred and forty cotton-plants from Tlacotalpam yield a pound of fibre, while in Texas two hundred plants are necessary. In the state of Guerrero the difference in favor of Mexican cotton is still greater, although they adhere to the old-fashioned method of cultivation, by the plough; and we might say that, except in the states of Vera Cruz, Durango, Chihuahua, and Coahuila, the methods of cultivation are just as primitive as in Guerrero. The best cotton in Mexico is that of Acapulco, in the state of Guerrero, where the fibre attains a length of thirty-seven millimetres; the length of the fibres in San Pedro (Coahuila) and at Lerdo (Durango) is thirty-five millimetres.

In this connection it is well to note the experiment of cotton-raising made by the Agricultural, Industrial, and Colonization Company at Tlahualilo, in the state of Coahuila. To Señor Don Juan Llemado it was left to illustrate, in a most practical way, to what extent cotton grows in this republic. This huge enterprise is developing into a fine agricultural district land which was previously little better than a desert, making it, if not literally to blossom as the rose, white with cotton-bolls. Standing upon the roof of the *casa grande*, in which are the offices of the company and the home of the administrador, and which is situated at the railroad terminus at the southern border of the property, a magnificent view is obtained of the main portion of the company's land, bordered on the east and on the west by low-lying mountain-ranges, and stretching away to the northern end of the valley beyond the reach of the eye. The entire valley, as far as it can be viewed from this point of vantage, is divided into immense fields of cotton and corn, dotted here and there with houses and corrals, indicating the location of the head-quarters of the haciendas into which the property is divided for its better management, and each of which has its overseer or superintendent. The development of this property was begun in the year 1888 by the Tlahualilo Agricultural Company, and at that time almost the sole vegetation was the scrubby mesquite growth which still covers the land not yet brought under irrigation and cultivation. After two years, in 1890, the company was reorganized as the Agricultural, Industrial, and Colonization Company, Limited, of Tlahualilo.

The fact that the word "colonization" forms a part of the corporate title of this company has misled many to suppose that it was a land company of a more or less speculative nature which had secured a tract of land with a view of selling it in small portions to settlers from other countries; and this view was strengthened in many instances by the belief that the negroes who were brought there from the United States were placed on small tracts of land which they were to cultivate on shares, and of which, if successful, they were eventually to become the owners. This impression is entirely erroneous; not an acre of the property is for sale, it being the intention of its proprietors to place the entire tract under cultivation and to sell the products in the open market, either in a raw or in a manufactured state. The negroes who were brought here, to the number of about two thousand, came as farm-laborers. The chief crop raised on the Tlahualilo lands is cotton, and the idea prevailed that this could be better cultivated by negroes from the cotton-producing States of the northern republic than by Mexican farm-laborers. This effort, however, was not successful, because the negroes had been taken from the large cities instead of from farming regions, and because of a distressingly fatal disease which broke out among them, and, again, because of the homesickness and despair which seemed utterly to demoralize them.

The Tlahualilo company owns about two hundred and forty square miles of land, which lies in one tract, with the exception of the Hacienda of San Fernando, the latter having been purchased in 1891 in order to obtain for irrigation a supply of water in addition to the grant of the government.

There are now under cultivation, chiefly in cotton and corn, about eighty-three square miles of land, and the company expects to have its entire tract under cultivation at the close of the year 1899. The lands depend entirely upon irrigation for moisture for crops, which is supplied by a vast system of canals and ditches aggregating in length at the present time over seven hundred and fifty kilometres. The water is taken from the river Nazas at a point near Lerdo, and flows through a huge canal to the point of distribution. This canal is of itself a small river, being seventy-two kilometres in length, twenty-five metres in width, and two and one-half metres in depth.

The growth of cotton and corn is almost beyond belief. The writer saw corn which had grown to the height of from sixteen to eighteen feet. The cotton is equally productive, many of the plants bearing one hundred perfect bolls.

As may be supposed, this immense estate requires a small army of laborers, and there are at the present time fully four thousand work-people employed by the company, who, with their families, make a population of at least six thousand five hundred people, all comfortably housed on various sections of the property. The farming machinery in use is another evidence of the magnitude of the enterprise. There are steam-ploughs, steam-threshers for the wheat, and steam corn-shellers. In addition there are over seven thousand ploughs, cultivators, etc., including planters, as well as cultivators for cotton, corn, and wheat.

The company now has about four million five hundred thousand dollars invested in its property. The enterprise pays a handsome profit, although these profits are to a great extent used in the erection of the industrial plant, the operation of which forms a by no means insignificant part of the business of the company.

The agricultural development of the land, as previously stated, is not the sole business of the Tlahualilo Company. The industrial branch of its business is much larger than one would expect to find in so remote a district. Two years ago the company erected an oil-factory, a soap-factory, and a cotton-gin, in which may be seen the most improved machinery for ginning and baling the cotton. An electric dynamo furnishes facilities for lighting the various buildings.

The company provides to the utmost extent for the benefit of its work-people. There is a resident physician for those who need medical attendance. There are a large and well-appointed school-house and teachers for the instruction of the children. No intoxicating liquors are sold on the property, and so important is this regulation deemed, not only here but on the other haciendas in that section of the country, that when the Mexican International Railroad was granted the right of way to build the branch road from Matamoros to Zaragoza it was stipulated in the contracts that the railroad company should not permit the sale of intoxicating liquor of any kind on any part of the property ceded for railroad purposes. When the barrenness of the adjoining territory is seen, then are fully understood the difficulties which this company has battled with and overcome; and then, too, is realized the fact that to secure the results mentioned above it was necessary that the owners and managers should possess an immense amount of energy, intelligence, and business ability.

The cotton consumed by the manufacturers of the country amounts to about two hundred and sixty thousand quintals per year, half of this coming from abroad. The annual production in cotton cloth, coutils, percales, and calicos reaches about three million eight hundred thousand pieces of cotton cloth, two hundred and eighty thousand of calico and percales, and two million seven hundred and thirty-five thousand of cotton in hanks, consumed by manufacturers of rebozos, sheets, napkins, stockings, and other articles. More than fifty thousand families live by the cotton industry.

Among the profit-bearing plants should be placed in the first rank the henequin.

Henequin, of all the textile plants which abound in Mexico, is the one which is the most assiduously cultivated. It seems to have originated in the peninsula of Yucatán, of which it has made the fortune, and appears to have been created especially for that desolate country, which before having undertaken culture on any scale was considered the most worthless district of the republic, fit only to receive exiled convicts. The henequin of Yucatán—which, by the way, must not be confounded with the plant of the same name which grows at Manila, and which is of another family—specially grows on stony ground, and particularly on rocks. It is even asserted that it draws all its nourishment from the atmosphere, and that its roots serve only to fix it to the soil. The henequin is produced by drageons. It receives two cultivations the first year and another each successive year. It arrives at its complete development at the end of four years. At the end of this time there are annually cut a certain number of leaves. The duration of the exploitation of the plant averages from six to eight years, and sometimes extends as long as fifteen or twenty years. Its fibre is very fine, finer than that of hemp, does not harden under the influence of moisture, nor even stiffen under the lowest temperatures, and does not call for the care necessary to be bestowed on flax and hemp. The cultivation of this plant is constantly increasing in Yucatán. It occupies the first place in the agricultural products.

Henequin began to be seriously worked in Yucatán in 1860, before which it was exported only manufactured in the shape of hammocks, ropes, etc., the whiteness and suppleness of which articles had attracted the attention of foreign merchants. The United States commenced to import the raw material, and the agriculturists of Yucatán were therefore forced to make their products known to European markets.

The general conditions of climate and the latitude of Mexico are as favorable as they could possibly be to the culture of the ramie-plant. In fact, latitude is one of the most important factors in its development. The length of the fibre varies under this influence from three to six feet, and a difference of two degrees of latitude may cause the length to vary one hundred per cent.

Nothing is simpler or more economic than the culture of ramie. As the plant is perennial, once developed it can give crops through several years, and the fibre not only loses none of its good qualities in growing old, but gains, on the contrary, in fineness, and, above all, in strength, to such a degree that the first crop is scarcely ever utilized. The number of crops per year varies with the climate. In the hot districts there can usually be made at least three.

A SCENE ALONG THE TEHUANTEPEC RAILROAD.

The zacatón, or dog's-tooth, is a wild plant found in abundance at Huamantla and in several other districts. Its root is highly esteemed in European and American markets for the manufacture of brushes, brooms, etc. Not only does it require no cultivation, but, on the contrary, is an undesirable weed, cumbering the ground, which otherwise cannot be utilized for any other crop.

The maguey manso, already referred to as the source of pulque, produces a fibre which has received the name of ixtle and which serves for the manufacture of ropes and coarse canvas. This fibre, as well as that from the leaves of the same plant, employed in the manufacture of paper, gives a product of remarkable fineness and solidity. All attempts at manufacture which have been tried with ixtle have succeeded admirably, and it is astonishing that they have not been followed by a more systematic development.

The pita, which abounds in a wild state in Oaxaca, gives a fibre resembling that of the ramie and answering the same purposes. Ropes made with Oaxaca pita are four times stronger than those of hemp.

The question of cultivating the india-rubber-tree in Mexico has been agitated considerably by private parties, as well as by the federal authorities of the republic, as the supply of rubber in the accessible regions is diminishing steadily, while the demand for it increases. Practical experiments in the cultivation of these trees, according to the officials of the Bureau of Agriculture, have demonstrated beyond doubt that this industry can be established with profit.

Young trees transplanted from a forest to a cultivated field in Soconusco have yielded rubber for more than thirty-five years, the present annual product averaging more than fifty pounds of gum for each tree.

Up to the present time the production of india-rubber in Mexico has consisted in the extraction of the gum collected by the Indians in a very primitive manner in the forests, where they find the trees which produce it. The plants themselves have not been cultivated, nor has the extraction of the juice been carried out in a scientific manner. The Indians tap the trees, gather the sap in the hollow of a piece of bark or in a pot and boil it, and the gum, formed in crude balls, is carried to market.

The Mexican gum deserves to be taken into consideration. The plants which produce it are found in considerable quantities in all the forests of the hot districts, and especially in those of the states of Vera Cruz, Tamaulipas, and Tabasco, and on the Pacific slope, on the coasts of the states of Guerrero, Oaxaca, Tepic, Chiapas, etc.

It is stated that in Tuxpán the milk drawn from rubber-trees is placed in earthenware vessels and whipped with a weed called *coyuntla*, which is an astringent that causes the milk to curdle, making the crude rubber.

The mulberry-tree, to which place is here given because it is the indispensable complement of the silk industry, grows in both hot and temperate climates. Under the colonial régime several successful attempts to plant mulberry-trees were made in Mexico.

The tree grows with great rapidity in this country. Besides the plantations of small shoots, there have been made considerable plantings of mulberry-seed, which have proved profitable.

The government has bought from both Japan and China eggs of the best class of silkworm and the seed of the more valuable kinds of mulberry. These last have been distributed in those districts where silkworm-raising has been carried to the highest development. The number of mulberry-trees cultivated in the republic at present exceeds two million.

Silkworm-raising has succeeded perfectly in several districts in the country, notably in the states of Puebla and Jalisco, in which latter there are already several silk-factories.

It is doubtful if there is any race of people—even the Irish or the French—who eat less meat than the Mexicans, and as to intemperance among respectable people, it is almost unknown. You will rarely see Mexican gentlemen drink anything stronger than claret wine; and they are equally temperate in eating.

The constant succession of fruits of every variety is in itself a resource which few other countries offer. It is not uncommon on the large estates to find that the climate gives a chance for every vegetable product to grow and flourish, the lowlands producing all the fruits and vegetables of the tropics, and the higher regions those of the temperate zone, according to their altitude.

The apples and peaches of Mexico, except in the colder portions, are not of the highest excellence, but the pears are very fine; indeed, there is one species of this fruit which is decidedly the best I have ever seen. It is not only very large, but its flavor is as delicious as that of the finest pear ever grown in the United States.

All the tropical fruits are produced in Mexico, and in fact the most exquisite fruits are grown in all the states.

In the hot country the most delicious fruits are the oranges, limes, guavas, anonas, chirimoyas, melons, zapotes, bananas, pineapples, watermelons, mameyes, and mangoes; in the colder and temperate regions, aguacates, apples, pears, peaches, apricots, plums, strawberries, and blackberries. Grapes, from which excellent wines are made, are cultivated in Sonora, Lower California, Puebla, and Oaxaca.

The entire Mexican coast produces these fruits spontaneously and in great abundance, the banana and the orange being the characteristic flora of these regions.

Baron Humboldt wrote at the beginning of the present century of the remarkable productiveness of the banana in Mexico, saying that the same spot of ground which planted with wheat would support one man, if planted with bananas would support twenty-five. In the districts near the sea, at from six hundred to seven hundred metres of altitude, great plantations of bananas may be made at about five cents per plant, including all expenses up to the day of bearing. At the end of the first year each banana-plant produces a crop.

Rice, one of the most precious gifts of nature, is produced in hot and moist places, and especially in Sonoma, the southern part of Morelia, Tamaulipas, Jalisco, Guerrero, Vera Cruz, Morelos, Colima, and Tepic.

Indigo is cultivated in Vera Cruz, Oaxaca, Colima, and Chiapas, and on almost all the coastlands.

The potato is raised in nearly all parts of the republic.

In Oaxaca the nopal (cactus) is cultivated especially for the cochineal, an insect from which is produced a fine and brilliant red dye.

The jalap (*Convolvulus Jalapa*) grows in a wild state, and is very abundant in the state of Vera Cruz.

The coasts of the hot district produce many other useful plants, among which may be mentioned sarsaparilla (*Smilax medica*), Tabasco pepper (*Eugenia Pimenta*), and the manioc (*Jatropha Manihot*), which produces starch, rice, and arrowroot.

But of all the fruits of Mexico I have eaten nothing finer than the tuna. It is both refreshing and exquisite in flavor. It is the product of one of the infinite varieties of cactus, of which I have seen as many as twenty on a single acre of land. One of these varieties grows to a height of from thirty to forty feet in the form of a beautiful fluted column, and is used to enclose gardens by planting close together.

The cactus which produces the tuna grows to a height of thirty feet and covers an area of twenty feet in circumference, with the leaves (if they may be called so) drooping over one another exactly like the shingles on a house. These leaves are from twelve to eighteen inches in breadth, and shaped like those of the smaller prickly pear of the North.

The fruit is about the size and very much the shape of a duck's egg. The combined flavor of a cucumber, a watermelon, and a lump of sugar will give some idea of this delicious fruit, which literally melts in the mouth.

In the valley of Mexico, toward Querétaro, the white tuna is found. Alfajayucán is noted for a very superior variety of this fruit, and from Querétaro on to Guanajuato, San Luis Potosí, and Zacatecas, is found the *Tuna cardona*, or red tuna, from which is made a most refreshing drink.

The chirimoya is a larger fruit than the tuna, and altogether delicious. The idea which occurs to every one on eating it for the first time is that it is a vegetable custard. Every American makes that comparison, thinking to say something original; but I have heard it at least a hundred times.

The "May-apple" also abounds in Mexico, or at least something very much like it. It is of the same size as the same fruit in the United States, and the flavor has all the peculiarities of the passion-flower. The fruit is exactly the same, except that it has a yellow rind like a lemon. It grows on a vine which is something like a grape-vine, instead of trailing on the ground as in more northern countries.

Spain, desirous of preserving for her wines the market of the American colonies and fearing rivalry, was always opposed to the cultivation of the vine (as of several other plants) in Mexico. If, after the declaration of independence, Mexico had not had so many struggles to

COFFEE PLANTATION ON THE INTEROCEANIC RAILROAD.

undergo and so many difficulties to conquer, it is almost sure that she would by this time have been counted among the richest of wine-growing countries. In fact, immediately after the conquest, and even before, there were timid essays in the plantation of vines, the results of which have always been encouraging. The vines of Parras, in the state of Coahuila, had and have still the highest reputation in the country; but the distance of Coahuila from the centres which would be able to consume her wines, added to the unfortunate economical situation of the country, prevented this industry from acquiring any importance.

As soon, however, as the complete pacification of the country was effected, and at the same time that improvements of all sorts were being pushed, the enterprising minister of public works bought vine shoots in France, Spain, and Italy, and distributed them throughout the country to persons capable of undertaking their cultivation. Inspectors named by the government, and competent in this cultivation as well as in wine-making, were charged to aid with their counsels the inexperienced cultivators and wine-makers. These attempts were crowned with full success.

Not only did the plant not degenerate, but its development everywhere has been surprising. At Ixmuquilpán the development of the plant is most satisfactory, and at the end of two years bunches have been obtained weighing over two pounds each.

The reports rendered by the inspectors show that the results obtained in Chihuahua, Zacatecas, Aguas Calientes, Hidalgo, and Puebla are very satisfactory, but nowhere else have they been so stable as at Juarez (Chihuahua) and at Aguas Calientes; Juarez above all being destined for a brilliant future, not only by reason of the conditions of her soil and climate, but also because of her nearness to the great North American market.

Unhappily, though the grape crops are good as regards quantity and quality, the wines still leave much to desire. The wine-making industry demands a great amount of experience and special knowledge, which are lacking among Mexican growers. Here is an opportunity for foreigners to step in and finish with profit what has been begun with such excellent promise.

The magnificent arboreal vegetation of Mexico embraces one hundred and fourteen different species of building timber and cabinet woods, including oaks, pines, firs, cedars, mahogany, rosewood, etc., twelve species of dyewoods, eight of gum-trees, the india-rubber-tree, copal, liquidambar, camphor, turpentine pine, mezquite (yielding a substance similar to gum arabic), dragon-tree, and the almacogo, or *Callitris quadrivalvis*, from which sandarach is extracted.

Among the oil-bearing trees and plants there are seventeen varieties, including the olive, cocoa-palm, almond, sesame, flax, and the tree yielding the "balsam of Peru."

The exploitation of the immense Mexican forests, which stand thick with splendid timber of the richest and most varied kinds, is most pitiable. Cuttings are made in every conceivable way except the right one, without care, without replanting, without prior selection of trees, so that there has resulted an enormous waste of the raw material and of time and labor. About the centres of population, notably in the environs of the capital, which formerly was surrounded with forests of trees that had come down from the ages, the cutting away of the trees has been so complete that at present in the valley of Mexico there are but few standing. It is necessary to go far therefrom to find forests, which are confined at present to the slopes of the mountains surrounding the grand valley. But despite this remarkable waste, there yet remains a forest worthy to be worked, beside which the part already worked seems to be but a trifle. The establishment of railways has enabled the working of extended forests of enormous extent and almost fabulous value. Really, only the central plateau has been vandalized; but the coast, so rich and so populous, and all the regions of the interior far from the centres of population, have been spared.

Business in dye-woods is in a very satisfactory condition. In general, the cost of working is much less than in timber-cutting, because all that has to be done is to fell the trees; they have not to be sawed, and the smallest pieces have the same commercial value as the largest. The principal dye-woods exported are the *palo moral*, brazil-wood, and Campeche-wood.

The first, which contains two coloring principles, yielding red and green, is usually employed as a yellow dye for cotton and silk, and particularly for wool. Other shades can be obtained by combination with indigo, Campeche, brazil-wood, and salts of iron, copper, etc. The *palo moral* grows wild in the states of Guerrero, Michoacán, and Campeche, the most valuable being that of the islands of Carmen, Tuxpán, and Tampico.

Indigo is cultivated specially at Judistán, and the annual crop is from one hundred and ten thousand to one hundred and thirty thousand pounds, worth nearly fifty cents per pound. At Tonaba there is rather more than half as great a crop, selling at from fifty to one hundred per cent. higher. An inferior grade of indigo brings from thirty to thirty-five cents per pound.

CHAPTER XLVI

MINERAL RESOURCES

MEXICO still seems to have inexhaustible wealth in her mineral resources. Some of her mountains are almost solid masses of iron or gold and silver ore. The innumerable enterprises for developing the country have produced, with more or less profit, colossal sums. If the work had been directed from the beginning with intelligent economy, the importance and profits of the exploitations would have been much greater. As for the riches already extracted from the principal mining regions, they are insignificant compared with those still shut up in the bowels of the earth.

Of the two branches of the grand cordillera, the western branch is much the richer in metal-bearing deposits. From the time when all these riches shall be developed with enough capital and sufficiently intelligent business management, the results attained will be surprising, particularly in the rich region comprised by the states of Sonora, Chihuahua, Durango, and Sinaloa, and in the still unexplored mountains of the states of Michoacán and Guerrero.

It may be said, without reference to political subdivisions, that the principal Mexican gold- and silver-mining deposits are found in a zone two thousand kilometres (twelve hundred and fifty miles) long by six hundred kilometres (three hundred and fifty miles) wide, and stretching from northwest to southeast. Outside of this district there are in other states mines which have been abandoned for a long time, but which to-day are being prospected.

It is impossible to state the degree of fineness of the ores, there being considerable variation. In some districts there is almost fabulous richness; in others there is only poor ore. The most celebrated mine in the country, the Valenciana, in Guanajuato, which is worked to-day with success, has given its best dividends with ores containing only five ounces of silver per quintal; and the same at Pachuca, where ores even less rich than those of the Valenciana have been giving the best results. These are large deposits of comparatively poor ore. The richer veins and irregular deposits have produced, and are still producing, masses of native silver of a grade so high as to appear almost fabulous. These cases are frequent in Sonora, Chihuahua, and Jalisco. At Batopilas a single mass weighed over one hundred and fifty pounds, and brought two thousand eight hundred and sixty-two dollars.

A vein of silver discovered by an Indian near Tastioto, Sonora, assays five hundred dollars per ton.

Of all the auriferous districts of the republic, El Cerro Colorado (Red Mountain), in the state of Chihuahua, is undoubtedly the richest. It is being worked at present by a Mexican company.

The zone now being worked, after thorough examination, is found to yield sixteen dollars of gold to the ton, and comprises about eighty thousand tons of ore. Gold has been found on the mountain-top, as well as on the slopes and base, hence it is believed that the mountain contains immense masses of rich ore not yet discovered. The system of reduction adopted, which has given excellent results, is by direct amalgamation, using the Huntington mills. This enterprise of Cerro Colorado has a brilliant future, and if the company now working there will continue with the same energy and skill that it is now manifesting, untold riches will be its reward.

The samples of meteoric iron found in Mexico are mentioned in almost every treatise on that metal. Magnetic iron abounds. Reference is made elsewhere to the famous iron mountain, and there are other deposits, which, without having so great importance as the latter, are very interesting. In the district of Coalcoman (state of Michoacán) iron exists in deposits which, while irregular, are often colossal. There are many remarkable and very rich deposits, notably that of Chorreras in the state of Chihuahua. Yet during the past few years there have been over two thousand miles of railway built with imported rails.

In 1892 there was transported from Chupaderos, state of Chihuahua, to the capital the most noted meteor ever found in the republic of Mexico. It broke in two pieces as it fell, both together weighing twenty-eight tons.

There are twenty-one states of the Mexican republic known as mining states.—Lower California, Coahuila, Chihuahua, Durango, Guanajuato, Guerrero, Hidalgo, Jalisco, Mexico, Michoacán, Morelos, Nuevo León, Oaxaca, Puebla, Querétaro, San Luis Potosi, Sinaloa, Sonora, Tamaulipas, Vera Cruz, and Zacatecas.

The number of minerals found in the republic is three hundred and twenty-four. There are twelve hundred and forty-seven mines in operation, and four hundred and forty-seven owned by different companies which are not worked. These mines produce gold, gold and silver, silver, copper, lead, cinnabar.

From our knowledge of ancient history of the great southwest we conclude that the civilization of the Toltecs and the Aztecs dates back to the seventh century, and from that time until the arrival of Cortez in 1519, over nine hundred years, we have evidence that these ancient and primitive people devoted a portion of their attention to working the precious metals. It is also evident that they mined in the most crude and imperfect manner, washing for gold and rough-smelting for silver. The process was imperfect in separating gold from silver, and much of their

TUNNEL, INTEROCEANIC RAILROAD.

silver carried considerable gold. Yet in their workmanship they showed high artistic skill and great mechanical knowledge. At the time of the advent of Cortez Mexico was rich in gold and silver in every condition of use and ornament. The value of the treasure that Montezuma brought to Cortez as a present to the Spanish king, according to Prescott's estimate, was seven million four hundred and twenty-two thousand dollars. This does not include a vast amount of ornaments and the priceless jewels that were retained by Cortez and his followers. This can be taken as some evidence of the vast wealth of the ancient Toltecs and Aztecs, though little of their gold and silver was brought to the knowledge of the greedy Spanish soldiery. Subsequently the Spaniards applied their knowledge of mining to the precious metals, and year by year extended their possessions and their facilities, introducing the use of quicksilver and approved methods aside from smelting. As time progressed we find the business of mining and that of treating or working the ores becoming separated, until shortly previous to 1810, the year of Mexico's greatest prosperity, the two were totally distinct. At this time the *rescatadores* bought the ores, hauling them to their haciendas, and reducing them by the most approved appliances then known. This system was carried on to an enormous extent, a vast floating capital being employed, and all classes being deeply interested in a fascinating and productive industry. Mining was extended to the northward, and soon the most ancient mining-ground of the Toltecs and Aztecs in Arizona and New Mexico, whence they had been driven to the south by famine and the attacks of the barbarous Red Indians, would have been again opened to the eyes of the world. But in the year 1810 occurred the great revolution which was the commencement of the internecine troubles and civil wars which disrupted this unfortunate country.

For fifteen years after the beginning of the revolution the products of the metals decreased immeasurably. The civil war destroyed the chain of communication between capital, which was buying and working the ores, and the miners or producers. Haciendas were ruined, and in many cases the machinery and works on the mines were destroyed. In all districts the principal mines were abandoned and machinery allowed to go to absolute ruin. The silver produced was only the gleaning of more prosperous times. The lower classes, by a desultory system, gathered only the rich surface-ores. The sole exception was the mines at Tazco, a short distance south of the capital, where there was a military station.

Humboldt, who in his studies of Mexican mineralogy is generally accurate, said, "The common feldspar belongs to the most ancient formations, as the mines of Pachuca, Real del Monte, and Moran, which furnish twice as much silver as Saxony, are contained therein. We frequently discover only vitreous feldspar in the porphyries of Mexico." The most ancient rock known is in the district of Guanajuato, the clay slate, which rests on the granite rocks of Zacatecas and the Peñon Blanco. It is ash-gray or grayish black, frequently intersected by innumerable small quartz veins, which pass into talc slate and schistose chlorite. In the mines of Valencia are discovered banks of syenite, hornblende slate, and true serpentine alternating and forming subordinate veins in the clay slate. Two different formations rest on the clay slate,—porphyry, at a considerable elevation, and the old freestone of the ravine and table-land of low elevation. The porphyry of the Sierra de Santa Rosa, of a greenish color, varies according to the nature of the base and the crystals contained. The oldest hornstone or compact feldspar is found passing into ptotonite or klingstein of Werner, which latter has a great analogy to the porphyry slate.

The veins of Guanajuato contain common quartz, carbonate of lime, pearl spar, splintery hornstone, calcareous spar, a little sulphate of baryta, and brown spar. The most abundant metals are prismatic black silver and red plunet or vitreous silver, mixed with native silver and silberschwartz. In the Catorce mine the gangue is decomposed, and contains lime spar, red ochre, and muriated and native silver. In Tazco and Real de Tehuilotepec are calcareous spar, lacteous quartz, gypsum, oxide of iron, galena, etc.

The district of Santa Eulalia, in the state of Chihuahua, a space of two square leagues, is thickly interspersed with veins of silver. Two hundred mines were worked, upward of fifty of them to a depth of six hundred feet, which would be the greatest limit, as the water and ore had to be carried out on the backs of the natives.

The famous vein of Guanajuato alone, since the beginning of the sixteenth century, produced three hundred million dollars, and during ten years of its greatest activity about eighty million dollars. The provincial treasurers' receipts from eleven principal mines during eleven years show a production of eighty million dollars. The silver exported from Vera Cruz annually equalled two-thirds of the silver extracted from the globe. The amount of production of the above mines, considering the crude manner in which they were worked in those days, shows conclusively that the ores must have been very rich and extensive. If these mines had been owned and worked by our present skilled miners, with modern appliances, the yield would have been fabulous. The total product of Mexican mines since they began to be worked is estimated at five and a half billions of dollars.

The last ten years have added a tremendous value to the mining interest, not only in opening up many new fields and generally stimulating the public mind, but also because of the more exact appliance of science to mining processes. The last link to bind the Mexican mineral world to American wealth is now being welded by the extension of the railway system through the republic. This once accomplished, there must be a legitimate mining excitement over Mexico which has not been equalled in her history. For no other mining region of North America has been so bounteously endowed by nature, not only as to ores of exceeding richness, but also as to extent of the mineral field, as Mexico.

The Spanish fathers must have become aware at an early date of the rich deposits of copper in the northern district of Lower California, and it was probably the first metal to receive their attention. That copper was mined to a considerable extent by the old mission padres is evident from the number of bells, kettles, implements, and utensils which were manufactured in a crude way in those days.

At San Telmo may be seen the ruins of an old foundry with its furnaces, and several caldrons are still there which were hammered out of copper mined in the vicinity.

At the San Fernando Mission, which at one time numbered about five thousand people, the most extensive work was done; and it is said that nearly all the mission bells in this district, as well as in California, were wrought in a primitive way by its priestly coppersmiths. One of the bells at the Rosario Mission, below San Quintin, marked "El Rosario" and dated "1810," was cast at San Fernando.

During the excitement at Alamo some years ago, and at Mexican Gulch, where the Viznaga mine is now pouring out a golden stream, spoons and horns were found, and decomposed sections of an antiquated arrastra, showing that these deposits were worked in the early part of this century.

Copper has been for a long time neglected in Mexico, and only recently has assumed any considerable importance, although its deposits are numerous.

Mercury has special interest in the Mexican mining industry, because of the process of treating silver ore generally adopted in the country. There are yearly consumed over seven hundred tons of mercury, of which hardly half is produced in the country, the rest coming from California and Spain. However, there are in Mexico important mercury deposits, the only trouble being that the miners have been so busy working silver, with which they are familiar, that they have let the mercury remain unworked and even unseen. This metal is found in several states, particularly in Querétaro.

Calamine is found in Mexico, but is not yet exploited; zinc is found in quantities in the form of blendes accompanied by silver ore. Antimony and manganese, while found in several mines, have not been worked. Although there are no mines exclusively of zinc worked in the republic, it is extracted in a few places, as in Vallecillo, in the state of Nuevo León, where silver-lead-mines are worked containing a great deal of zinc ore, which is separated and exported to Germany.

Platinum is found in the state of Hidalgo. A European company with the necessary capital would probably succeed. There are also found nickel and osmium at several points in the country.

Lead, as necessary as mercury for treating silver ores, is found everywhere,—above all, in the form of galena and in small quantities as carbonate.

Metallic lead, which may be mined, and from which silver is extracted, is found in enormous masses at Lomo de Toro (state of Hidalgo) and in several other quarters. Large deposits of

THE BEND, ON THE CUERNAVACA AND PACIFIC RAILROAD.

silver-lead ores are found at Sierra Mojoda, state of Coahuila, and are being worked advantageously. Most of these ores go to the Monterey smelters.

Mexican mining can be suspended, developed, or retarded according to the wish of the proprietor, subject only to police regulations and those touching the safety of the miners. The government of Mexico, desiring to develop the mining industries of the republic, has taken a very important step by passing a mining law that will induce American capitalists to enter the promising field of its yet but partially explored mineral regions.

The principal deposits of sulphur are at San Antonio, Guascamán (San Luis Potosí), Mapimí (Durango), and the volcanic region of Michoacán (Taximasoa), Popocatepetl, and several districts in the centre and north of Lower California.

The marble of Galeana (Chihuahua) is comparable to that of Carrara; that of Tecali, which, although a marble, is known to every one in the United States under the name of Mexican onyx, is of admirable transparency and variety of color.

The state of Nuevo León produces a great variety of colored and white marbles, and the same might be said of almost all the other states. The gray, black, and other colored marbles, more or less beautiful, of Orizaba (Vera Cruz) constitute to-day one of the vastest and most important interests in Mexico. The quarries are very numerous, and their exploitation is developed day by day.

There is no marble or other stone which has ever compared in beauty with the Tecali Mexican marble or Mexican onyx. For centuries before the conquest the Aztec artists and architects found in this marble their favorite material, which was so highly prized that they considered it too sacred for common use, and so devoted it almost entirely to religious structure and decorations. Its Indian name tecali is merely a corruption of the Aztec word teocalli,—a large mansion,—a name which the Indians gave to their temples. In the days of Cortez altars and baptismal fonts were always made of it when it could be obtained. While the ordinary grades probably surpass in elegance any similar material, it is only in the light and dark grained, the ivory-colored, the brilliantly banded, and the dark-red varieties that there is had a full realization of this stone at its best. Under the touch of a skilled hand it becomes almost a gem. It owes its combination of colors to iron and manganese. It is as hard as marble, but susceptible of a higher polish. In the quarries it comes in detached masses of from a few inches up to ten or twelve feet. The inferior qualities that lack color are sawed into very thin slabs, so thin as to be almost transparent, which are then colored and pencilled to make a fair counterfeit of the real article, after which the side that is painted is covered with a coating of very fine cement, giving it the appearance of having been merely sawed and then polished. All the quarries are small. The most famous, La Pedrera, in the district of Tecali, twenty-one miles from Puebla, is less than three acres in extent, and the average quarry not over seven feet, but the value of the material taken from this small area is hard to realize. The material obtained is a very fine quality of green, from very light to very dark, sometimes showing a slight tinge of red or pink.

The most abundant precious stone is the opal. One of the heroes of the war of independence, General Guerrero, has several diamonds which were given to him by one of his soldiers, who found them during an expedition in that part of the Sierra Madre which crosses the state of Guerrero. The deposits which yielded these precious stones, and concerning which the general has given but very vague information, have been vainly sought by explorers. There have also been found in Mexico the topaz, the ruby, the emerald, and the garnet.

The most celebrated salt-mines in Mexico are those of Peñon Blanco (San Luis Potosí), their products containing from seventy to eighty per cent. of pure chloride of sodium. In the same state are found the equally important salt-mines of Tapado and Zamorelia. On the coast of both oceans there are a great number of salt-mines, those most worked being the mines of Yucatán.

Until 1881 Mexican geologists asserted that there was no mineral coal in Mexico, but since that time investigators have found deposits in various parts of the country, particularly one in the state of Sonora, in which the percentage of carbon is so high as to cause General Rosencranz to give it the name of "black gold." Government commissions have found coal in Sonora, Michoacán, Vera Cruz, Guerrero, Oaxaca, Puebla, and other states. There are also deposits in the north, in the states of Chihuahua and Coahuila. Coal is also found in the states of Tlaxcala and Hidalgo, where it is not worked. The most important of these deposits are those of Sonora, Puebla, and Coahuila.

Despite the fact that the coal discovered is of unusual richness, the Mexicans have never worked the deposits. The first important purchase was made in Coahuila by Mr. C. P. Huntington. This coal contains seventy-three per cent. of fixed carbon, and has a heating power of eighty-two and four-tenths per cent. The very first year that Mr. Huntington's mines were worked they yielded one hundred and fifty thousand tons, and they are now producing two hundred and fifty thousand tons a year.

Mexico uses about five million gallons of petroleum per annum. Crude petroleum springs running freely are to be seen on the banks of several rivers, some of them having a natural flow three inches in diameter. This industry has not been developed.

Attention may be called to abundant and easily worked sources upon the Gulf of Mexico, and above all those of Macuspana (state of Tabasco). They have not been worked, except to a trifling extent in the state of Vera Cruz, where there are rich deposits.

All along the Gulf coast there are traces of asphalt, and in the northern part are deposits thereof. This asphalt may be broken into blocks and floated down the river to the sea-coast, there to be collected and loaded on vessels.

Lower California contains, besides silver and copper and gold, mica, alum, saltpetre, borax salt, and sulphur. The little islands of Rasa, St. Teresa, and Palos contain phosphates, of which there are exported about fifty thousand dollars' worth per year.

The legal taxes in taking title to a mine are one dollar for admission and declaration and five dollars for adjudication. The costs of advertisement are charged to the claimant, as well as the tax of two dollars per league to the member of the delegation who makes the adjudication.

Mines and deposits of every inorganic substance may be exploited without authorization from the owners of the land on which they are found; these, however, reserving their rights in coal, building-stone, mineral springs, and placers of all metals except gold and platinum, and of precious stones.

The Mexican government, desirous of favoring the development of the mining industry, and understanding that the small legal claim of two hundred metres square allowed to one person would not attract foreign capital, gives large companies special concessions, embracing a considerable extent of territory, and permitting the working of many veins, thus diminishing the fleeting character of enterprises of this kind. A mining company may have a maximum of twenty claims in ordinary cases and thirty where the company works newly discovered mines or takes up work in an abandoned mining district. The maximum quantity of land that may be taken up is one million eight hundred thousand square metres. All special concessions made to companies last ten years, after which the companies come under the general law. They must invest in working their mines at least two hundred thousand dollars. This sum is exempt from all federal taxation except that of timber.

The name Atotonilco is very common in Mexico, and always indicates the proximity of warm mineral springs.

Sponges, mother-of-pearl, and shell—which can hardly be deemed mining products, yet which cannot be classed among agricultural productions—are found in abundance of the best quality on both coasts, and are already worked regularly in Vera Cruz, Yucatán, and Lower California. The government, in order to develop this branch of industry, has already made very liberal concessions to companies desiring to follow this profitable line. It is an infant industry, but well worthy of recommendation,—above all, because the capital necessary to establish it is very small, while the profits are high.

At Yucatán tortoise-shell is manufactured with considerable skill into articles of ornament.

CHAPTER XLVII

RAILROADS AND TELEGRAPHS

THE time has gone by when Mexico was isolated from her fellow-republics and the world at large by lack of means of communication. At present she has large and rapidly developing facilities of transportation of matter and communication of thought.

The first concession granted for the construction of a railway in the Valley of Mexico was issued on October 12, 1852, the concessionnaire being Count Cortina, who is often and favorably mentioned in Madame Calderon de la Barca's "Life in Mexico." The charter was for a line from the city of Mexico to Tlalpam, passing *en route* through the towns of Tacubaya, Mixcoac, Coyacán, and San Angel. The count was a very brilliant and versatile man, being at once a littérateur, a journalist, a man of business, and a conspicuous figure in society. But he did not succeed as a railroad-builder, and the concession lapsed. The next charter was granted on August 13, 1856, to Mr. George Luis Hammecken for the construction of a railway from Mexico to Tacubaya. This line, which was no other than the present one, was bought by the Mexican (Vera Cruz) Railroad in 1865.

The railway era of Mexico may be dated from the year 1880, when the charters were granted under which the two great systems of the country, the Mexican Central and the Mexican National, were commenced. These charters were dated respectively the 8th and the 13th of September, 1880; and then followed the flood of concessions for railways which, if all had been carried out, were more than sufficient to create a complete net-work of rails, covering the whole country from north to south, from east to west.

MAJOR ROBERT B. GORSUCH.

The development of railway construction in Mexico since 1880 has been really remarkable, and the benefits which have resulted to the republic are incalculable. From a turbulent nation, always in civil war, without security on its highways for travellers or protection for capital and business; without any export trade, and with a stationary import trade; without a sure revenue; without credit in the financial markets of the world; its only means of communication the heavy diligencia drawn by twelve or fourteen mules and making not over seventy-five miles a day; its transportation of merchandise limited to pack-mules and clumsy carts, whose rate of travel was at most fifteen miles in twenty-four hours, Mexico has been transformed by steel rails and the locomotive into a nation possessing six thousand five hundred and ten miles of railway, and these are daily increasing, connecting all its important cities, and creating centres of trade; with a rapidly growing export trade and an annually increasing import trade; a stable and strong government inviting foreign capital and foreign enterprise into the country and affording them the fullest protection; with an established credit throughout the financial world, and with peace, security, prosperity, and contentment reigning throughout the land from the Rio Grande to its southern limits, from the Atlantic to the Pacific.

Of the existing railways, eight hundred and ninety miles have been built by native capital and native engineers and are managed entirely by Mexicans, and five thousand six hundred and twenty miles by foreign capital and foreign engineers, and are managed by foreigners, mostly English and American.

The first concession for the creation of a street railway system proper was granted under the Empire, in 1865, to a Frenchman, Carlos T. Arnoux, and after being renewed on February 19, 1866, was finally declared to have been forfeited on November 13 of the same year. But no great progress was effected in the creation of a tramway system until 1878, when the District Railway Company was brought into existence. Concessions were obtained in quick succession for the lines uniting the city of Mexico with all the other towns and villages in the Valley. An American company, with Mr. Thomas H. McLean as president, has now come into possession of the street railways of the city of Mexico, and is extending them rapidly.

The great railway of Mexico, from the traffic and mileage point of view, is the Mexican Central, whose system extends over eighteen hundred and fifty-five miles, the main line being from Mexico City to Ciudad Juarez, on the Rio Grande frontier, with branch lines to Guanajuato, San Luis Potosi and Tampico, Pachuca and Guadalajara. The scenery on the line of the Mexican Central is characteristic of the country in all its variations. On the northern end, leaving Juarez, you pass through the prairies of the state of Chihuahua; then through the rocky ranges of the state of Zacatecas, filled with minerals of every kind, where mines have been worked for over three hundred years; through Aguas Calientes, with its luscious grapes and hot baths and great American smelting-works; then through Irapuato, with its delicious strawberries, and Celaya, with its tempting dried and candied fruits; then through Querétaro, with its historical and romantic reminiscences of the collapse of the ephemeral empire Napoleon attempted to raise on the ruins of a republic under a hapless Austrian prince; then through Tula, with its Toltec ruins and fine agricultural lands; now through the imposing Nochistongo cut, a huge monument to Spanish misspent efforts to drain the Valley of Mexico in 1607; then the capital of the republic is approached through cultivated fields and ranches where herds of cattle are pasturing; then, at last, after an entertaining ride of twelve hundred and twenty-four miles in luxurious Pullman cars, through ever-varying scenery, you enter the city of Mexico, where once were the mystic halls of the Montezumas, and where now are all the attractions of a charming climate, novelties beyond description, rich in traditions and romantic reminiscences of the past, all replete with interest for the tourist.

The Mexican Central's division from near Aguas Calientes to San Luis Potosi and thence to the splendid port of Tampico presents in some places the wildest, grandest scenery it is possible to imagine; it passes through deep, rugged cañons and then winds through lands as rich as nature can make them, and covered with an exuberance of vegetation all the year round.

The Mexican National is next in importance, taking the second place in traffic and miles operated. Its system covers one thousand and fifty-two miles, and consists of its main line from the city of Mexico to Laredo on the Rio Grande, with a branch to Morelia and Patzcuaro and another to El Salto.

The scenery on the line of the National is at some points grand and picturesque.

The Mexican Railway is next in traffic importance. Its system embraces three hundred and twenty-one miles, consisting of the main line from Mexico to Vera Cruz, with a branch to Puebla and another to Pachuca. Among the contracting parties was Mr. Thomas Braniff, the well-known American resident and millionaire, whose fortune is associated with the steady progress of the country. Mr. Braniff's financial ability was exercised most opportunely during a critical period in the construction of this the first railway venture from the coast to the capital city, and he is now actively connected with several of the most progressive industries established during recent years.

The Mexican Railway Company, the original pioneer railway in the republic, is organized with British capital; its head office is in London, and its rolling stock of the English pattern. The main line leads from the Buena Vista station in the city of Mexico, seven thousand three hundred and forty-nine feet above the sea, two hundred and sixty-three miles by an average descending grade to Vera Cruz, at the sea-level; but at one point (Ocotlan) the line is eight thousand three hundred feet above the sea. Most of the seven thousand three hundred and forty-nine feet of descent is made in a distance of twenty miles between Boca del Monte and Maltrata, this twenty miles (on the right side of the train) being the best worth seeing of the whole line; but of this later. So precipitous is the grade that the Indian who sells fruit and flowers at one of the half-way stations has time to clamber down the cañon road to Maltrata before the train gets there.

ACROSS THE ISTHMUS OF TEHUANTEPEC.

In many parts of the line the scenery is grand. Leaving the city of Mexico, it passes through the great pulque district which supplies the popular national beverage, and then winds down around and among wooded and steep mountains, where the scenery is enchanting and the engineering is admirable and bold.

The narrow-gauge Interoceanic Railway in part competes with the Mexican Railway. Its system covers five hundred and thirty miles, its main line being from Vera Cruz to Puebla and Mexico and southward from Mexico through the state of Morelos to Ixtla, with a branch line from Puebla to Matamoros, Izucar, and Chietla. From Mexico it also passes through the pulque district to Puebla; thence to Perote, an old Spanish fortress; Jalapa, the capital of the state of Vera Cruz, called the "City of Flowers"; thence to Vera Cruz, touching many intermediate towns. The other part of the main line runs from Mexico to Amecameca, where is the famous shrine of the Sacre-Monte, visited annually by thousands of pilgrims.

This railway purchased all the concessions granted by the Mexican government to Señor Don Delfin Sanchez, who constructed all the lines. Through the great executive ability of this latter gentleman the line is not only the best but the most cheaply constructed in the country.

COLONEL JOE H. HAMISON.

This road is considered by the Mexicans themselves as of such great importance in the development of their resources that President Diaz in person specially requested the writer to inspect it from one end to the other, a task which was rendered much more easy, while its results were much more thorough, by a most comfortable and well-equipped special train.

The Mexican International Railway, a short, standard-gauge route to Mexico, and the only standard-gauge road to Monterey, has its eastern terminus at Ciudad Porfirio Diaz, opposite Eagle Pass, Texas, where it connects with the Southern Pacific system. Trevino, formerly called Venadito, two hundred and twenty-four miles from Ciudad Porfirio Diaz, is the junction with the Monterey and Mexican Gulf road, and Torreón, three hundred and eighty-four miles from Ciudad Porfirio Diaz, with the Mexican Central road. At Sabinas the line branches to the San Felipe coal-mines; at Hornos a branch runs through the cotton district of the republic to San Pedro. From Monclova its line to Sierra Mojada runs, and its Durango extension commences at Torreón, and is of great importance to the country. It is the finest equipped line in Mexico, and its road-bed, bridges, and culverts are alike first-class.

The San Pedro branch runs through the cotton district of Mexico. Over sixty thousand bales of cotton are annually shipped over it to mills in the city of Mexico, Hercules, and other large cotton-factories in the republic. The International Railway comprises five hundred and seventy-three miles; in addition to its main line from Eagle Pass, or rather Ciudad Porfirio Diaz, on the Mexican side of the Rio Grande, to the city of Durango, it has branch lines to Hondo, to San Pedro, and to Velardeña.

The main line leaving Porfirio Diaz strikes the Central at Torreón, and thence runs to Durango, the capital of the state. In its course it connects many flourishing towns, and passes through grazing-lands, agricultural districts, and mining regions ; at Durango it taps the greatest iron mountain in the world. Its branch from Sabinas runs to the great coal-field of San Felipe.

Major Robert B. Gorsuch is the official representative of Mr. C. P. Huntington in all his great enterprises in the republic. He makes his home in the city, and is the most distinguished American that has ever lived in Mexico. He came from New York early in 1850 to commence the construction of the Vera Cruz Railroad. He has taken an active interest in every railroad development in the country, and his complete study of everything that has tended toward the material progress of Mexico has made him the authority on all important

TWO TUNNELS ON THE INTEROCEANIC RAILROAD.

matters pertaining to the growth of the country. The great men of Mexico are his personal friends, and to his rare store of solid and general knowledge of the republic I am indebted for much valuable information.

The Hidalgo and Northwestern was begun in 1880 by native capital and Mexican engineers. Its main line is from Mexico to Tulancingo, with a branch to Pachuca, and traverses the great agricultural region of the northern part of the state of Vera Cruz and the water-shed of the broad Tuxpan River.

The Mexican Southern Railway, from Puebla to Oaxaca, three hundred and twenty-eight miles, passes through a rich and extensive agricultural country in its whole length. It touches the towns of Tehuacan, Tecomovaca, Tomellin, Huitzo, and Etla, as well as many others of less importance. Oaxaca is one of the historic places of Mexico, and gave the republic Benito Juarez and Porfirio Diaz. A short distance from the city are the wonderful ruins of Mitla, the vestiges of an Egyptian civilization, and the great cypress-tree at Tula, the trunk of which measures one hundred feet in circumference. The Mexican Southern began operation in 1891, and for a short distance parallels the Interoceanic Railway.

When we consider how important a city Oaxaca has been without the railway, we may form some idea of how it has now commenced to take giant strides in population, commerce, and influence.

The Mexico, Cuernavaca and Pacific Railway, though the last of the thirty Mexican railways to begin construction, is specially worthy of mention for its beautiful scenery and unequalled panoramas. The line is destined to reach the Pacific port of Acapulco. Forty-six miles of this road have been completed from Mexico City to Las Tres Marias, with active building now in progress and preliminaries going on toward the building to its Pacific terminus.

This is, without question, the scenic road of Mexico. Leaving the city, it runs through pretty suburban farms, gradually ascending to Contreras, where one has a complete view of the Valley of Mexico, with its old capital at your feet. Here you have a panorama embracing at least fifty miles in length and twenty-five miles in width, with the lakes of Texcoco, Chalco, and Xochimilco and the white walls of over twenty villages and Chapultepec Castle gleaming below. All the way up the mountain-side from Contreras to Arenal this vast panorama is in view. Then you pass the foot of the old Ajusco volcano, which centuries ago bathed the country in lava, through which the line now runs. Next the wide forests of Huitzilac are reached, where huge pine-trees, bending to the breeze, wave you a welcome. At Tres Marias,—or the Three Marys, of whom there is an interesting tradition,—three thousand feet above Mexico, you see the broad valley of Cuernavaca four thousand feet below, stretching out seventy miles, green with the cane-fields of the sugar plantations and dotted with the villages which surround the mills. There, too, is the beautiful city of Cuernavaca, with its picturesque suburbs and orchards full of coffee-plants and fruit-trees. The route of this road is also made interesting by legends of the past, the crumbling ruins of ancient cities, fortresses, and temples, the mysterious caverns trending and winding for miles underground, in which subterranean rivers flow, fishes and birds abound, and the most fantastic forms of stalactites are found; and here is the palace the conquering Cortez built for a residence, which the visionary Maximilian occupied when weary of politics and the din of arms.

HON. THOMAS BRANIFF.

These roads are sufficient to give an idea of what may be seen and studied in Mexico while travelling with comfort and, if you wish, with luxurious ease and every commodity at command.

Colonel Joe H. Hampson is the young president of this road,—another American who has reflected lustre from the United States. He is no ordinary man. Resolute and indefatigable, every one regards him here with pride and affection as a typical American whom success and fortune have left unspoiled, a worthy continuer of the great traditions of the American railway-constructors in Spanish-speaking lands. Open-handed, liberal to a degree, a born commander of men, Hampson is of the Cecil Rhodes type, a developer of new regions, one of those men who were born for great affairs.

These new lines, pushing on to the Pacific, Huntington's in Northern and Hampson's in Central Mexico, will enable Mexican manufactures, working on a silver basis, to reach out for the west coast trade of South America. And it is believed that the Mexico, Cuernavaca, and Pacific road will open up extensive coal-fields in the state of Guerrero, cheapening fuel over a large region.

After fourteen years of work and ten million dollars of expenditure, the National Tehuantepec Railroad, running across the Tehuantepec peninsula from Salina Cruz on the Pacific side to Coatzacoalcos on the Gulf side, has been completed. This railroad is just now recognized as one of the most important railroads in the world. It is one hundred and twenty-two miles long, and the Mexican government owns and controls the line. The Tehuantepec Railroad will in time revolutionize the freight traffic between San Francisco and New York, because the route is shorter than by the Isthmus of Panama by fifteen hundred miles. An international interest has been awakened in this Mexican enterprise, and the route to China from important foreign ports is shorter by seven hundred miles than *via* the Suez Canal.

By a strange freak of topography, at Tehuantepec Isthmus is the only break in the Sierra Madre Mountains from Guaymas to Panama, a distance of nearly two thousand miles. At Salina Cruz, where the railroad terminates, the greatest altitude is only seven hundred feet above sea-level, and there is a natural break of thirty miles across through the low mountains, making an easy passage for the road. Here, also (at Salina Cruz), is a fine open roadstead. The harbor on the Gulf side is superb, having a depth of thirteen feet six inches of water, with a hard clay formation and no sand-bars. After crossing the bar, and for a distance of thirty miles up the Coatzacoalcos River, there is a continuous depth of forty feet of water, doing away with the necessity of lighters, an unavoidable and heavy expense at Panama.

When all improvements are completed, the commerce of the world will seek this route for trade between Europe and California, the western parts of Mexico, the Pacific States, and the western coast of South America; besides, this route must be preferred to Suez, particularly in trade with Chile, Peru, and Ecuador.

The Tehuantepec Isthmus improvement provides for the development of two great harbors and the construction of the Tehuantepec Railway. At Coatzacoalcos, the harbor on the Atlantic side, the contract will call for the expenditure of two million five hundred thousand dollars. At Salina Cruz, on the Pacific side of the isthmus, it is estimated that four million five hundred thousand dollars will be spent.

Very elaborate will be the work of building a harbor on the Pacific side of the isthmus. Salina Cruz is an open roadstead with a depth of fifty feet of water only a little way out from the shore. A harbor is to be made by the building of two breakwaters. One will be three thousand five hundred feet long, the other will be an elbow and will have a length of eight hundred feet. The contract adopts the ideas of Mexican engineers, which are a compromise or combination of all the proposed solutions for this harbor problem. Rubble and concrete will be used in the construction of the breakwater, which will be practically a sea-wall. The height of the wall from the foundation to the top of the parapet will be seventy feet. There will be sixteen feet above water at high tide. At the base, on the sea bottom, this marine breakwater will have a width of three hundred and fifty feet. The thickness will narrow as the wall rises, and at the parapet the wall will be twenty-four feet. Six years is the contract time allowed for the completion of the Salina Cruz harbor.

The contractor who is completing the twenty-million-dollar contract at Vera Cruz is the one who has undertaken the harbor improvements at Coatzacoalcos and Salina Cruz, with the reconstruction of the Tehuantepec Railway and the concession to operate it for fifty years. He is Sir Weetman Pearson, an Englishman, the foremost contractor in the world. He built the drainage-canal to relieve the city of Mexico. He is building the Blackwell tunnel under the Thames; he is constructing irrigation-works in Egypt at a cost of twenty-five million dollars. The character of his achievements inspires confidence that is having great effect on Southern Mexico.

For a distance of fifty miles up the Coatzacoalcos and Uspanapa Rivers the landscape is one long stretch of low and level country of extremely fertile soil and covered with a luxuriance of tropical vegetation that is not surpassed in the world. Birds of startling plumage brighten the scene, and the water, clear as crystal, cuts its way to the sea through bowers of green rich in color and gay with song. This is the native home of cacao, from which chocolate is made. In a picturesque casa by the water-way one may enjoy the most palatable dish ever tasted. It is prepared by the Indians from a green chocolate nut mixed with fresh cheese and covered with slightly boiled juice of the sugar-cane. The little Indian village of Jaltipan is said to be just as it was when Cortez met the beautiful Aztec princess there. It was from that village that Cortez wrote to Spain describing a new paradise. What is attracting a large amount of American capital is the coffee industry, and here the advantages for profitable production are unequalled. Seldom are found such depth of soil, such evenness of temperature, and such abundance of rainfall, combined with cheap and quick transportation, as in the new coffee districts in this Tehuantepec isthmus. The temperature never rises above ninety-two degrees and never sinks below sixty. The trade-winds from the Pacific sweep across the snow-capped peaks of the Sierra Madre range and are forced through the break at Tehuantepec as through a funnel.

ALONG THE CUERNAVACA AND PACIFIC RAILROAD.

To reach Mexico from New York I have found the Pennsylvania road by far the best route. The beautiful scenery along the Horse-Shoe Curve up among the Alleghanies is a fitting preface for a journey to picturesque Mexico. From the Pennsylvania system you make the best connections at St. Louis or Chicago to reach either of the Mexican borders with fewer changes and more personal comfort.

At Chicago take the Santa Fé for El Paso, Texas, where you pass the Mexican line at Juarez; at St. Louis the Louisville and Nashville connects at New Orleans with the Southern Pacific for Eagle Pass and Ciudad Porfirio Diaz. This latter route I would advise in returning to the East in winter from Mexico, as you gradually get into the colder climate without feeling the change.

To reach Mexico by water, the Ward line offers every desirable facility. It makes weekly trips between New York and Progreso, Tampico, and Vera Cruz, and touches every two weeks at Tuxpam and Campeche.

The remarkable growth of postal business led the government to reduce by one-half the rates on all inland correspondence from July, 1895; but even with that reduction the receipts

BUENA VISTA STATION, MEXICAN RAILROAD.

of the postal service of Mexico in 1895 show an increase of one hundred and twenty-seven thousand six hundred and forty dollars over any previous year.

One of the things which the prosperous administration of President Diaz can point out with pride is the wonderful development of the telegraph system of the republic and the excellent way in which it is managed. Morse's invention reaches every city, town, or place of any importance, and it is operated in an efficient, business-like manner. Few telegraphic services in the world are to-day more efficient and well managed in the interest of the public than Mexico's federal telegraph. Every office throughout the country runs like clock-work and on strict business principles.

For the following information on the Mexican telegraph system I am indebted to Mr. J. A. Soni, of that department in Mexico City.

"To the personal efforts of one of its learned citizens, Señor Don Juan de la Granja, belongs the honor of having imported into Mexico the electric telegraph. While serving his country as consul-general to the United States, Señor de la Granja witnessed with keen interest the rapid development of Professor Morse's wonderful invention, and he returned home to form a company to erect telegraph lines. The government subscribed liberally to the enterprise, and Señor de la Granja was soon in possession of the necessary capital to start his labors on a line from the city of Mexico toward Vera Cruz. On November 5, 1851, he reached the little village of Nopalucan, and the line to that place was inaugurated the same day amidst great festivities. Six months after, on May 19, 1852, the entire line to the port of Vera Cruz, four hundred and ninety kilometres in length, was opened to public services. The laying of telegraph lines to Toluca, Guanajuato, and San Luis Potosi soon followed, but always by private enterprise. So all the lines remained for years outside government control.

"But at the downfall of the Emperor Maximilian, in 1867, the owners of the Guanajuato and San Luis Potosi lines having taken part in the struggle against the republic, Juarez laid an embargo on their lines, and thus gave birth to the federal telegraph system, which then measured six hundred and seventy kilometres. The government proceeded then to develop the system, and gradually reached the principal cities.

"In 1876, when General Diaz was elected president, Mexico had seven thousand nine hundred and twenty-seven kilometres of federal and four thousand nine hundred and twenty-seven kilometres of private telegraph lines with one hundred and thirty-five offices in all. At present the federal government's system measures forty-five thousand kilometres in length and serves three hundred and forty-two offices; while there are numerous telephone lines, measuring thirteen thousand kilometres in length, and independent telegraph systems, in every state, belonging either to the local governments or to private parties. These local systems bind together one hundred and sixty-four different places and measure in all nineteen thousand five hundred and seventy-six kilometres. Besides these, there are the telegraph lines belonging to the railroad companies, ten thousand kilometres in length, and four hundred and twenty-two offices; making a grand total of seventy-four thousand five hundred and seventy-six kilometres of regular telegraph lines and nine hundred and twenty-eight offices.

"The federal lines extend their benefits to all state capitals, all commercial places, and all towns on the northern and southern frontiers, as well as to all ports on the Pacific and the Gulf of Mexico. As to the local systems, they reach every town in the states to which they

BARRANCA NEAR TRES MARIAS, ON THE CUERNAVACA AND PACIFIC RAILROAD.

belong. In fact, it can be said that every place of any importance in Mexico can now be reached either by telegraph or telephone.

"For its international communications Mexico has four great submarine cables, two of them belonging to the Mexican Telegraph Company and the other two to the Central and South American Telegraph Company. The cables belonging to the Mexican Telegraph Company are

TELEGRAPH OFFICE IN THE FEDERAL DISTRICT.

laid in the Gulf of Mexico, one of them from Galveston, Texas, to Coatzacoalcos, and the other from Galveston to Tampico, Vera Cruz, and Coatzacoalcos; those belonging to the Central and South American Telegraph Company, from Salina Cruz on the Isthmus of Tehuantepec down to Valparaiso in Chile. Thus we may well consider Mexico as the bridge for telegraphic communications between Europe and the United States and all Central and South American countries on the Pacific Ocean."

CHAPTER XLVIII

FINANCIAL AND BUSINESS OUTLOOK

MEXICO is literally a money-making country, as she digs from the bowels of the earth a raw product which, when conveniently put into masses of uniform weight and appearance and stamped with her trade-mark, becomes the most widely circulated and demanded medium of exchange the world has ever known.

Although the ancient Aztecs do not appear to have had regularly stamped coin, their commerce was not exclusively confined to an exchange of commodities. They had certain values of different articles which took the place of money, and of which Clavigero enumerates five kinds. One of these was the cacao bean, which was counted by *xiquipillis*, or lots of eight thousand, or in sacks of twenty-four thousand each. For articles of common daily necessity their usual money was scraps of cotton cloth called *patolcuachtli*. Expensive objects were bought with grains of gold carried in quills, and for cheaper articles copper pieces cut in the form of a T were used.

After the conquest the first mint was established in 1538 in Mexico by Don Antonio de Mendoza, the first viceroy. The coinage of colonial times was subdivided into four kinds. The first was *moneda macuquina*, irregular polygonal coin stamped by hand, with a cross, two lions, and two columns on one side and the name of the reigning Spanish sovereign on the other. These were used from 1538 to 1731. Then there was the *moneda columnaria*, or pillar coin, used from 1732 to 1771; the *moneda de busto*, or bust coin, in usage from 1772 to 1821; and the coinage struck during the war of 1821 and 1822. After this war there were two distinct categories,—the imperial and the republican.

The total issue of macuquina coins was seven hundred and sixty million seven hundred and sixty-five thousand four hundred and six dollars; of pillar coins, four hundred and sixty-one million five hundred and eighteen thousand two hundred and twenty-five dollars; of bust coins, nine hundred and twenty-nine million two hundred and ninety-eight thousand three hundred and twenty-seven dollars; making the total colonial coinage two billion one hundred and fifty-one million five hundred and eighty-one thousand nine hundred and fifty-eight dollars. The total coinage of money in Mexico now amounts to considerably over three billions of dollars.

The monetary unit of Mexico is the *peso* (piastre) of silver, 902.7 fine and weighing 27.073 grammes. In all Mexican mints any gold which the silver contains under a certain proportion is left in, so that we find the dollars of the states of Guadalajara and Durango to contain two per cent. of gold and those of Oaxaca four per cent. of gold.

Of coins there are the *águila*, or eagle, of twenty dollars, and the *onza de oro*, or gold ounce, of sixteen dollars, besides fractional gold pieces. Then there are the *peso*, the *toston*, or fifty centavos, the *peseta*, corresponding to the American "quarter," and, as further binary divisions, the *real*, *medio*, and *cuartilla*. Since the decimal system has been adopted the other small silver

ORGANOS, THE LARGE CACTUS PLANT, OAXACA.

pieces have disappeared. In all commercial transactions the dollar is designated by the same mark as in the United States.

The exportation of the Mexican dollar to Oriental countries is a regular commercial operation. The demand for this kind of money in London is constant, and has no serious influence on its value. While Mexico cannot in one sense be compared as a silver producer with some other countries,—as, for instance, with the United States or with Bolivia,—these last export their silver in the shape of ingots; but Mexico sends out hers in the form of a manufactured article, —the dollar,—for which there is a market in which no one will dispute with her the supremacy.

It is very strange that the hold which this Mexican eagle dollar has had in the Orient has never been loosened by any rival. In 1772 Spain struck a Spanish pillar dollar, avowedly moulded on the Mexican eagle in weight and fineness. At one time it commanded in China over eight per cent. premium. In 1887 the Spanish government decided to demonetize it, and then received from all parts of the world twenty-two millions of those dollars, for which it paid gold, although intrinsically the coin is not worth eighty cents in gold. Hong-Kong had so put it upon the market in 1886, and the Chinese government undertook to aid it by receiving it for customs duties, but neither merchants nor the Chinese themselves liked it, and, although it was a better executed coin than the Mexican dollar, it was quoted at a discount.

The design on one side of the Mexican coins, representing an eagle resting on a cactus, with a snake in its beak, is a picture-story of an Aztec legend that runs thus: In the early part of the fourteenth century, while the prowess of the Aztecs was at a low ebb and they wandered among the salt marshes and reeds of the valley, a commission came down from heaven to Tenoch, one of their chiefs, to the effect that when they should see a cactus growing upon a rock, and on the cactus an eagle perched devouring a snake, then and there they should build a temple to the god of war, who in turn would ever after guard and protect them, and elevate their country to the dignity of a great nation. And it came to pass, one day in the year A.D. 1325, on the banks of the lake Texcoco they beheld a sight just as prophesied, and Tenoch camped on the spot and immediately began the erection of a temple, as commanded, and called it Tenochtitlan. On that spot to-day stands the beautiful city of Mexico, and the legend is perpetuated in the memory of the people by the illustration on the national currency.

It is by the establishment of banks that Europe and America can give the country the capital necessary for developing her agriculture and industries. The flourishing condition of Mexican banks is proverbial. Of the five great ones only the "National Pawn-Shop" has ever failed, and that is now in a flourishing condition.

The Banco de Londres y México, or London and Mexican Bank, was originally established in 1864 as a branch of a London bank doing business with South America. Notwithstanding the political events of the period, good results were obtained, but were not published separately from the general accounts presented at the shareholders' meeting, although the fact was recognized in the report of the directors. When the banking law was decreed by the Mexican government it became necessary to reorganize the bank and domicile in the republic, and, several local capitalists having expressed the wish to join interests with the bank, a contract for the sale of a portion of the holding, to be represented by a separate issue of shares, was entered into and approved by the government, and a new law decreed granting the bank valuable privileges.

The commercial situation may be summed up in these words,—lack of active capital. This has always been the case, and even while American and English capital now goes into the country, the insufficiency of capital is still manifest. After the war for independence internal difficulties, civil war, and two foreign wars prevented the national capital from being put into active circulation. Every one, as in the East, hoarded his cash. No one wished to invest, and the country vegetated in a state of uncertainty for the upper classes and complete misery for the lower ones. Then, after peace was established, people got used to prosperity in a quiet sort of way and did not wish to start anything new. They have not yet got quite over that state of affairs.

A statement in regard to the amount of business done by and with Mexico should prove highly acceptable in this connection, as should, also, a series of hints and suggestions to business men throughout the world relative to opening or enlarging commercial relations with her merchants and people.

The material and pecuniary progress of Mexico since 1877 cannot be better demonstrated than by the figures which show that the producing industries and business of the country have been more than doubled since that date. In 1877, when General Porfirio Diaz first became the guiding genius and shaped the destiny of the republic, the exports were twenty-nine million two hundred and eighty-five thousand six hundred and fifty-nine dollars; since that time they have more than trebled, showing that the administrations which have governed the country since 1877, and which have followed the policy initiated by General Diaz in that year, have wonderfully developed the productive industries of the country, and, as a natural consequence, the pecuniary interests of the nation have grown in proportion to the prosperity of its producing industries and business.

HUSKING COFFEE.

As yet, this great republic, prominent as she is in mining and agriculture, has not distinguished herself as a manufacturer, finding, heretofore, that it paid better to purchase the manufactures of other countries and pay for them in her almost limitless productions of the ground. Yet a change is coming. The principal manufactures in the country now are, in the order of their importance: cotton, nearly four million pieces of goods being produced annually, valued at fourteen million dollars; wool; paper; earthenware; metals; brewing, principally in Monterey and Toluca; canned fruit is being produced from a factory at the port of Todos Santos.

Iron-foundries are numerous, and, by reason of the excellent quality of the Mexican ore, give very good results. However, the more important pieces having been for some time already cast, and the demand being limited, the production is confined to car-wheels and to ordinary merchant iron.

There are in Mexico several shops where they make cane-mills, turbine-wheels, etc. Foreign establishments, however, compete with these to the disadvantage of the local concerns.

Although acids are so necessary to the mining districts, there are but two manufacturing establishments producing them. Sulphuric, hydrochloric, and nitric acids are manufactured at great profit, and there is room for many more establishments of the same character.

The rebozos of Tenancingo and the serapes (a sort of multi-colored wrap) of Saltillo and of San Miguel are the best liked.

At Tepic there is a bleachery with an output of sixty thousand yards weekly, which, in conjunction with another establishment at Guadalajara, is aiding the country to take care of itself in this line. A factory for making printed goods is also working well, so that before long all that part of the coast about San Blas should be supplied with home-made goods.

The principal wool-manufacturing establishments are three in the Federal District, making one hundred and sixty-two thousand pieces of cloth per year; three in the city of Mexico, making one hundred and fifty thousand pieces of cloth and carpets; five in the state of Puebla, making five hundred and fifty thousand pounds of wool yearly, serving for serapes, jorongo,

GROUP OF TEHUANTEPECANAS.

plaids, etc.; three in the state of Hidalgo, producing one hundred and twenty-five thousand pieces of cloth; one in the capital city, and several in the state of Guanajuato, the most important of which, at Celaya, produces about eighty-five thousand pieces of cassimere and cloth and about fifty-five thousand yards of carpet when running, but just now it is shut down. There is also one in Ensenada, which produces very fine goods.

For centuries hammocks have been articles of use and barter in the state of Yucatán, and hammock-making is quite a prominent industry in a republic where so many persons are indisposed to physical exertion, and where the great heat renders it desirable to have a cool and easy substitute for the ordinary couch. Hammock beams and hooks are found in the buried cities.

There are several paper-mills, the production of which is important, as it supplies the principal printing establishments for their periodicals and classic works.

The third great manufacture of the country is pottery, which is carried on everywhere, particularly in the states of Guadalajara, Zacatecas, Guanajuato, and Puebla. Each district has its special designs in shape and color and its distinctive quality of ware. For instance, in Guadalajara the usual ware is gray, soft-baked and polished, and often quite elaborately decorated in gold, silver, and brilliant colors; from Zacatecas comes red, hard-baked, glazed ware, rudely decorated with splashes under the glaze; Guanajuato produces a dark brown or gray ware having a soft, rich glaze, with ornamentation in low relief; and in Puebla there is made a coarse porcelain with a thick tin glaze. Some parts of the republic produce a curious iridescent copper-glazed ware. For table use the usual ware is heavy, in white and blue; but in the Federal District there are two quite extensive factories making fine grades of porcelain.

There is ample field for the investment of capital in cotton-mills, paper, and other manufactures. Mexican woollens as now made are of superior quality, and thousands of people are refusing to buy the more expensive, but no handsomer, English goods. Tailors are supplying their growing demand at prices less than one-half of those charged for European textures. Mexico is growing more cotton every year, and will soon be able to supply herself without bringing in American cotton; and as the growing and manufacturing are done on the basis of cheap labor and silver money, Mexico may well enter the lists as an exporter of cotton goods.

In this connection it is interesting to know that the first spinning- and weaving-mill in Mexico was built in Puebla, and called "La Constancia." Later, in 1835, another mill was built there, and called "El Patriotismo"; and about the same time another was built at Tlalpam, in the Valley of Mexico, and called "La Magdalena." In 1842 the first attempt at making print cloths was tried in Puebla, but nothing of importance was effected in this line until 1870. Now there is no part of the country that has not its cotton-mills of greater or less importance.

Cotton has for centuries been a staple product in Mexico. Cortez, it is recorded, received many presents from the Indians of cotton cloths of native manufacture. Think of it! cotton cloth was actually made in Mexico years before the United States was occupied by white men!

It must interest all who propose settling in Mexico or investing there to know the conditions concerning the acquirement of land,—where it is to be had, of what owners, at what price, and under what conditions.

Among the many sources of revenue from which the government of Mexico may draw may be reckoned the public lands. At the time of the declaration of Mexican independence the crown rights, which comprised all the territory included within the kingdom at any one period and all additions thereto in the way of conquest, reverted to the republic of Mexico. In 1863, during the presidency of Juarez, there was passed a law which defined very simply the baldios lands, or those lands which have not been destined to public uses by the authorities legally empowered so to do nor ceded by the same to individuals or corporations having the capacity for acquiring them. This law of 1863 enabled any inhabitant of the republic, except certain foreigners, to claim up to about six thousand two hundred and fifty acres of the public lands at the prices fixed by the government tariff and under conditions fixed by the law. This law of 1863 was supplemented by the colonization laws of 1875 and 1883, authorizing the government to grant private parties or companies the right to search for, claim, and survey certain public lands within certain zones or districts to be agreed upon, the private party or company receiving in recompense one-third of all resultant lands or of their money value at tariff rates.

Within a few years the lands on both sides of the Paseo de la Reforma, from the statue of Cuauhtemoc up to Chapultepec, were opened for public purchase at moderate prices. Competent engineers were employed in surveying the lots, fixing the boundaries, and so on. The active demand for the lots directly fronting on the Paseo induced speedy building up to the very gates of the forest of Chapultepec, and made this one of the finest avenues in the world. In Tacubaya lots increased over sixfold in two years.

A very large proportion of the public land of Mexico is fertile, well watered, and in every way desirable. Intending purchasers will do well to buy government lands, as they are cheaper than others and no question can arise as to the title.

A study of the resources of Mexico would not be complete were it to omit the great industry of cattle-raising. This business is carried on in all parts of Mexico,—on the plains of Chihuahua and Durango, in the Bajión, in all the valleys of Michoacán and Jalisco, and in the plains and valleys of the coast. Where rains are insufficient to produce corn crops, as is the case in considerable portions of Chihuahua, Durango, and Coahuila, the grass is sufficient for grazing and even the fattening of stock. Generally, however, thin stock from the northern portions of the republic is fattened on the haciendas in the southern and central portions. Of late years the business of cattle-raising has grown in the states of San Luis Potosí, Tamaulipas, and Vera Cruz, and, though yet in its infancy, is still very important.

Not only is the country well fitted by its climate for the cattle industry, but, with its large unoccupied territories well supplied with running streams and its abundant yield of corn, it would be difficult to find another country so well adapted to compete for the trade of Europe as is Mexico.

In short, in a country with such a healthy climate, such good breeding facilities, such excellent harbor accommodations and good railroad services, the day cannot be far distant when the cattle industry of Mexico will have attained enormous proportions.

CHAPTER XLIX

MEXICO AS A WHOLE

MEXICO is preeminently the land of mystery of the Western world. It contains abundant traces of a civilization far older than any other on this continent, and, now that a key to the Maya inscriptions has been found, it is reasonable to expect that systematic exploration will result in reconstructing, at least partially, the history of the vanished race, and throw some light on the interesting question of its antiquity as well as of its origin, and with it give us some knowledge of what is now the prehistoric period of North America.

It is scarcely possible to overestimate the importance of the movement now on foot in Mexico to have the archæological treasures of that country properly explored. A bill has been passed by the Mexican congress to empower American scientists to make archæological excavations in that country, provided the objects found be divided equally between the two countries. This is a liberal proposition, and will, doubtless, be accepted readily by scientific explorers everywhere.

Among the features of which Mexico can boast are the richest and most productive silver-mines in the world; the cradle of civilization on this continent; the ruins and romance of historic and prehistoric America; the Cholula pyramid,—the Tower of Babel of Indian tradition; the spot where the first known European set foot on this continent, to which he gave his name,—the place, the coast near Tampico, the man, Americus Vespucci; the largest meteorite in the world; the statue of Charles VI. on the Paseo in the city of Mexico, the first and, according to some authorities, the largest bronze ever cast in America, and, according to Humboldt, the finest equestrian statue in the world next to that of Marcus Aurelius at Rome; the stoutest tree on the continent and perhaps in the world, at Tula, one hundred and fifty-four feet two inches in circumference six feet from the ground; Popocatepetl, according to the latest figures, the highest mountain on the continent; the largest American church building, in the Mexican cathedral, and the most beautiful, in that of Puebla; the first pulpit and the first church structure in the New World, at Tlaxcala; and the largest bell in America, and one of the largest in the world, in the Mexican cathedral. This bell is said to be nineteen feet high. The "monarch of bells" in the Kremlin at Moscow is twenty feet high and weighs four hundred and forty-four thousand pounds, but it is cracked and useless, while Mexico's bell is sound and serviceable.

In historic associations and relics of the past there is the same diversity. There are reminders of Diaz, of Juarez and Maximilian, of General Scott and Santa Anna, of Spanish viceroys and Hidalgo, of Cortez and Montezuma, and of the unknown builders of pyramids and palaces that antedate the beginnings of recorded history in America. Among its natural attractions are semi-tropical Orizaba, only eighty miles from the Gulf of Mexico, with its Swiss mountains, mountain-torrents, and picturesque buildings, its Javanese coffee, palms and bananas;

attractive and picturesque Guadalajara, on the Pacific slope, with its lake, its waterfall, the Niagara of Mexico, and its cañon that boasts of the temperate zone at its top and the torrid zone at its bottom; and to the southward Oaxaca and the famous ruins of Mitla.

Mexico is more foreign in appearance than nine-tenths of Europe. Her twelve millions of natives are either pure Indian, direct and unadulterated descendants of the Aztecs and other Indian tribes, or mixed Indian and Spanish, or (much the smallest class) pure Spanish. Four-fifths of the people have some Indian blood, two-fifths are pure Indian, and about one-third can neither speak nor understand Spanish, and use their original dialects. In the outward appearance of the men, women, and children and in their habitations, costumes, and habits it suggests in its different sections and among its varied peoples now Europe in Moorish Spain, now Asia in Palestine, now Africa in Egypt.

CARRYING PULQUE.

In some Mexican homes there are reminders, in architectural effects and in stucco-work, in horseshoe arches and graceful columns, of the Moorish influence upon the Spaniards during the period of Moorish occupation of Spain, while one always finds in its Indian dark-skinned people reminders of the African and Asiatic. In the small villages and country sections where the millions of Indians dwell Oriental scenes are plentiful. The dark-skinned men, with bright eyes and white teeth, dressed first in white cotton and then draped in a serape,—a shawl by day and a blanket by night,—are distinctively Oriental, and the effect is only heightened by the immense sombreros upon their heads or the sandals upon their feet.

The Mexican horseman is even more dashing and picturesque than his Old-World counterpart. As in Spain, the city's heart is often a plaza, with a stand for band-music, the cathedral facing the plaza on one side and the palace or government building on the other.

All classes of people are polite and charitable to one another, and are wonderfully kind and gentle in manner. The women are beautiful when very young, but age rapidly. There are picturesque scenes along the streets of the town Saturday nights, when the men sit in groups playing cards and various games and all classes are apparently happy.

In some parts of the country the method of doing the family wash is as primitive as picturesque, and would make a pretty picture if caught by a snap-shot kodak. The women stand along the river banks, just as they do in parts of Brittany and Holland, and dip the clothes in and out of the running stream, while their children and babies roll and frolic about in sand or perch upon the stones, their melting dark eyes and slips of bright color making a theme for the brush of Millet. The women of the working class spend much of their time sewing. There are many sewing-machines, upon which the native girls do good work. These women also make the wooden jar, olla, used for holding water. The olla is porous, and will keep water agreeably cold for a length of time. The women dress generally in a calico skirt and sash of some bright color, and a rebozo. The latter is composed of a long blue shawl with fringed ends wound about the head and shoulders. A black shawl instead of the blue rebozo is considered more elegant and distinguished. Bonnets and hats are worn by the upper classes, of course, but only since the advent of the railroad, which has at last penetrated the upper portions

A FIELD OF MAGUEY PLANTS.

of the country. The women, often in gay colors and draped in the rebozo, which half conceals the face, suggest Asia or Africa rather than America or Europe.

Mr. Theodore W. Noyes, a Washington (D.C.) editor, and a very close observer, says, "The Egyptian shaduf finds its counterpart in the well-sweep of Irapuato, where strawberries are grown and sold every day in the year, and where irrigation is resorted to, as in Egypt, systematically and on a large scale. In the absence of trees and rocks the Egyptian shaduf is small, is composed of prepared timbers, and the counterpoise to the well-bucket is an immense hunk of dried, hardened Nile mud. The Mexican shaduf generally utilizes a forked tree, and swings across it a long, tapering trunk or branch, and the counterpoise consists of a large single stone or a mass of stones fastened together. Though Mexico stretches farther south than Egypt, the two countries lie, speaking generally, between the same parallels of latitude; but the altitude of Irapuato is over five thousand feet above the sea-level or the level of the Nile, so that the same degree of undress is not expected or found in the Mexican as in the Egyptian shaduf-worker. I saw, however, in the neighborhood of Irapuato, two Indians as well-sweeps working side by side, who were dressed only in white cotton loin-cloths, and who looked like the twin brothers of shaduf-workers whom I have seen and photographed on the Nile."

And again he says, "The Mexican woman, with her baby at her back securely fastened in the rebozo, which throws the infant's weight on the mother's shoulders, is to be compared with the Egyptian woman, whose 'rebozo' covers her face while the child straddles her shoulders,

DRAWING PULQUE, IN TLACHIQUERO.

holding to her head and leaving her hands as unfettered as in the Mexican fashion. There are no Egyptian camels, but even more numerous donkeys, the patient burros. The Indian villages, whether of adobe or of bamboo, with thatched roofs and organ cactus fences, and whether alive with goats, donkeys, or snarling curs, are African in effect. There are Aztec picture-writings resembling the Egyptian, the paper being made from the maguey instead of papyrus. The Aztecs employed captives on great public works, as in Egypt. Mexico thus has pyramids, much broader based than those of Egypt, though not so high, and idols quite as ugly. Gold ornaments, beads, masks, and other highly prized antiquities are found on the tombs, as in Egypt."

CHAPTER L.

GENERAL SUGGESTIONS

To enable readers of these pages to best open and most profitably maintain social and business relations with Mexico and her people, some appropriate hints may not here prove amiss. Those here given have the advantage of having been inspired during actual residence and of being the result of wide travel and close observation.

It is remarkable how little not only Europeans but Americans know concerning Mexico. A great many know that there is such a country as Mexico, and that is about all. It is not long since that a very successful business man in the United States, on being told that the city of Mexico had a population of over three hundred thousand, expressed himself as incredulous on this point, saying he had always had the impression that it was not over twenty-five thousand.

Those who are seeking the trade of people speaking a different language from their own should accommodate themselves to the language spoken by the expected customers. This is the law of trade. English-speaking people who desire the trade of Spanish-speaking countries should pocket their pride or any theories which they may have as regards the genius or value of their mother-tongue as compared with any other. A knowledge of Spanish greatly aids one in opening out business with Mexico, whether he goes there or remains at home and transacts his business by correspondents, although English is spoken very generally throughout Mexico.

It is pleasant to note that in American towns which have commenced to have large business with Mexico Spanish classes have become quite popular among business men.

It may be interesting to all non-Mexicans to know what the laws are as to who are Mexicans and who are considered foreigners.

Those are considered Mexicans who are born in the national territory and of fathers who are Mexicans by birth or naturalization; those born in the national territory of a Mexican mother and of a father who may not be legally recognized as a Mexican, and those who are born of parents who are unknown or of unknown nationality; and those born outside of the republic of a Mexican father who has not lost his nationality. Should he have lost his nationality the sons shall be considered as foreigners, but shall have the right to declare their intention of considering themselves Mexican within a year following their twenty-first birthday. Those born outside of the republic of a Mexican mother have this privilege, supposing she has not lost her nationality. If the mother shall not have been naturalized her sons will be foreigners, but will have the right to declare themselves Mexicans as in the case before mentioned. A foreign woman who marries a Mexican is considered a Mexican, even during her widowhood. Those born outside of the republic but who resided there in 1821 and swore to the Act of Independence are also residents if they have not changed their nationality. Those Mexicans who lived in the territory ceded to the United States and have fulfilled the required conditions to keep their nationality are also Mexicans. In a similar way are those in territory ceded to Guatemala. Those foreigners who were naturalized according to the present law; those who acquire real estate in the republic, provided they do not declare their intentions to preserve their original nationality; foreigners who have children born in Mexico, provided they do not prefer to preserve their original nationality; and all foreigners who serve the Mexican government officially, or who accept from it titles for public offices, are citizens of Mexico.

Those are considered foreigners who are born outside of the national territory and are subject to foreign governments and have not been naturalized in Mexico; the sons of a foreign father or of a foreign mother born in the national territory, and who have not declared their intentions; those absent from the republic without license from the government, on account of studies, of public interest, of commerce or industries, or the practice of a profession, who let ten years go by without asking permission to extend their absence. Mexican women who marry foreigners retain their character as citizens even during widowhood; Mexicans who are naturalized in other countries, or who officially serve foreign governments without license of the Mexican Congress; those who accept foreign decorations, titles, or offices other than literary, scientific, or humanitarian without permission from Congress are classed as foreigners. Every foreigner can be naturalized who complies with the requirements of this law.

It surprises those who visit Mexico to find that almost everywhere the methods of cultivation are the same as those employed by the ancient Egyptians. A Mexican plough has a wooden beam and a small iron shoe which scratches a furrow about five inches broad and the same depth. Its work is supplemented by a three- to five-pound hoe, and there is a saw-tooth sickle. The plough is practically nothing but a forked stick, the shorter fork being iron-shod and the longer one lashed with raw-hide thongs to the yoke of the oxen that draw it. With such primitive appliances it need surprise no one to learn that it takes about four men and four yoke of oxen to do the work that is done by one man and one horse in the United States.

The difference between the present Mexican way of ploughing and that prevailing in this country is even less marked than that between the two methods of threshing. There are few districts in which the grain is not threshed by simply driving horses or mules around in a ring into which the sheaves are tossed. As to winnowing, that is done by tossing the grain and chaff into the air with scoop shovels.

In the matter of local transportation of grains, there are employed on the farms ponderous two-wheeled carts, with three pounds of dead load for every pound of merchandise hauled.

The Indian population, taking into account the greater activity of which it is susceptible, and which will be the natural consequence of the increase of wages and of the demands which the development of civilization brings about, and also the economical transformations introduced by improved methods of tillage, can furnish sufficient working force to develop double the amount of lands and manufactories already worked.

The cultivation of tropical plants will certainly give considerable profit. The branches of cultivation in which peasants are past-masters—the culture of the vine, the olive, the mulberry, and the cereals—are also very lucrative.

In general it may be said that the cost of living in Mexico is low. In the interior towns and villages the necessaries of life are cheap, although coffee and tea are dear. The latter is seldom used or even seen in the interior. Butter is very expensive, and but little used. The food is rich and highly seasoned.

Rents are high, not because the landlords are rapacious, but because house-building is expensive, by reason of the annual tax of twelve per cent. on the rental of houses, in addition to the necessary defrayal of pavement, drainage, water, and stamp taxes by the owners of the property.

During the Spanish dominion the government of New Spain, as Mexico was then called, was systematically hostile to strangers, and after the independence the country was very much busier with civil war than in appealing for immigrants. It may be said that the period for immigration into Mexico is only now commencing, and if we consider that peace reigns in the country so completely that it seems to be permanent, every one will agree that there are very few countries which present to the immigrant the advantages which will be found in Mexico. No other country in the world offers to every comer one hundred acres of land absolutely free. Given the conditions of climate and fertility of soil which have been shown in these pages and the immense mineral wealth of which it has been impossible to give here more than an imperfect account, there only remains to address a few words of advice to those who may be tempted to partake of a part of Mexico's wealth.

It may be said first to the intending colonist or immigrant, if you have no money and only strong arms and good habits, do not come to Mexico, for you will find as rivals several millions of Indian workers, also with good habits, who have arms sufficient to work the farms there, and who will content themselves with salaries which would render you more miserable in Mexico than you would be in any other country.

In Mexico the torrid and frigid zones are in close proximity, and within a few hours of each other changes that represent thousands of miles north and south are encountered. Rice-fields and plains where thousands of cattle graze are near neighbors.

One of the greatest advantages, and one that will serve to advance its material development, is that labor troubles are unknown. Such a thing as a strike or confusion among laborers is never dreamed of. The best of labor is always available at a very low figure. Peon labor, which can be trained to accomplish very skilful work, can always be secured at from thirty-seven and one-half to seventy-five cents per day in Mexican silver. All labor and supplies are paid for in this metal, which is not at a discount in the country. This fact, taken in connection with the additional fact that all exports can be sold on a gold basis, gives still further advantage in the way of a successful and profitable investment of capital. There is hardly any section of the country that is not easily accessible to the principal trade centres. All towns not having easy water connection are within easy access of the railroad.

The old idea that the Mexican people can never be induced to change from the customs of their ancestors is fast losing its grasp. The people are finding out that there is more money to be made for themselves by the adoption of progressive customs; that the credit of their institutions can be greatly enhanced by the same; and that the civilizing influence of the American people can be made of great benefit to them and those who are to come after them. And the railway, while undertaken as an investment enterprise, is really bringing into the country a splendid revolution in the condition of affairs which no one can thoroughly appreciate who has not studied this system and the opportunities that it has opened up.

The various climates of the country resemble one another very much in some ways. There are no sudden changes, no extremes of heat or cold, no heavy prolonged storms, but a temperature between summer and winter.

It is a most erroneous opinion that health is more precarious and disease more virulent in Mexico than in the north. This idea is without the least basis in fact. Foreigners in Mexico who conform to the conditions of the country are as healthy as they would be at home. There are thousands of families in the United States who would gladly settle in Mexico if they but possessed definite and reliable information about this republic,—if they only knew that there is no excessive cold, that on the same lands a thousand different kinds of produce can be raised.

A careful study of the business conditions and opportunities of the republic of Mexico develops two facts,—viz., that the resources of the country are almost illimitable and that the application of proper business methods will bring results that are most satisfactory. Mexico is, in short, the coming country.

Reciprocity, said Confucius, is the one word which sums up the whole moral life and coins moral sentiment into current exchange. In its modern commercial sense it indicates the line of moral action between nations; the line of reciprocal exchange or trade between two republics, like Mexico and the United States.

Blaine's watchword of the times—"reciprocity"—should be exemplified in Mexico. The United States is the elder brother among American republics, but Mexico is the closest and nearest of sisters, and in many ways their interests are identical.

Of little value to Mexico is the temporary presence of traders from across the Atlantic compared with the more permanent presence of thousands of Americans in that neighborly spirit which establishes personal relations. The trader from the older countries of the East comes to make what money he can and return with it. The American seeks out places for location, invites friends to visit him, who enter with zest into the opening up of the resources of the country, all of which helps on the desired interchange of ideas and experiences between the neighboring republics and cements their natural relationship. Mexico is in need to-day of many of the things which the people of the United States have already wrested from the hand of nature, while the restless spirit of the American is equally in need of the sphere of mental activity which many of the partially developed resources of Mexico offer.

How can this neighborly fellowship be brought about? Simply by greater knowledge of the resources and advantages of each republic. Knowledge must be distributed, facts must be made known, a mutual interest between the republics must be created, and then the harvest of mutual advantage will come.

The United States and Mexico mutually assisting in each other's development might become well-nigh independent of the rest of the world. They can produce anything that can be produced on the globe. All they need is to know each other better and then to work together according to the dictates of that knowledge. And this comprises the moral relations of nations.

Silver is adding to the permanent wealth of Mexico, because it pays for labor which is transmuted, under intelligent direction, into things that will outlast the currency question, which must some day be settled.

Mexico is on a silver basis, with the shield of the government's protection thrown impartially over all enterprises. A spirit of mutual co-operation between the people and the railways exists, and out of the fall in silver a great benefit has come to Mexico. As out of apparent evil good has come, Mexico will probably continue to stick to the efficient silver dollar which has served her so well. To-day the republic of Mexico is, without doubt, attracting more attention than any other country on the globe.

The explanation of the great interest shown in this land of the Montezumas can easily be made. The wealth of her resources is beyond the comprehension of the human mind; the climate is the finest under the sun. President Porfirio Diaz and his loyal cabinet, who so ably manage the general government, together with a judiciary among the most scholarly anywhere on the continent, with governors and other officers loyal to their country, make Mexico the most stable and law-abiding republic under the sun.

When the first international railway was projected, alarm and apprehension were felt throughout the country. It was thought that the Americans were about to penetrate into the country through that opening, into which Uncle Sam would insert the thin end of the wedge that was to split Mexico from top to bottom. But a few years have proved the contrary, and shown that Mexico is strong enough to stand alone.

There is a deep prejudice among the better class of Mexicans against the average American who settles in Mexico. In this connection it is well to state that some of the Americans who are most prominent in Mexico by no means represent the best class of citizens in the United States. Many of them are there for the sole purpose of making money, and are lacking in the good manners and solid, fine qualities of the best people in the United States.

It is hardly fair, however, though it may be natural, for intelligent Mexicans to judge of the refinement, culture, and honest purpose of the average American citizen by the emigrants from Northern cities whom they too often see.

The predictions of Humboldt and Stevenson will soon be realized, and Mexico will become a great and powerful nation, the bulwark of Latin America against aggression from the north. Mexico, freed from the curse of recurring revolutions, her people devoted to the arts of peace, must inevitably maintain her sovereignty and fulfil her destiny as a nation of the first rank.

www.ingramcontent.com/pod-product-compliance
Lightning Source LLC
Chambersburg PA
CBHW022144300426
44115CB00006B/335